QUESTIONS OF COMMUNICATION
A Practical Introduction to Theory

second edition

QUESTIONS OF COMMUNICATION
A Practical Introduction to Theory

second edition

Rob Anderson
Saint Louis University

Veronica Ross
Greenville College

Bedford/St. Martin's
Boston ◆ New York

Sponsoring editor: Suzanne Phelps Weir
Managing editor: Patricia Mansfield Phelan
Project editor: Jessica Zorn
Production supervisor: Joe Ford
Art director: Lucy Krikorian
Photo research: Inge King
Cover design: Evelyn Horovicz
Cover art: Ron Chan

Library of Congress Catalog Card Number: 97-65198

Manufactured in the United States of America.

3 2 1 0 9
f e d c

For information, write:
Bedford/St. Martin's
75 Arlington Street
Boston, MA 02116
(617-426-7440)

ISBN: 0-312-17086-6

Acknowledgment

The Way to Teach by Ric Masten. Sun Flower Inc. Presentations, Carmel, CA.
Reprinted by permission of the author.

contents

8. Changing Minds

9. The Influence of the Media World

preface

We're pleased with the enthusiastic response from so many teachers and students who found the first edition of *Questions of Communication* informative and readable for introduction to communication theory courses. The invitation to do a second edition gives us the opportunity to explore new ideas and apply the valuable feedback that our careful readers have been so willing to give.

The philosophy that guides *Questions of Communication* remains the same. We're convinced that a communication theory course can be inviting and accessible while also being intellectually rigorous.

the importance of curiosity

We wrote this book for students and teachers who are curious about how communication works. Not everyone is. Many people are content to ignore why some friends understand them more readily than others, or why some relationships are satisfying when others fall flat. Some people don't particularly care if electronic media might be changing how they perceive the world, or why certain messages might be morally defensible when others are not. However, students majoring in communication *are* curious about these kinds of issues and, we've found, are willing to exercise their intellectual curiosity when sincerely invited to do so. Although it is important to know the skills of communicating (e.g., public speaking, interpersonal sensitivity, small-group decision making, and interviewing), skills alone are not enough for a specialist in communication. At the same time, students may lose their enthusiasm for the field if they encounter too much abstract

theoretical material all at once. We think students should be introduced to theory in practical and relevant contexts.

A number of excellent comprehensive textbooks are available to introduce communication theory to students who have taken the first course in communication. In our experience, however, none of these books quite fits the needs of our own students to study theory in an involving, personalized, and pragmatic way, while also recognizing that ideas can be exciting on their own merit.

We wrote *Questions of Communication* with the needs of students and teachers in mind, not as a book for sophisticated researchers. New undergraduate communication majors will have plenty of opportunities to probe the intricacies of specific theories in upper-level courses. Here, we want to introduce mainstream communication theory by respecting and attempting to address students' real questions. Somewhat more streamlined in scope and more integrative than most theory books, this text is appropriate for lower-level nonskills courses in communication theory, which are often among the first courses a student takes in the discipline. The book could also be a main text in a course that introduces the discipline to new majors.

Our approach to communication theory uniquely depends on a number of special features:

- We emphasize the role of questioning more than the compulsion for answering or resolving every question. Knowledge is built more by developing the ability to ask and seek answers to intelligent questions than by receiving packages of answers from experts. Focused questioning is the one theme that most consistently cuts across methodological and theoretical divisions in studying communication. Although as authors we take broadly interpretive, qualitative, or applied roles in our own work, we also have a healthy respect for quantitative and behavioral social science research. Genuinely helpful communication theorizing is motivated by curiosity and characterized by systematic approaches to phenomena, whether those approaches are quantitative, qualitative, or (increasingly) both.

- We emphasize that theory and practice are not opposites, but two perspectives on the same process—that is, the process of learning. Effective theories help communication specialists with such practical tasks as writing, reading, speaking, and listening.
- We emphasize the role of students as learners in the context of higher education. Our explanations of theories include numerous examples and research findings specifically relevant to the campus context.
- We emphasize that communication theory is not a disciplinary possession but an enterprise that unites many scholars in the humanities and social sciences. Therefore, this book supports a broadly based general education or liberal arts philosophy. In other words, we argue that the most practical education is liberalizing and expansive, and through it, we can improve the dialogue among the disciplines.
- We emphasize the need to clarify and integrate theoretical concepts, rather than enumerating many of the diverse categories, terms, and abstractions that are more appropriately covered in advanced courses. We believe that introductory students should be excited by the possibilities of their subject, not intimidated by elaborate lists of concepts and subconcepts. The Glossary, for example, provides brief definitions for basic concepts discussed in the text, to

encourage students to build a core vocabulary for understanding research in the discipline.

- We emphasize a narrative tone, "talking" readers through basic ideas and encouraging new and individualized questions. In addition, we sometimes illustrate ideas through narratives interwoven throughout a chapter; the narrative helps readers relate their learning to real-life problems.
- We emphasize ethics as a frame for all communication problems and choices. Chapter 10 is devoted to ethical theory and philosophy, but ethical issues are important in all chapters.

In addition, two special sections are included at the end of each chapter to help students and teachers interact with the book as a stimulus for learning:

- **Summary: "Testing the Concepts."** Instead of the traditional end-of-chapter summary we use a question-and-answer format to focus students' attention on particularly important or interesting topics. We include these focused questions, which are similar or nearly identical to those asked by students in our classes, in order to test the implications and practicality of chapter content from a student perspective. The questions and responses should also generate further questions and class dialogue—and maybe an argument or two.
- **"You, the Researcher."** These sections include a wide range of projects and activities designed to stimulate students' out-of-class investigation and exploration of related topics. Students are asked, for example, to conduct informal research that could stimulate class discussion or personal reflection, or to do more formal studies in which they collect data through interviews, mini-experiments, and observations perhaps for a research paper or report. Each chapter includes several research projects from

which the student or teacher can select one or more that are appropriate to the course. The activities illustrate the range of communication research, thereby reinforcing the researcher's role in theory building. We hope students realize in this way that theorists don't specialize in armchair noodling, but are also active investigators. In the introduction to "You, the Researcher" in Chapter 1, we include some guidelines for research that involves human subjects.

A new *Instructor's Manual,* written by Deborah Stiencker of Arapahoe Community College, is an interesting and effective pedagogical resource for use with this text. It includes course syllabi, examination items, and assignments, as well as teaching strategies, examples of theory in practice, and proficiency goals for students.

changes for the second edition

Although we have not changed the approach and basic themes of the book, readers of the first edition will notice a number of differences in this new edition. We want the book to be even more accessible and readable for both students and instructors. Specifically, the second edition incorporates the following major revisions:

- A new chapter, Chapter 7, "Living across Cultural Borders" describes an important area of communication research about which many students are curious. Intercultural situations are no longer regarded as mere arenas for applying generic interpersonal and media theories. We now recognize the concept of culture itself as a vital part of the ongoing academic conversation about communication. In addition to introducing basic cultural concepts and theories, Chapter 7 surveys several influential cultural studies and critical approaches to cross-cultural conflict as well as an exemplar theory that integrates social science research: Kim's cross-cultural adaptation the-

ory. This new chapter will help students enter the contemporary conversation about multiculturalism by integrating and applying both cultural studies and traditional social science theories.

- Another new chapter, Chapter 11, "Discipline, Interdiscipline, or Field?" ends the book with conceptual and career issues that are relevant to students about to enter more advanced classes in their communication program. Such students often have many "questions of communication" about the nature of the discipline or "interdiscipline" they've chosen to study. The emphasis on questions about the discipline and coherence in this new chapter will assist students in understanding the communication major in the context of a broadly based liberal arts program. We've found that "communication theory" or "introduction to the major" courses are the best places to address such questions.

- The Introduction (formerly Chapter 1), on learning styles and college life, has been streamlined and reorganized. In addition, its new title more appropriately identifies the opening chapter as a prelude to the book. We found that many faculty and students appreciated the emphasis on learning styles and college life, but some preferred to move more directly to chapters focusing specifically on communication theorizing. The new organization allows teachers increased flexibility in making assignments, while still introducing students to the same ideas.

- The second edition divides the text into five parts, giving students a better sense of the book's structure. However, the topics inevitably build on each other (and therefore overlap) from section to section. The chapters in Part One, "Asking Communication Questions," invite students to consider the process of communication inquiry itself, including how to define essential concepts. The chapters in Part Two, "The Outer and

Inner Contexts of Communication," ask how physical, social, and cognitive contexts influence communication. In Part Three, "Interpersonal Processes," the chapters focus on interpersonal theories about rules, relationship management, symbolic and narrative interaction, and dialogue. The chapters in Part Four, "Cultural, Public, and Mediated Forms of Communication," widen the focus to include theories about the dynamics of the public arena. Finally, in Part Five, "Issues of Ethics and Coherence in Communication," the two chapters serve as a capstone for the communication theory course, asking students to consider why theories of ethics are important as well as why the discipline of communication asks difficult questions about its own identity.

- Several chapters have been revised in ways that are relevant to student readers. Chapter 1 widens the discussion of how quantitative and qualitative research contribute to communication theorizing, while Chapter 3 now probes more into how online or computer-mediated communication affects the contexts of communication. Chapter 4 looks more closely at semiotics and postmodernism, areas that many humanities students are also encountering in literature, history, and media analysis courses. Chapter 6 includes a new section on dialectical theory and an expanded discussion of social exchange theory. We more thoroughly emphasize the everyday use of persuasion in Chapter 8, supplementing the discussion of rhetorical theory. Chapter 10 includes new material on the highly influential theorist Jurgen Habermas and on ethicists' recent interest in communitarianism.

- In order to highlight the interdependence of many communication theories and concepts, we have introduced "Links" throughout the text to call attention to where various topics are discussed elsewhere, perhaps in different contexts. In addition, some

"Link" boxes preview related topics that are developed later in the book.

- We have also developed a special boxed feature for the new edition. Each chapter now includes boxes that summarize, amplify, or exemplify important topics discussed in the text. This new feature is designed to help students identify and focus on critical concepts within each chapter.

- The Glossary, still subtitled "An 'Access Vocabulary' in Communication Theory," has been expanded.

- The end-of-chapter sections, "Summary: Testing the Concepts" and "You, the Researcher," have been updated to include many new relevant questions and projects.

- Finally, we have tightened the writing style throughout, and have updated many examples, sources, and descriptions.

appreciations

Although any extended writing project demands a great deal of "alone time" and cooperation between coauthors, we appreciate the support provided by many people who might not even know how much they've helped. Our families, Dona, Eric, and Neil Anderson, and Steve, Chris, Jennifer, Alexa, and Corey Ross, remain not only loving and genuinely patient, but also professionally helpful in many ways. We continue to be grateful for conversations many years ago with Dr. Kevin E. McClearey of the Department of Speech Communication at Southern Illinois University at Edwardsville, talks that helped to launch this book. Other colleagues and friends graciously read drafts of the first edition and gave us their informal suggestions on how to improve the text: Dr. George M. Killenberg, professor of mass communication at the University of South Florida at St. Petersburg; Dr. Noreen Carrocci, dean of the College of Arts and Sciences at the University of St. Thomas; and Dr. Cecelia Keener of the Communication Department at Greenville College. We also thank Deborah Stieneker for the *Instruc-*

tor's Manual, and for the excellent quality and depth of her important contribution.

Many of the earliest "reviewers" of this text were our questioning and thoughtful students at Saint Louis University, Greenville College, Southern Illinois University at Edwardsville, and the University of South Florida. They went beyond remembering concepts to involve themselves in genuine learning. You'll meet them indirectly in these pages. They continue to ask exciting questions about communication, and to confront faculty—as they should—when they think we might be bluffing.

Since the publication of the first edition, many students at Greenville College have, with remarkable good will and skillful tact, helped us improve the book by offering their suggestions for revision. We have also learned much from three colleagues who used the first edition in their classes and gave us their students' feedback: Dr. Mara Adelman of Seattle University, Dr. Michael Hanna of the University of South Alabama, and Dr. Robert Strain, formerly of California State University–Fullerton and now at Saint Louis University. Dr. John Pauly and Dr. Karla Scott of Saint Louis University shared their valuable impressions of the text and helped us make needed revisions. David Crowson of the University of Alaska was kind enough to point out an error in one chapter, and Ed Phillips of Southern Illinois University at Carbondale went out of

his way to share his impressions of the theory-building process described now in Chapter 1.

The editors, staff, and reviewers at St. Martin's Press have encouraged this book at every stage of its development. We remain indebted to the early interest and support of Cathy Pusateri and Jane Lambert. We are also grateful to Suzanne Phelps Weir, the current communication editor, whose skillful encouragement has been important to us. Amy Horowitz, our project editor for the first edition, and Patricia Mansfield Phelan, managing editor, who oversaw the second edition, were both extremely helpful in coordinating changes and polishing the manuscript.

We are also grateful to the reviewers engaged by St. Martin's Press for their expert feedback and suggestions, which have improved the second edition significantly: Mara B. Adelman, Seattle University; Marjorie Fish, St. Cloud State University; Kenneth D. Frandsen, University of New Mexico; Betsy Gordon, McKendree College; Michael Hemphill, University of Arkansas; Randy Hirokawa, University of Iowa–Iowa City; Cecil Kramer Jr., Liberty University; Pamela McWherter, University of Alaska; Jonathan Miller, Rider University; Russell Proctor, Northern Kentucky University; Gregory J. Shepherd, University of Kansas; and Gregory Spencer, Westmont College.

Rob Anderson
Veronica Ross

QUESTIONS OF COMMUNICATION
A Practical Introduction to Theory

second edition

Jean-Claude LeJeune/Stock, Boston

introduction: college students, ethical assumptions, and constructed knowledge

"do we have to *memorize all this* stuff?"

1

The Way to Teach

(It isn't so much having a question to ask, rather the ability to create one)

and so

he let them have their games

until the tide was fully out

   and when it was

he came upon the rocky beach

a may-pole of a man

among the shouting children

and bending down beside a magic pool

   peering in

he waited

till a ring of faces gathered

at the edge of this attention

then slowly reaching through the mirror

gave a sea anemone

   a punch

who did what sea anemones will do

quickly folding in

on what should have been a lunch

   WOW!

he said—eyes popping

then abruptly rising

but keeping in mind the length of his legs

moved on up the beach

   the children scrambling behind

   with questions

RIC MASTEN, *SPEAKING POEMS* (1979, p. 32)

"AT THE EDGE OF THIS ATTENTION": SOME DIRECT TALK ABOUT HOW TEXTBOOKS ARE WRITTEN

Ric Masten's poem "The Way to Teach" suggests what college and university communication classes can accomplish. Anyone who wants to learn can benefit from being with other curious learners, preferably those who can model the process of asking questions and listening alertly for possible answers.

After decades of teaching and learning about communication, we've noticed that sometimes people don't understand our excitement about the behind-the-scenes reasons that make the communication process interesting and involving. Communication students typically enjoy meeting people and look forward to learning how they can speak and listen more effectively in their everyday lives. Learning about communication is a stimulating opportunity to learn about people. Meeting people is an indispensable part of an education in communication.

However, consider another side to the study of communication, one that applies to students who intend to specialize in communication—as managers, trainers, teachers, personnel directors, or public relations practitioners, for example. If this applies to you, then keep in mind that your co-workers, clients, and fellow students will expect you to function effectively as a resource and, occasionally, as a troubleshooter. Thus, in addition to good communication skills, you will need to develop an awareness of communication as a broad field of study. Speaking, listening, writing, and reading skills are not enough. Effective communication specialists are also able to suggest workable alternatives, direct people to helpful readings, and explain interpersonal and public communication topics clearly without being simplistic.

Our premise in this book is that communication study is a complex, intellectually exciting, and pragmatic calling. Let's examine this statement claim by claim. First, studying communication is complex because human society is ultimately founded on **communication,** which we will define for now as the development of shared meaning through messages. What human activity, then, is unrelated? Almost everything from solitary contemplation through the most carefully coordinated advertising campaign can be understood by considering its relationship to communication. Specific behaviors such as complimenting a friend or choosing a class to take have communication implications, as do general cultural patterns such as preferences for certain types of art or literature.

Second, communication study is intellectually exciting in part because it poses a paradox, a situation of self-contradiction in which an assertion or recommendation cannot logically be possible. For example, the request "Be spontaneous!" is paradoxical because if its request is followed literally, the listener would not behave spontaneously (Watzlawick, Weakland, & Fisch, 1974, pp. 62–73). Similarly, we inevitably experience paradoxes as we study communication by communicating about it. Although this sounds odd, the problem—which researchers term **reflexivity**—is common and unavoidable. The dilemma it poses is like a person with poor eyesight trying to see his or her glasses clearly. The person needs the glasses to see in the first place, and yet wants to see the glasses clearly, too. If you want to analyze how human language works, can you escape using language to analyze itself?

Curiosity leads us to question our lives; it seems natural to wonder "why?" when confronted with our own existence. In his well-known book *The Lives of a Cell* (1974), biologist Lewis Thomas discusses the dilemmas of human personality, mind, and language. For example, you might assume it would be useful for communicators to strive for precision (and you'd often be right). Yet, paradoxically, according to Thomas, too much precision will create problems:

> Ambiguity seems to be an essential, indispensable element for the transfer of information from one place to another by words, where matters of real importance are concerned. It is often necessary, for meaning to come through, that there be an almost vague sense of strangeness and askewness. Speechless animals and cells cannot do this. The specifically locked-on antigen at the surface of a lymphocyte does not send the cell off in search of something totally different; when a bee is tracking sugar by polarized light, observing the sun as though consulting his watch, he does not veer away to discover an unimaginable marvel of a flower. Only the human mind is designed to work in this way, programmed to drift away in the presence of locked-on information, straying from each point in a hunt for a better, different point.
>
> If it were not for the capacity for ambiguity, for the sensing of strangeness, that words in all languages provide, we would have no way of recognizing the layers of counterpoint in meaning. . . . (pp. 94–95)

Although we will never see the glasses clearly, we shouldn't become discouraged by the paradox and quit looking. Simply asking questions that yield ambiguous answers creates a condition of learning.

Essentially, this is what Masten's poem, "The Way to Teach," is about. We are doing something essentially human when we explore questions that have no set answers. According to Thomas (1983), the shared ground inhabited by all who study social life is "bewilderment": "What we have been learning in our time is that we really do not understand this place or how it works, and we comprehend our own selves least of all. And the more we learn, the more we are—or ought to be—dumbfounded" (p. 157). In order to learn anything new, we must first learn to respect the mysteries, and then to place ourselves near those who ask the questions that address the mysteries. We watch and listen, placing ourselves "at the edge of this attention," in Masten's words (1979, p. 32). Saying that you are interested in communication without being curious about, and often bewildered by, the "whys" behind it seems like a contradiction of terms.

Third, communication study is pragmatic because it is useful. Later we'll develop an argument for how practical communication theory can be, but you should know that we recognize no distinct boundary between *theory* and *practice*. These terms, which suggest emphases or approaches in learning, are interdependent. A theory cannot be taken seriously unless it is linked to concrete experience and put into practice. Conversely, concrete experience, to be useful, has to be evaluated, generalized, and made transferable to new situations. Theory-building is our method for accomplishing this transfer.

Finally, communication study can be thought of as a calling. The scientist-philosopher Michael Polanyi (1962) observed that some personal commitments seem to come from both external and internal sources. A *calling*, as he discussed it, emerges from a situation to which someone must form a response, an external circumstance that the person discovers is relevant to self and worthy of commitment. Its existence is neither wholly objective and external nor wholly subjective and internal, but personal. That is, a calling develops from someone's particular perception of what is important in the world. It's not caused; it just seems to develop gradually. However, people can solidify a calling by the substance of their choices. We've noticed that many of our students choose their majors, and thus their careers, in roughly this way. Although studying communication at first seems to be the "right thing" to do, students are not yet clear about the exact nature of their commitment. They find some classes and assignments more interesting, relevant, or useful than others. To respond to the calling, we suggest that you investigate the full range of commitments it requires. Someone who enjoys meeting people and for whom interpersonal communication is "fun" may, on that basis alone, choose a communication major. But a communication specialist needs to possess much more than basic communication skills or a pleasant disposition. Interactional and intellectual commitments are both essential.

Most readers will encounter *Questions of Communication* in an undergraduate class for communication majors that emphasizes ideas rather than skills. Skills are important, but they're emphasized elsewhere in the curriculum. While reading this book, you'll be able to decide the extent to which you'll join in the intellectual curiosity that supports the calling you've tentatively accepted. We hope you'll understand through these chapters that asking questions about ambiguities of human communication can be challenging and interesting.

Throughout this book, we make several assumptions, some of which may seem unusual at first (this is the "direct talk" mentioned in the heading for this section):

1. *You—as students—are the primary audience for this book.* That is, when writing, we let the needs of students guide us. *Our* central "question of communication" was "How can students best merge the intellectual and the interactional facets of their calling?"

2. *You aren't the only audience for this book.* In the text, we also address the concerns of those who teach communication theory courses as a forum for ideas that range across the social sciences and humanities. These faculty have direct experience in advising students how to integrate ideas so that the broad shape of liberal arts learning is emphasized. We've tried to provide stimulating raw material for that synthesis, while also covering the range of topics traditionally associated with communication theory. In addition, our audience includes *any* reader interested in learning more about communication.

3. *The chapters are meant to be easy to read.* This is relative, of course. Comic books would be easier to read. So would *People* magazine. Quantum physics and continental postmodern philosophy are likely to be harder. But we understand that the specialized terminology of social science, however necessary, can intimidate readers. The text invites you into that language without drowning you in its detail. Wherever possible, we introduce ideas by discussing examples and practical applications in direct everyday language (not just with technical definitions). You might think

of this book as a doorway into communication theory, where you will learn much about the topic but not all the details you may eventually want to know. We provide some brief lists to help you understand the shape of an idea. But generally we avoid long laundry lists of the seven factors of this and the six exceptions to that, and we also bypass most of the ins and outs of academic hairsplitting and infighting. The discipline's many professional journals provide lively forums for discussion and argument. Students intrigued by the concepts in this book will be better prepared to investigate the professional literature.

4. *The chapters are also meant to be hard to read.* We don't apologize for this. A simplistic narrative account of a complex concept only trivializes learning. Part of the responsibility for your understanding of the concepts in this book is ours, and the other part is yours. We are guided here by E. F. Schumacher's (1979) explanation of the classical notion of *adaequatio:* In any situation that calls for learning or appreciation (a class or a symphony, a novel or a parlor game), the perceiver must be at least adequate to the demands of the situation, or else its messages will seem meaningless, as a foreign language might sound like gibberish and its writing appear to be mere squiggles on paper. For example, it's easy for someone who knows nothing about classical music or the structure of symphonies to listen to Beethoven and then proclaim: "This is boring and too hard to listen to. A bad piece of music." It's easy to say that Picasso is a poor artist if the observer refuses to learn anything about the kind of art that Picasso is attempting. This doesn't mean that criticism is out-of-bounds or unjustifiable. Rather, it means that critics should be responsible enough to make themselves adequate to comprehend the nuances of messages. Think of a topic in which you are "adequate" in terms of Schumacher's notion of *adaequatio.* If you're a jazz musician, you would wince at hearing someone describe jazz as "all sounding alike." If you're a fan of science fiction literature, you would consider it unfair if someone new to the field dismissed Isaac Asimov and Phillip Jose Farmer, two very different writers, for the same reasons.

Try to withhold blame or praise for particular communication theories until you've done your best to understand the system of thought to which you're responding. This might require you to reread sections of the book you find difficult or to look up the meanings of unfamiliar words in a dictionary. Remember, part of your education involves responding to, not just receiving, information and knowledge. This leads us to a valuable distinction between two types of responding.

THE DOUBTING GAME AND THE BELIEVING GAME

Many people use the noun *intellectual* as a put-down, a kind of synonym for what used to be called an "egghead." Intellectuals, to some, are people who live only "in the mind," people who are not sufficiently connected to the real world to be able to know the differences between common sense and ivory tower abstraction. Some intellectuals are probably like that.

When we say that communication theory is an *intellectual* study, we define that term in a precise way. To Peter Elbow (1973), an intellectual is "someone who tries to figure out what is true by means of the best processes available, and uses them in a rational, disciplined way to try to avoid deluding himself" (p. 148).[1] If this is what an intellectual does, then Diane Sawyer is an intellectual journalist, Spike Lee's movies are intellectually motivated, and Barbra Streisand manages her career as both an entertainer and an intellectual. In other words, intellectuals do not live entirely "in their heads." Rather, they are grounded in practical experience *and* they use their full mental potential to solve human problems.

Elbow (1973), a well-known writing teacher, reinforces two attitudes central to intellectual life when he refers to the **doubting game** and the **believing game.** By "games," Elbow means that we not only hold these attitudes in our heads, but that we use them to develop rules for acting in the world (much like the rules of board games). The games are described in this introduction to provide a better handle on what you'll be asked to do in your course. Any significant learning, Elbow claims, ultimately depends on the willingness to play both the doubting and believing games.

The doubting game has profoundly influenced modern scientific research. In fact, the meaning of science has in many ways been defined through doubting. When you "play" the doubting game, you look for errors, find faults, and try to pick apart whatever you're looking at so that you can see what's wrong. Doubt, in this sense, emphasizes logic, method, technique, precise control, definition, and analysis. In a doubting game approach, the world is sliced into segments so that its flaws and problems can be noticed more readily. Someone playing the intellectual doubting game responds to a new idea with skepticism: "What's wrong with it? When won't it work? Who can't use it?"

If guided by the believing game, however, you discover that belief is more than the absence of doubt (Elbow, 1973). The object of the believing game is not to disprove but to support and clarify. Therefore, when confronted with a surprising, disagreeable, or ambiguous message, a believing game communicator's first response might be "In what ways is this true?" or "How could this make good sense from the other person's point of view?" The believing game assumes a willingness to suspend doubt, argumentation, and premature conclusions in favor of momentarily accepting the plausibility of another's position.

LINK

The Chapter 1 discussion of theory building includes a more detailed definition of what science has meant throughout history.

---

[1] We use gender-neutral language, and suggest this practice to students out of fairness, accuracy, and a sense of gender equality. However, some otherwise relevant quotations predate this usage, or their authors have made different stylistic decisions. We have chosen to present such statements in their original form, without attempting to make the value judgment (by inserting "[sic]" or by other means) that the authors were mistaken. For example, inserting "[sic]" after *mankind* in a quotation implies wrongly that the original statement contained an error at the time it was written rather than employed a prevalent literary convention.

Although both approaches are reasonable in different contexts and are often interdependent, the believing game may be more central to such tasks as understanding and building communication theories and doing literary criticism. Moreover, the believing game often sets the stage for the doubting game; we can be realistic in our distrust of a concept only after a sincere attempt has been made to perceive it as valid in the same way and in the same spirit in which it was offered.

To illustrate this point, consider the professional responsibilities of the family counselor. A counselor working with a family hears a young boy complain that his parents never listen to him. One approach (based on the doubting game) would involve correcting the boy by pointing out his error: "But just the other day, your mom and dad sat in this office and listened to you complain for twenty minutes!" Such a strategy might be intended to help the boy understand that his complaint is not reasonable. Another approach (based on the believing game) would focus on tentatively accepting the truthfulness of the boy's perception even though the external evidence seems to deny it. Only by establishing the potential believability of the boy's position can that position be disproved (or shown to be valid). Whether he's right or wrong, he feels ignored, and that's his reality. Until he is confirmed at some level, he'll miss the validity of alternative views. In other words, in situations where meanings are uniquely constructed and personally held, the doubting game must be tempered by the believing game.

The study of communication involves much more than memorizing the meanings of terms associated with various theories. Recall is not what developing theoretical appreciation is all about. Instead, *Questions of Communication* will help you become a better critic of communication and, ultimately, a better theorist yourself. You'll still need to master a basic vocabulary to become "adequate" to discuss the theories. But as you read, you should be both a believer and a doubter. Believe that these theories made good sense to their originators and followers and in the context of the theorists' assumptions about human behavior. Unless your background knowledge and creativity approximates that of the theorists, the believing game is absolutely essential (although this assumption in no way makes others' theories and concepts more correct than your own in the long run). Give the theories a chance, and then apply reasoned skepticism consistent with the doubting game. You may ultimately accept or reject the new learnings, but you'll at least have given them a chance.

STAGES AND TYPES OF LEARNING

Developing a critical attitude is one of the primary outcomes of higher education. Even so, many first-year college students are unaware of the attitude changes they're likely to experience as a result of their undergraduate education. They believe they've come to college in order to "get" an education, but researchers have found that the most successful students often use their personal experience to "build" an education.

Two particular research studies have contributed significantly to our understanding of how adults learn in college and other educational environments. Both studies can be thought of as providing *developmental theories*, in that they attempt to explain how people progress to more sophisticated forms of learning over time. They also emphasize human communication, but they do not claim overtly to be "communication research." Perry's 1970 study focuses on the experiences of male students at Harvard from 1954 to 1963. Belenky et al.'s 1986 study, which builds on the Harvard research and on Gilligan's (1982) studies of women's "voice" issues, suggests that women's and men's learning styles differ somewhat in formal and informal settings.

We summarize each study briefly in the following sections. The studies are important because (1) their findings suggest learning choices that are especially appropriate for communication theorizing; (2) they provide *typologies* or category systems, of communication within the particular context of adult learning; and (3) you can use them to begin to diagnose your own learning perspectives. However, keep in mind that a typology cannot describe precisely the experiences of all individuals progressing through college life or model all potential subgroups within an overall learning population. Both studies examined here are based on in-depth interviews with many people over extended time periods, and as such they are helpful in providing clues and generalizations. But neither study can claim definitely that "this is how it is" with students, with women or men, or with learning. There are too many different kinds of campuses, types of students, and goals for learning.

perry's harvard study

While some students always expect teachers to provide clear-cut and well-defined answers to questions, other students expect to accomplish at least some of their learning by comparing ideas or solutions to problems with others. Perry's (1970) Harvard study attempted to determine whether a four-year college education helps students develop more flexible and contextualized qualities of learning, replacing more simplistic forms in which students try to understand the world "in unqualified polar terms of absolute right-wrong, good-bad" (p. 3). In other words, after four years of communicating in college, can students perceive the world in more of its subtleties and shades of gray?

Perry's findings suggest that many college students progress through stages of learning—from a simplistic *either-or* or *yes-no* stage of seeking answers to a more personal learning style based on a pluralistic worldview and a commitment to make learning more personal and practical. Despite the unique personalities of respondents, the study notes that groups of students tend to define learning in similar ways at certain points in their college careers. Perry calls these attitudes "positions" to indicate how students move from one attitude to the next as they progress toward a college degree. He identifies nine such positions, though for the purpose of this summary, we can discuss them in five categories (see Box I-1).

L I N K

Chapter 4 describes how perceiving more subtle meanings is related to what constructivist theorists call *cognitive complexity*.

Perry's study found that college is a profoundly life-changing experience for most students and that they often are not fully aware of how they change as they progress through the educational experience. In some ways, being in college is very different from the rest of our everyday lives, so much so that we might be tempted to contrast it with the "real world." Nonetheless, college life is a real-world activity. In higher education, students encounter a complex mix of different viewpoints that reflect a pluralistic society. In higher education—just as in the workplace or family—students' appreciation of the role of communication is the crucial factor in determining how they balance authorities, theories, learning styles, and personal commitments.

Harvard's undergraduates progressed through identifiable stages of development as they gradually became committed to personal beliefs and more open

BOX I-1

PERRY'S POSITIONS OF LEARNING

- *Duality:* Students are both certain about and protective of their long-held ideas; ideas encountered in college either fit a student's current thought (are probably right) or don't fit (and are probably wrong). ("Don't confuse me with facts—I already know what I believe.")
- *Multiplicity:* All reality is fundamentally negotiable, because authorities often can't even agree among themselves; no position is necessarily any better than another. Students begin to respect multiplicity and disagreement. ("I know researchers say attribution theory works that way, *but I don't agree;* in my family things are different.")
- *Relativism:* There are many possible points of view, but the truth of each one is always relative to context and circumstance; every truth seems "up for grabs." ("Compared to what?" is a typical inquiry from a relativist.)
- *Commitment foreseen:* Going beyond the dilemmas of relativism, many students begin to order their tentative commitments with a stronger sense of identity and more position-taking on issues. ("Although studies in family communication may never be conclusive, I tend to think the social exchange model is the most realistic approach.")
- *Commitment:* Although learning is developed flexibly, it is also guided by the student's personal commitments. The learner realizes that others' views are not only different, but also potentially persuasive. Students in this position have a strong sense of personal identity and also are comfortable with constant change. ("Even though my family and I have always thought of ourselves as staunch conservatives, I learned a lot from the readings on Marxist theory in my political science course.")

Source: Perry, 1970 (pp. 57–176).

to the views of others. Not all of the students experienced their education in this way, but enough did to allow Perry to identify a general pattern.

belenky and colleagues' *women's ways of knowing* study

The Harvard study was based on interview data collected from male Harvard students. Agreeing on the importance of this developmental communication study, another research team set out to explore what the Harvard study did not: the experience of women in various contexts of formal and informal learning. Belenky, Clinchy, Goldberger, and Tarule (1986) wanted to know if women's styles of integrating new experiences might differ from those of men.

In interviews with women learners, Belenky et al. found enough similarities to produce a typology similar to that of Perry. However, they noted several important differences. For example, women tend to elaborate on their experiences differently. In Perry's (1970) study, doubt is a prerequisite to the development of contextual and relativistic thinking that supports personal commitment. *Confirmation*—recognition, assurance, social support—follows. But Belenky et al. found that for women confirmation, not doubt, is the more common prerequisite (pp. 193–194). They speculate that a different pattern of socialization may lead women to start the learning process with an interest in relational support, rather than with a need to doubt. (Remember, however, that such studies illustrate only the *tendencies* of certain behaviors to illustrate men's or women's experience; they do not suggest what is "right" for men or women to do. Some men, for example, more closely approximate the Belenky patterns than do many women.)

Belenky et al. also noted that men and women tend to use different metaphors to describe their experiences. (A *metaphor* is a figure of speech that asserts a sameness about different things, as in "That exam was a killer.") Whereas men tend to speak of *seeing* things in new ways, women more commonly use a metaphor of *voice* to describe their intellectual development. Thus, for example, a man might say, "I see what you mean," "These stories appear to be similar," or "I noticed that you wrote another memo," while a woman might comment, "That speaks to me," "These stories sound similar to me," or "I hear you."

Another difference between the Perry and Belenky studies is that the latter identified "perspectives" instead of a series of sequential "positions" or stages. Belenky and her colleagues weren't surprised that a study of a pluralistic institution with strong traditions such as Harvard would tend to socialize its men toward pluralistic assumptions in a readily identifiable set of stages. Yet studying women in more diverse contexts simply yielded different perspectives that researchers were not as ready to claim as a distinct developmental sequence. Belenky et al. identified five such perspectives (see Box I-2).

The Belenky et al. study has contributed to how we think about learning in general, as well as to our understanding of women's communication styles. Although the researchers do not identify precise developmental stages, there are similarities between their categories and Perry's typology. Effective learning involves constructing answers that are contingent on context and interpretation

L I N K

See the discussions of confirmation in Chapters 6 and 10. If you were a teacher, how could you ensure that your students—male and female—experienced confirmation in your classes?

BOX I-2

BELENKY ET AL.'S PERSPECTIVES OF LEARNERS

- *Silence:* Women in this perspective feel as if they have no voice or that they cannot contribute meaningfully to intellectual or social conversation. They are often dependent on others to think and speak for them. They possess little or no motivation for learning, and they lack confidence when they fear authorities will contradict them.
- *Received knowledge:* The received knowledge learner collects the wisdom of others and may even pass it on. Although she listens well to voices of authority, she doesn't believe she could be a voice of authority for others. This category is similar to Perry's "dualistic" position with one important difference: Whereas men who accept a dualistic position become psychologically aligned with the authorities who supply them with answers, women who are received knowledge learners experience the authorities as distant and separate from themselves.
- *Subjective knowledge:* These women elevate subjective knowledge and disregard or reject the external answers provided by experts. Subjective knowledge learners claim to know things intuitively and experientially, often with a distrust of language, rational analysis, and abstraction. If another person's argument contradicts the personal experience of the subjective knower, then the truth of the argument is considered immediately suspect.
- *Procedural knowledge:* Women in this perspective tend to believe that the answers to important questions can be discovered in the procedures that have guided others in their quest for knowledge. Thus, procedural knowledge learners set out to attain such "how-to" knowledge in order to gain entrance into the game of competence. They seek the formulas necessary for success, and are suspicious of teachers unwilling to provide them. At times, these learners may advocate what feminist theorist Mary Daly (1973) calls *methodolatry*—an exaggerated faith in the ability of "proper" methods to produce good results. Belenky et al. identify two basic types of procedural knowledge: *separate knowing* and *connected knowing*. Unlike the more objective knowledge-is-out-there assumptions of the separate knower, the connected knower shares the subjectivist's distrust of external authority and emphasizes the values of sharing, perspective taking, and cooperative development of ideas.

(continued)

within a pluralistic society. Learning is itself a "question of communication," in that it evolves not from pronouncements or prescriptions but from learners' participation in a dialogue of differing perspectives.

Communication specialists might draw a simple lesson from these two studies. Readers who approach this book from the perspectives of "commitment" (Perry) and "constructed knowledge" (Belenky et al.) will find their task much

BOX I-2 (*cont.*)

- *Constructed knowledge:* This perspective involves a process of "integrating the voices." Women who learn this way share many of Perry's assumptions about personal commitment, including its role in guiding learners through the complicated choices of a contextualized world. For constructed knowledge learners, answers should be neither received nor intuited, but constructed by real people on the basis of their firsthand experiences. Self and other are both necessary for constructed knowledge. An answer can tentatively address a situation, but it does not necessarily persist across situations. These learners are flexible—when contexts change, they expect the answers and actions to change as well. As one respondent commented, "Circumstances change. Our way of looking at things change[s]. Time may have given us what we think are right answers, but it also gives us a different set of problems" (p. 138).

Source: Belenky et al., 1986 (pp. 23–152).

more rewarding. In this book, we attempt to engage students in an ongoing conversation about communication, rather than just presenting facts for memorization.

KNOWLEDGE IN AN ETHICAL FRAMEWORK

As you read the preceding section on learning perspectives, you might have considered questions such as these: "How much faith do I place in my own ideas and feelings?" "How certain am I that I'm right?" "How willing am I to listen to others' ideas and feelings, and which of these ideas can I trust?" "Am I willing to accept opposing points of view as valid?" "Do I give appropriate credit to people who invest their time and energy in studying human problems, or do I too readily believe or dismiss their notions?" "Do I sometimes defend my ideas simply because they're mine?" "To what extent do I state my views to others in a way that reflects what I think they might want to hear?"

These questions not only reflect potential problems in everyday living, but they also imply an ethical foundation to theorizing and researching. Theorists are, in a word, learners, and the "texts" they study are usually not the text*books* written by authors, but the social practices of everyday communication. Theorists are learners at a more basic level than they are defenders of a particular dogma. Although we like to think of theorists as committed to learning and as having an open attitude toward knowledge, they too face dilemmas of how to express their theories.

Throughout this book, we suggest at least implicitly that any investigation has ethical implications. The process of learning always involves decisions about

L I N K

Chapter 10 describes in detail some general approaches to ethical decision making as well as specific ethical systems for communicators.

what is right or wrong, good or bad, positive or negative. People with knowledge often have power, but they cannot avoid **ethics**—the study of the criteria on which moral judgments of right and wrong are made. They only avoid ethical awareness. Suppose you believe knowledge is only gained by reception. This seems innocent enough, but it is hardly a benign belief if you insist that your instructors tidily package answers for you at the end of each class session. Other students, of course, will be affected by this event, and their learning expectations might be different. How you express your beliefs will affect the direction your group will take, and this gives you a kind of power.

Although we will discuss ethics in more detail later, we now should clarify our ethical perspective for communication education. In general, we believe learning and teaching about communication are ethically defensible to the extent that all persons concerned:

1. Remain open to being persuaded by the statements of others, whether they are experts, peers, neither, or both.

2. Be willing to try out new ideas, even those viewed by others as "mistakes." Invite others to experiment also. In this spirit, communicators may share insights creatively, without unnecessary defensiveness.

3. Accept that multiple perspectives on reality are held as valid by different people, especially in different cultural contexts. For example, did you read the accounts of the Perry and Belenky et al. research projects with an attitude of dismissing either men's or women's learning styles as deficient? Is it possible to learn the distinctions first as simply *different*, rather than *better* or *worse* in an overall sense? Remember, too, that scholars often disagree on what counts as evidence or backing for a knowledge claim. Accepting multiple perspectives as valid does not mean that you must agree with all those perspectives. Rather, it means that you are willing to participate readily in Elbow's "believing game" by attempting to experience the level of commitment that another person has toward a particular perspective or point of view.

4. Attempt to test any tentatively held knowledge by applying criteria developed by social consensus. That is, people interested in developing new learning should understand the social context in which their learning occurs. A learner who is unaware of the existing research in a field of study—called the field's *literature*—is not sufficiently prepared for further learning. Remember, however, that the consensus of judgment in any area of study at any given time does not represent the only possible judgment or even the best one (see Chapter 1). It simply means that accumulated wisdom should not be ignored.

5. Live with ambiguity, but treat contradiction as a signal to start questioning things. Not everything will be or needs to be explained. However, when two "accepted" facts, ideas, or definitions seem to contradict each other, and it seems they both can't be true, regard that as an invitation or challenge for further study. You may end up finding a paradox or mak-

ing a genuine contribution to your understanding of communication—
but in either case, the ambiguity will be worthwhile.

6. Evaluate knowledge claims against your personal experience and the
everyday pragmatism of what works. In other words, when you take a position, hold it tentatively, and until you learn otherwise, trust your own experience. After all, personal experience is your own accumulated (but
usually unsystematic) research. This doesn't mean that you mistrust the
experience of others, but that your own life forms one basis for evaluating it. In addition, accept the responsibility of introspection; ask yourself
questions that test your experience and probe your prejudices, moral assumptions, and beliefs about cause and effect.

Boiled down, this ethic can be summarized as the art of open questioning—
an art that is ultimately also scientific. Everything else, in a sense, flows from the
questions that we're curious or courageous enough to ask. In words that summarize the premise of this book, biologist Robert McFarlane (1992) explains why education should emphasize not the accumulation of facts but the questioning of
previous assumptions:

> Science, from one perspective, is the art of phrasing questions and identifying
> their attendant assumptions. Its basic tenet is that nature has no secrets. The
> obstacles to furthering knowledge lie in formulating the right questions and
> in circumventing ambiguous answers, never an easy task. The best practition-
> ers know that incisive questions and skillful analysis will ultimately yield their
> reward. Artful questions may require new technology, often from unrelated
> disciplines. New questions may require fresh insight, unencumbered by the
> baggage of past experience, and a probing mind to test old concepts. The im-
> portance of the proper question is often overlooked, by experienced observer
> and novice alike. (p. 31)

TESTING THE CONCEPTS

At the end of each chapter is a brief section like this one, designed to summarize
major themes in a question-and-answer format. Its purpose is to supplement the
opinions of the authors with others' voices. Although we have written and streamlined the questions, most of them have been adapted from spontaneous questions
asked over the years by our students. They will stimulate your thinking about the
implications of communication topics and reinforce the practicality of communication theory. The questions may suggest other questions to you. Your instructor is probably hoping you will ask them in class.

"I don't feel a 'calling.' I'm just taking this class to fulfill a requirement. Does this chapter apply to me?"

Although most students who take a communication theory course are communication majors, we realize that many are not. Even for them, a serious discussion of the complexity of communication and its connection to learning should be helpful. What it takes to *learn* more effectively and what it takes to *communicate* more effectively are essentially the same thing: Ask relevant questions about reality, be open to others' answers, and find a way to develop a realistic commitment to the answers you build for yourself.

"I've been communicating since I was a baby. Why is it so important to study something I already know how to do and have done naturally for so long?"

Like anything else that's worthwhile in life, solutions to communication problems are not lined up in neat rows. Tentative answers are often puzzled out individually by people who are basically experimenters in their own lives. "Can other people's solutions help me and you, though?" is a valid question. Sometimes the answer is yes, but sometimes it is no. Communication theorists are like consultants—their responsibility is to survey the solutions persons reach individually and to note the patterns that, when generalized, could apply to the rest of us.

"When I play 'the doubting game' in the classroom, I come across as argumentative; but if I believe everything the instructor says, I become a robot. Is there a happy medium?"

Yes. The happy medium is to avoid concentrating on either one or the other, emphasizing instead a blend of doubting and believing. In the questioning you do in class and elsewhere, the best clarifications come when you buy into a topic enough to believe that it's important, but not so much that you accept answers without question. Accepting professors' opinions as absolute facts is dangerous for you and your professors. The danger for them is that they will cease to learn and question themselves.

"As a woman, I've often felt that no one listens to me in class, so I practice silence as a defense mechanism. How can I learn to speak up? Is there a theory to explain this?"

(VR): Often, women feel less self-assured in college, and believe that men will dismiss their comments as "emotional" or "trivial." As an only child, and a daughter at that, I often heard my father (obviously from another generation of communicators) make comments like, "You don't know what you're talking about; stay out of this." After years of similar verbal and nonverbal responses from men, silence became a protective buffer.

Questions that integrate both doubting and believing are an effective first step to becoming more assertive in classes. Use your questions to break the silence, but also to speak up for the things you do understand from your reading and your own experience.

"Why the emphasis on ethics? Shouldn't science and the search for knowledge be value-free?"

We emphasize the importance of ethical alertness, here in the Introduction as well as in Part Five, because no social knowledge can be considered seriously apart from potential applications. Ethical theory is a practical way of evaluating the uses to which theories of communication might be put. Asking and answering such questions as "What works?" and "Why does it work?" will only take us so far; they will give us insights into our options in public life. Beyond this, though, asking the ethically oriented "whether" question (whether we should in fact do such things) is the practical ground on which communication options must be evaluated.

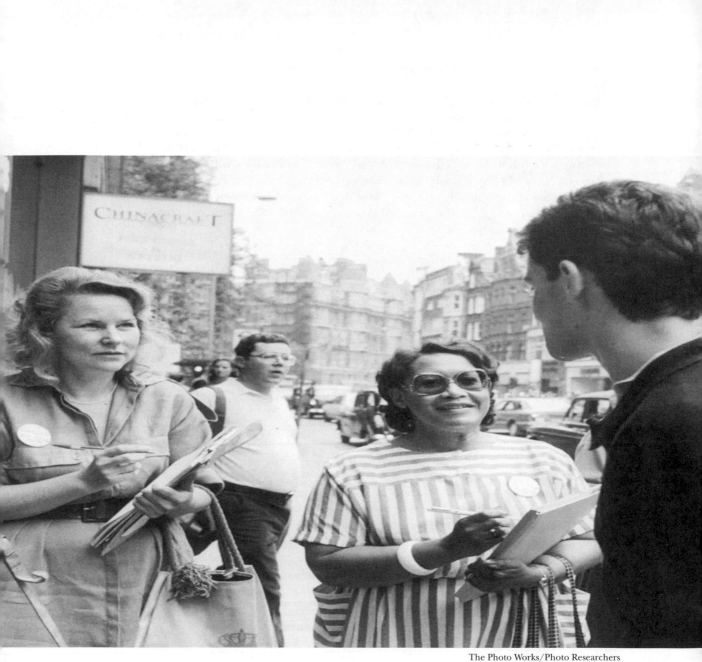

The Photo Works/Photo Researchers

asking, observing, theorizing, checking, asking...

"how do we learn about communication?"

1

There is a continuum of seeing what is to be done and doing it, and seeing what has been done and reviewing it, reseeing it and redoing it. Theory and practice are continuous. And by our practice may ye know our theories.

M. C. Richards, *The Crossing Point* (1973, pp. 81-82)

Some years ago, a highly motivated and intelligent student named Ted took a communication theory course taught by one of the authors. Throughout the term, Ted read with relish, wrote creatively and intelligently, and contributed consistently to class discussions. He was hungry for learning—and he fully digested the material. In short, he was a teacher's dream.

Ted also questioned the text, the teacher, and other students. He wouldn't settle for easy answers. "What else?" he would ask. "How do you know?" "Who says so?" "What are some alternate explanations?" "Why couldn't it be another way?" Such persistent questioning can be a teacher's nightmare because it's not always easy to respond to highly inquisitive students. But Ted questioned so sincerely, persistently, and selflessly that it was obvious that he wasn't showing off. "Put up, or shut up," he seemed to say. He wanted the rest of us to put up our own best ideas. He would not settle for a mere survey course where terms and names were memorized and tested on exams. Ted represented a style of learning we should remember when deciding how to teach and learn communication theory.

Ted demonstrated the most fundamental attitude of scientific learning—the willingness to ask meaningful questions. He wanted the course to stress ideas and thereby to prepare him to *theorize* more effectively. He wanted to participate in theory-building, rather than just observe the theories that others have built. We'll consider this process of *theorizing* in more detail later in the chapter. For now, we can think of theorizing as a way of making an educated guess, an explanation-in-process, open to change.

Throughout this book, we stress the importance of theorizing, of approaching communication from the standpoint of the questions that motivate theorists. This is a practical as well as challenging introduction to the study of communication. As you read the book, you may notice that it is unlike a traditional textbook in its style of teaching. You will learn about communication through your own questioning and theorizing.

Ted wanted to become either a communication specialist in a large organization or a college teacher. He'd declared a major and made a commitment to learn as much as possible about it. He had, in short, found a *calling*—a decision to submit "to the vast area of information and belief surrounding his selected field of inquiry" (Polanyi, 1967, p. 79). Most professions, and especially academic ones, are described in terms of inquiry, which is just another way of saying that professionals are expected to ask a lot of questions and to be persistent in seeking answers.

When writing this book, we assumed that our readers were responding at least tentatively to a calling. We also assumed that by enrolling in a course that goes beyond basic communication processes, you are seeking assistance in becoming a better questioner. Although you might have chosen to study communication because of your skill in conversation or public speaking, you also should know that the discipline has a rich intellectual heritage. Effective communication specialists in such areas as management, training, public relations, marketing, journalism, and teaching possess not only good performance skills but also the ability to theorize. As social scientist Kurt Lewin has observed, nothing is as practical as a good theory (1951, p. 169). Theories help us apply what we understand in one situation to new or unexpected experiences. What could be more practical than that?

We cannot assume that you share Ted's learning style or personality. However, because all communicators must make assumptions about their audience, we can assume that you share Ted's curiosity about communication and that you have a calling. Your curiosity and your calling will combine to make your education in communication both personally relevant and professionally valuable.

In this chapter, we will accomplish several goals. First, we will attempt to demystify the term *theory.* "Oh, that's just fine in theory," people often say, "but it'll never work in practice." By saying this, they imply that theory is lofty, abstract, and, worst of all, impractical. Instead of this dismissive attitude, think of academic theorizing as simply a logical extension of the everyday process of learning. Second, we'll relate theorizing to an attitude of availability to show how crucial this attitude can be. Third, we will explain the more formal theory-building cycle of communication studies, the components of a theory, the research process through which theories are developed, the functions of theory in the academic world, and some criteria for evaluating theories. Finally, we will discuss theory-building goals to show what theorists hope to accomplish in their work.

THEORIZING AS AN EVERYDAY OCCURRENCE

Imagine that you play tennis every Saturday morning with a group of friends. You usually look forward to the event, but on this particular Friday night you feel tired, weak, sickly, and not in the mood to exercise tomorrow morning. You'd rather stay home and do some low-level activity. You seriously consider calling your tennis partners to cancel out.

Just then, your housemate comes in and says: "I hope you aren't planning anything tomorrow morning; that's the only time I can make all those phone calls you promised you'd help with. I'm counting on you." Suddenly, playing tennis tomorrow morning looks like a good idea. You reply, "Hey, I'd like to help, but I have a tennis game every Saturday morning, remember?" Something interesting has happened here. Even though your housemate has just suggested the exact kind of activity you were considering a moment ago, you object to it. Why? Let's consider several possible reasons:

1. You say no because you want to teach your roommate a lesson about assumptions.

2. You say no because you have compared rationally the consequences of inconveniencing one person versus inconveniencing several people.
3. You say no because you dislike making phone calls and weren't serious when you promised to help.
4. You say no because you are selfish.
5. You say no because you just realized how much you enjoy playing tennis.

Note that each explanation relies on a different implicit theory about the situation. But as our hypothetical example illustrates, analyzing human behavior even in everyday situations is a complex task because many possible explanations can account for a single action. How, then, do we identify the most appropriate explanation(s)?

Studying communication theory offers general clues, criteria, and definitions. Although such clues may not apply to *particular* persons, events, or relationships, they can help us make sense of our world. The act of theorizing is more than guesswork, and even more than enlightened guesswork. This leads us to an expanded definition of the concept: *To theorize is to respond to meaningful questions with tentative answers*. Although the term **theory** was originally associated with seeing and vision (Williams, 1976, p. 266), it now refers to the explanations people use to resolve the ambiguities of life. (A word we sometimes use similarly, *speculation,* is also related etymologically to vision.) People speculate and theorize all the time, though at various levels. In our hypothetical example, we might refer to the five explanations in the list as (1) behavioral teaching theory, (2) rational theory, (3) clinical psychological theory, (4) human nature theory, and (5) self-realization theory. But all of these "theories" are merely guesswork. A systematic approach is what distinguishes serious theorizing from simple speculation.

A formal theory (in a scientific sense) presents *a set of tentative answers built in response to focused questions, often phrased as propositions and described systematically.* Although it may sound odd to refer to answers as "built" rather than discovered, this is precisely what we intend. The answers are not "out there" waiting to be found; rather, they have to be invented from the intellectual materials at hand—insights, clues, concepts, and data. You have an answer only after you've worked to build one, not when you've passively received one.

One communication theorist working within social psychology has systematically researched the kinds of behaviors we hypothesized about earlier. Brehm's (1966) theory of *psychological reactance* cannot claim to describe the motives of all real people caught in similar Saturday morning predicaments, but it can highlight continuities in human communication behavior that help explain the interaction. (Communication specialists are more likely to want to understand the inner workings of such events—and to be asked to explain them—than are everyday people!) Brehm's theory, in short, predicts that people tend to react to situations in ways that protect their range of options. Therefore, if your housemate's expectations were perceived as a threat to your freedom of choice about how to spend your Saturday morning, you would most likely react by asserting your right to choose. By expressing your desire to play tennis, you are also telling your roommate that you want choices. Brehm's theory, then, is based on a perceived connection between how people speak and their psychological needs.

Notice the similarities between Brehm's research and what any observer could do on the spot. In both situations, the person theorizes to structure ambiguous events by offering tentative answers in response to focused questions. Although the everyday theorist doesn't have the same capacity to conduct research as the professional theorist, the fundamental process varies only in that the professional can be more systematic in finding evidence to support or reject a hunch. As researcher John Gillin (quoted in Natanson, 1963) explains:

> Every "normal" human being is, willy-nilly, a theorizer. This is merely to say that no normally intelligent member of the species . . . can look at anything without formulating a theory (or following some traditional formulation) about what he observes. To take a very trivial example, Joe Doakes hammers a nail into a board and the nail crumples. Doakes says to himself (if he has no audience), "That must be hard wood instead of soft wood." That statement of Doakes is a theoretical conclusion or theorem from certain implicit postulates. It is meant to explain the result he had from trying to drive the nail. Furthermore, it is a verifiable theorem. There are certain methods available to Doakes to determine whether or not the piece of wood involved is in fact northern oak or southern pine, or something else. Thus, everyone theorizes. (p. 11)

Similarly, Dillon (1990) suggests that "practice is not a matter of brute action but conception and reflection. It is knowledge-in-action, an enactment that is informed by an understanding at once theoretical and empirical and practical. Hence the far-off realms of theory . . . are nearer to practice than we may have guessed. They are not worlds apart. They form the one world of questioning" (p. 1).

Schön's (1983) discussion of **reflection-in-action** shows how closely tied theory and practice should be (see Box 1-1). The most effective practitioners may have developed a storehouse of useful techniques, but more importantly they are willing to revise their behavior in light of ongoing informal theories and are open to change. According to Schön, practitioners who "overlearn their routines . . . may miss important opportunities to think about what [they are] doing." They may find themselves "drawn into patterns of error [they] cannot correct" and be "selectively inattentive to phenomena that do not fit the categories of [their previous] knowing-in-action" (p. 61). In effect, not just all practice, but all perception of the world becomes theory-dependent (Hanson, 1958). We cannot perceive any new circumstance meaningfully without bringing previously learned generalizations to bear on it. Approaching each situation as if it were brand new is psychologically impossible.

L I N K

Brehm's theorizing about psychological reactance attempts to account for a widespread and persistent tendency in human behavior, not just how individuals may react to others in certain situations. As such, his search was for what theorists call a *covering law* of behavior. See the discussion of covering laws later in this chapter.

THE ATTITUDE OF AVAILABILITY

You are a theorist of relational negotiation in the workplace when you object to a supervisor loudly criticizing a new employee in front of the entire staff. You are a

BOX 1-1

DONALD SCHÖN (1983) ON THEORISTS' "REFLECTION-IN-ACTION":

- "When someone reflects-in-action, he becomes a researcher in the practice context. He is not dependent on the categories of established theory and technique, but constructs a new theory of the unique case. . . . He does not keep means and ends separate, but defines them interactively as he frames a problematic situation" (p. 68).
- "Many practitioners, locked into a view of themselves as technical experts, find nothing in the world of practice to occasion reflection. They have become too skillful at techniques of selective inattention, junk categories, and situational control, techniques which they use to preserve the constancy of their knowledge-in-practice. For them, uncertainty is a threat; its admission is a sign of weakness" (p. 69).

Clearly, improvisational jazz musicians and good freelance basketball players are skilled in constructing "new theories of the unique case" because they cannot afford to rely on previous techniques. In the communication professions, which roles do you think depend most on Schön's reflection-in-action type of theorizing? Reporters? Organizational consultants? Teachers? Why?

Source: Schön, 1983 (pp. 68–69).

theorist of family communication when you decide to ease tension by suggesting that more activities be done together with siblings, parents, partner, or children. You are a theorist when you decide that the friend you've written to for five Christmases but who has never responded is no longer interested in maintaining your friendship. In each case, you have asked yourself a question, collected some informal evidence, and formed a tentative conclusion. Your theory about each would include general expectations for relationships and particular expectations for these unique relationships. Although in the last example a letter from your friend might convince you otherwise, your current decision that the friendship is over would remain in place until further data became available.

As the preceding examples illustrate, each insight into communication has to integrate both the general and the particular. Effective theorists learn that generalizations do not mean that the expected outcomes will automatically fall into place. Exceptions or variations will always occur at the level of concrete particulars; if too many exceptions occur, the basic theory must be revised to account for them. At some point in most theory courses, a student will "disagree" with a scholarly theory by citing a personal example ("That theory isn't right—my parents

were completely different"). Although the student's experience may very well be
valid, it is not a true disagreement with the theory itself, but simply an exception
to it or a variation on a theme.

At the core of scientific theorizing are the abilities to adjust the generalizations as the particulars change and to develop generalizations that one knows
will not contain all possible particulars. This kind of flexibility is also psychologically healthy, as one psychiatrist (Kubie, 1961) reminds us:

> The measure of health is flexibility, the freedom to learn through experience,
> the freedom to change with changing internal and external circumstances, to
> be influenced by reasonable argument, admonitions, exhortation, and the ap-
> peal to emotions; the freedom to respond appropriately to the stimulus of re-
> ward and punishment, and especially the freedom to cease when sated. The
> essence of normality is flexibility in all of these vital ways. The essence of ill-
> ness is the freezing of behavior into unalterable and insatiable patterns. (pp.
> 20–21)

Another way to describe this psychological flexibility is to say that the effective
communicator—and, therefore, the effective theorist—is *available* to change.
Availability is necessary to theorizing in four major ways:

- Curiosity
- Willingness to be surprised
- Adequate knowledge
- Appreciation of multiple perspectives

First, the theorist should be curious. Theorizing, in fact, demands curiosity—
a willingness to ask "Why?" while also accepting that complete explanations are
not possible. Curiosity is intimately related to the process of creativity, another
process that can't be taught readily. Curious people tend to be satisfied with neither a situation of ambiguity nor a state of supposedly complete explanation.

Second, the theorist should be willing to be surprised and to accept the
consequences of surprise (usually the loss of certainty). It may be uncomfortable
at times to recognize how limited your own perspective may be. In her essay "Seeing," Pulitzer Prize–winning writer Annie Dillard (1975) tells the true story of a
group of cataract sufferers born sightless. After surgeons discovered techniques
for performing safe operations to let them see the world, these newly gifted people reacted very differently to their personal miracles. Some described the task of
viewing the "dazzle of color-patches" as "tormentingly difficult" (p. 28). A young
girl, upon visiting a garden, stood transfixed in front of what she called "the tree
with the lights in it" (p. 30). Other patients described their newfound ability to see
as intimidating, uncomfortable, even threatening. Some refused to open their
eyes or to make sense of the new images before them, preferring instead the comfort of depending on others' interpretations of the visual world.

You may have been intimidated by a new area of study or other event that
helps you identify with the fears these persons encountered in their new world of

vision. But for theorists and others, learning cannot take place without a willingness to be surprised.

Third, a theorist should be knowledgeable. Curiosity doesn't develop in an information vacuum, nor does it develop in an environment in which a single set of assumptions predominates. Anthropologists, who theorize about human variability between cultures, understand this well. According to Gregory Bateson (1980), all knowledge is based on sensing differences (pp. 31–32). Thus, to understand where you are or what you are doing, you must also learn about places other than where you live and about the behavior of strangers. Mary Catherine Bateson (1990)—a prominent scholar and the daughter of anthropologists Bateson and Margaret Mead—emphasizes the need to be knowledgeable about things beyond your own most comfortable surroundings. "One of the great steps forward in history," she writes, "was learning to regard those who spoke odd-sounding languages and had different smells and habits as fully human, as similar to oneself. The next step from this realization, the step which we have still not fully made, is the willingness to question and purposefully alter one's own conditions and habits, to learn by observing others" (p. 57). Theorists become knowledgeable, and therefore more effectively curious, when they read and experience widely in seemingly separate areas.

Therefore, the theorist should understand and appreciate multiple perspectives on communication, perspectives that are held both concurrently and provisionally (Littlejohn, 1982). Being curious means that you continue inquiring even after you've developed a perspective on an issue. If you are an expert in the theory of group decision making, for instance, could you ignore new theories of how individuals develop verbal plans for upcoming interactions? Surely not, because the perspectives overlap. You'll continue asking, synthesizing, and asking some more. Abraham Kaplan's (1964) *law of the instrument* refers to the unfortunate tendency of a theorist or researcher to view *all* problems in light of *one* technique, methodology, or perspective. Just as the child who discovers a hammer will also find many things in need of hammering (to use Kaplan's analogy), the single-minded Marxist theorist might see *only* exploitation in economic power relations and the experimentalist might be convinced that quantitative laboratory studies comprise the *only* valid type of communication research.

Remember Ted—the inquisitive student we told you about at the start of the chapter? One afternoon late in the term, he enlivened a theory discussion with a question that went something like this: "Well, we've studied all these different theories. Systems of this, laws of that, rules, principles, blah, blah, blah. Which one is right?" Although only Ted knew for sure, the instructor's theory was that Ted understood the implications of his question and looked forward to the kind of discussion it would generate. The class eventually concluded that it was not useful to claim any one theory supreme or correct. Because theories tend to be developed for different reasons, to explain different phenomena, or to examine similar phenomena in different settings, it is probably unwise to wish for a single theory to unite all communication studies.

The diversity inherent in theorizing enriches the field. Donald Campbell's (1969; 1986) model of scholarly or scientific knowledge as a fish's scales helps us

L I N K

Chapter 4, which explores cognition and personal experience, includes an extended discussion of perception and its relationship to theorizing about communication.

understand why. Each small scale, which represents a specialty or theoretical insight, overlaps with other small scales until the entire fish is covered. No one scale (specialty) can or should cover the entire fish (field), but the coverage is sufficient if we coordinate the overlapping. Such diverse scholars as literary critic Wayne Booth (1990, pp. 325–327) and philosopher of science Michael Polanyi (1967) advocate similar models. Polanyi (1967) calls his notion the *principle of mutual control* in science, and claims that it works well because of the "chains of overlapping neighborhoods" (p. 72).

Communication theory, therefore, is not a horse race in which the various explanations (and explainers) are straining to win, place, or show; it's more like a convention in which the various points of view are given forums and opportunities to be influential. We will discuss the evaluation of theories later in the chapter (some theories, as you might expect, are more useful than others in helping us understand communication). But by discussing what motivates successful theorists, we have demystified the process of theorizing somewhat. Let's consider what professional communication specialists do when their curiosity motivates them to explain human interaction systematically.

> **LINK**
>
> Recall from the Introduction that building theories is remarkably similar to being a successful college student. As good learners progress through college, they tend to become more tolerant of others' opinions, more comfortable with ambiguity, and more willing to construct personal commitments. In other words, they become effective theorists.

THE THEORY-BUILDING CYCLE IN COMMUNICATION

science as methodical inquiry

Leonard Hawes (1975), the author of one of the few book-length discussions of theory-building—as opposed to theory-surveying—in communication, describes the *scientific attitude* in plain language:

> The scientific attitude refers to an ever-present curiosity on the one hand and an ever-present suspicion on the other. The curiosity is manifested in the asking of questions and the suspicion is manifested in the uneasiness with existing answers. This uneasiness generates new questions. In the process of asking new questions and questioning old answers, there is no one method or procedure to follow. There is an array of approaches which is, in part, influenced by the scientist's style of thinking. But even within particular approaches, there is no consensus regarding what constitutes an appropriate question or an appropriate method for attempting an answer to the question. (p. 23)

Note that Hawes not only reinforces curiosity as a motivation for science, but also suggests that scientists must be familiar enough with existing knowledge to say, in effect, "we haven't learned enough; this doesn't seem to explain what it needs to explain." Human knowledge usually is advanced when curious people shake their heads and mutter, "I don't know . . . yet." The "yet" is crucial. Moreover, the scientific method is more open to revision and based more on the subjective, creative arguments of scientists struggling to solve human problems than most people assume (Kuhn, 1970). Perhaps most important, Hawes emphasizes, current knowledge should not breed complacency but cycles of reconsideration.

Several times, we've used the word *science* without defining it. It is a common word that is usually presented without definition. But we should examine it more closely. Despite its aura of objective precision and its association with such academic fields as chemistry, biology, and physics, *science* is a relatively new word in the English language. From its earliest known usage in the fourteenth century until the middle of the nineteenth century, it typically referred to methodical inquiry, often theoretically based. Literature could be studied "scientifically"; so could religion or political strategy. In the twentieth century, however, *science* generally refers to the objective observation of and inquiry into areas where experimentation, specification, and control (rather than personal experience and interpretation) are appropriate (Williams, 1976, pp. 232–235).

Late in the twentieth century, however, we seem to be returning to a wider definition of science in the social sciences (which usually include not only communication, but also psychology, sociology, anthropology, and political science). Thus, a scientist today is not necessarily someone who conducts precise experiments that measure objective truths (see Fay, 1996). Certainly, experimentation plays an exciting role in the scientific community's attempt to understand human behavior. But the social scientist does not assume that controlled laboratory methods are the only way to do so. As we will use the term in this book, *science* is *the systematic attempt, through various methodologies, to ask and answer meaningful questions while remaining open to alternate answers.* Researchers who are careful observers and who employ **qualitative methodologies** (which explore and describe the qualities of phenomena) or **quantitative methodologies** (which focus on isolating, counting, and analyzing units of phenomena) are scientists when they respond to their curiosity with systematic questioning. Qualitative researchers may refer to themselves as *interpretivists* (those who study relatively intangible and subjective patterns of human interpretation) or as *naturalistic researchers* (those who study communication in natural settings). Quantitative researchers, in contrast, tend to be *experimentalists* (those who structure laboratory comparisons of how different groups and individuals communicate in certain ways) or *survey researchers* (those who use questionnaires or precision interviews to collect data and illustrate general trends among social communicators). In practice, however, qualitative researchers are not averse to counting things if it advances their understanding, and quantitative researchers often engage in interpretation and speculation. The distinction is not as clear-cut as a textbook discussion might imply. Still, most researchers, if pressed, will align themselves with one label or the other.

Historically, both quantitative and qualitative scholars have been systematic, thorough, and, considering our previous definition, scientific in their missions. The vast majority of scholars in both areas of research acknowledge the value of quantitative and qualitative studies as well as the many variations within each approach. However, they sometimes disagree about the relative importance of their respective contributions to our knowledge of communication. Quantitative scholars, for example, claim that their methodological precision gives them more control over observations and experiments, allows them to study larger and more varied groups of people, results in better generalizations, and is a more objective means of gathering data than qualitative studies. Quantitative scholars also argue that their methodology delineates cause-effect relationships more precisely and, therefore, produces data that is empirically valid.

Qualitative scholars counter that cause-effect attributions of quantitative research far too often assume one-way influence (i.e., a particular cause directly creates a particular effect), and that most quantitative studies are conducted in artificial settings that cannot truly represent real-world situations or complex issues of race, class, gender, and power. Qualitative scholars believe that their method of studying dynamic communicating in natural settings preserves the subjectivity essential to learning about communication systematically. While each group understands the reasons why scholars are attracted to the other camp, they tend to disagree about the relative significance of their contributions.

In two recent works, communication scholars Janet Beavin Bavelas (1995) and Mary Anne Fitzpatrick (1993) address the folly of methodological narrow-mindedness. Bavelas questions the basis of the distinctions between quantitative and qualitative methods, suggesting that the widely accepted dichotomies (e.g., empirical/nonempirical, statistical/nonstatistical, objective/subjective, deductive/inductive, hypothesis testing/exploratory, artificial/natural, not generalizable/generalizable, and laboratory/real world), when they are applied to distinguish quantitative from qualitative research, are more misleading than instructive. Bavelas (1995) claims that "A highly restricted choice of methods inevitably stunts the growth of theory. . . . [I]f we reject polarization we may discover new, previously unexplored combinations of both approaches" (p. 51).

Similarly, Fitzpatrick (1993) writes that "as a discipline, we are not capitalizing on the mutual relevance of each other's work. The shocking disdain we have for each other's intellectual contributions is holding us back" (p. 124). Fitzpatrick supports a *realist philosophy of communication science* that would draw upon and synthesize the best empirical traditions of both quantitative and qualitative research. At their extremes, single-minded quantitative research can be too sterile and too reliant on a "hard determinism," while single-minded qualitative research can be too relativistic in its emphasis on unique cases and researcher involvement (pp. 123–124). Fitzpatrick's realist approach, which stresses objectivity, causality, and "soft determinism" within a context of social interpretation, "supports a variety of methodologies" (p. 124).

BOX 1-2

SCIENCE INVOLVES:
- Methodical questioning
- Appropriate suspicion about answers
- Qualitative and quantitative research methods
- Dynamic objectivity
- Linkage with human values and concerns
- Ethical and rhetorical engagement

Another important critique has stimulated a deeper understanding of the scientific enterprise. Biophysicist and feminist theorist Evelyn Fox Keller (1985) argues that traditional Western science was long based on a male model of knowing. In this model, a separation between knower and known was assumed, analysis was the tool, and domination of nature by "mankind" was the goal. Keller claims that the male conception of science restricted women's participation; defined as "unscientific," women were excluded because their skepticism of objectivity contradicted the concerns of established scientists. Viewing the traditionally objective model of science as incomplete rather than "wrong," Keller believes science should strive for what she terms *dynamic objectivity,* which "grants to the world around us its independent integrity but does so in a way that remains cognizant of, indeed relies on, our connectivity with the world" (p. 117). Dynamic objectivity "makes use of subjective experience . . . in the interests of a more effective objectivity. Premised on continuity, it recognizes difference between self and other as an opportunity for a deeper and more articulated kinship" (p. 117). Keller's suggestion may be said to integrate Elbow's doubting and believing games, quantitative and qualitative research methods, and the objective and subjective realms of human knowledge (see Box 1-2).

As these and other communication scholars suggest, the traditional scientific attitude is helpful, but it ought not serve as the *only* stimulus for theory development. Humanistic thought, sometimes erroneously viewed as opposed to science, is actually a complement to it. Scientific and humanistic inquiry can be rigorous, sustained, committed, and based on theory. Researchers in the humanities perhaps emphasize theories of interpretation, valuing, and subjectivity more than the so-called social scientists. If anything, the subject matter of the humanities is more open to speculation and theorizing, though it may be less open to verification. Qualitative research methods are thus prevalent in the humanities, but this may be seen as complementing social science rather than competing with it. Social science and humanities scholars are, in effect, teammates (Brown, 1987; Farrell, 1987; Montagu, 1962), and this book reflects their interdependence. As one humanities scholar puts it: "In spite of the trappings of objectivity in which we like to drape our psychological, educational, social, and artistic theories, the knowledge they have to offer is always indeterminate in the sense of being relative to the values behind them. When we ask for objective solutions to social or artistic problems, we are asking for brain surgery with a monkey wrench" (Hardison, 1972, p. xx). Researchers in the humanities often search in different places for their answers, asking different research questions, but ultimately the overriding goal is the same: "How can we better understand the human animal?"

The theories you will read about in this book were developed by real, flesh-and-blood people who were and are smart, knowledgeable, insightful, and creative in some ways, and—since they're human—probably short-sighted and narrow-minded in others.

Science is built on the work of theorists who attempt to be systematic, but it is also marked by a messy collection of arguments and comparisons, mistakes and happy accidents. Science progresses as much by wrong answers as it does by accurate ones. But those wrong (or inappropriate, or unhelpful, or irrelevant) answers have to be identified as such. Doing science isn't just doing the study, but also fleshing out the implications of the study afterwards in the context of other work by other scholars, in other places, at other times, with other subjects, with other methods, and perhaps with other expectations.

Science is less like a sterile laboratory than it is like two other metaphors— the playing field or the town meeting. The playing field metaphor reminds us that scientists play by rules that are commonly accepted and have expectations that are relatively well understood. This is part of the *ethical* dimension of communication theory that applies even at the early stages of inquiry (see Box 1-3). For example, investigators should not allow personal biases to affect the results of a study, should not exploit human participants with whom they work, and should not falsify data. They should attempt to share their results with other scientists and describe their methodologies accurately enough to allow comparisons with other studies.

The town meeting metaphor reminds us that science is an arena that is, in some ways, essentially *rhetorical*. **Rhetoric** is the purposeful process of forming and processing messages to achieve personal and social goals. The scholar presents theories to the scientific community expecting them to be understood, agreed (or disagreed) with, and persuasive. They often aren't. As theorist Klaus Krippendorf (1989) points out, "the history of communication research is not so much about communication but about creative scholars, about researchers talking to each other and playing with ideas" (p. 77). In other words, scientists don't just *do* science, they also *argue* science. This doesn't imply that they yell and scream at each other (well . . . maybe some do). Instead, they theorize in public. And, in a sense, they advertise.

the cycle

Scientists advance their claims and argue through a process shown in Figure 1-1. Let's examine each of these stages in detail, considering some of the various building blocks of theories. Remember that even though we use the term "theorizing" for one particular step in the cycle, the whole cycle really characterizes the theory-building process, not just that step. Our description is cast as if you, the reader, were the theorist.

LINKS

• Chapter 8 describes how communicators may change their minds as a result of public and interpersonal rhetoric.

• Habermas (see Chapter 10) describes a communicative rationality that (ideally) governs most modern scientific arguments. His approach to dialogue helps explain how scientists and other communicators find procedures for reaching consensus.

BOX 1-3

ETHICAL INQUIRERS:
- Attempt to be aware of personal biases.
- Acknowledge how bias influences conclusions.
- Do not exploit human subjects.
- Report results truthfully.
- Share results openly.
- Describe their methods thoroughly, to invite further study.

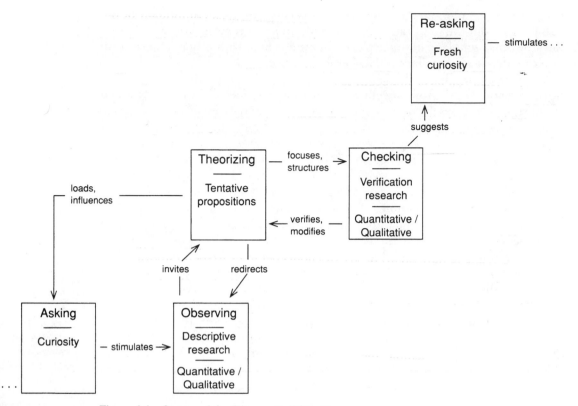

Figure 1-1   Stages of the Theory-Building Process

   1. Asking. At this initial stage in the theory-building process, you are confronted with a problem, situation, or phenomenon that you are unable to explain. It may involve a state of ambiguity or, as Dewey (1933) says, a *felt difficulty*
(the realization that something is wrong). Perhaps your felt difficulty is simply a
curiosity about what else is "out there," and you feel compelled to explore it. Perhaps you're not satisfied with your current understanding of something you consider intriguing. Whatever the problem may be, at this stage you begin to ask
questions: "What if?," "What else?," "Why is a certain result so regular?," and others. Asking ideally leads to observing, an attempt to gather information relevant
to your questions.
   2. Observing. Through observing, you are able to focus your questions in
ways that may lead you to possible answers. In a sense, systematic observing surveys the relevant landscape and provides a context for your questions. You read,
watch, plan, and notice differences as they arise. Many researchers specialize in *descriptive research,* which charts conceptual territories by gathering information
about them. Often the goals of such research are exploratory; for example, linguists use surveys to map the speech variations among people in various geo-
graphical regions within a culture, and public opinion pollsters profile attitudes
of the electorate. Although descriptive research is sometimes unfairly regarded as

less prestigious than other research traditions, it is a crucial component of the theory-building cycle. Observing is interdependent with the next step we'll consider, theorizing.

   3. Theorizing. At this stage, you bring your critical and creative powers to bear on the problem you face. You begin to build tentative answers and construct explanations that make sense and are reasonably consistent with your data. You also develop a **research question**, which asks as clearly as possible what relationship between behaviors can be found in a focused investigation, and a **hypothesis**, which is a tentative statement of truth. Smith (1988) supplies examples: "Do stereotyped portrayals of women in television entertainment programs affect the self-concepts of young female viewers?" is a research question, and "Different value systems of parents and their college-age children are linked to unwanted verbal conflict" is a research hypothesis (p. 24). Although theorists phrase hypotheses as statements rather than questions, the assumption is that all hypotheses are in effect open questions. If you hypothesize, "Quitting my part-time job will improve my grades," you are expecting to have twenty or so extra hours per week to spend studying. But whether you will actually devote all twenty hours to studying and improve your grades are open questions.

   Theorizing also involves other aspects of clear thinking and communication (see Box 1-4). Theorists build theories from **concepts**, complex or abstract ideas that are identified by special terms to aid our understanding and discussion of them. Consider, for example, the highly abstract concept we refer to as *attitude*. Without the term, it would be difficult to discuss the concept at all, for it is essentially an abstraction that we have invented to help us understand the tendencies of people to behave similarly in certain circumstances. The conceptual term *attitude* refers to predispositions to act, choose, or evaluate in certain ways.

   Concepts are not "things," then, until you name them; they are transitory tendencies that must be inferred from other observations. When we label tendencies as "attitudes," though, we can study them *as if* they were "things."

   A concept has both attributes and variables. **Attributes** are those properties the theorist claims are present whenever the concept is discussed (e.g., attitudes are usually considered to have cognitive, affective, and behavioral components). **Variables,** particularly important notions to scientists, are properties that may be present in varying degrees, such that "there may be some of the property present or a lot of it" (Dubin, 1969, p. 35). Attitudes vary in their direction and intensity, as well as their expression. Theorists therefore could speculate about levels of these variables under different conditions. As Bergmann (1957) reminds us, "a

---

BOX 1-4

THEORIZING:

- Responds to a problem with *research questions* and *hypotheses*
- Identifies *concepts*, which have both *attributes* and *variables*
- Organizes concepts into *propositions* that are backed by evidence

concept is neither true nor false, only propositions are. A concept is neither valid nor invalid, only arguments are" (p. 50). Therefore, to be observed, the basic building blocks of theories—concepts—must be assembled into *propositions,* which are the formal claims the theorist wants to assert to the scientific community. They are the academic equivalent to a lawyer's "brief." A proposition differs from a hypothesis in that the theorist has already collected much of the evidence needed to support the claim made in the proposition.

4. *Checking.* The propositions of any theory cannot be considered apart from the process by which they were developed. Thus, at this stage of the theory-building process, *verification research* (as distinguished from descriptive research) is used to check or verify hypotheses and tentative answers. As you might guess, verification research goes beyond a survey of the behavioral landscape to probe for answers in areas where the theorist most expects to find them. As a theorist, you would check on your earlier hunches, often with quantitative experimental or highly focused qualitative methods such as interviewing or participant observation. Of course, you should not strain to verify your theory. Confirmation of your theory could result from the checking stage of the cycle, or further testing could refute the theory's propositions. Generally, confirming or refuting a theoretical assertion is not the task of a single study, however sophisticated it may be. Researchers first familiarize themselves with what is called the "literature" of their field—research that's already been conducted—then look for areas in need of further study.

Researchers must be as open to evidence that refutes their hypotheses as they are to evidence that supports them. This is why experimental researchers create *null hypotheses,* which are overt statements that remind the researcher not to expect (because of the potential for bias) significant differences in a given direction. A null hypothesis says, in effect, "Although the hypothesis that brought me to this point might give me a certain expectation, I will overtly remind myself to expect *no* difference as I manipulate variables and look for results within this study. Therefore, I'll have more confidence in the actual results, knowing that there is this check on the bias of expectation."

Sometimes even scholars overlook the connection between theorizing and researching. In the introduction to his influential book on theorizing, Dubin (1969) warns against this oversight. He advocates "bridg[ing] the gap" between theory and research, and he views the "bridge" not as a static connector but as facilitating "traffic" between theory and research (p. 2). In this sense, theorizing is not primarily an armchair activity of speculation, but it actively recognizes interdependent relationships among asking, observing, theorizing, checking, retheorizing, and re-asking.

5. *Re-asking.* The results of the checking step of theory-building must be fed back into the total system of questioning reality. New questions and new theories develop to reenergize the theory-building cycle. As philosopher of science Karl Popper (1968) notes, "theories are nets cast to catch what we call 'the world': to rationalize, to explain, and to master it. We endeavour to make the mesh ever finer and finer" (p. 59).

L I N K

After reading several more chapters, review this distinction between concepts and variables. Choose a theoretical approach from a later chapter—for instance, rules theory from Chapter 5. From a list of its concepts, try to identify some variables associated with the concepts. Compare your reactions with those of other students in class.

the functions of theorizing

Effective theorizing gives us answers about the world that help society in three primary ways (see Box 1-5). First, when they provide a sense of order with which we can clarify and understand complex processes, theories fulfill an *organizing function*. A good theory simplifies a complex process without oversimplifying or overgeneralizing it.

1.

Second, when theories give us a reasonably good idea of what to expect in the future, they perform a *predictive function*. A good theory thus helps us make decisions that may not even have been anticipated before the theory was developed.

2.

Third, when theories stimulate further research and speculation, they fulfill a *heuristic function.* "Theory serves as matchmaker, midwife, and godfather all in one," writes Abraham Kaplan (1964, p. 303). This could be true whether others agree or disagree with your theory; in either case, your theory encourages others to prove or disprove its validity by conducting further research. Even if a theory proves to be technically inaccurate or even wrong, such as some predictions of the theory of general relativity or Freudian psychoanalysis, it has served society well if it can fuel people's curiosity and stimulate attempts to correct errors.

3.

evaluating theories

Evaluating a theory, whether it is your own or a professional scholar's in the field of communication, involves asking questions that are based on relevant *criteria*— the standards by which one can fairly judge the quality or accuracy of a claim. A common set of criteria used in evaluating theories of communication asks questions about the theory's parsimony, consistency, refutability, and imagination.

checklist for evaluating a theory.   The following informal checklist of questions can help you evaluate theoretical explanations in this book and elsewhere. Use the criteria and questions in the checklist in conjunction with the functions of theories discussed in the previous section.

1. *Criterion of parsimony. Is the theory sufficiently complex to explain the processes and events it claims to represent, but not overly complicated or repetitious?* When a theory organizes and explains many things without proliferating unnecessary propositions and concepts, it meets the criterion of parsimony. In applying this criterion, remember that no theory can reproduce reality exactly; therefore, a theory should not be criticized for being incomplete just be-

BOX 1-5

WHAT GOOD THEORIES HELP US DO:
- Organize and clarify complex processes
- Predict future outcomes
- Stimulate further curiosity and research

---

cause it isn't *congruent* with all experience. Einstein once said that good science doesn't try "to give the taste of the soup" (quoted in Rudner, 1966, p. 69), reminding us that no matter how thoroughly we describe the characteristics of soup or the reactions of someone tasting it we cannot expect theory to be as satisfying as the experience itself. In other words, theory cannot reproduce reality but it can help us manage our understanding of it.

Note here that parsimony does not necessarily mean that theories should be simple. This criterion only warns about the dangers of unnecessary complexity, and these are not the same things.

2. *Criterion of consistency. Does the theory avoid contradicting both itself and known external findings currently accepted as true? Is it, in other words, consistent?* This criterion is often the object of intense scientific dispute. You can ask questions like the following to determine if a theory does not meet the criterion of consistency: Are basic concepts defined in different ways in different parts of the theory? Are different effects predicted in similar situations or conditions, without adequate explanation? Philosopher of social science Alfred Schutz (1967) discusses what he calls people's *stock of knowledge at hand,* which they bring to bear on everyday problems (p. 81; see also Gurwitsch, 1974, pp. 118–124). This expectation is developed by both social and personal experience, and the individual uses it to evaluate new explanations as they are offered. Any new theory should attempt to explain how it is consistent with, or why it deviates from, the "stock of knowledge" developed by ordinary people in ordinary situations.

3. *Criterion of refutability. Is the theory open to tests that could potentially refute it?* Popper (1980) calls this the "falsification principle." Since this term might suggest that a purpose of theories is either to falsify or to unmask falsification (neither is necessarily true, although both have undoubtedly happened!), we will call this the criterion of refutability. According to Popper, genuinely helpful theories are vulnerable to criticism; they do not make such grandiose claims or such vague predictions that proponents of the theory could claim that any phenomenon might fit under the theory's umbrella. Rather, they are open to being disproved, if warranted by the evidence. (The reasoning behind this criterion is discussed briefly earlier in the chapter.) As systematic researchers know, searching for confirmation alone is to invite confirmations wherever one looks. Popper (1980) notes that "some genuinely testable theories, when found to be false, are still upheld by their admirers—for example by introducing ad hoc some auxiliary assumption, or by reinterpreting the theory ad hoc in such a way that it escapes refutation" (pp. 22–23). He cites astrology as an example of an everyday theory that some people use to guide their communication decisions but that does not meet the criterion of refutability:

> Astrology did not pass the test. Astrologers were greatly impressed, and misled, by what they believed to be confirming evidence—so much so that they were quite unimpressed by any unfavourable evidence. Moreover, by making their interpretations and prophecies sufficiently vague

they were able to explain away anything that might have been a refutation of the theory had the theory and the prophecies been more precise. In order to escape falsification they destroyed the testability of their theory. It is a typical soothsayer's trick to predict things so vaguely that the predictions can hardly fail: that they become irrefutable. (p. 23)

4. *Criterion of imagination. Is the theory imaginative and interesting?* This criterion, more subtle than the others, is also one that many otherwise effective theories do not fully meet. It implies that how a theory is presented rhetorically, not just how it is developed and researched or how precisely it predicts consequences, contributes significantly to its ultimate acceptance. As researcher M. Scott Poole (1990) wrote, "a good theory should be exciting; it should make us enthusiasts. We should be able to have fun applying the theory to different problems and contexts" (p. 237). But what is exciting to one person might spell boredom to another: 0–0 soccer matches? Computer programming? Theorizing about why conversations develop as they do? And, we should note, imagination is ultimately the least useful and most potentially misleading of the four criteria for evaluating a theory. Clever and attractive explanations may seem imaginative, while failing to meet other criteria and being backed by scant testable research. Successful theories catch our attention with striking metaphors, analogies, and visual models that illustrate the patterns accounted for by the theory. *Metaphor,* a vivid comparison that highlights an important factor or relation, is crucial to both the theory-building process and the evaluation of a theory. Sociologist Richard Brown (1977) argues that "new metaphors not only represent appearances, they change them and even create new ones. New metaphors lie at the heart of new theories" (p. 99).

Consider, for example, how Frank E. X. Dance's (1967) reading in DNA research incorporates both metaphorical and geometrical representations of his theoretical approach. As shown in Figure 1-2, his model

Figure 1-2 Dance's Helical Spiral Model
Source: F. E. X. Dance (Ed.), *Human Communication Theory* (New York: Holt, 1967), pp. 288–309. Reprinted by permission.

BOX 1-6

TO EVALUATE A THEORY, ASK:

- Is it unnecessarily complicated? (The *criterion of parsimony*)
- Does it have internal contradictions or unexplained inconsistencies? (The *criterion of consistency*)
- Is it capable of being refuted or tested by gathering persuasive evidence? (The *criterion of refutability*, or *falsifiability*)
- Does it stimulate creativity and enthusiasm among theorists and researchers? (The *criterion of imagination*)

resembles a "helical spiral." Although the figure doesn't capture much detail about communication, it vividly suggests the central feature of Dance's perspective: Communication might *appear* to be a clear-cut activity in which messages are exchanged between communicators, but it is actually a circular process that constantly changes over time to a different level or plane. The helical nature of the image shows that nothing ever stays unchanged as communication occurs; neither people nor their meanings "hold still" and the impact of communication widens. (The implications of this viewpoint are discussed in detail in Chapter 2.) Dance's metaphor is intriguing, as it reinforces his idea that communication could be represented in nonlinear and dynamic ways, not just as message-sending from a source to a receiver.

WHAT DO COMMUNICATION THEORISTS HOPE TO ACCOMPLISH (OTHER THAN BUILDING THEORIES)?

One educational theorist claims that most types of learning can be phrased in response to three basic questions: (1) "What?" (2) "So what?" and (3) "Now what?" (Borton, 1970). Effective communication theorists also address these questions. They ask "What?" questions to pinpoint areas in need of further study: "What do we not know about . . . ?" They ask, "So what?" (phrased as *why* questions) to identify the importance of their tentative answers: "Why is this approach distinctly useful?" or "Why is it important for other people to know about these insights?" And they address "Now what?" questions to set the stage for larger issues of future social planning: *"Now* that we have this new insight into communicative processes, *what* social significance might it possess?" Thus far in this chapter, our discussion of communication theory has been focused on the first two questions. In this section, we will place communication theorizing in a larger framework by asking: "Now what?"

BOX 1-7

> ## SHOULD THEORIES OF HUMAN INTERACTION LEAD TO LAWS, RULES, OR BOTH?
>
> - *Covering law theorists* attempt general macroscopic explanations that apply widely across social and cultural contexts.
> - *Rules theorists* rely on specific explanations that demonstrate how behaviors become regularized in particular contexts.

covering laws or rules?

Theorists need to ask whether their theories and research will eventually add up to anything that's socially significant: "Now what?" (see Box 1-7). Can we advance far enough to discover some nearly invariant and generalizable principles applicable across many different types of people and situations? Some theorists think so; they search for **covering laws** that will help explain and predict human behavior on a macroscopic scale (see Berger, 1977). Our earlier discussion of psychological reactance theory is an example of a theorist's attempt to create a covering law of human behavior: that people will tend to protect their behavioral options in communication with others (Brehm, 1966).

Other theorists, in contrast, aim to identify the specific **rules** that guide people's unique communication choices within particular situations. In this case, the theorist looks not at general human tendencies but inside particular cultures, organizations, and occasions for insight into how people regulate their communication with others (see Pearce & Cronen, 1980; Shimanoff, 1980). In this sense, then, rules refer not to the things people are *compelled* to do, except in the sense that there might be social pressure if rules were violated. They refer to the regularities, decision-patterns, norms, and expectations underlying what people *actually* do. Rules theorists try to understand the criteria people use, largely unconsciously, when speaking and acting in public. Communication rules are inferred by observing people in action, though no attempt is made to generalize such rules to universal laws. It is this emphasis on specific contexts that is the chief difference between rules approaches and covering laws approaches: "A rule is a followable prescription that indicates what behavior is obligated, preferred, or prohibited in certain contexts" (Shimanoff, 1980, p. 57).

We consider in later chapters a number of theories that take essentially one form or the other, and in Chapter 5 we discuss some of the most influential rules-based approaches. But for now, it is important to note controversy in the communication field over the relative value of covering laws approaches and rules perspectives. Should we aim high to establish which grand laws regulate human behavior across situations, and perhaps even somewhat deterministically? Or should we aim toward more immediate episodes, establishing which contextual rules regulate the specific communication behaviors of humans within situations, adopting an assumption of more human choice and control? This question was

L I N K

Recall the distinctions we made earlier in the chapter between quantitative and qualitative research. Quantitative researchers who identify themselves as behaviorists often adopt philosophical positions consistent with laws approaches. Qualitative researchers, who tend to rely more on interpretation, often identify with rules approaches. Although there are many exceptions, why do you think this general tendency might have developed?

See Chapter 6 for a more detailed discussion of Kenneth Burke's distinction between action and motion, and why it is important for defining human nature.

long debated in the professional journals and conventions. The current status of the controversy is that it seems to be a non-issue. Many scholars today recognize that both approaches can yield fruitful results.

Still, the distinction is interesting, and implies somewhat distinctive philosophies of human nature. Are human communication behaviors primarily mechanistically determined? In the **motional view of behavior,** humans are "put in motion" principally by potentially predictable forces. Or do humans make choices independently, choices that largely determine their own fate? In the **actional view of behavior,** humans internally choose to initiate their own actions.

systems theory

The motional and actional views of behavior are supplemented (and sometimes informed) by yet another approach to interaction and causality, the systemic view. Many contemporary scholars synthesize scientific assumptions about interaction by applying **general systems theory** (GST) concepts (Bertalanffy, 1968; Ruben & Kim, 1975). Systems theorists argue that change in human relations is neither primarily caused from the outside in, nor chosen from within, but is a process of mutual adjustment among relationships within a system. GST, perhaps the definitive interdisciplinary effort, was biologist Ludwig von Bertalanffy's (1968) attempt to argue that the same basic principles guide all dynamic systems—including biological, human, environmental, political, and social systems.

General systems theory is not without its critics, however. Some see it as belaboring the obvious, untestable, and not terribly fruitful in generating new research (Phillips, 1976). But since the publication of Watzlawick, Beavin, and Jackson's influential *Pragmatics of Human Communication* (1967), many communication theorists have taken most of the theory's claims for granted. Systems theories assume that it is more fruitful for researchers to study relationships rather than individual persons, behaviors, or things.

Rapoport informally defines a *system* as a "bundle of relations" (quoted in Davidson, 1983, p. 26), while Davidson (1983) reminds us that those relationships are intangible: "A system is a manifestation of something intangible, but quite real, called organization. A system, like a work of art, is a pattern rather than a pile. Like a piece of music, it's an arrangement rather than an aggregate. Like a marriage, it's a relationship rather than an encounter" (pp. 26–27). Thus, for example, students who gather to try out for a play have established only minimal relationships with each other and, therefore, are an "aggregate" of persons in Davidson's terms. But the play's cast, once chosen, forms a system of relationships and roles that takes on an organization all its own. That system cannot be analyzed simply by looking at the actors or their individual motives. The entire system must be taken into account. This notion of wholeness influences our more formal definition of a **system** as *a unit of analysis in which a change in any part affects all other parts and all relations among parts.*

Fisher (1982, pp. 198–201) describes the basic concepts within systems theories of communication, which we have paraphrased and extended here:

Synergy

1. *Holism and nonsummativity.* These terms mean that you won't be able to understand a system by analyzing the separate components of the system and then adding them up ("summing" them) to try to get a picture of the whole. The whole cannot accurately be predicted by examining parts of the system, because it is by their *interaction* that the whole is formed. "The parts of the system are less important than the connectedness of the parts" (Fisher, 1982, p. 199). Theatrical directors and athletic coaches sense this when they refer to the "chemistry" in their casts and teams.

2. *Openness.* This term refers to how a system interchanges information with the environment outside its boundaries. In human systems especially, the boundaries are to some extent open, allowing the interchange of information between the system and outside elements. To the extent that the system becomes closed to outside information (perhaps feedback from rehearsal audiences), it begins to exhibit *entropy*—that is, it becomes increasingly disorganized and unpredictable. The system quits learning. An open system exhibits *equifinality,* which suggests that any given state or configuration of the system can be arrived at by various actions of system components. For example, there are many ways for the cast to interact with each other and the director to produce a given outcome, such as favorable reviews for the play.

3. *Hierarchical organization.* Each system is simultaneously: (a) its own distinctive organization, (b) a part of a larger system (a subsystem), and (c) a collection of smaller systems (a suprasystem). Systems theorists thus realize that their "unit of analysis," whatever they choose to study, could be studied in vastly different ways just by taking alternative macroscopic or microscopic views. The system under study, then, is known as a *holon* (Koestler, 1967), that could be studied as a system in its own right, as a component of a larger system, or as an environment for a collection of smaller systems. A communication theorist interested in theater, for example, could study a cast as a holon, therefore, or might be more interested in studying a more complex holon comprised of the system formed by the cast, the script, the set, the director, the stage crew, the musicians, and the audience—the show. Individual actors could serve as holons too, if studied as system organisms comprised of psychological and biological subsystems. And so the analysis could go (perhaps infinitely?) in either direction.

4. *Organized complexity.* A system provides itself with ever-increasing states of differentiation. In order to survive and thrive, a system must take into account many different kinds of information, especially external feedback (see Box 1-8), to create complex internal structures for processing alternatives. Most systems are in a state of dynamic, always-changing complexity in which flexibility of response is a major criterion. Imagine analyzing as a system the mind of an improvisational actor such as Robin Williams or Whoopi Goldberg. The complexity of their talent involves changingness, not complicated stability. Thus, the whole issue of *causa-*

BOX 1-8

FEEDBACK

In communication theory, **feedback** refers to any message from your environment that can help you assess how effective your previous messages were in accomplishing certain goals. Good feedback serves as a control mechanism by which a system adapts flexibly within its context.

- *Examples:* Grades provide feedback for students, but so can such informal behaviors as a teacher's interpersonal responsiveness, attention, friendliness, and perceived annoyance. In addition, students' performance on an examination or assignment provides teachers with feedback on how well they're meeting their goals of helping create effective learning.
- *Types:* Positive feedback enhances or reinforces a tendency within a system. Negative feedback inhibits or regulates a system tendency, by imposing a predetermined desired level or criterion. How do you think grades might function as positive feedback for students? How might grades function as negative feedback?

tion, or the assumed connections between some events and changes in other events ("What caused her to react to that comment that way?"), becomes problematic and complicated in systems theory. This is why systems theorists are skeptical of single or linear explanations (causes) for phenomena.

5. *Self-regulation.* This term refers to how a system regulates itself internally by balancing the relations among its components, or the characteristics or properties of those components. Although the environment always has some effect on a given system (e.g., a theater's acoustics will subtly influence how loudly the actors will say their dialogue), each communication system establishes an internal *homeostasis,* or balance of relations, that allows it to generate its own distinctive kinds of information and to set its own goals.

General systems theory is less a theory of communication than it is a *theory about theorizing* about communication. Nevertheless, it helps us organize our ideas about communication theory. If you consider systems approaches as ways to organize your communication thinking, then many of the concepts we describe later in this book can be organized in terms of a systems framework.

Now what? How might such a framework alter your worldview? Systems theory might lead you to any number of discoveries—that everything within a system is connected; that a system's components are all vulnerable to change; and that change is a function of the system itself, and is not just a direct cause-to-effect sequence. For example, consider a systems-oriented response to the question, "What's wrong with this office?" A systems theorist would not reply, "The office is

BOX 1-9

HUMAN SYSTEMS, AS "BUNDLES OF RELATIONS," CAN BE ANALYZED BY UNDERSTANDING:

- *Holism/Nonsummativity* (You can't predict the behavior of a system merely by considering the sum of its parts.)
- *Openness* (How the system interchanges information with the environment outside its own boundaries)
- *Hierarchy* (How any system can be seen as comprised by smaller subsystems, and as components of larger systems)
- *Organized Complexity* (How a system becomes differentiated within itself in order to deal with ever-changing tasks)
- *Self-Regulation* (How the system regulates itself by establishing an internal balance of relations)

---

managed by an incompetent supervisor" because it cannot be assumed that the boss alone makes the office ineffective. Instead, a systems theorist would first think of the office as a holon, with its own inner and outer ecology, and then ask further questions: "Do any extra-system requirements and information influence the supervisor's behavior?" "Would any other supervisor in the same office be subject to the same influences?" "To what extent have subordinates invited or influenced the behavior of the supervisor?" Systems theory, in short, looks beyond easy answers in response to communication questions. In its emphasis on connection and relationship, it asks us constantly to consider "What else?" "Who else?" "How else?" and "Why else?"

TESTING THE CONCEPTS

"Is Ted real?"

Definitely. He is real in two ways. First, he actually took a theory class with content similar to the one you're enrolled in now. But more important, Ted's attitude and motivation represent the real-life qualities of successful communication students. Such students, like Ted, expect to be seen as unique individuals. They ask their instructors to explain the implications of issues presented in class, and they insist on having their own voices heard in a group.

"I'm not at all theoretical. I want to study the practical. Why is it important for me to analyze all these theories of the communication process?"

In order to be a practical communicator, you should first understand how you've come to know what you do about communicating. Whether you realize it or not, you theorize about many aspects of life without thinking of it in that way. As you go about your daily activities, you question why something happens or doesn't happen, take your observations into account, then check them out. Ultimately, if your tentative conclusions aren't helpful, you'll question some more. When you do this, you are developing a theory about some everyday occurrence. If you are curious, are willing to be surprised, are experienced at trying things out, and respect others' views, you already have experience in theory-building. By fine-tuning this process and learning from others' theorizing, you become more comfortable and more effective in applying communication skills. What could be more practical?

"Should all theorists become researchers, too?"
In one way, yes. Most scholarly work assumes that theorists work from data. Ideas shouldn't come from thin air, nor should they remain there. That is, theorists have the responsibility to show how their theories are, or can be, practical and useful.

But in another way, the answer is no. One type of theorist (who is still a researcher, we'd argue) doesn't attempt to demonstrate practicality just by creating data. Instead, this theorist/researcher also synthesizes the work of others into a more coherent larger pattern or whole. In the discipline of communication, many theorists fulfill this role well. We especially recommend the work of Julia Wood (1996), Frank E. X. Dance (1967; 1982), Stephen Littlejohn (1996), and W. Barnett Pearce (1989). This role doesn't suggest a lack of originality; these and other scholars have made many original contributions to communication theory. Skillful synthesis is itself a kind of research.

"Several times you mentioned 'mystery' in relation to communication theory. Can't we just let some things *be* mysterious, without overanalyzing them?"
This question, common in communication classes, uncovers an important problem: As indicated by the experience of some writers, "analysis can become paralysis." Overanalyzing the communication process, or even becoming excessively aware of it while it happens, can disable communicators.

But the major reason for studying theories of communication is not to guide your moment-by-moment choices of language and behavior while in conversation with others. Practical theories provide the backdrop against which specific problems, as they arise, may be understood. In the language of *gestalt psychology* (a historical branch of psychological research that focuses on perceptual problems), this is called a *figure/ground relationship*. The ground, the backdrop, surrounds and provides context for the figure, or object of perception on which you wish to focus—and to understand one you need to understand the other. A communication specialist who serves as a resource to others in an organization must be able to provide insight and clues that help people deal with the inevitable dilemmas of communication. The specialist who responds with useful suggestions or explanations based on theories of communication, however tentative they may be, is far more competent than one who says, "I'm sorry, but communication is just too mysterious to be understood."

To understand the nature of mystery is to respect the unknown, the undiscovered, perhaps the undiscoverable. The mysterious demands our attention, but makes no promises and often won't yield to our solutions. The world refuses to sit still as a puzzle waits to be solved. Of course, some aspects of communication may always remain a mystery. Some theorists have begun to examine the role of mystery in guiding how humans relate to each other (Goodall, 1991; Pearce, 1989). This is exciting work. You might want to investigate the topic in a special class project or independently.

"Since theories are really similar to positions taken in arguments, who can settle the arguments? Who decides?"

No board of appeals governs an academic discipline. There are no elections for choosing the "best" theories, although a journal once ran an article listing and ranking influential communication theorists (Beniger, 1990). Instead, a theory is considered successful if it is used by other theorists and if it helps people organize concepts and ideas better than they could before the theory was developed. Many theoretical arguments are never "decided," because observers inevitably disagree about what constitutes a good account of social phenomena.

Try to think of theoretical arguments not as formal debates, but as ongoing conversations within an intellectual arena, where the give-and-take of fact and opinion continually modify all positions within the dialogue. Thus some positions that once seemed mutually exclusive or even contradictory in this scholarly interchange might later be modified by the conversation into theories that are actually compatible.

"You stress the importance of asking questions, sometimes even more than answering them. Are all questions good?"

Not necessarily. Some contemporary philosophers of communication, notably Gadamer (1982, pp. 325 ff.; Palmer, 1969, pp. 198–201), believe that a genuine or true question always presumes an openness to experience (or a willingness to be surprised, in the language we used earlier in the chapter). Genuine questions therefore address issues about which the questioner *does not already know the answer.* Ambiguity doesn't just stimulate a question, it is the very presumption by which a question is defined. This is why theorizing is so exciting, and far from being the "dry" subject many new students assume it to be.

Gadamer (1982) contrasts true questions, however, with false and/or distorted ones (p. 327). Although false questions masquerade as true questions, they are actually presuppositions and assertions in disguise. They presume not to discover answers, but to know them already. As such, they don't invite new learning as much as they warm over and assert what we already know. As an example, consider how attorneys use cross-examination in a courtroom. Some lawyers are taught in law school that when they have to ask a witness a question to which the lawyer doesn't already know the answer, then the case is in deep trouble indeed. The lawyer is an advocate with a case to present, and a "side" to represent. Although this may be necessary in the legal field, it is not what Gadamer has in mind as genuine questioning. Nor can it be a model for inquiry in the creative arts and sciences.

A sentence that ends with a question mark may not be a true question, then. And a theory to which a theorist is irrevocably committed is not a true theory. In both cases, the questions are false.

Y O U,   T H E   R E S E A R C H E R

In this and the following chapters, we'll suggest some useful projects for you to try. These suggestions will range from small teasers to tasks involving library research or experience-based excursions that could serve as the basis for term papers. They are designed to give you a taste of what it's like to be a practicing communication scholar. They may also stimulate class discussion and help you see the links between the chapters and possible applications in your own life. Most can be accomplished effectively in a relatively brief time period.

Before you begin working on these activities, however, there are a few things you should keep in mind. First, even though the projects involve research, they in no way approximate the complexity of the research studies discussed in this book. Most of the communication theories you will learn about in this course are a result of scholars' years of commitment to studying the field. Therefore, while the activities are designed to be interesting and practical for you, they will not supply results that can verify or refute scholarly theories.

Second, because our focus in this book is on asking questions in order to theorize, many of the end-of-chapter activities also have basically descriptive or exploratory research goals. Experimental research, with its emphasis on precise control of variables, is usually too complicated and intricate to simulate in class activities.

Finally, some of the research projects ask you to collect data from other people, such as other students or faculty members on campus. A very important point: *Before beginning any activities that require others' cooperation or participation, students and faculty should make themselves aware of any campus guidelines for the conduct of research with human subjects.* Most colleges and universities now require (usually through a clear and succinct policy) prior approval for any studies, formal or informal, that require the willing or unwitting participation of other persons. Check your institution's regulations, usually described in a faculty handbook or in other general campus publications.

1. Carefully read the past week's editions of your local newspaper, or the previous four issues of a national newsmagazine (including the editorial, sports, and cartoon sections). Copy in a notebook all sentences that mention the concept of *theory*. In addition, note when and how your friends use "theory" and "theoretical" in everyday conversation. Which, if any, of the sentences use the concept in a negative context in your opinion (e.g., a book review that refers to the author's point of view as "merely theoretical")? Which, if any, of the sentences refer to the concept in a positive or neutral context (e.g., a science article that cites Einstein's "theory of

relativity" to explain . . .)? Discuss how—and how often—our culture tends to employ the concept of theory.

2. Draw a diagram, or construct with any materials at hand a three-dimensional representation, showing how each of the following is a "system." (You may need to talk with friends or other students to learn more about how each system is composed of components, properties, and relationships.)

- A stereo system (including such audio components as amplifier, pre-amplifier, tuner, tape deck, CD player, turntable, patch cords, speaker cables, and speakers)
- A sports team (e.g., softball, baseball, basketball, football, soccer, volleyball)
- The organization of a restaurant's kitchen
- Photosynthesis in a plant

You have just created "a systems **model**." A good model, which we'll discuss in more detail in the next chapter, simplifies and represents the basic operation of a complex process without *over*simplifying it. In a model, the relationships become clearer, although complexity must be sacrificed.

3. Conduct a series of interviews to determine how the concept of theory is used in other disciplines. Interview three faculty members from departments other than communication, one from each of the following areas:

- Natural sciences (e.g., chemistry, biology, physics, astronomy)
- Social sciences (e.g., sociology, anthropology, psychology, political science)
- Humanities (e.g., literature, philosophy, art, music, languages)

Begin each interview by introducing yourself and explaining the purpose of your interview. Then ask this question: "How does a new theory in your field get accepted or rejected?" Respond to the professor's answer with whatever follow-up questions or comments you think are appropriate, based on your reading of this chapter. Take careful notes, or if the interviewees agree, tape-record the interviews. Finally, compare your findings to this chapter's discussion of the theory-building cycle. Do the various disciplines have anything in common? If so, what? Are there any significant differences? Do these professors use such terms as *science, research,* and *verification* in ways similar to or different from their colleagues in other fields?

Jeffry Myers/Stock, Boston

the flow of communication

"when have we communicated*?"*

Communication: A Cure?

Defining Communication Realistically

Communication: Continually Changing?
What Is a Process?
The Difficulties of a Process Orientation

Mutuality and Transaction
Individualistic Approaches: One to Another?
Mutualistic Approaches: Both Sides Now?

Meaning
Meaning Is Processual
Meaning Is Personalized
Meaning Is Co-Constructed
Meaning Is Multidimensional

Intention and the Definition of Communication: A Controversy

Models of Communication

Summary: Testing the Concepts

You, the Researcher

> To learn to be human is to develop through the give-and-take of communication an effective sense of being an individually distinctive member of a community. . . .
>
> JOHN DEWEY, *THE PUBLIC AND ITS PROBLEMS* (1927, P. 154)

Communication techniques have become marketable commodities in today's consumer culture. It sometimes seems as if the world is divided into two almost equally large groups—the people who want to be saved by the techniques, and the experts who offer such salvation. As teachers of communication, we have mixed feelings about this trend. Although communication is now recognized as an important problem, we think it is inappropriate to imply that an academic field of study is a technique-centered social fad. But in many ways, regrettably, some people seem to be trying to make it just that.

Popular culture, at least in North America, is infatuated with the companion concepts of communication and relationship. Television and radio talk shows, advice columns, and everyday talk at parties and offices all seem to point to a "lack of communication" as a root cause of society's maladies. "More" communication and prescriptive techniques are packaged for marriage partners, families, committees, football teams, and organizations, as though communication were a medicine. After we take a prescribed dose, presumably we'll hurt less.

COMMUNICATION: A CURE?

Two recent stories in major urban newspapers, coincidentally on the same day, illustrate our popular preoccupation with "communication." One front-page article reported that a mayor telephoned an owner of a sports franchise and subjected his secretary to obscene namecalling and taunts. The columnist ended the story by wondering if this was a case of too much impulsive anger, "or just not enough communication?" (Koman, 1990, p. 4).

In the other article, the manager of a baseball team that had lost ninety-five games the previous year is interviewed about his leadership style. Unidentified players had accused him of being "unfairly critical and uncommunicative." But now, the interviewer discovers, "community" has become a high priority for the manager, who claims that "communication is crucial to managing a ballclub" (O'Neill, 1990, p. 3D). Of course, he's right; communication is indeed crucial. But the team's poor record the previous year was not caused by a *lack* of communication any more than the mayor's bad manners were. Both incidents were examples of particular kinds of communication, not examples of its absence. Communication is crucial because without it, there wouldn't have been a "last season" for the manager, and indeed there wouldn't have been a team.

In most academic theories, communication is neither a fad nor a handy self-help tool, but the basic process that constitutes human cooperation and conflict in the first place. Recall, from the Introduction, our preliminary definition of *communication* as a process in which people interpret messages in order to co-ordinate their individual and social meanings. Through communication we co-operate in sharing meanings in order to achieve some sort of coordination in relationships.

You might ask, "If communication becomes a fad now and then, what's wrong with that?" While some fads are trivial, such as the hula-hoop, others can be harmful, such as spiked heels on women's shoes or diets that produce rapid weight loss without medical supervision. Still, you might ask, "But what could be detrimental about a preoccupation with communication, a central process of human understanding? Who could fault modern society for trying to improve relationships through more understanding?" Unfortunately, the understanding of communication that often accompanies this goal is subtly dangerous. Communication is trivialized when it is viewed simply as a medicine or self-help treatment that can be prescribed in greater or smaller doses. People who try "more" communication as a fix-it technique often find nothing is fixed. An open and honest conversation—presumably "good" communication to many people—may reveal that the speakers actually like each other less than they originally thought they did, or that they feel less motivated to listen to or agree with each other. Ventilating feelings in an office or family setting, presumably to add more communication, can increase, not decrease, resentment and conflict.

Studying communication theory provides alternatives to this popularized communication-is-the-answer philosophy, but they are not as neat and tidy. Contemporary theorists understand communication not so much as a single answer to human problems, but as the central process by which we become human in the first place, and the process by which we can understand the everyday problems we face. Therefore, communication is not itself an answer, but to understand communication more fully is to know more about *how life's questions get asked.* Theorists have not developed a single unified, sophisticated, and definitive description of communication to replace the simplistic view of it as a fad. Nor are they likely to do so.

Researchers develop alternative explanations for communication and different models of it that attempt to illustrate its processes. Communication theory is necessarily a *pluralistic,* not a unified, field. Studying these explanations can be frustrating because they often contradict each other. However, studying them can also be eminently realistic and practical. Another way of stating the major theme in this chapter is that communication is the only way we can live, behave, and develop symbolic relationships. It is not just a therapeutic medicine to take when something is wrong with a relationship at home or work.

This chapter describes some basic facets of communication about which most current theorists and researchers agree. First, you'll read about communication as the process through which people use messages to create human environments for relationships. This definition will be contrasted with a more simplistic information-transmission definition. Second, we'll explore the implications of the concept of *process.* Third, we'll discuss the impact of a relational or mutualistic, rather than an individualistic, perspective, using *transaction* as an explanatory key. We'll use the knotty problem of *meaning* to test the practicality of our vantage point on communication. Finally, we'll consider whether sender/speaker intention is necessary in a helpful specification of communication. This brings us back full circle to where the chapter begins—with the claim that an appreciation of the flow of communication (though more complex and less intuitive than a sender–receiver model) is actually more practical for communicators, researchers, and theorists.

We also have a secondary agenda in this chapter. It includes previewing some of the concepts that we'll return to often in the remaining chapters of the book. Another goal is to show that communication, an interdisciplinary venture, is not owned by any one academic discipline or even a family of disciplines. We'll cite authorities in communication, psychology, sociology, anthropology, philosophy, economics, literature, biology, and other fields to stress this important point. Practical communication theory comes from all directions, not just from the social sciences, the humanities, experimental studies, or communication scholars. The symbolic nature of human interaction provides a hub for theorists of many persuasions and disciplines.

DEFINING COMMUNICATION REALISTICALLY

Ancient Roman and Greek teachers had a creative explanation for how people communicated. They believed that Mercury (Hermes to the Greeks), the god with wings on his feet and cap, grabbed an idea from one person's head, skewered it on his spear, and then thrust it into another person's head in an unambiguous, irrevocable act of delivering the goods (Thayer, 1968, p. 3). Mercury, "the messenger," came to be known also as the god of commerce; you can still see his image today portrayed in the logo of a prominent national floral delivery company.

You may be amused by this Mercury "model of communication," assuming that it's too superficial to account for all the complex variables of human interaction. And, of course, it is. Yet contemporary Western culture retains the single most misleading and possibly dangerous concept of the ancient transportation-of-an-idea notion. By believing that Mercury could transfer an idea, the Romans assumed that the idea supposedly delivered to the receiver was *the same idea formerly found only in the brain of the sender.* However, isn't an idea (or an image, intention, or feeling) an intangible, an interpretation, and a personalized, unique meaning? As such, it cannot be transferred as a whole to another person; rather, it can only be hinted at or suggested in fragments, largely because other communicators share in the same cultural stock of ideas. But consider the words used today to oversimplify this amazingly intricate process: *transmitting, conveying, feeding back, exchanging, delivering.*

A classic volume of research findings, influential with social scientists for years, informed readers that communication is "the transmission of information, ideas, emotions, skills, etc., by the use of symbols" (Berelson & Steiner, 1964,

p. 527). Similarly, influential philosopher A. J. Ayer (1955) claims that in typical conceptions of communication, "the connecting thread appears to be the idea of something's being transferred from one thing, or person, to another" (p. 12). Unfortunately, some prominent dictionaries of social science also reinforce this transfer/transmit theme (Corsini, 1984, p. 249; Goldenson, 1984, p. 160; Theodorson & Theodorson, 1969, p. 62; Wolman, 1973, p. 69).

Michael Reddy (1979) refers to this preoccupation as the **conduit metaphor** (a conduit is a pathway or channel through which a substance moves from one place to another). Reddy shows how conduit thinking is deeply embedded within the English language (Reddy, 1979; see also Lakoff & Johnson, 1980). If we think and speak in English, says Reddy, we cannot completely escape conceptualizing communication in conduit terms. Our language makes it seem natural for us to consider ideas, feelings, and intended meanings as objects to place into containers (words, language) for the purpose of sending them to other persons. However, reminding ourselves that this metaphor misstates the complexity of the communication process is a step toward a more realistic understanding.

As Lakoff and Johnson (1980) show in the following examples, it's difficult to understand conduit thinking as a metaphor because we are so thoroughly immersed in certain linguistic assumptions. Yet, listening closely, we can hear the metaphor in everyday talk:

It's hard to *get* that idea *across to* him.

I *gave* you that idea.

Your reasons *came through* to us.

It's difficult to *put* my ideas *into* words.

When you *have* a good idea, try to *capture* it immediately *in* words.

Try to *pack* more thought *into* fewer words.

You can't simply *stuff* ideas *into* a sentence any old way.

The meaning is right there *in* the words.

Don't *force* your meanings *into* the wrong words.

His words *carry* little meaning.

The introduction *has* a great deal of thought *content*.

Your words seem *hollow.*

The sentence is *without* meaning.

The idea is *buried in* terribly dense paragraphs. (p. 11)

W. Charles Redding (1960) reported that in his workshops for middle- and upper-level managers, almost 100 percent of executives agreed with this initial characterization of communication: "When Person X 'communicates' with Person

Y, what happens is that he transmits meanings (information, facts, ideas, etc.) . . . to the mind of Person *Y*" (p. 101). The rest of Redding's workshop was devoted to encouraging people to change this natural, but fallacious, assumption to a more realistic one.

Another organizational communication specialist (Haney, 1973) warns students not to forget completely about transmission; although *something* is conveyed from place to place in an act of human speech, it isn't meaning: "Some neural impulses are sent from the brain to the abdominal muscles (for air power), the larynx (for phonation), and the articulatory organs (jaw, teeth, tongue, glottis, lips, and so forth) and A is now *transmitting.* Transmitting what? Words? Thoughts? Meanings? Ideas? Feelings? The Message? No—vibrations—simply compressions and rarefications of molecules in the air" (p. 183). When we move molecules through speech or create symbols or images in other ways, we create the conditions in which meanings can be partially accessible to others. But the inner state of a communicator never travels from person to person. We take messages as clues that others are somehow attempting to connect with us. Then, as if building the same bridge but starting from different shores, we tentatively begin to construct a corresponding message. If we want to continue building the bridge, we monitor each other's progress and direction and try to use compatible methods. We acknowledge the inevitability of trial and error. We know the meeting can never be exact. The bridge, admittedly imperfect, only comes into being at the meeting, however. Only then do the two sides meet with something in common. To avoid being misled by yet another metaphor, think of the bridge as people's common access to cooperation and coordination, not as their way to share exactly the same thoughts and feelings.

This notion of commonality is at the root of all purposeful communication, in etymology as well as in function. In communication, meaning is created that is common to the participants. *Communication, common, community, commune, communion*—the similarities among these words are not accidental (Williams, 1976, pp. 62–63). The shared meaning is not the property of individuals, nor is it transmitted from one to the other; rather, it is pooled between them. The center of two separate beings, the link, becomes their communication. Are they two beings any more? Yes and no. Yes, they remain separate and unique. No, their communication has, in a sense, made them one functioning unit, a system with interdependencies.

Despite the interdependent relationship among communicators, communication is not always pleasant or strategically planned. Some people call every disagreement or conflict a "communication breakdown" and any confrontation of different values a "communication gap." They assume that if the other person just understood them well enough, if they could just "get their idea across" better, the disagreement would disappear. Conflict is seen as evidence of a lack of communication, and a signal to inject more of this magical stuff into the conversation. However, with better understanding comes dual possibilities—we may agree with or appreciate each other more *or* less.

Communication as a process is omnipresent and, therefore, neutral. Although personifying concepts is always somewhat inaccurate, another metaphor might help here. Communication, in a sense, doesn't care what happens through its workings. Of course, people care about communication, but it doesn't return the favor. Communication is much more like a constantly shifting environment than a tool for ensuring the results we individually or collectively want. We don't work with it as much as we work within it. Communication theorist W. Barnett Pearce (1989) provides an insightful summary of this point: "The process of describing forms of communication is made more important because the discovery that we live in communication transmutes communication from a secondary to a primary role in human life. Rather than a means by which 'internal' states are expressed and 'objective' facts represented, communication is that process by which 'persons,' 'institutions,' and 'facts' are constructed" (p. xvi).

COMMUNICATION: CONTINUALLY CHANGING?

what is a process?

A realistic definition of communication should not rely on jargon. Still, this chapter has presented a number of common terms in fairly restricted ways. One example is the notion of a process. In everyday talk, the claim that something is a process implies that events occur sequentially. We "use" a process to accomplish a pre-set goal or to make sure a problem is solved smoothly. In this sense, parliamentary procedure is a good process for running meetings, and one form of rationality could be learned by applying John Dewey's process of reflective thinking. When we speak of "processing paperwork" and "word processing," we imply movement toward a defined end. Such ways of referring to process are reasonable and valid.

The flow of communication, however, is best described by a different notion of process, one developed by prominent philosophers and theorists (Johnson, 1946; Kress, 1970; Whitehead, 1930). In communication theory, process usually doesn't refer to a sequential way of doing things. Rather, when communication is said to be a **process,** theorists are in tune with contemporary scientists, who argue that the world is not composed of discrete and isolated *things* that affect each other in neat packages of cause and effect called *events*. The scientific concept of process is fundamentally ecological; it suggests that everything is interlinked, sometimes even to the point that it's hard to tell where or when one thing begins and another ends. We may choose to simplify our explanations and discuss "events," implying as we do that they have clear-cut beginnings and endings. For example, you might simplify how we talk about persons and imply that Professor Jones was the "same" person with the same attitude before and after you complained about your grade. These are compromises of everyday speech, through which we convince ourselves that the world is manageable.

A more realistic idea, though admittedly harder to grasp, is that nothing is static or unchanging. The universe is in constant flux, movement, and adjustment, much of which we can sense only indirectly with our human perceptual apparatus. Thus, for example, Professor Jones's attitude did change after your conversation, but perhaps not in the direction or magnitude you would have liked. Nor was your teacher the same person after your talk, since all people are constantly affected by their surroundings. Communication is, in a fundamental way, neither an accomplishment nor a simple event. It is a process of continual change that is impossible to slow down or stop. There aren't snapshots or instant replays of communication, then, because when it's frozen or analyzed into an event, it ceases to be living communication anymore.

Because human communication is a process in constant creative flux, and one that cannot be stopped or manipulated at will, we have to use artificial verbal concoctions such as "components," "stages," "conclusions," and "causes," among many others, to aid in our understanding of it. But as process theorists remind us, we do not discover these phenomena in external reality. The concepts are manufactured and then layered over the reality we experience in an attempt to make that reality appear more manageable. Philosopher Alan Watts (1975) asks, "Can we think of the heart as separate from the veins, or the branches from the tree? Just what exact delineations distinguish the bee process from the flower process? These distinctions are always somewhat arbitrary and conventional, even when described with very exact language, for the distinctions reside more in the language than in what it describes" (p. 13).

Brenda Dervin (1993) has recently suggested that if theorists want to remain true to what they profess in their classes and business consultations, they would do more of what she calls "verbing." As Dervin describes it, verbing is a way of reminding ourselves that whatever noun labels we use, we are really studying fluid *processes,* such as "thinkings and emotings, listenings and arguings, positionings and vacillatings, cooperatings and contestings, polarizings and nuancings, categorizings and hierarchializings, nounings and verbings" (p. 51). She admits that such terms sound clumsy, but still we need the reminders. Although the communication discipline earnestly encourages students to adopt a process-centered theoretical perspective, too many researchers still tend to "posit the subject as moving from one state to another. The emphasis is on the states, not the moves" (p. 51). It's a matter of not practicing what we preach: Unfortunately, Dervin claims, we often "focus on entities, not process; on nouns, not verbs" (p. 51). For example, Dervin would advise researchers studying how people get angry with each other to define their task as studying the *process* of people's "emotings" rather than the *things* we imagine as "emotions."

the difficulties of a process orientation

As Watts (1975) and Dervin (1993) illustrate, the nature of language presents problems to anyone who studies it from a process orientation. The separations and distinctions signified by words are absent in our everyday flow of experiencing. Language, indispensable in human experience, imposes a kind of artificial order on that experience. Therefore, theorists and researchers face an especially difficult challenge. To be as precise and clear as possible, they invent more and more specific linguistic category systems called *taxonomies* with which to describe a complex world. But if the communicative world exists more as relationships-in-

LINKS

• Dervin (1993) argues that the communication "field has already done more to move the social sciences from noun theories and methodologies to verb theories and methodologies than any other field" (p. 52). For more ideas on communication as an academic discipline—for some new "conceptualizings"—see Chapter 11.
• See Chapters 8 and 9 for discussions of how persuasion and media studies researchers have relied upon *constructs* (such as "attitude," "mind," and "gratification"), which are noun-based definitions of the topics being studied. In your opinion, is Dervin saying this research is invalid, or is "nouning" sometimes a necessary evil?

flux rather than as things, the boundaries described *by* the words actually belong *to* the words. Philosopher Alfred North Whitehead (1930) shows how *spatialization* (the cutting of reality artificially into static categories to ignore the world's inherent "fluency") "is the shortest route to a clear-cut philosophy expressed in reasonably familiar language" (p. 319). Unfortunately, the clarity that results from spatialization may be only a false security. As Watts suggested earlier, the bee process *is* the flower process, and vice versa. By using artificial linguistic divisions (would Dervin remind us to say "dividings"?), students of communication risk removing themselves from the very process they seek to understand.

Scientist Werner Heisenberg (1958) grapples with a similar problem in his **uncertainty principle.** He argues that researchers cannot study a phenomenon in isolation; the very methods used to observe and measure nature interfere with and alter natural processes. We end up studying, in other words, what may be happening *only because we're studying something* (see also Zukav, 1979, pp. 132–136). Researchers can never be completely sure whether some observed effects have been influenced by the observations themselves. Because the world is itself in a process of constant change, research cannot be conducted independent of that process.

Another problem with the process orientation is simply stated but its implications are complex and frustrating. Process thinking doesn't sound practical at first. It *feels* like our lives have starts, stops, and turning points, even though conceptually we might agree that processes are ongoing and in constant change. Our direct experience of communication, therefore, seems to contradict our process understanding of it. Despite all our reminders in this book, you probably still think of your personal relationships as capable of being frozen, stuck, stopped, started anew, and in many ways manipulated like objects. Intellectually, you may agree that communication is always flowing in some new direction and that it's impossible to freeze it long enough to study it precisely (even though we attempt to do just that). "Stop the world! I want to get off," screamed a character in a famous Broadway play. Communication theorists face this dilemma every day. Their theories attempt to explain how people manage events, explanations, and transitions, such as fault finding, leave taking, and conversational turn taking, in their lives. They "punctuate" sequences of actions through individual attention and relational redefinitions.

In fact, *punctuation* is used by some theorists to describe how people structure their experience in terms of their perceptions of when things start, stop, change, renew, and so forth (Bateson & Jackson, 1964; Watzlawick, 1984). Periods, commas, and other punctuation marks help readers understand how writers structure their messages. In writing, punctuation is an attempt to provide order. (That last sentence "ended" where the period signaled its conclusion.) Analogously, two communicators who blame each other for starting an argument are "punctuating" the disagreement differently. (I might think our argument last night started because we ended up seeing the movie I chose, and that the argument has passed. You might attribute the argument to my prior unwillingness to listen to your suggestions and thus consider the argument still in progress. Sound familiar?) A recognition of the effects of punctuation has saved many relationships: it permits the talk to shift from blaming to discussing the reasons for different punctuations.

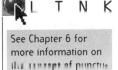

L T N K

See Chapter 6 for more information on the concept of punctuation.

A process orientation is practical, therefore, because it can give us a clear mind in times of interpersonal crisis and help us focus on real, rather than illusory communication problems. Here are some of its reminders for everyday application:

- Something is always happening to change the developing flow of communication. As one communication book proclaims, "nothing never happens" (Johnson, Senatore, Liebig, & Minor, 1974). Complacency, despair, and stagnation—despite being experienced as "real" emotions and frustrations—don't adequately describe a world in constant change. The future may or may not be brighter, but it will be different from the present and the past.
- Data is always available. Since relationships don't vanish, interpretive clues remain. For example, your roommate may stop talking to you as punishment for some personal insult. The process of constructing meaning continues, however, and you begin to notice how your roommate looks at you or how long she stays away from the apartment or how she fidgets while watching television. All of these acts are potential messages, and as Watzlawick, Beavin, and Jackson (1967) point out, once you are in a relationship, it's impossible to avoid communication. Although some scholars advance a more restrictive definition of communication based on the intentions of communicators, the reminder is still valid. Potentially helpful data for clarifying an interaction is always available.
- You cannot change only one part of a process or fiddle with only one variable. Although you may hope to do so, you will inevitably be frustrated by what communication theorists call *interdependence* or *wholeness*. Changing any one part of the whole will affect the relationships among the other parts of the whole, and thus the other parts will relate to each other in new ways. Thus, for instance, if you work in a small office and change your relationship with the boss (by becoming more competitive, let's say), that is not "just between the two of you" and "nobody else's business." Your co-workers may or may not be tactful, but they are not, technically speaking, mere observers of a process. They are inextricably part of the process, and their experience is affected by all changes in the office. Changing one relationship affects the dynamic of the entire group, perhaps in unpredictable ways. It is practical to be better able to predict such system, effects.

Communication creates interdependent systems out of the accidental collections of persons, and then it sustains those systems dynamically. As B. Aubrey Fisher (1978), one influential analyst of human systems, explains:

Two adults and three children may constitute a mere "aggregate" or a "heap" (system-theory jargon for a nonsystem). But when they live together as a family and affect each other in the day-by-day living together, they constitute a collective system called family—identifiable as a single unit. The individual identities . . . become amalgamated into the collectivity . . . such that what happens to one (for example, an illness, a broken teen-age heart, a loss of job income) affects every other member of the family unit. (p. 197)

Family systems also comprise neighborhoods, which can also be analyzed as systems themselves. The various levels of systems analysis can, of course, stretch in both directions, larger or smaller, from any system upon which you might be focusing. (See Box 2-1.)

MUTUALITY AND TRANSACTION

Interdependence, ecology, and *system* have become hallmark terms of contemporary culture. No longer is it realistic to think of the United States as being self-sufficient with regard to world resources, as the oil policies of Mideast countries often demonstrate. And decisions made by students in small sequestered apartments in Beijing, China, some years ago profoundly affected macroeconomic and diplomatic strategies debated in the world's major capitals.

individualistic approaches: one to another?

In the United States especially, a preoccupation with the self still seems to drive our attitudes about communication. When we want to compliment or advise someone, what do we tend to say? Here is a brief list of typical comments that illustrate the individualistic bias in our talk; the list suggests in both obvious and subtle ways a predominant informal *non*processual "theory":

"You're so self-reliant."
"He's an independent thinker."
"She's her own person."
"You've learned to meet your own needs."

BOX 2-1

PRACTICAL REMINDERS FROM THE PROCESS ORIENTATION OF COMMUNICATION

- Conditions, states, and meanings can't be frozen; tomorrow may not be better or worse than today, but it will not be another today.
- Humans constantly interpret life by using messages as data. Instead of assuming that communication is not happening, assume that it is, and then ask, "How?"
- Beware of the assumption that "it's nobody else's business." Communication relationships are interdependent on many levels, and observers are inevitably participants, too

"He's self-actualized."

"She's really made something of herself."

"You're a self-starter."

"He's into self-help and self-development."

"She has power over others."

"Be yourself."

"Do what you think is right."

"Decide for yourself."

"Take your future in your own hands."

"Make your own decisions."

"Be the captain of your own fate."

"Look out for number one."

Taken singly and in context, these statements seem reasonable. After all, people do "make personal decisions" and some "have power over others." But as a group, such comments emphasize the individual's contributions to communication and largely neglect how others influence communication outcomes. Some social scientists with an interest in communication bemoan this trend, including Bellah, Madsen, Sullivan, Swidler, and Tipton (1986). After conducting extensive interviews, they conclude that the American tendency toward individualism—one that has been helpful in many ways—has now become potentially "cancerous" (p. vii). Similarly, sociologist Charles Derber (1979), in an analysis of conversational narcissism, argues that "America is developing . . . not toward greater community or cooperation, but toward an intensification of the entrenched individualism" (p. 93). *Conversational narcissism* refers to people who believe they must monopolize conversations to prove themselves effective communicators.

LINK

Clearly this kind of individualism (whether "cancerous." as to Bellah and his colleagues, or not) has implications for theories of communication ethics. See Chapter 10 for a discussion of a *communitarian ethic,* which is meant to counterbalance ethical systems that emphasize individual rights.

The *individualistic orientation* of communication defines communication in terms of what one person does *to* others by aiming messages that may either hit or miss designated targets. Similar to Reddy's (1979) conduit metaphor discussed earlier in this chapter, communication is assumed to be made up of message manipulations that are controlled by a sender and designed for a receiver. Communication is an *"I"* process; *I* communicate *toward* or *at* you. In this sense, then, communication appears to have a well-defined intention, and, if the target is hit with the intended message, it produces predictable effects in the receiver. This model of communication implies that a well-chosen message will "work" for the sender, unless there is interference (sometimes referred to as **noise**) in the transmitting **channel** (the medium through which messages are conveyed).

Early studies of persuasion provide examples of this approach to communication. The studies presume that the receivers of persuasive messages are relatively passive, unlike the senders (Hovland, Janis, & Kelley, 1953). However, receivers were not found to be cognitively inert in processing messages. Aiming to identify the personality characteristics that affect message reception, this line of research focuses less on how receivers affect the persuasive relationship than on how persuaders do so by targeting their messages.

mutualistic approaches: both sides now?

Although the notion that communication moves from individual to individual may seem reasonable, most theorists now recognize a more *mutualistic orientation,* one that focuses on relationships rather than individuals (Reardon, 1987, pp. 125–158). This approach also incorporates the concept of **transaction** (Dewey & Bentley, 1949), which implies a relationship between system elements in which the definition of each element depends on changes in the other elements within the same system, such that nothing can be defined in isolation (see Box 2-2).

A diverse assortment of academic fields has applied transactional theory in their research. Transactional psychologists have used the concept to probe the processes of human perception (Ames, 1951; Bruner, 1986; Toch & MacLean, 1962). Literary critics have applied transaction and allied concepts to the analysis of poetry and other literature (Clark, 1990; Rosenblatt, 1978). The theoretical and practical relevance of transaction in the fields of mass communication and journalism also has been explored (Killenberg & Anderson, 1989; Wenner, 1985). Mainstream communication theorists have used it to emphasize a general state of reciprocity and mutual causality in interpersonal relations (Barnlund, 1970; Hall, 1977; Mortensen, 1972; Rasmussen, 1976; Stewart, 1990; Windahl & Signitzer, with Olson, 1992).

Dewey and Bentley (1949, p. 116) point out that the word *transaction* customarily refers to the deals or negotiations that result in agreements, or to the straightforward exchange of goods and services. But since Dewey introduced the concept around 1930, its meaning has become somewhat more specialized.

In order to understand communication transactionally, consider the following scenario: You attempt to establish a new friendship with a person you've noticed in class. You do everything you can think of to be friendly to her—you walk to the water fountain with her at break, you suggest studying together, you even offer to tape a class session you know she'll miss because of a dental appointment. Despite your efforts and good intentions, she seems aloof and non-committal. Why? One way of explaining the communication situation is to assume that she is just a quiet person. You might call her "shy," if this explanation makes sense to you. But Dewey and Bentley (1949) point out the problem of such an explanation, and suggest that the basis of this human difficulty is the activity

BOX 2-2

TRANSACTION

"Transaction designates . . . an ongoing process in which the elements or factors are, one might say, aspects of a total situation, each conditioned by and conditioning the other" (Rosenblatt, 1978, p. 17, emphasis added). Dewey and Bentley (1949) note further that transactional thought is distinguished from the "self-actional" and "interactional" approaches to communication.

of naming. We sometimes try to name things and their characteristics as though meaning comes directly to us from those things in a linear fashion. They call this kind of understanding *self-actional.*

An alternative way of explaining your predicament would be to assume that your actions in some way made her back off from you. In this case, you would begin to criticize yourself: "That was stupid. I'm too pushy. I caused her to respond to me that way." Or you might think that her quietness caused you to respond with a nurturing or helping attitude. This is a somewhat more sophisticated view of the situation because it assumes a two-way flow of action. Unlike your first explanation, which relies on a single external factor (the student's shyness), the second explanation allows for the possibility that *you* may have influenced the other person's behavior. Based on this analysis, you may conclude that you and your classmate reacted to each other's actions. This type of understanding, which recognizes the causes and effects of actions and reactions, is what Dewey and Bentley (1949) call *interactional.*

In 1949, when Dewey and Bentley published *Knowing and the Known,* most researchers in the fields of science and social science sought self-actional explanations. Although Newtonian physics and some explanatory systems in psychology had moved toward a more interactional perspective, the relationship between the *processes* of naming and the named (or between knowing and the known) was not adequately recognized until the publication of Dewey and Bentley's book.

Let's try some hypothetical thinking about our previous example. Suppose that your classmate's quiet behavior wasn't necessarily an unchangeable component of her personality that can be objectified—"thing-ized"—by calling it shyness. At the same time, imagine that you didn't *cause* that behavior, nor did she somehow *cause* your nurturance or friendliness. What you're supposing here, then, is that the world isn't composed of isolated objects with necessary attributes (self-actional), and it also isn't like a tabletop of billiard balls that only move when they're hit or caused to move by external objects (interactional). So-called common sense encourages self-actional and interactional explanations; they are simple to provide.

Dewey and Bentley (1949) adapted the term *transactional* to describe explanations that depend not on objects but on the active relationships that connect them. They regard this kind of relational thinking as most consistent with the complex nature of the world. Again, let's be practical. Being practical doesn't mean always adopting the most obvious or the simplest explanation; maybe it's *truly* practical to take complex factors into account, and in their proper context. Dewey and Bentley (1949) bring a transactional approach to communicating down-to-earth with common terms: "In ordinary everyday behavior, in what sense can we examine a talking unless we bring a hearing along with it into account? Or a writing without a reading? Or a buying without a selling? Or a supply without a demand? . . . We can, of course, detach any portion of a transaction that we wish, and secure provisional descriptions and partial reports. But all this must be subject to the wider observation of the full process" (p. 134). In other words, we cannot isolate things from each other if we hope to understand them more clearly.

The transactional perspective thus recognizes that all parties in a communicative relationship are mutually engaged in defining both themselves and each other. Toch and MacLean's (1962) influential article on perception presents several excellent examples. In baseball, for instance, a pitcher is defined as a player who takes the role of throwing the ball toward the plate so that the batter can try to hit it. But the pitcher cannot be defined in terms of his or her activity alone, because without the batter, pitching cannot occur (throwing, maybe, but not pitching). The same is true of the batter, whose role is dependent upon that of the pitcher. Neither can function without the other in a game of baseball. Nor can we *define* a batter or a pitcher without including both of them in our definition. Furthermore, although competition seems to dominate the two players' relationship, it is the transactional character of the game that allows for cooperation and teamwork to exist even among competitors.

The act of speaking, therefore, cannot be analyzed outside of the context of listening for a similar reason. Speaking is *defined* in part by listening. We understand a person's behavior only by placing it in the context of a larger relational process. Neither speaking nor listening could function without the other. Similarly, your classmate's "shyness," if that's the label you choose, may be accounted for transactionally as a function of the context in which it occurs, rather than as a personality trait that belongs to her and for which she is responsible, and not as a simplistic reaction to your behavior. In short, it belongs to the relationship.

MEANING

Some of the most derogatory statements we can make about another person's speech might include "It doesn't mean anything" and "You don't mean what you say." We obviously use the word *meaning* in very different ways. When it is used to refer to the overall significance of something or someone, a message that I understand but consider trivial will seem "meaningless" even though I have interpreted it and attributed my own personalized meaning to it. In another sense, *meaning* refers to the specific socially agreed-upon codes that we call language, as well as to the different abilities of persons to share in that code. At the start of an introductory physics course, for instance, you might say that you do not yet know what "quantum" means. The word is semantically meaningless to you, but in a larger sense it is meaningful to your relationship with the professor and the course. Perhaps you also develop hazy associations connecting the term with other, more familiar concepts of physics.

How can we analyze meaning, then? Obviously, it is a key concept in communication, for without some notion of how meaning develops, we cannot tell whether communication has occurred or whether it has been successful when it does occur. **Meaning** can be defined generally as *the conscious pattern humans create out of their interpretation of experience, whether that interpretation is relatively subjective and personalized* (Boulding, 1956) *or sociocultural and interpersonal in origin* (Mead, 1956).

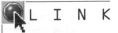

L I N K

Thinking transactionally, of course, is closely related to other central concepts of this chapter. Through its transactional nature, communication constitutes human experience. Transactional thinking depends on a process orientation, since it discourages analysis that depends on separate "things" that exhibit their own properties. It illustrates the interdependence feature of systems theory. With transactional thinking, perception is a matter of creativity, not certainty; we don't *receive* meanings as much as *conceive* them. You can easily see why individualistic general theories of communication (or of subfields such as persuasion, counseling skills, teaching, conversation, or many others) evolve into more sophisticated mutualistic modifications. See Chapter 11 for a discussion of the evolution of the discipline of communication. Its beginnings can be traced from speaker-centered concerns that are fundamentally individualistic and self-actional to process concerns that are fundamentally mutualistic and transactional.

However, defining meaning doesn't necessarily make it measurable. As anthropologist Victor Turner (1986) observes: "Obviously, there is much that can be counted, measured, and submitted to statistical analysis. But all human act[s are] impregnated with meaning, and meaning is hard to measure, though it can often be grasped, even if only fleetingly and ambiguously. Meaning arises when we try to put what culture and language have crystallized from the past together with what we feel, wish, and think about our present point in life" (p. 33). This view of meaning has four interconnected implications for communication theorists (see Box 2-3 on p. 67).

meaning is processual

Meaning is not a constant or a package, but a process that changes with the flow of time. It not only has a history, but also tends to persist until it is contradicted. Its forward reach is supported by the images humans construct from previous meaning-making.

According to economist and social theorist Kenneth Boulding (1956), the meaning of any new message for an individual is the change it produces in the person's existing image of the world. All communicative action that is meaningful, therefore, is embedded in a historical framework. What something means is largely determined by how it is perceived at any given moment.

L I N K

See Chapter 4 for more on how personal experience can help shape your unique images of the world.

meaning is personalized

Describing the meaning *of* a circumstance implies that we attribute meaning *to* the circumstance. The meaning of any word you look up in the dictionary does not exist in the word itself but in the consciousness of those who use the word in speaking or listening. The dictionary, really more a public opinion poll than a repository of meanings carried by words, simply reports on how the majority of educated speakers develop interpretations when they use words. Although the conduit metaphor suggests that words can "contain," "carry," or "send" packages of meaning, most contemporary theories support the notion that words and other messages point to meanings that are uniquely personalized.

L I N K

Theories associated with *hermeneutics* in some ways dispute the assumption that meaning is personalized. The work of one prominent hermeneutic theorist, Hans-Georg Gadamer, is discussed in Chapter 6.

meaning is co-constructed

Although meaning has a personalized subjective component, it is not ultimately a product of isolated *intrapersonal* (within-the-person) interpretive acts. In fact, if communication is transactional and mutualistic, how can meaning—the fuel of communication—be wholly an individualistic invention? Rather, the ground rules of communicative meaning are intersubjective. Meaning emerges from relationships because it is in relationships, not in our heads, that our lives are led.

For example, suppose we ask you, "What is your meaning for a B grade?" Obviously, your personal history is involved. What kind of grades have you already received in the class? What's your GPA? Have you previously cared much about what grades you received? Your personal feelings and goals are also uniquely involved.

Your goals for this class may be different from those of the student sitting at the next desk, and therefore you're gratified to get a B while she is terribly disappointed with one. But we also need to recognize that our meanings for messages constantly emerge from our real and inferred relationships with others. For instance, your relationship with the professor provides the context for the grade, and you understand that the grade is in part a relational message. Dr. Jones has power, advanced knowledge, and prestige, so it perhaps seems fitting that she evaluates you. The grade doesn't come from outer space, but instead originates in her reasoned attempt to give you feedback. Your grade for Communication Theory 201 does not really attach directly to the work you turned in, but is mediated through the relationship of you and your work to Dr. Jones and her expectations, perceptions, and interpretations.

Martin Buber's (1965b) philosophy of dialogue shows how this kind of meaning exists within the realm of human life he called *the between:* "We tend . . . to forget that something can happen not merely 'to' us and 'in' us but also, in all reality, between us. Let us consider the most elementary of all facts of our intercourse with one another. The word that is spoken is uttered here and heard there, but its spokenness has its place in 'the between'" (p. 112). The genuine location of meaning, Buber suggested, is not within the psychology of persons, nor in an abstract faith in spirit, but instead in the meeting of persons in their relationship— that is, "between" them. Buber affirms the mutualistic dimensions of meaning while also acknowledging that persons do in fact develop personalized meanings unique only to them. By walking the "narrow ridge," as he put it, between the two extremes of interpretation, Buber acknowledged the I-nature of unique experience, but simultaneously stressed the We-nature of communication and meaning-making.

L I N K

For more on Buber's philosophy, see the discussion of mutuality in Chapter 6 and the section on dialogic ethics in Chapter 10.

meaning is multidimensional

Finally, meaning evidently can't be reduced to a single, easily articulated message. It develops in the complex patterns we use to organize and interpret our world (Blakemore & Greenfield, 1987; Young, 1978). It is, therefore, multidimensional.

But much of our everyday talk seems to assume the opposite: that meaning is sent to receivers from senders in tidy packages ("I know exactly what you mean!"). A sequence of words may seem to constitute a speaker's single utterance: "I'd like to turn my paper in late." And it seems reasonable for us to ask the student, "What do you mean?" But by asking that question, we assume that it is possible to state *the* meaning "behind" the statement or *the* meaning that presumably motivates and expresses the intention of the statement. In most communication, however, multiple, complex meanings (many of which the speaker is unable to articulate) stimulate the statement. Although the speaker may have in mind a certain persuasive intent or even what Infante (1980) and others call a "verbal plan," many other meanings are unconsciously and *simultaneously* represented by the comment. In our example, then, the student who says "I'd like to turn my paper in late" may also mean that he or she (1) is overburdened, (2) seeks empathy from

BOX 2-3

MEANING: CREATING PATTERNS OF INTERPRETATION FROM EXPERIENCE

Meaning is:

- *Processual* (always changing).
- *Personalized* (inevitably varying somewhat among both individuals and groups).
- *Co-constructed* (not just inner thought, but intersubjective).
- *Multidimensional* (involving many levels and possible interpretations).

the professor, (3) is ashamed to request an extension, (4) wants to remain tentative about the request, (5) hopes the professor will reconsider the policy of weekly papers, and (6) dislikes the professor but expects to mask that feeling (among many other possible meanings). When we speak, we have multiple intentions, many of which we may not be fully aware of or acknowledge consciously.

Some theorists and philosophers use the term **polysemy** to describe the dependence of symbolic communication on the multiple meanings that can arise from interpretation (Condit, 1989; Ricoeur, 1981; Rommetveit, 1987; Ullmann, 1966). Symbolic communication is highly polysemous because whenever we say a word we are laying open all the possible meanings for the word that reside in the language. Puns, tact, sarcasm, spontaneous verbal surprises, and verbal playfulness all emerge from the polysemic possibilities of interaction. A person speaking a word is, in effect, inviting listeners to participate, not just as receivers, but also in the construction of mutual meanings. Context, therefore, not simply the word, must be considered in developing meaning. From the transaction, both parties have the opportunity to discover something new about themselves.

L I N K

For more on language as a symbolic system, see Chapter 4. Regarding polysemy, why do you think it is impractical to assume that human-to-human understanding can be completely accurate or total?

When we communicate, we not only express what we already believe, intend, or plan; we also discover new beliefs, intentions, and so on. Anthropologist and conversation analyst Michael Moerman (1988) helps us understand how the multidimensional nature of meaning affects our informal communication. If meaning were instead one-dimensional, we could assume that, as message senders, we are in charge of expressing our own predetermined beliefs or intentions. We could also evaluate our talk by using this simple criterion: "Did I accomplish my objective?" But are speaker and listener really accomplishing different things, or are they both involved in one coordinated process? Moerman's investigation of *overlaps*—occasions when people find themselves speaking simultaneously—led him to conclude that mutuality in communication is highly pronounced, so much so that "the conscious actor cannot be the author of his or her talk" (p. xi). As a result, we are never completely in charge of our own speech, much less in control of our communication relationships. Practically speaking, then, it seems unreasonable to blame other people for their intentions in communication, knowing full well that we, in our relationship with them, are co-conspirators even in the communicative conditions we deplore (e.g., insults, slights, put-downs, interruptions, and the like).

INTENTION AND THE DEFINITION OF COMMUNICATION: A CONTROVERSY

The study of communication had a speaker-centered, rhetorical focus for centuries (Stamp & Knapp, 1990). The intent of the speaker was of prime concern, and definitions of communication tended to be molded by the communication events (speaker-to-audience) in which scholars were most interested. Later, as our interests broadened to include interpersonal communication, listening claimed our attention as well. We needed to refocus the concept of communication in order to take into account unintended effects, as well as intentions from a listener's point of view. Why is a speaker's intention to form overt messages any more crucial, for example, than a listener's intention to gain new meaning through interpreting messages?

One particular approach was accepted as a truism within communication studies for many years. Watzlawick, Beavin, and Jackson (1967) asserted "the impossibility of not communicating" in interactional situations, presumably where the parties are aware of each other's presence. This was proposed as a tentative *axiom*—a firmly established claim that needs no further support—so they were reasonably confident about their conclusions. Because they identify communication largely with behavior, Watzlawick and his colleagues claim that communication is unavoidable. All behavior has communicative potential. Their contribution, simply put, is that communication can be seen as a constantly occurring environment for human experience. Two persons who are together cannot stop communicating because they can't avoid behaving in some way, and any behavior has message value when the other person attributes meaning to it. Silence, absence, lack of eye contact, and other nonverbal behaviors, intended or not, all might constitute communication from the perspective described in Watzlawick, Beavin, and Jackson's *Pragmatics of Human Communication* (1967, pp. 48–51).

Introductory to communication books and basic interpersonal communication texts repeated the axiom often, solidifying its acceptance. Communication scholars expanded their interest in the unintended effects of messages in interactional environments. Researchers could study almost anything because all types of human action could potentially fit under the conceptual umbrella of communication.

More recently, however, some scholars have renewed their interest in a narrower definition of communication. Arguing that if communication is conceived as everything, nothing really is specified, these theorists (Infante, Rancer, & Womack, 1990; Motley, 1990; Scott, 1977) want to distinguish communicative behaviors from other human processes, such as perception and nonsymbolic nonverbal behaviors. According to one approach within this more restricted area of focus,

L I N K

This controversy surrounding the two main approaches to studying communication reinforces a similar point made in Chapter 1 about theorizing. It is not necessary for theorists to prove that their definitions or concepts are "right" in order to conduct research or make stimulating contributions to scholarly understanding. We believe it is a strength of a discipline when different theories can test each other, calling forth perhaps clearer conceptions, while still stimulating separate programs of research. It is by this process that knowledge advances.

"human communication represents the execution of the individual's most recently adopted communication plan" (Infante, Rancer, & Womack, 1990, p. 11). By placing communication primarily within an individualistic framework, these authors portray it as an outcome of the separate intentions of its participants. Without denying the importance of process-centered views of reality, such theorists advocate restricting the definition of communication to achieve greater conceptual clarity.

Despite their different areas of focus, both of these approaches to the study of communication offer valuable insights. The broader transactional approach can help us understand the complexity of communication, while the narrower individualistic approach can help clarify some communication concepts more precisely. We tend to agree with Stamp and Knapp (1990) on this issue: "For interactional participants, the most important aspect of intentionality may not be what an encoder really intends to accomplish with a particular message or what attributions a decoder makes about the message but how the interactants in the relationship ultimately negotiate the two perspectives" (p. 296). "Communication" therefore, is also a useful label for what happens when participants aren't fully aware of their intentions at all, but are aware of the relationship between them.

MODELS OF COMMUNICATION

Several times in this chapter, we've used the word *model* in different contexts. Although in everyday life a *supermodel* can be someone who displays expensive clothing for potential buyers, a *role model* is someone who supposedly behaves in an exemplary way, and a carefully constructed *model airplane* duplicates the colors and relative dimensions of the full-sized plane, a communication **model** serves a somewhat different purpose than advertising, emulation, or copying.

A model of communication—or of any other process, object, or event—is a way of simplifying the complex interactions of elements in order to clarify relevant relationships, and perhaps to help predict outcomes (see Box 2-4). McQuail and Windahl (1993) define a model as "a consciously simplified description in graphic form of a piece of reality. A model seeks to show the main elements of any structure or process and the relationships between these elements" (p. 2). Because not all aspects of a complex process can be modeled, even if they are known, the theorist constructing a model must make a challenging set of choices. Of the many different factors that comprise the process, which ones can be omitted without doing a disservice to its essence? What static symbolic or visual elements (words? lines? arrows?) may substitute appropriately for the dynamic reality of communication? Modelers abstract and generalize the empirical world, hoping for a kind of truth to emerge from their creativity. A model can be physical, visual, or verbal. However, most attempts at communication modeling have been combinations of the visual and the verbal, and have had largely instructional goals.

Modeling the next version of the Ford Escort is a big challenge for Detroit's carmakers, and the thoroughness of the engineers and the extent of their knowledge might surprise you. But they have something tangible to shape and to sub-

BOX 2-4

EFFECTIVE COMMUNICATION MODELS:

• Clarify, explain, and help to predict outcomes of basic processes by skillful simplification.

• Avoid oversimplification by ensuring that essential elements are retained.

• Can be physical, visual, or verbal depictions, although most models of communication combine strong visual elements with written explanations.

---

ject to wind tunnel and other tests. Modeling communication in a way that captures the essence of the process presents very different challenges. Communication is hard to get hold of because it doesn't sit still.

Everyone carries models in their heads all the time, whether they know it or not. One scientist (Bross, 1970) notes that "all of us are accustomed to using verbal models in our thinking processes and we do it intuitively" (p. 14). The questions become: Are your verbal models of how communication works sophisticated enough to do you any good? Will they help you predict what kinds of responses are necessary in any given situation? Will they help you decide how to assist another person in mutual cooperation? Will they help you troubleshoot in times of conflict or misunderstanding? In other words, are they *practical?* We believe that contemporary communication theory has shown individualistic models to be impractical. Such a model seems simple, even elegantly so (see Figure 2-1 for an example).

But what is omitted? The process nature of communication is neglected, as is the recognition that all participants actively contribute to outcomes. Although the changing character of the communication process cannot be fully captured by any static model, we can build in such factors as feedback to suggest that communication is not a one-way phenomenon. Some feedback models of communication attempt to suggest that communication depends on the two-way, cause-and-effect interactions of message/feedback/response. One example is shown in Figure 2-2.

What became known as *information theory* was based on a similar feedback model (Shannon & Weaver, 1949). Information theory, which developed from research conducted at Bell Laboratories in the 1940s, had a profound effect on the vocabulary of communication theorists at mid-century. It considered *senders* as sources of information who encoded messages designed to be transmitted through *channels* for the subsequent decoding of *receivers*. An intended message

L I N K

If you haven't already done so, complete Exercise 2 in the "You, the Researcher" section of Chapter 1. It asks you to diagram a rudimentary communication model. If you completed the exercise earlier, reexamine your work to see if it meets the criteria for an effective model of communication.

Figure 2-1 An Individualistic Model

Figure 2-2   A Simple Feedback Model

becomes a *signal* when it is encoded, and that signal assumes the status of message again when it is successfully decoded by the receiver. Any channel through which a signal moves is considered to have a certain degree of *noise,* which is any interference in the system that reduces the chance that the decoded signal will match the encoded one. Information was defined as a message or set of messages that reduce uncertainty for the receiver; its measure was the *bit,* the amount of information necessary to reduce uncertainty roughly by half. Information theory illustrated well the communication problem of *channel capacity and efficiency* (how many messages can be decoded accurately in a given period of time), and helped define how senders and receivers reduce uncertainty in mediated, especially technological, situations. However, because it largely neglected the problems of meaning, mutuality, and process in favor of intentionalistic communication assumptions, it does not shed much light on process and change in communication relationships and doesn't function particularly well as a general model of communication.

Some theorists have despaired of ever adequately capturing "process" changes in communication, and have settled for presenting lists of relevant variables as their models. One such attempt, Berlo's (1960) variables model of communication, is shown in Figure 2-3. Any understanding of communication starts with the ability to identify its essential elements. Therefore, the primary purposes of the variables model are (1) to clarify the "ingredients" that affect the tasks of encoding and decoding and (2) to show how senders and receivers use similar personal (skills, attitudes, knowledge) and contextual (social system, culture) cues to understand both the code and the content of messages as they are sent through channels.

Unlike these more static models, Dance's (1967) helical spiral model of communication emphasizes the changing nature of the process, though to the exclusion of everything else (see Figure 1-2 in Chapter 1). Still, by following the flow of communication with the spiral, we see clearly that communication is not a linear transmission but one that travels indefinitely in circles, back upon itself—never to the same place it started, but to a new position that is itself already flowing into something yet newer. So, when you reply to me, it is to a changed me, and with a broadened perspective. Dance attempts to illustrate this by a spiral that ever-widens into infinity.

Finally, the transactional perspective of communication, discussed at length earlier in the chapter, differs significantly from those of the self-actional and in-

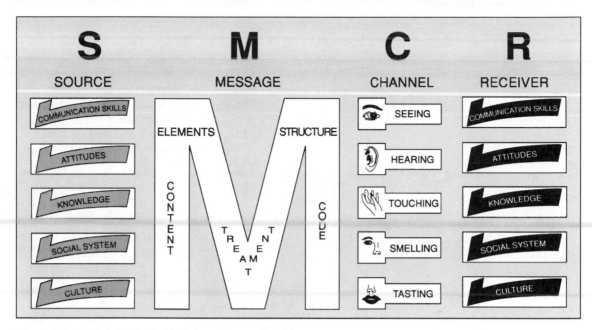

Figure 2-3 Berlo's Variable Model

Source: "A Model of the Ingredients in Communication" from *The Process of Communication: An Introduction to Theory and Practice* by David Berlo, copyright © 1960 by Holt, Rinehart and Winston, Inc. and renewed in 1988 by David K. Berlo. Reproduced by permission of the publisher.

teractional approaches. Instead of aiming or trading messages, communicators build relationships. A transactional model developed by Barnlund (1970), shown in Figure 2-4, may appear cluttered and complicated at first, but notice how many mutualistic assumptions he acknowledges with some relatively straightforward symbols. The two persons (P_1 and P_2) each represent simultaneous encoding (sending) and decoding (receiving) functions enfolded within personal experience. Encoding (E) and decoding (D) are depicted not as alternating subprocesses of communication, but as mutually dependent ones. Each contributes to what the communicators are building together. In effect, the persons represented in the model do not "transfer" meaning "across" to each other but agree to "meet in the middle." Each still has access to his or her private cues (C_{PR}) (e.g., unique feelings, insights, values) in what some psychologists call a *phenomenal field*—the array of cues available for individuals' interpretation at any given time. In addition, both parties share access to a field of public cues (C_{PU}), though the meanings of these will differ for each communicator.

Still, there are deficiencies and compromises in such a model; it, too, is an oversimplification. To make it more explanatory, you might imagine that Figure 2-4 has built in, as inherent factors, the variables Berlo mentions. Imagine that the negotiation process illustrated by the "relationship" between communicators is

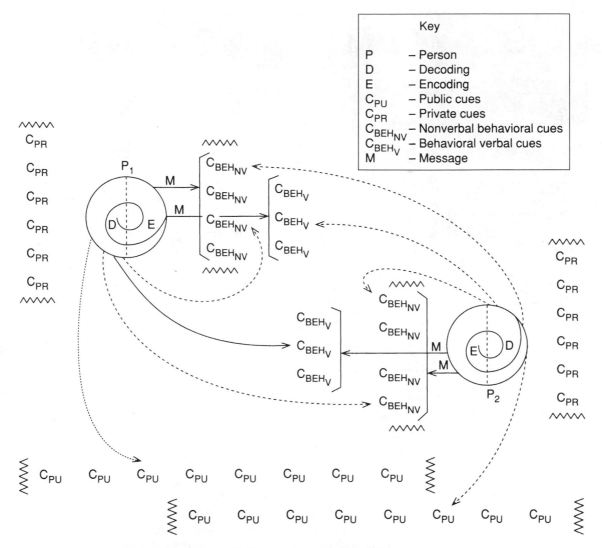

Figure 2-4   Barnlund's Transactional Model of Communication

Source: "A Transactional Model of Communication" by D. C. Barnlund. From *Foundations of Communication Theory,* edited by Kenneth K. Sereno and C. David Mortenson. Copyright © 1970 by Harper & Row. Reprinted by permission of Addison Wesley Educational Publishers Inc.

constantly in flux in the way Dance suggests, adjusting to accommodate the messages communicators contribute to it. If your mental model can integrate these ideas, then your understanding of communication will be theoretically more solid and pragmatically more useful.

T E S T I N G   T H E   C O N C E P T S

"If people understood each other better, wouldn't there be fewer conflicts? And if so, does this mean communication and conflict are opposite processes?"

If communication allows people to understand each other better, some conflicts would be resolved. Many conflicts result from misunderstanding and ignorance. Yet many conflicts result from *accurate* interpretations, too. Therefore, improving communication might also improve people's understanding of why they disagree, and, in fact, deepen their disagreement. Communication is a neutral process, not a prescription for a "good" life but the only way human life can be understood.

"Isn't the conduit definition of communication easier to understand than the mutualistic definition?"

Yes, but its simplicity is misleading. The conduit metaphor makes the problems of communication appear more manageable than they really are; it also encourages people to take simplistic solutions seriously.

"Should I agree with the broad definition of communication (all behavior can be communication) or the narrower definition (only intentional messages are communicative)? Which is right?"

Both approaches can be helpful, but neither is necessarily "right." What does *right* mean? There's no holy definition of communication hidden somewhere in a golden shrine, so to what can theorists compare their definitions? Definitions should be compared with each other, and with suitably applied criteria of appropriateness (see Chapter 1). Thus, if it helps you to define communication broadly (or narrowly), do so. However, make yourself aware of the arguments of other perspectives as well.

"Does this chapter mean that no one can ever fully understand me?"

In a sense, yes. Your inner meanings (images, feelings, and so forth) may not even be fully understood by you. And how many people can read your mind? So, no one can ever fully understand you. But the other side of this story is important to remember, too. Meaning is not just an intrapersonal issue (within personal cognition and experience), but an interpersonal one, too. Buber (1965b) says meaning resides in the "between" of relationships, and in this way communicators can be said to have full access to understanding relational meaning.

"Shouldn't science search for the one Truth? How can communication study be scientifically based if the discipline tolerates conflicting theories and definitions?"

A truly scientific attitude is one that remains open to new and different interpretations. In the scientific world, nothing is fixed or unchanging. That's why textbooks are constantly being revised in the scientific disciplines. Further conflicting theories encourage science to re-energize itself continually. Communication theorists cannot realistically attempt to identify a single theory that explains all of what we call communication.

"Isn't *transaction* just a fancy way of saying communication is two-way?"
No. It is a fancy word to some people, but it implies much more than the two-way trading of messages. It is a theorist's way of noting that communicators simultaneously affect and define each other, and neither party can fully control these effects. You can't change another person without simultaneously being changed. Examples: You can't be persuasive without someone else being persuaded. No one can be a leader without followers. (If they don't define themselves as followers, who are you leading?)

"So what? How can what I've learned in this chapter change how I communicate to my friends?"
It may not. At least, it won't change things directly. But it may change how you *think about* your talk with others. For example, you might consider why you used the phrase "communicate *to* my friends" in your question, rather than "*with* my friends." If communication is basically mutualistic, an attitude of *with* could mean that you'd be more ready to invite others' reactions, and more able to understand how others' meanings may affect yours in subtle ways. Personal theorizing and personal behavior are intimately related.

"I always thought meaning was in words. Why don't words mean what they mean?"
To counteract the misleading aspects of the conduit metaphor, try to think of words as stimulating people to create meanings within communication relationships. If the meaning was "in" the word, then the same word would trigger the same reactions in all people who know the word (which, of course, is not at all what happens). Although the nature of language as a code ensures that native speakers of the same language generally will not diverge very far from each other's meanings, this results from habit and agreement, not from any inherent meaning in the words themselves.

Y O U ,   T H E   R E S E A R C H E R

1. Try some speculative, introspective research. Think creatively about objects or events with which communication might be compared.

   - Think in terms of analogies: How is communication like a frisbee? A rubber band? A key? A sporting event? A lightbulb?
   - Questions: How is communication also unlike these analogies? What other analogies can you think of? How are these analogies similar to or different from communication models? Which of the analogies are most similar to the conduit metaphor? Least similar?

2. Simulate on a smaller scale and with a different audience Redding's (1968) informal survey of executives described in this chapter (see p. 53–54).

- Type on a sheet of paper the linear and one-way definition he used to stimulate discussion with business executives ("When Person X 'communicates' with Person Y, what happens is that he transmits meanings (information, facts, ideas, etc.) . . . to the mind of Person Y" (Redding, 1968, p. 101). Make five copies and give them to five different friends who are not in your communication class.
- Below the definition, ask your friends (your study participants, in terms of research) to write brief reactions to the following questions: (A) Does this definition make sense? (B) Would someone who believes communication works this way be successful in most organizations? (C) If you could change anything about the definition, what would it be?
- Researchers *hypothesize*, or make educated guesses, about the outcomes of their studies. A hypothesis is based upon prior research findings, but is not meant to bias upcoming results; researchers are willing to be surprised by whatever reactions *these* participants have. (In fact, as discussed in Chapter 1, quantitative researchers often employ what they call a *null hypothesis*, which states explicitly that no significant differences will be found between, for example, two groups that are compared. This move is to counter the inherent biases of researchers to expect or desire particular kinds of significance in their findings.) Here, simply make your best educated guesses about the participants' specific responses.
- Determine how to code your results. For example, of the five respondents, how many believe Redding's definition (which was a purposely inaccurate statement) captures the essence of communication? What other good questions about the results could suggest categories into which you could code the results?
- After you have compiled results, compare your findings with those of other students. Do most of the participants responding to the surveys seem to agree or disagree with linear, one-way, self-actional perspectives on communication? Do they have confidence in the effectiveness of one-way models? If they believe an inaccurate conception to have practical value in organizations, what does this tell you about contemporary organizations or how we need to prepare people for them?

3. Try some secondary or supportive research on professional versus popular definitions of communication. In your school's library, find three recent articles about communication in professional journals such as *Communication Theory, Communication Monographs,* or the *Journal of Communication,* and three articles about communication in popular magazines, such as *Redbook, Reader's Digest,* or *Psychology Today.* Read the articles closely to see whether communication is defined explicitly or implicitly. Take notes on what you find. Compare the popularized definitions with the professional ones. What did you discover?

Peter Vandermark/Stock, Boston

the context of communication

"are we part of
an ecology
of physical and social
settings?"

The conceptualization of knowledge of and about a context is often rendered in the static language of photography: we are taking pictures of a scene; this is what you see in it. But the scene was not the same before the photographer entered, and it changes after the picture is taken. . . . What is even more confounding is that a context is given meaning in sentences uttered by the participants who, in turn, are influenced by those utterances to "see" the context in their own interpretive ways. What one person "sees" as the context is not necessarily what another person "sees" (or responds to) in it, even though their roles may be clear to the researcher and to them and despite the fact that they share precisely the same physical environment.

H. L. GOODALL, JR., *LIVING IN THE ROCK 'N' ROLL MYSTERY* (1991, P. 29)

66 "What did you say?" "What was he talking about?" "What did she have to say about the proposal?" "Let them talk it out." "Let's reason together." Speech sometimes seems to define human life, and often it is the basic criterion by which we judge the differences between humans and other animals.

But what about the rest of human existence, aspects of interaction that aren't verbal and are shared with other living beings? In addition to what you may assume to be the verbal core of experience, what else is relevant to communication? If human symbols are at the center of our lives, what other communication factors lurk at the edges?

Although it is tremendously important that we humans speak, does it matter where and when we speak, and what else might surround or accompany the words we address to each other? Although it may seem as if our focus in this chapter is with what the popular media call *body language* or what scholars term nonverbal communication, we are in fact interested in something broader that could be called *context*. As Cody and McLaughlin (1985) suggest, "We need to know more about how situational applications, interactional constraint, and impinging environmental cues operate in the real world to influence behavior" (p. 303). What is needed, they write, is "ecologically sound understanding" (p. 303).

CONTEXT

Context is challenging to define because it refers to everything in a frame of interest *except* what you're focusing on. Normally, a definition is a way to focus on or specify a concept. Defining *context* becomes a paradox of sorts because to define the term, the definer has to place in the foreground of perception that which *by* *definition* is not foregrounded. Once we analyze context it ceases to *be* a context. Perceptual and Gestalt psychologists talk about the *figure/ground relationship,* in which a *figure* is the focus and the *ground* is composed of the perceptually deemphasized background stimuli against which the figure is perceived (Bolles, 1991; Koffka, 1935). Context is the ground for communicators.

Context is not a "thing," nor is it an organized collection of things that can be isolated or analyzed precisely. When you read a newspaper article, for instance, the article becomes the figure or text. Its placement on the page (e.g., at the bottom of page eight next to the obituaries) is not only an aspect of the text but also of the *con*-text. Notice that context can be a mixture of both verbal and nonverbal elements in a communication environment. Moreover, context is not just a given in communication; rather, it is achieved and elaborated on by communicators. In face-to-face communication, Nofsinger (1989) explains, context is often created and modified through conversations. Although not all communication is conversation, of course, theorists usually regard context in the same way as a dynamic and ongoing social process, not as a static variable.

Understanding the influence of context means that it might be significant that a particular *communication cue* (a simple message or interpretable act, such as an oral or written statement, a gesture, a logo, a picture, or an advertisement):

> appears after an earlier one (rather than before it);
>
> is printed in **bold** type in a company newsletter (rather than in standard type);
>
> is uttered in a whisper in church (rather than at normal volume);
>
> is said to one particular person in the presence of others (rather than in private);
>
> is broadcast by a radio station late at night (rather than in prime time);
>
> is presented unknowingly by a person's clothing, such as when certain colors or types of clothing are accidentally associated with urban gangs (rather than intentionally); and
>
> is in the foreground as other events take place in the background (rather than vice versa).

These examples illustrate that context is an ecological concern for communicators. An *ecology* is an environmental system in which everything interrelates and in which organisms are studied in relation to their environment (Hawley, 1986). Changes in any part of the system affect the other parts of the system. Developing contextual awareness is a question of noticing the connections between messages and their social, intellectual, and physical settings. Messages aren't offered one at a time, but in complex mosaics that are impossible to take in all at once. Too much focus on individual elements makes you "miss the forest for the trees," a particularly apt cliché that emphasizes context awareness.

Ecological assumptions guided Barker's (1968) study of a small town community. He concludes, among other things, that children's actions could often be more accurately predicted by the behavioral patterns expected of the *places* in which children communicate than by the "behavioral tendencies" or personalities of the children themselves (p. 4). Many communication students are surprised to learn that context can have more impact than personality on how communication develops.

L I N K

Barker's ecological study provides a practical reminder that's consistent with a systems theory approach. See the section devoted to general systems theory in Chapter 1.

Therefore, understanding the context of communication events is practical in several respects. It helps us distinguish kidding from criticism, sarcasm from sincerity, and silliness from seriousness. Through context, we learn that a crowded city bus is not an appropriate setting to discuss a marriage proposal, and that timing is crucial in planning when and where, not just how, to ask your supervisor for a day off. Often it's not just what is said that's crucial but *where* and *when* it's said, *what else* is said in the same situation, and *what else* is expected. A *text* is often important only because of a certain context.

Given the importance of context, then, it is not surprising that some theorists and researchers specialize in the study of communication contexts. In this chapter, we'll discuss two major types of contextual communication: (1) the more immediate *physical and psychological context* surrounding a particular communication episode, and (2) the broader *social context* or interactional setting in which communication occurs. The distinctions are important to note if we hope to translate theoretical insight into everyday pragmatics. Can we know what is right or wrong, or good or bad, to say without context awareness? Is it appropriate to tell jokes when meeting someone for the first time? Although you may have a generalized answer for this question based on your personality and previous experience, would that answer change if we stipulated that you'd meet your partner at a dinner party, or alternatively, at a new job on the assembly line, or at the funeral of your friend's father, or at a TV station where you're being interviewed on the air?

PHYSICAL AND PSYCHOLOGICAL CONTEXT: NONVERBAL LIFE AND THE THEORY OF IMMEDIACY

The verbal and nonverbal message systems are not independent or autonomous. They depend on each other for context. Yet it is the nonverbal system that more nearly completes our picture for what context means, and for that reason we'll concentrate on it in this first section.

the nonverbal message system: how is it theoretically important?

While verbal symbols can serve as contextual cues for other verbal symbols, most analyses of communication context focus on the nonverbal realm. This is understandable if you realize that words are only a tiny fraction of all the stimuli available to humans when we interpret situations and ideas. Most of what we learn comes from nonverbal messages or artifacts. Most of our ability to interpret verbal messages depends on nonverbal information.

Thus, theorists have developed assumptions about the impact of both intentional and unintentional nonverbal messages (see Box 3-1):

BOX 3-1

UNDERSTANDING THE NONVERBAL MESSAGE SYSTEM MEANS THAT YOU:

- Analyze context, not just the messages themselves.
- Understand messages within contexts as defining relationships.
- Know that nonverbal communication is always part of your communication experience.
- Realize that when a nonverbal message and a verbal message contradict each other, people tend to trust the nonverbal.
- Acknowledge that the nonverbal message system involves a complex set of visual/auditory codes, contact codes and place/time codes.

1. *The nonverbal system invites contextual analysis.* Indeed, its contextual nature is one reason why theorists refer so often to **metacommunication,** the ability to communicate *about* communication (*meta* is a prefix indicating something's self-reference) (Watzlawick, Beavin, & Jackson, 1967). Metacommunication tends to regulate human interaction. For example, if you put down or criticize your friend while also smiling, your smile is a signal to your friend about how to interpret your comment. While we converse, we simultaneously offer nonverbal commentaries on how our verbal offerings should be taken.

2. *The nonverbal system emphasizes relationship-defining messages,* rather than the content-specifying, naming messages of the verbal system. Language employs many symbols that stand for aspects of the object world by arbitrary social agreement. Thus, for example, the word *book* and the object you hold in your hands right now relate to each other only because of a social code or agreement. But once we're participants in that agreement, the letters *b-o-o-k* call to mind the object, even when the object is absent. Language enables us to communicate at a distance.

   In the nonverbal system, messages assume a more immediate and direct connection to what is being expressed and to the relationship of the communicators. The meaning of a book might be indicated by showing an actual book to a listener. Nonhuman animal communication is based on this relation-defining function, rather than category-naming, (though some people like to think their pets are capable of both): "When I open the refrigerator and the cat comes, rubs against my legs, and mews, this does not mean 'I want milk'—as a human being would express it—but invokes a specific relationship, 'Be mother to me,' because such behavior is only observed in kittens in relation to adult cats, and never between two grown-up animals" (Watzlawick, Beavin, & Jackson, 1967, p. 63).

3. *The nonverbal system cannot be avoided.* Linguist Mary Ritchie Key (1980) writes that her "beginning premise is that when human beings interact, language . . . may or may not occur, but extralinguistic correlates always

occur" (p. vii). The nonverbal system can neither be ignored nor turned off as if it were a faucet or light switch. Nonverbal messages constantly surround us as perceptual or psychic backdrops for whatever else we are doing. Because we seek meaning and closure, it is paradoxical (from an observer's point of view) to perceive literally a "blank look" or a "noncommittal gesture." The gesture or the look is ultimately interpreted in some way. Nonverbal messages can also exist even in the negative—silence or absence, whether intended or unintended, may be interpreted by others as contextual cues.

4. *The nonverbal system is typically more believable and persuasive than the verbal.* Listeners presented with a verbal and a nonverbal message that are contradictory tend to assume that the nonverbal cue is more true or genuine than the verbal one, other factors being equal. Thus, for example, a speaker who, while sweating profusely in a cool room, claims, "I'm not nervous!" will probably be viewed as nervous. Similarly, someone who scowls, turns red, and shouts, "I'm not mad!" will be perceived as angry.

5. *The nonverbal system is behaviorally complex.* Despite scholarly debate over what behaviors to study and what terms to use to describe them, a basic vocabulary of nonverbal theory has emerged in recent years. We have borrowed the following typology from Burgoon, Buller, and Woodall (1989), but will describe each technical term briefly in everyday language:

a. Visual and auditory codes

Kinesics: The study of the meanings of body movements, macro (major) and micro (minor). (Much of this research is based on the work of anthropologist Ray Birdwhistell [1970].)

Physical appearance: The study of how variables such as height, weight, and demeanor affect interaction. (For a fascinating discussion of the effects of such factors on male–female relationships, see Nancy Henley's *Body Politics* [1977] and "Body Politics Revisited" [1995].)

Vocalics: The study of how voice can create the context for understanding words (e.g., by its rate, pitch, volume, or tone).

b. Contact codes

Haptics: The study of how people develop meanings for touch behaviors.

Proxemics: The study of distance as a communication message.

c. Place and time codes

Environment: The study of how meaning is affected by where people interact; the study of environment may be direct and physically based, such as the effects of urban housing design on interaction (Yancey, 1977), or it may be indirect and technology based, such as the effects of electronic media on workplace interactions (Acker, 1989).

Artifacts: The study of the communicative potential of object display; it can involve explicit *object language,* such as showing someone the fish you just caught, or the ring you just bought, or implicit effects such as the jacket you're wearing.

Chronemics: The study of how people communicate different messages through the manipulation of time; it can involve being late, early, and "on time," for instance.

Clearly, theorizing about human relationships must take nonverbal messages into account. It is their implicitness that makes them so important (Douglas, 1975). Nonverbal messages are a crucial component of our study of communication context.

immediacy

Psychologist Albert Mehrabian (1981) developed his **immediacy theory** of implicit communication while studying nonverbal messages, although its basic concepts can be applied to language use as well. The theory identifies three levels of emotional response: *attraction, dominance,* and *arousal.* At various times, Mehrabian also has called attraction "liking," "evaluation," or "positiveness"; dominance has been discussed as a "power," "potency," or "status" issue; and arousal has been discussed also as "responsiveness." People reveal their attraction to another person by body language and movements, by eye contact, by haptic (touching) messages, or by physical proximity (closeness). The cues here are what Mehrabian calls *immediacy cues;* they signal a desire by one communication partner to be directly "with" the other as much as possible. We might illustrate dominance over others by such relaxation cues as "arm position asymmetry, sideways lean, leg-position asymmetry, hand relaxation, neck relaxation, [or] reclining angle" (Druckman, Rozelle, & Baxter, 1982, p. 29). Likewise, emotional arousal is significantly more apparent with nonverbal behaviors than it is with the spoken word. Words like "I love you" are more meaningful to an intimate partner when accompanied by "immediate" activities such as a hug, a kiss, or a gentle touch to the face.

Mehrabian's concept of immediacy is important for understanding context. If much of the meaning in social situations is dependent on nonverbal cues, as Mehrabian and other theorists have shown (estimates range as high as 93 percent), and if human relationships are largely maintained and defined nonverbally (Weitz, 1974), then we should understand more about the environments that facilitate and impede immediacy. Berger and Luckman (1966) established a philosophical basis for a *here-and-now* contextual focus among communicators. "Here" indicates an immediate spatial dimension; communicators often desire direct physical access to each other, traditionally in face-to-face situations. "Now" indicates an immediate temporal dimension; communicators want to know others are available to them in the present moment, not on some future occasion. To what extent, then, does environmental design affect immediacy?

physical settings: environment and space

people and environment Psychologist Robert Sommer (1969) has devoted much of his career to researching the effects of personal space, environment, and the effects of human-designed physical settings (e.g., architecture) on communication. His view of communication is part of an overall perspective on humanity: As creative creatures, we cannot escape the effects of environment, even insisting on constructing our own. "All people are builders, creators, molders, and shapers of the environment; we are the environment," Sommer says (1969, p. 7). Not only do we select our environments but we begin changing them from the onset of our interactions within them. Human presence changes everything. Students personalize their rooms with flags, posters, stuffed animals, sports equipment, and mementos from the past. Newly married couples cannot wait to purchase their own place in order to reconstruct and redecorate it to their tastes.

To some extent, homes reflect the personalities of those who live within them. One of the authors recalls visiting friends in Levittown, Pennsylvania after being gone for a number of years. What had once been streets of identically constructed houses were now individualized dwellings, each reflecting its owners' communication preferences. Clearly, we change and construct our environments. But Sommer's conclusion—that we *become* the environment—is more radical.

Consider, for example, how the seating arrangement in a small group setting (such as a classroom) can predict communication patterns. Sommer (1969) conducted such a study, focusing on the seating positions people tend to choose for rectangular and round tables. Students who were asked to make diagrams of themselves and another person at a rectangular table "overwhelmingly chose a corner-to-corner or face-to-face arrangement for casual conversation," but not for other communication tasks. When a cooperative activity was the goal, the students chose a side-by-side arrangement, but for a competitive activity they chose a face-to-face arrangement or, on occasion, a distant seating pattern (p. 62). Thus, the seating patterns tended to represent and symbolize visually the cognitive and experiential evaluations of the participants: side-by-side seating represented a mutual orientation toward a common direction, whereas face-to-face seating permitted a maximal orientation toward the other, simulating confrontation and/or mutual exchange of ideas. Similar findings resulted from the study involving round tables. Most pairs who wanted to talk cooperatively used adjacent chairs, whereas "competing pairs chose to sit directly across from one another" (Sommer, 1969, p. 63).

In addition, Sommer (1969) studied small student groups in a natural setting, the college cafeteria. (Recall from Chapter 1 that *naturalistic research* is so termed because the researcher studies a communication phenomenon in its naturally occurring setting or context [Lincoln & Guba, 1985].) He found that the "spacing of individuals . . . is not random but follows from the personality and cultural backgrounds of the individuals involved, what they are doing, and the nature of the physical setting" (p. 68). In other words, communication outcomes depend not only on people's personalities and tasks, but also on their environments.

In many college classes that encourage discussion, the instructor suggests a circular seating arrangement. In fact, it has become a hallmark of many communication faculty, distinctive from colleagues in some other departments—and annoying to countless maintenance staff on campuses who have to arrange desks in

 L I N K

See Chapter 1 for a review of the role of naturalistic qualitative research within the theory-building cycle.

rows at the end of each day. Although this arrangement might seem to be an idio-syncracy, it is actually founded on research that investigates classroom interac-tion when students are in rows. As shown in Figure 3-1, where students sit in a tra-ditionally set-up classroom has a dramatic effect on how often they contribute to class discussion, and how often teachers will note their presence. Students who sit within the smaller triangle tend to contribute significantly more to class discus-sions than do students who sit outside it but within the larger triangle. And those who sit outside both triangles tend to contribute the least (Hurt, Scott, & Mc-Croskey, 1978, p. 95).

In another study, Sommer (1974) focuses on the negative consequences of what he calls **hard architecture** in human-designed environments. The charac-teristics of hard architecture include a lack of permeability; a high expense of con-struction, alteration, or razing; clearly marked status levels; the selection of ma-terials and furnishing based on ease of purchase and maintenance; and uniformity in design and layout (pp. 25–26). Sommer contends that hard archi-tecture can inhibit communication because it is planned to resist human imprint. To inhabitants, it seems "impervious, impersonal, and inorganic" (p. 2). He also argues that much of today's architecture cuts us off from one another (or, in Mehrabian's terms, decreases our chances for immediacy in nonverbal relations). Examples include windowless offices in which workers are separated by cubicles and apartment buildings that stack families on top of each other.

Many of our readers are college students and faculty who spend much of their time on campuses that discourage human immediacy. Many of these insti-tutions (although attractive to look at) seem similar to penitentiaries in design and

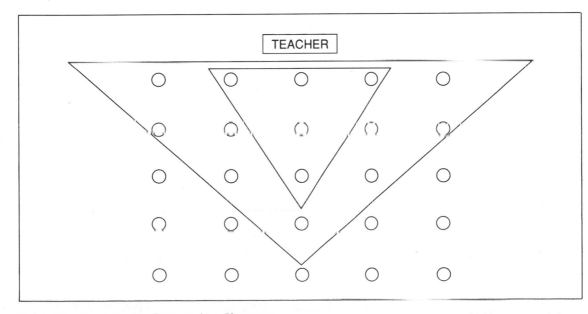

Figure 3-1   Contribution Patterns in a Classroom

construction. Buildings may be large blocks of brick and glass that are set apart, multilayered, and compartmentalized. Landscaping is often black asphalt and rock with some trees, flowers, and color at the fringes. Some classrooms are windowless cubes. Sommer (1974) writes, "I have never taught in a classroom that had even a single picture on the wall. There were no flowers or green things of any kind and no tropical fish, terraria, or tapestry. The classrooms lacked all of those things that would convert a bare room into something lived in" (p. 95). Although most financially strapped universities are unlikely to invest in an aquarium or attractive carpet for every classroom, and although university classes are obviously less likely to be "homey" than elementary classrooms, it isn't difficult to read the educational philosophy of architects from the kinds of rooms they design for educational communication. Generally, the rooms are more hard than soft, more impersonal than personal, more institutional than human, more efficient than inviting or spontaneous. Maybe your classrooms aren't like this. We should not be surprised, then, if the students and faculty within such hard environments sometimes have hard reactions to each other—like manipulation, objectification, or dismissiveness—when more immediate and responsive attitudes would be the ideal.

Sommer also includes airports in his indictment of hard architecture: These "funnels and tunnels," as he calls them, "rank high in any list of socially destructive buildings" (1974, p. 70). Regarding the impersonal and anticommunicational nature of the waiting areas, Sommer writes: "To see [the family] sitting dumbly side by side in the shiny plastic chairs is heartrending" (p. 75). Because the seating is arranged to discourage conversation, often members of a group will stand in front of those seated so that they can form a social circle and thereby communicate more directly. Although some newly designed airports may have been designed with "softer" assumptions, other terminals of public transportation, such as bus stations, typically maintain hard design characteristics.

Try to think contextually about other kinds of physical environments also. For example, Blair, Jeppeson, and Pucci (1994) analyze the design of the Vietnam Veterans Memorial in Washington, D.C. They show how the structure is purposely nonfunctional and in some ways inefficient for visitors, how it suggests a variety of possible interpretations, and how it invites visitors into certain kinds of communicative experiences that reflect the political nature of the memorial. As an example of postmodern architecture, the Vietnam Veterans Memorial "attempt[s] to 'speak' not only to architects about technical architectural matters, but also to viewers and users of buildings about substantive socio-cultural matters. It questions and critiques ideas as well as architectural forms" (p. 359). (See Box 3-2.) In this sense, architecture is not only a context in which communication occurs; it can also be analyzed as a communication text or message.

When Sommer says that people "become" their environment, whether in a classroom, a home, or an airport, he is implying that the social presence of any one person becomes part of the overall context for other persons. And if so, how do we arrange ourselves with and for each other? This was the research question asked by anthropologist Edward T. Hall.

BOX 3-2

POSTMODERN THEORY: A PREVIEW

Although the controversies surrounding postmodern theory are covered in Chapter 4, it is useful to note here some of the defining characteristics of *postmodernism.* It is a way of looking at the world that largely ignores many traditional assumptions of Western civilization, such as rational predictability, concrete meaning, the scientific method, and clear understandings that fit into an overall explanation. "Modernists" have long applied these expressions of rational thought since the Enlightenment in the eighteenth century. Modernists offered a coherent type of rationality that would presumably apply to thinking whatever the culture or time. But "postmodern" thinkers see the world in a different way, arguing that language itself and new forms of media have created an age in which meanings are increasingly harder to pin down, tougher to specify. Whereas modernist theorists work for specification of meaning, postmodernist theorists claim that our old ways of being sure about things aren't realistic anymore. We've lost our assurance that we can distinguish the real from the phony, so the former distinctions that seemed so solid just don't help, and may even inhibit our learning. Obviously, ours is a time in which both modernist and postmodernist trends influence us. The implications for communicators are unsettling.

people and space. One of the authors of this book recently experienced a telling example of contemporary society's concern with "personal space":

> I was visiting EPCOT Center and Disney World with my family, on a day when temperatures exceeded 100 degrees. In addition to the typical crowds, two large international groups were looking for entertainment. Our family had crammed a two-week vacation into four days. After I had been pushed, shoved, stepped on, and plowed into for the thousandth time, my younger son, ever-affectionate, kept walking up to me and placing his arm around my shoulders. In a moment of desperation, what should have been a touching episode became a caustic one. I snapped, "Get away! I need some room. You're invading my space." For the next several hours, I walked alone, feeling isolated, and deservedly so.

The "you're invading my space" concern is common in contemporary society. We encounter its many variations ("Get out of my face!") in television commercials, magazine articles, and everyday speech. But why is space so important to communication context? Because, as anthropologist Edward T. Hall (1959) emphasized, "space speaks." By that he means people often provide valuable information about themselves and their relationships by how they choose to place themselves relative to other people and external objects. The study of such spatial messages is called *proxemics*. Hall (1966) found in his research with USA subjects that communicators tend to make four relatively distinct distance choices. The first category, touching to eighteen inches, is called *intimate distance*. When we become psychologically close with others, we are more ready to allow them into this space. *Personal distance* ranges from eighteen inches to four feet. Students and professors, managers and employees, or new acquaintances might still consider this an uncomfortable distance, especially in most North American cultures, where it connotes close emotional involvement. In the personal distance area, persons experience the feeling of being invaded. Nonverbal theorists sometimes refer to this phenomenon as the "protective bubble" of space, within which most people will feel threatened by someone's uninvited advances. *Social distance* ranges from four feet to twelve feet. Many business situations, such as those involving salespeople and customers, fall within the social distance range. Finally, *public distance*—more than twelve feet—is usually reserved for public occasions that are relatively impersonal or performance oriented, such as public speaking (Hall, 1966).

A good example of the communicative use of physical space can be seen in the movie, *War of the Roses*. When the Roses were first married, they could not get close enough, a fact especially well symbolized by their interaction at the dining room table. Previously, they were happy in their small apartment, where they sat corner-to-corner at a small square table, holding hands and enjoying their time together. But at their new residence, their dining room table is larger and longer. At first, they sit next to each other at the larger table, but as their marriage deteriorates, they take seats at opposite ends of the table. By the end of the film, their table has grown to about four times its original length, a symbol of the distance between them and, ultimately, of the end of their marriage. They both want a divorce, and the physical distance is both symptom and symbol of their psychic devastation.

Proxemic messages also contribute to Mehrabian's immediacy phenomenon. When Albert Scheflen (1974) researched the developing rapport between psychotherapists and clients, he could discern a clear link between subjective involvement and patterns of proxemics and posture. Therapists tended to shift from backward leaning with arms crossed, for instance, to forward leaning with arms and legs uncrossed. Scheflen concludes that "the subjective experience of rapport . . . occurs in connection with the assumption of a characteristic pattern of postures" (p. 85). He calls this the *rapport constellation*. The therapist thus signals a more immediate involvement not necessarily with words, but also by shifting the bodily context in which the words are spoken and heard. Interestingly, in the forty-minute therapy sessions studied by Scheflen, this shift tended to happen as a "climax" around the twentieth or twenty-fifth minute, after which the sequence of nonimmediate to immediate is repeated (p. 86). Moving toward or away from another person is often experienced as a direct commentary on the relationship, whether or not we mean it as such. It's simply a part of what anthropologist Ray Birdwhistell, a pioneer in nonverbal theory and research, calls "learning to be a human body" (1970).

SOCIAL CONTEXT: COMMUNICATORS AND TECHNOLOGIES IN SITUATIONS

In social situations, we interact with other people, taking them into account and coordinating our actions toward them with our own personal goals. While *social* situations are often contrasted with *personal* ones, it's difficult to conceive of a social situation without also considering individuals, and vice versa (Stamp, Vangelisti, & Knapp, 1994, pp. 170–171).

In this section, we'll review two schemes for organizing social context, one that has been useful traditionally for communication scholars (Ruesch & Bateson, 1968), and one that is a more recent reorienting suggestion (Lievrouw & Finn, 1990). In presenting these ideas, we aren't implying that they are the only two ways to analyze social context, but only that these alternatives suggest a wide range of conceptual possibilities.

social levels of communication

Ruesch and Bateson (1968), argued that how researchers choose which levels of social communication to examine will influence how much and what kind of detail they're likely to find. In other words, studying social situations is like using a microscope: "As magnification increases, the area of the field must decrease. . . . Depending upon whether [the researcher] focuses upon large or small entities, he will see the various functions in greater or smaller detail" (p. 274). If you decide to study larger units or levels of social organization, you will find less resolution of detail. Four basic levels of communication are distinguished by Ruesch and Bateson, each with progressively more systemic complexity.

level i communication.   This is the "within one" level of *intrapersonal* processes, in which inner physiological and psychological messages are perceived by a communicator. The person is considered a system of communication in and of itself. Thus, when you contemplate whether to enroll in a class, to complain about your new car, or to go to the library, you're processing inner messages at this level. Although Level I communication is not a context of social interaction, it is the necessary prelude to one. Intrapersonal processes, of course, assume that there will be external social influences, such as in the development of the self-concept, for example.

level ii communication.   This level could be termed the "one-to-one" level, or, as the communication literature refers to it, the dyadic situation. In the **dyad,** a two-person system, each communicator observes and participates in the two-way communication that develops, and this presents dilemmas. According to Ruesch and Bateson (1968), individuals tend to specialize in either observation or participation, and are not realistically able to do both equally well. Some information inevitably will be overlooked in the dyadic mode. Job interviews, dates, marital arguments, and counseling are examples of Level II communication.

L I N K

Chapter 4. "Personal Experience." will describe several theories associated with cognitive contexts for communication. Think of contexts as being both external and internal: if this chapter concentrates on the outer phenomena of context, the next chapter will focus on inner context.

level iii communication.   At this level, communicators engage each other in *group* situations. The context is marked by an unequal division of functions among the communicators in the group, as in a hierarchical organization or a group with designated leadership roles. The group can be seen as having a *center* and a *periphery*, with messages being sent in a primarily *one-way* fashion. Ruesch and Bateson (1968) identify two types of messages (and therefore sublevels) at this level: The "one-to-many" message is sent to people at the periphery by someone at the center of the group (e.g., when a corporate chief executive distributes a letter to employees about impending layoffs), whereas the "many-to-one" message is sent to the center by those at the periphery of the group (e.g., when union members request a meeting with the CEO to discuss the layoff policy). Modern businesses at this level are often organized for specialization involving relatively narrow one-way messages and roles rather than for dialogue.

level iv communication.   At this final level, also known as the "many-to-many" level, **cultural communication** takes place. As Ruesch and Bateson (1968) explain, "In addition to intrapersonal, interpersonal, and organized group networks, which are variously perceived as such by the individuals, there is a host of instances in which the individual is unable to recognize the source and destination of messages, and therefore does not recognize that these messages travel in a network structure" (pp. 281–282). Such *cultural* networks, therefore, operate invisibly from the standpoint of individual actors within the culture(s). However, these networks are no less important to communication. Rather, the pervasiveness of the sources and destinations of such messages simply makes them hard to pin down because they are so pervasive. Level IV messages may be *space binding* (bringing people in different places "together" for a time while attending to the same set of messages, such as our culture-wide system of advertising) or *time binding* (integrating past and present, such as a team of archaeologists publishing a book about an ancient and nearly forgotten culture). Clearly, analysts focusing on this level would have to become very familiar with the media of mass communication in modern societies.

One innovative study in this vein is Donal Carbaugh's (1989) *Talking American: Cultural Discourses on "Donahue."* The author analyzed numerous Phil Donahue talk shows, fleshing out a number of themes Americans seem to use implicitly in their talk about self, social roles, relationships, and the notion of communication itself. He notes, for example, that *Donahue* participants talked about self as if it were a possession, and as if "self" exists along the three dimensions of "independent–dependent" (in relationships), "aware–unaware" (of self-concept and of others), and "communicative–closed" (about the content of social choices). A cultural theme inferred by this research was that the optimal American self is *independent, aware,* and *expressive* (1989, pp. 61–86). Remember that if themes are truly cultural, they don't just represent Donahue's shows; they don't originate with these interviewees, these expert guests, these audience members, or even from the television medium itself. They can be studied there because they have no real identifiable source. Cultural themes are spread throughout the culture; they are for all practical purposes sourceless and pervasive.

LINKS

- See Chapter 7 for a detailed discussion of theories of cultural communication.
- See Chapter 9 for more information about how media have changed the reach of our communication messages.
- If your teacher agrees, try another kind of link, too. With the notion of "context" in mind, check into the organization of two or three other communication theory books from your campus library. We predict that you'll find the order and division of topics by authors not only varies quite a bit, but that topic organization seems at least somewhat artificial or arbitrary. This is because *most* communication topics can be couched as contextual in terms of their companion topics, and authors can make strong cases for why their organizations are more basic than the alternatives.

Ruesch and Bateson (1968) organize their system in terms of these four levels of communication. However, they also show that each level is composed of four basic communication actions: *evaluating, sending, channel choices,* and *receiving.* As shown in Figure 3-2, they illustrate their model as a cone that is subdivided into these basic human activities.

a communication systems model of social context

A good example of a recent attempt to conceptualize social contexts in a new way is Lievrouw and Finn's (1990) model emphasizing the role of *mediation* in human interaction. If a process is said to be "mediated," we mean that its success depends in part on some other entity, such as a technology or, in the case of labor–management mediation, a third-party negotiator. Traditionally, communication scholars have viewed some forms of communication as mediated (e.g., television and newspapers) and other forms as nonmediated (e.g., face-to-face dyadic communication). Traces of this traditional distinction are present in

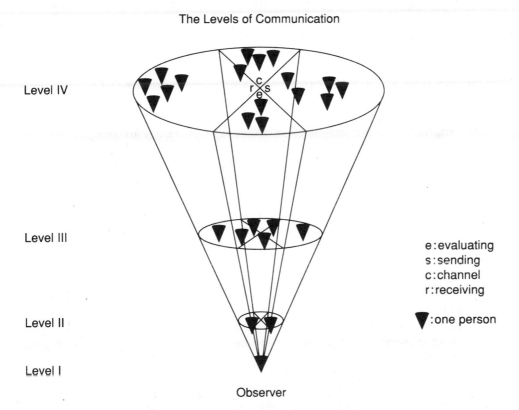

Figure 3-2 Ruesch and Bateson's Social Levels of Communication

BOX 3-3

RUESCH & BATESON'S SOCIAL LEVELS
(CONTEXTS) OF COMMUNICATION

I. Intrapersonal (within one)
II. Dyadic (one-to-one)
III. Group (one-to-many/many-to-one)
IV. Cultural (many-to-many)

Source: Ruesch and Bateson (1968).

Ruesch and Bateson's (1968) model of the social levels of communication. According to Lievrouw and Finn (1990), however, the distinction is misleading because all forms of communication, including face-to-face (FtF) interaction, may be viewed as mediated. Interpersonal situations typically emphasize one or more of the five senses, which are mediated at least by "natural channels" of light and air, they argue. Furthermore, "most scholars of interpersonal communication do not think of FtF communication as mediated because the descriptive phrase itself, 'face-to-face,' dismisses the dimension of space (distance) as important. Yet distance is a relevant variable" (pp. 41–42). The question isn't *whether* communication is mediated, but *how.*

Lievrouw and Finn's (1990) systems model of social context suggests that the three fundamental dimensions of any communicative act are temporality, involvement, and control. *Temporality* is how people experience time in their communication relationships. *Involvement* refers to how persons bridge both physical and psychological forms of distance. Through involvement, individuals become more engaged with others and with themselves in cognitive, affective (emotionally based), and sensory ways. Finally, *control* refers to the exertion of influence in social settings. Through awareness of the control dimension, communicators understand how much control is inherent within a situation and the balance of control distributed among participants.

Mapping these variables into a three-dimensional model (shown in Figure 3-3), Lievrouw and Finn (1990) create a "space" within which different types of communication systems are described in terms of their mediation and social characteristics. Temporality is represented as a continuum ranging from simultaneous to nonsimultaneous events, while involvement is represented as a range of persons' low to high involvement in the situation. The control continuum ranges from receiver-oriented through equal control to sender-oriented control.

Figure 3-3 shows Lievrouw and Finn's dimensions model before specific systems and social networks are located within it. Next, the authors place various mediated social contexts into the space to illustrate the extent to which each depends differently on temporality, involvement, and control. Thus, for example,

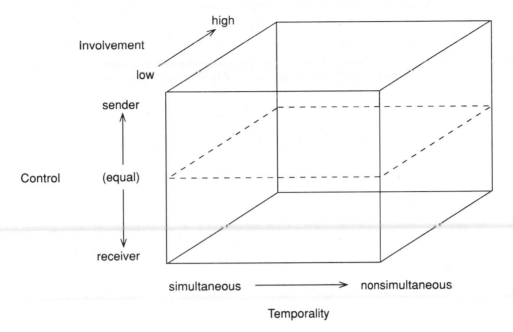

Figure 3-3 Lievrouw and Finn's Dimensions of Communication Behavior
Source: L. A. Lievrouw and T. A. Finn, "Identifying the Common Dimensions of
Communication," in B. D. Ruben and L. A. Lievrouw (Eds.), *Mediation, Information,
and Behavior* (pp. 37–65). Copyright © 1990 by Transaction Publishers. Used with
permission.

the position of database systems technology (item 14) in Figure 3-4 reflects its (1)
high degree of receiver-based control, (2) nonsimultaneous usage (i.e., user and
designer are not co-oriented at the same time), and (3) low degree of user involvement. As this example illustrates, Lievrouw and Finn's model invites a rich
analysis of communication contexts.

The ability of the communication systems model of social context to chart
different kinds of mediation provides a valuable clue to an emerging area of theorizing about computer-mediated communication that could be termed *access
theory* (Anderson, 1997). Conceiving of a new communication context as based on
access to messages rather than on message *reception* contrasts with our traditional
assumptions of how communication works. Older media contexts presumed that
senders direct and deliver messages to receivers. Though computer users still are
able to transfer messages in this way, most of the new *online culture*—which is ex-
emplified by databases, e-mail, chat rooms, bulletin board systems, and virtual
reality—does not depend on senders knowing the presence and placement of receivers (Heim, 1987, 1993; Landow, 1992; Lanham, 1993; Snyder, 1996). In fact,
the phenomenon of *hypertext*, presumes that access processes of reading and listening are really forms of co-authorship; the reader/listener determines not only
when access occurs, but also through a series of self-controlled choices affects the

L I N K

The communication
systems model of so-
cial context (Lievrouw
& Finn, 1990) is rele-
vant to Joshua Mey-
rowitz's (1985) the-
ory of mediated place,
discussed in Chapter
9. According to Mey-
rowitz, some forms of
electronic mediation
have changed not only
the ground rules for
developing and ex-
pressing personal
identity, but also how
we think about inter-
personal relationships

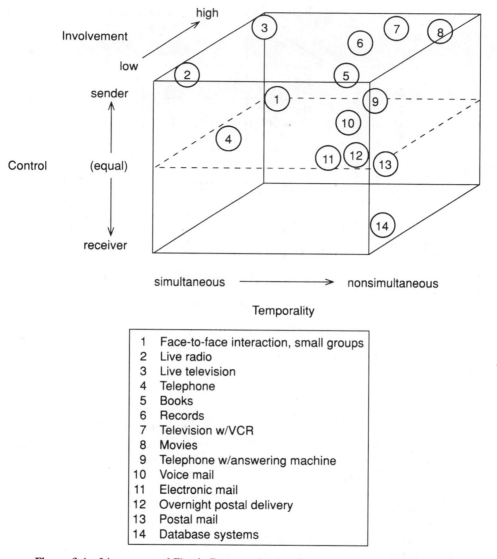

Figure 3-4   Lievrouw and Finn's Communication Systems, Arrayed within Dimensions of Communication Behavior

Source: L. A. Lievrouw and T. A. Finn, "Identifying the Common Dimensions of Communication," in B. D. Ruben and L. A. Lievrouw (Eds.), *Mediation, Information, and Behavior* (pp. 37–65). Copyright © 1990 by Transaction Publishers. Used with permission.

---

ultimate and unique shape of the experience. According to language theorist Ilana Snyder (1996),

> [Hypertext] is an information medium that exists only on-line in a computer. A structure composed of blocks of text connected by electronic links, it offers

different pathways to users. Hypertext provides a means of arranging information in a non-linear manner with the computer automating the process of
connecting one piece of information to another. . . .

A hypertext is constructed partly by the writers who create the links, and
partly by readers who decide which threads to follow. . . . Hypertext differs
from printed text by offering readers multiple paths through a body of information: it allows them to make their own connections, to incorporate their
own links and to produce their own meanings. (p. ix)

In contrast to the long-held directedness theories of communication that have always assumed that audiences were to some extent targets of speakers, writers, and
broadcasters, we clearly have entered an era that Gozzi and Haynes (1992) call
"distant presence." Communicators contribute messages to databases and virtual
forums, for example, and other communicators can subsequently *access* those messages, but the messages are not actually sent *to* receivers. Digitally mediated systems
are not propelled by producers, and they thereby blur the traditional distinctions
between producers and consumers, and between senders and receivers. The lis-
tener/reader of a hypertext message chooses how to co-produce the message.
This, as a recent commercial said, changes everything. The new psychological
and sociological communication contexts of the twenty-first century will also be
molded by *virtual reality,* in which seemingly immediate experiences can be digitally packaged to be deferred—at a communicator's choice—to later times and
other places.

Still in its relative infancy, online technology is more prominently used by
some cultural groups than others. Lievrouw and Finn (1990) remind us that all
analyses of mediated systems must exist within an overall cultural context. The authors extend their model to show how the cube must itself exist within cultural assumptions about communication. They write: ". . . communication cannot take
place unless culture, relationship, and content have been accounted for. Without
these contextual elements, the attempt at communication will be nonsensical. In
any given communication situation the context may influence communication
and vice versa" (p. 55).

Like any tentative model, Lievrouw and Finn's is incomplete. Yet, considered
alongside the Ruesch and Bateson system, it helps us to clarify how disparate concepts can fit together. Both approaches demonstrate how social contexts not only
influence what is communicated between people, but how it is communicated. Applying them to an emerging theoretical terrain of electronic access, we can also
glimpse the future.

TESTING THE CONCEPTS

"Does a contextual approach to communication mean that I'll never be able to 'pin
down' what people mean, or what causes them to act the ways they do? Will meaning *always* be contextual?"

In all likelihood, people will continue to be held accountable for their words and actions in most situations. Most philosophies of social science, after all, assume that humans are actors, not reactors, and that we are for the most part capable of choosing our own destinies. However, learning about the influence of context provides useful reminders: that meanings are not neat and tidy packages but are more like interpretations negotiated under the ground rules of differing contexts. This is why it is extremely hard to "pin down" such meanings. It is a matter of developing communication tolerance.

In another sense, an ecological approach to context does present some problems for determining causality because it relies on a systems model of communication. Consider, for example, the specific context of family interaction; a systems approach helps to explain the intricate dynamics of relations among parents and children. If all changes in a system are interconnected, as the model suggests, it would be difficult at best at any point in time to point to X and say with certainty that it "caused" changes in Y. This causal ambiguity is the basis of a feminist critique of systems theory applications in counseling and mental health disciplines (Cottone, 1992, pp. 262–267; Walters, Carter, Papp, & Silverstein, 1988). In a context of family violence against women, systems approaches seem to come dangerously close to implying that women somehow could share part of the responsibility for male violence! In terms of power, roles, and relational control, the causality, and thus the responsibility, appears more linear and more attributable than an ecological systems approach would indicate. Other feminist theorists are not as ready to sacrifice systemic or ecological assumptions (Goldner, Penn, Sheinberg, & Walker, 1990). Cottone (1992) argues for a middle-ground "contextualist" paradigm that more realistically allows for attributions of somewhat linear causality, without sacrificing the overall transactional insight of systemic-relational theory. In other words, you can still recognize the importance of ecological relations without assuming that victims are partially to blame for conditions of domination. Some things happen because *he* or *she* or *they* decided to make them happen, not because the "context" of a relationship or social situation "caused" them.

"Sommer sounds like he's criticizing 'hard architecture.' Is there ever a place for it? Does it serve any useful functions?"

Sommer's value judgments are displayed in his critique of the so-called hard architecture of airports. But it is also possible to argue that for the majority of travelers using public transportation, privacy-oriented waiting areas (e.g., where the seats do not face each other) are more functional than personalized waiting areas (where soft and inviting seating is designed to encourage conversation, even among strangers). In some other contexts, such as a congregation facing forward while sitting on the wood pews of a country church, inviting more comfortable interaction would defeat the primary purpose of the gathering. Effective planners of organizational meetings, workshops, and group gatherings understand that the psychological, physical, and social components of a situation must be coordinated with the purpose of the particular meeting involved.

"Do people automatically know what kind of communication I intend when I choose, for example, the 'social distance' of four to twelve feet?"

No, not automatically. But because of a variety of social context expectations, they probably could make an educated guess about what you would *not* discuss at that distance. For example, marriage proposals and intimate gossip are unlikely in this context because they usually demand more immediacy cues. Remember, too, that Hall's (1966) study is based on a relatively narrow sample—middle-class and mostly white Americans from the Northeast. Many people would not fit his pattern exactly. In two follow-up chapters, Hall presents evidence on distance differences noticed in other cultures (pp. 123–153).

"Do chat rooms and other online contexts fit into the categories of Level 2 (dyadic), Level 3 (group), or Level 4 (cultural) communication in Ruesch and Bateson's model?"

Here is an example of why traditional communication analyses must adapt to new forms of mediation and presence. Although many online relationships develop in an essentially dyadic way, the phenomenon known as "lurking" complicates that assumption. Lurking occurs when a person observes an online "chat" without contributing to the conversation. While most chat rooms identify the screen names of all users logged on to a room, in some cases it may not be possible to know how many lurkers there are. It becomes hard to know where the center and where the *periphery* might be in any online group. Formerly, the various social means of production were typically centralized in positions of power, while consumers were at the periphery; how does that change when literally anyone can create his or her own Web page on the Internet, becoming a potential information source for millions of other people? Finally, the *Internet* itself, that formally and informally interlinked worldwide network of computerized users and information, is obviously a "many-to-many" context, which is how Ruesch and Bateson defined Level IV.

Y O U,   T H E   R E S E A R C H E R

1. Keep a small notebook in which you can jot down brief observations and notes as convenient through the day. Carry the notebook with you for three days, and:

   - Pay especially close attention to any ongoing relationship in which you talk to the same person several times a day.
   - At the end of each day, make a list of the comments that could be easily misunderstood if a hypothetical eavesdropping reporter simply

quoted you or the other person accurately, but did not specify the verbal or nonverbal contexts in which statements were made.

Analyze the statements and incidents. Which were dependent on a physical or psychological context? On a social context? Draw some conclusions about how hard or easy it is to distinguish among the types of context.

2. Visit three different third-grade classrooms. Observe (a) what is displayed on the walls; (b) what objects and materials are prominent in the room; and (c) the arrangement of desks and other furniture. Then consider the following questions:

- How might these features of context affect student learning?
- Which contextual features are purposely intended to promote learning? Which are not? In both cases, whose choices do they represent?

After formulating your research hypothesis (see Chapter 2), write a brief paragraph describing a study you could do on the effects of context in elementary classrooms. Discuss your proposal in class.

3. Videotape or audiotape a television program that features political discussion (e.g., *The McLaughlin Group* or *Meet the Press*). Identify *episodes* (sequences of talk that seem to have identifiable beginnings and endings) in which the literal meaning of a person's words are—in your opinion— clearly the opposite of what that speaker intends. For example:

- Are the speakers using irony, sarcasm, or another speech strategy that depends on contextual awareness?
- What contextual factors signal the "proper" ways the words should be taken?

Play the excerpts for four friends whose political orientations differ (e.g., two Democrats and two Republicans). Later, interview them to discover if there were any striking differences of interpretation that might be attributed in part to the political affiliation of the observer. Then ask yourself: "What are the limitations of such an investigation, considering the small sample size?"

Research communication or social psychology journals to find at least one study that is basically an expanded version of your informal investigation. How did the researcher(s) deal with the problem of sample size?

4. Visit the waiting area of an airport or a bus terminal, and take notes on its design. Note how the seats are arranged and what materials they are made of. How do these features encourage or discourage communication among travelers? What assumptions about communication in this context might have guided the designers? In answering these questions, try to apply as many concepts from this chapter as possible. Discuss your findings in class.

5. Conduct an analysis of your classroom. First, compile a comprehensive list of its features. Describe the features in neutral terms (e.g., not as having "ugly green walls" or as "too small," but as "light green" and "14 by 23 feet"). Then write a brief essay about what the room's features reasonably allow you to infer about the educational philosophy of its designers or architects.

Erich Hartmann/Magnum Photos

personal experience

"what's happening *inside our heads*
when we communicate
and why do we need *to know?"*

The formulation of experience which is contained within the intellectual horizon of an age and a society is determined, I believe, not so much by events and desires, as by the *basic concepts* at people's disposal for analyzing and describing their adventures to their own understanding. Of course, such concepts arise as they are needed, to deal with political or domestic experience; but the same experiences could be seen in many different lights, so the light in which they do appear depends on the genius of a people as well as on the demands of the external occasion. Different minds will take the same events in very different ways. . . . Every society meets a new idea with its own concepts, its own tacit, fundamental way of seeing things; that is to say, *with its own questions*, its peculiar curiosity.

SUSANNE K. LANGER, *PHILOSOPHY IN A NEW KEY* (1951, P. 17)

Susanne Langer, one of the most prominent intellectuals of the twentieth century, consistently stressed the importance of asking good questions about human symbolizing. She describes why personal experience depends on concepts that, in fact, aren't entirely personal or private at all. Personal questions are also necessarily social questions. Our personal concepts develop in the social climate in which we live. Symbolic communication supplies us with these concepts, and we assume that thinking with them is natural, normal, and real. Therefore, what people assume to be true about their personal experience shapes the kind of communication that develops between them and other people. These assumptions do not *determine* the communication, of course. But it's helpful to have a general understanding of how the human mind processes information, solves linguistic problems, develops a sense of self, and applies its assumptions to others' messages. Why is this knowledge practical for communicators?

THE ASSUMPTIONS OF EXPERIENCE

A friend of ours traveled to Japan, where he taught interpersonal and intercultural communication to Japanese students. Bob thought he had carefully prepared himself for the many cultural differences he'd find in Japanese classrooms. Instead, he found himself surprised by the extent to which the classroom behavior of many students differed from his expectations. In lectures and classroom discussions, he was forced to test his assumptions about student interest and learning. Some of the students seemed so passive and unexpressive, so ready to write down his every jest and offhand remark. Were they bored? Were they grade-hungry robots uninvolved in participative learning (as he might have assumed in an American classroom)? Or were they simply demonstrating a different style of involvement, a different type of personal experience? He soon discovered that most of his students were interested and involved, but that their involvement was experienced and demonstrated differently.

Bob brought with him to Japan a certain mental model of expected student behaviors, despite his intellectual awareness that Japanese and American interpersonal styles differ. He was therefore surprised when actions that violated his model could still be considered good student behaviors by others. We're not referring here to an inexperienced person, but to a bright, scholarly, sensitive, and worldly educator who'd been teaching for decades, even in culturally diverse classrooms. If he could be surprised by the extent of the cultural differences he encountered, there's a lesson here for the rest of us. As Langer suggests in the chapter-opening quotation, all humans build inner models naturally and normally to structure the world, making the unmanageably complex dither of stimuli more comprehensible. We rarely consider how unique and idiosyncratic our models or expectations may be, and how easily they can contradict those of other people and groups.

surprise

It would be simple to assume that Bob simply increased his knowledge about Japanese students and then naturally improved his communication with them. But the process was more complicated than that. He realized that to learn about the students, he would have to learn something about his own cognitive patterns as well.

Cognition refers to those processes of mind through which people come to know, perceive, understand, remember, and evaluate aspects of their world. If our friend had assumed that the Japanese students' cognitive styles were basically similar to his own, he would have cut off his chances to learn about them and to learn about himself as well. He had to recognize not just that the styles differ but also *how* they differ. By doing so, he gained a better understanding of his own experience as well, recognizing his response to this situation was not the only possible human response. He was, in a word, surprised. (See Box 4-1.)

As we noted in Chapter 1 on theory construction, surprise is a vital element in the process of explaining or understanding anything. Jerome Bruner (1986), a prominent contemporary researcher of the human mind, claims that surprise is an "extraordinarily useful phenomenon to students of mind" because it provides a "window on presupposition" (p. 46). In other words, it shows us what has been taken for granted. When you are surprised by something or someone, you are engaged in a process of learning. You are forced to abandon the model of mind on which you'd been relying, and to imagine new possibilities. Our interest in Bruner is stimulated by the shape of his career, which has ranged from his early cognitive and narrowly psychologistic notions of the human mind to more recent concerns with the interpersonal and transactional dimensions of communication (Bruner, 1979, 1986, 1990).

sensing self from "who you aren't"

Any cross-cultural experience reminds us, if we're alert, how little we understand about our own ways of thinking and feeling. Again, surprise is a key. Anthropolo-

L I N K

In the terms used by cultural theorists—see Chapter 7—our friend, while in Japan, was a *sojourner* or *stranger*. He gradually discovered more effective ways to adjust, creating an identity that was not quite either an "American" way of being a teacher or a Japanese way, but a third way, a blended kind of cross-cultural teaching style. To balance this example, Chapter 7 will describe the story of another sojourner, a Japanese student attending a U.S. university.

BOX 4-1

PHILOSOPHER ROLAND BARTHES IS SURPRISED IN JAPAN

Roland Barthes (1989), a French philosopher and literary critic, explains his experience with communicating in Japan:

> Today there are doubtless a thousand things to learn about the Orient: an enormous labor of knowledge is and will be necessary (its delay can only be the result of an ideological occultation); but it is also necessary that, leaving aside vast regions of darkness (capitalist Japan, American acculturation, technological development), a slender thread of light search out not other symbols but the very fissure of the symbolic. . . . The author has never, in any sense, photographed Japan. Rather, he has done the opposite: Japan has starred him with any number of "flashes"; or, better still, Japan has afforded him a situation of writing. This situation is the very one in which a certain disturbance of the person occurs, a subversion of earlier readings, a shock of meaning lacerated, extenuated to the point of its irreplaceable void, without the object's ever ceasing to be significant, desirable. (p. 4)

Barthes first traveled to Japan before Western media influence was as pervasive as it is today. His poetic writing style, translated from the French, is difficult to grasp in English, but it is worth the effort. Reread his description several times, while asking yourself questions about what experiences he might be recalling.

gist Edward T. Hall (1977) suggests that this social phenomenon can be explained by a systems approach to communication: When the mechanisms of the human nervous system work smoothly, they utilize *positive feedback*—that is, feedback that tends to support or reinforce the directions being taken by previous perceptions, assumptions, and expectations. The organism remains essentially unaware of its own patterns of processing information. To use a computer analogy, the program is functioning smoothly. Cognitive processes become so integrated and seem so natural that they are taken for granted and, in a sense, become invisible. Hall (1977) puts it this way: "People's nervous systems are organized according to the principles of *negative feedback;* that is, the whole thing works so smoothly and automatically that the only time the control system is consciously brought into play is when the input signals deviate from the norm. Therefore, people individually and collectively are for the most part unaware of the patterns and reference signals governing behavior" (p. 54; emphasis added). The "great gift" we can give each other, writes Hall, is not a direct knowledge of otherness, but a *knowledge of self* that comes through contact with others who are sufficiently different (operating as negative feedback that contrasts with an individual's own assumptions).

You find out *who you are* by meeting *who you aren't*. A clear sense of self doesn't simply emerge from a stable cultural experience. Instability plays a role as well. You have to be shaken somewhat by communicating with people whose per-

L I N K

Reviewing the definitions of *feedback* and *system* in Chapter 1 will clarify this discussion.

sonal experience tests your own—or as Hall (1977) says, people who are "members of the opposite sex, different age groups, different ethnic groups, and different cultures" (p. 44). Intercultural communication becomes a valuable proving ground for trying out our cognitive assumptions.

Whatever our social contacts, we can develop perspective by looking inward at the ways humans make, or avoid making, decisions and interpretations about messages. Studying this process should increase tolerance for the distinctive behaviors alien to us that seem so natural or normal to others.

By now, you've noticed that this chapter on personal experience is not primarily concerned with the brain and its physiology. It's not just about psychology either, though psychologists have long explored this territory. Rather, our focus is on where inner private experience and outer social experience intersect. You'll learn about theories that try to explain:

1. human *perception,* the process of translating messages or input from the senses into awareness
2. human *language,* the system of symbols with which we make sense of and express that awareness
3. human *cognitive organizing systems,* which connect our personal experiences into a patterned whole

In addition, throughout the chapter we discuss how people develop what is commonly called a *self.*

Although it may seem as if this chapter's main topics—perception, language, cognitive organization, and self—have been arranged from simple to complex, the arrangement we chose for them is actually an arbitrary one. We could have arranged the topics in nearly any order because each is as complex as the others and each contributes equally to our understanding of how the others work. Perception is influenced by language, for example, and vice versa. A particular person's sense of self influences how she or he mentally organizes the world, and vice versa.

PERCEPTION, NOT RECEPTION

perception and activity

Perception is usually defined as the process by which an organism assimilates, makes sense out of, and uses, sensory data. In normal human perception, for example, we use our senses of sight, sound, smell, taste, and touch to provide clues to what goes on around us. This seems simple enough, but let's consider a few examples:

Juan, a new college student, is a little late to class on the first day of the semester. He parks his car and walks quickly to Bryce Hall. He's grateful to see that the professor has not yet arrived, and that there's time to choose a seat toward the back of the room, relax a bit, catch his breath, and look around. What does he see?

Jill, a first grader on a field trip to the zoo, steps off the school bus, holding hands with her teacher, Mr. Jones, and her best friend, Kate. She's excited because this is her first visit to a zoo. But she's a little scared, too, because the animals she'll see here are real. She wonders if any animals might bite or escape from their cages. As she walks through the front gate with other excited children and some parents, she hesitates, and Mr. Jones and Kate gently tug her hands. Jill's eyes open very wide, as she tries to take it all in at once. What does she see?

Marsha might look calm to others sitting in the doctor's waiting room, but they don't notice her constant flexing and unflexing the muscles just above her knees. They have no idea that she's worried about missing the rest of the high school soccer season just because of this stupid strain or twist or whatever it is. Marsha's mind is racing: "Where's that nurse, anyway?" "Who has all day to sit here?" She absently picks up a *Newsweek* and leafs through it. What does she see?

Although these examples focus on only one sensory capacity, they illustrate that perception is more complex than is commonly assumed. The *commonsense* answer to the question, "What does he or she see?" would be that they saw what was *in* the setting to be seen: Juan, we might assume, sees students fidgeting nervously, maps hanging on the wall, and paint chipping off old radiators, among many other physical features of the room. Jill could see the reassuring smiles of zoo attendants as well as the bars safely separating the kids from the hippos. And Marsha might see an interesting article on high-definition television, an advertisement for the new Volvo, and a column suggesting that it's more common to sue a lawyer than one might think. All of these assumptions might be safe if human perception were an objective process in which our brains receive data through our senses and record what is available to perceive. But it's not. Perception helps us make sense of outside information, but humans aren't simply sponges for soaking up stimuli. Juan, Jill, and Marsha might not see any of these things at all, due to their cognitive and emotional preoccupations.

The commonsense view of perception is represented by the simple diagram shown in Figure 4-1. Do we simply receive stimuli (S) and store them as internal

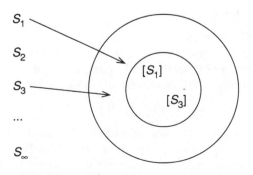

Figure 4-1   A Commonsense View of Perception

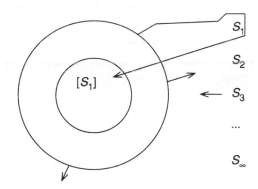

Figure 4-2 Perception as an Active Process

representations of the outer world? Or, is the process more dynamic, fluctuating, creative, and active than such a model indicates? Although still an oversimplification, Figure 4-2 better illustrates the usual pattern of human perception. In this model of **selective perception**, we are active in the process, in that we "reach toward" and select some stimuli and systematically ignore (or filter out) others. Nor are our inner representations necessarily "close" in form or function to an objective outer reality of stimuli. The unique experience of each of us appears to become immediately a part of the experience of perception. The external stimuli (e.g., S_1 in Figure 4-2) enter our consciousness in a form modified somewhat by our previous experience—our expectations, values, attitudes, beliefs, and other cultural assumptions. Of course, some types of stimuli, such as an unexpected loud noise or turning a corner and bumping into someone, can be thought of as incoming and inevitable. However, most perceptual activities do not support the commonsense assumptions that we see what's there to be seen, hear what's creating sound in our immediate environment, and so forth.

selectivity

Research on selective perception has shown that we miss much of what can be perceived in our environments and that what we do notice is selectively perceived, interpreted, and retained (Toch & Smith, 1968). Some scholars even contend that if we were to attempt to attend to and process all available stimuli at any one time, the result might be madness. Birdwhistell (1970), for instance, estimates that, at any given point in time, as many as ten thousand bits of "minimally discernible" sensory information are available to persons *per second* (p. 3). Processing all of this information at once would be impossible. Instead, the human mind compensates by *pre-deciding*, on the basis of *perceptual salience* (perceived importance to the self), what is most important to it. It then monitors the environment, scanning for stimuli that, at that moment, are the most relevant, dangerous, interesting, or applicable to the self.

When considering selective perception, keep in mind three things: (1) selectivity is built into our sensory experience, (2) selectivity is not total, and (3) selectivity seems to support an internal strain toward consistency (see Box 4-2).

BOX 4-2

Perception:
The Active Selection of Stimuli

- Perceptual expectations are built into experience itself. We see and hear, for example, as much with our personal values as we do with our eyes and ears.
- Selectivity in perception does not mean perception is completely arbitrary or idiosyncratic. Different people can and do agree about many perceptions.
- Perceptions are often selected to support an inner consistency among a person's beliefs, attitudes, and values.

First, selective perception is not a matter of perceiving worldly objects accurately and subsequently dismissing, distorting, or deselecting them internally. Instead, the evidence suggests the counterintuitive conclusion that expectations and selection habits become integrated with our sensory apparatus *directly*. As Boulding (1956) observes:

Even at the level of simple or supposedly simple sense perception we are increasingly discovering that the message which comes through the senses is itself mediated through a value system. We do not perceive our sense data raw; they are mediated through a highly learned process of interpretation and acceptance. When an object apparently increases in size on the retina of the eye, we interpret this not as an increase in size but as movement. Indeed, we only get along in the world because we consistently and persistently disbelieve the plain evidence of our senses. The stick in water is not bent; the movie is a succession of still pictures; and so on.

What this means is that for any individual organism or organization, there are no such things as "facts." There are only messages filtered through a changeable value system. (pp. 13–14)

As an example, let's consider the experience of a medical school physiology student. As reported by Llinas (1987), the medical student had a thorough understanding of the physiology and functional anatomy of the visual system. He understood the technical reasons the retina, the motor neurons, and the other parts of the eye contribute to how sight functions. But he confided to his professor (with some courage, we imagine), "I still do not understand . . . how I see" (p. 351). Llinas (1987) explains why:

This problem arises because we forget to tell our students that seeing is reconstructing the external world, based not on the reflecting properties of light on external objects but, rather, on the transformation of such visual sensory input (a vector) into perception vectors in *other sets of coordinate systems*. Indeed, we should have reminded our students that in order to see one requires first to have moved within the world and to have established, via the use of natural coordinates, the properties of objects with respect to our own physical attributes (the weight of each object, its size with respect to that of our body, etc.). It would be clear then that it is only through the ability that our brain has to transform measurements in one set of coordinates (the visual system) into comparable sets of measurements (visually guided motor execution) provided by other sensory inputs (for example, touch from fingertips) that one can truly develop the necessary semantics to be able to understand what one sees. . . . It is easy to demonstrate that in order to see we must interact with the external world by means of movement. In adult man, visual reversal following the wearing of inverting prism goggles can occur only if the subject is allowed to move about while wearing the goggles. *In short, then, we are able to measure and recreate universals on the basis of our own physical properties because, through interactions between our brain and the rest of our body, a set of natural coordinates has been embedded in our central nervous system.* (pp. 351–352)

In other words, neither the anatomy of sight nor any of the other senses can by itself explain "seeing" or perception. Instead, understanding perception involves recognizing that there is a **semantics** (an organized structure of meanings) for how mind and body work together to create our links with the world. In other words, the senses don't simply deliver information for the mind to process. Instead, mind, brain, and the senses are all part of the same system. This is why we see, hear, and feel with our hypotheses as much as with our eyes, ears, and skin.

Cognitive psychologist Jerome Bruner (1983) concludes that because hypotheses guide our perceptions, we are "never indifferent, always tuned, ever readier for some events than for others" (p. 95). And in a striking thought, another neuropsychologist asserts that perhaps babies would never learn to see unless they were allowed to roam through an environment, touching things while experimenting with hypotheses (Gregory & Miller, 1983, p. 62).

In one study of children's sensory perception that gained the attention of the news media, Bruner and a colleague asked children to describe the relative size of coins (Bruner & Goodman, 1947). The estimates the children gave were consistent only when their economic background was factored into the analysis (i.e., children from low-income families tended to perceive the coins as larger, whereas children from high-income families perceived them as smaller). Somehow a perceptual crossover developed, in which "perceived value" and "perceived physical size" were merged (Bruner & Goodman, 1947; Bruner, 1983, pp. 69–70).

These types of studies help us understand the phenomenon known as the *self-fulfilling prophecy,* in which we seem to see and hear what we've already preordained for ourselves (Rosenthal & Jacobson, 1968). This may set up the conditions in which an outcome becomes literally real primarily because we have expected it into existence. For example, if you expect to dislike your new roommate before you even meet her, you might accentuate the negatives in your initial impressions of her and act defensively towards her. Then, in the self-fulfilling part, her behavior, in

L I N K

Our perception of the world is intimately linked to the hypotheses we make about the world. This leads us to a disturbing suspicion: Does our culture provide subtle lenses through which we *think* we observe "facts" but actually we find what we *expect* to find? For more on this issue, see the discussion of cultural influences in Chapter 7. As Bolles (1991) summarizes: "When perception is the issue, prejudice often turns up under the guise of science. As recently as the 1960s, scholarly journals published articles about perceptual differences between men and women in which the authors took for granted a woman's "natural" subordination to men. Researchers in South Africa published articles supporting the policy of apartheid by reporting that cultural differences between the local races are so profound that education cannot change perception. Psychologists in the German Third Reich too were interested in the problem of illusion and culturally different perception. Not all work that supports a social prejudice is wrong or sloppy, but all of it is suspect. It is too easy for men, whites, Germans, or the British to assume that the perceptions of a man, white, German, or Britisher are the correct ones." (p. 108)

L I N K

Review the discussion of theory-building in Chapter 1. How might scholarly research be affected by self-fulfilling prophecies? What safeguards could help to prevent this problem?

turn, may be modified when she perceives (correctly) that your reaction to her is negative and doesn't seem fair. Finally, when you notice her negativity, you conclude that it confirms your initial expectations.

The second characteristic of selective perception is that it is not total. Just because you desperately want your team to play well, your perceptual system will not normally distort the final result of a lost game. Selectivity operates within certain boundaries of experience. We do not necessarily filter out new information because it conflicts with what we already know; many other variables can intervene. If, for example, a teacher requests that you follow certain study habits that contradict those you've used successfully over the years, you might choose not to ignore, neglect, or distort this new information. The information might appeal to you, in which case you may try to integrate it with what you already know about studying. Recognizing the gap between what you already know or expect to happen and what is new or surprising is called *learning*.

Bruner (1960) described learning as involving three "almost simultaneous" processes: acquisition, transformation, and evaluation (pp. 48–49). *Acquisition* is how a person perceives something that's different from what was known before, explicitly or implicitly. *Transformation* is how the mind can change newly acquired information to make it fit unanticipated situations. *Evaluation* is the process of checking whether the information can be successfully applied in new situations. In recent years, Bruner has emphasized communication more in his explanations of learning (1983, 1986, 1990). His newer work emphasizes that learning is fundamentally "collaborative" and, in many ways, an interpersonal phenomenon (1983, pp. 127–133; see also Vygotsky, 1962). In essence, he argues, humans learn by comparing their inner experiences with new external information in the context of immediate (e.g., face-to-face), or imagined and indirect (e.g., reading) human interaction.

The third characteristic of selective perception is that it appears to maintain an inner consistency among attitudes. Traditionally, social psychologists and most quantitative researchers in communication have treated *attitude* as a key cognitive variable. An attitude was presumed to be an inner disposition to behave in certain ways that are preferred to other behaviors. Thus, an attitude is defined in terms of external behaviors and is based on an external metaphor (the "attitude" of a boat is its tendency to lean or list to one side). Of course, an attitude is an inferred or hypothetical construct within the mind.

Consistency theorists believe that *homeostasis,* or system balance, is a preferred state of being for humans, although this can never be achieved in a static way. People's minds are too complex and the stimuli of experience too changeable. Simply stated, individuals' attitudes do not always fit neatly with each other within personal experience. They might clash with, diverge from, or contradict previously believed or taken-for-granted perceptions. What happens then?

Let's consider how you might react to these two conflicting bits of information: (1) that Professor Samily is your nicest and most effective teacher, and (2) that you've just heard she's been charged with plagiarism by the university. You attach a positive value to her, and also to the university. Yet the university, at least in this one instance, negatively values the professor. These facts, when considered side by side, seem to create a kind of psychological tension or discomfort, which has been researched as *cognitive dissonance* (Festinger, 1957), *incongruity* (Osgood & Tannenbaum, 1955), or *imbalance* (Heider, 1958) in different scholars' work.

In order to restore internal harmony or minimize disharmony, you might engage in one or more cognitive tactics, such as *denial* (a direct change of value placed on one of the objects), *bolstering* (adding perceptions to one of the objects), *differentiation* (splitting one of the objects into two parts, each of which is perceived differently, and then achieving balance with one of the new notions), or *transcendence* (perceiving the two inconsistent objects as a whole, and relating them together to a third object in a balanced way) (Abelson, 1967). In the student–professor example, denial might occur by an internal attitude adjustment in one direction. Your position toward the professor might change (e.g., "Maybe she just fooled me and isn't as nice or effective as I'd thought"). If you choose bolstering, you might attach additional perceptions to your original ones to achieve balance: "I never realized how much pressure professors must feel in doing their research, if even Dr. Samily feels like she has to stretch the rules." Using differentiation as your cognitive tactic, you'd separate one side of the imbalanced system into two or more distinct parts, and then would define one subpart as relevant: "Actually, it's not the university that's accusing her, but only that jealous colleague." Finally, if you opted for transcendence, you might make this rationalization: "I see both Dr. Samily's classroom success and her alleged plagiarism as two parts of what makes a university so complex. Besides, universities are still better places to be than corporations." Of course, our statements in this paragraph are only examples, and cannot begin to indicate the full complexity of human attitudes.

LANGUAGE IN-FORMS PERSONAL EXPERIENCE

A number of communication-related theories focus on the role of language in inner experience. They ask important questions: Does the human capacity for language form the groundwork for effective thinking? Or, is thinking itself linguistic, our only basic way to process information? Although theorists address these issues somewhat differently, they generally agree on the importance of language. Whether thinking *is* language itself or thinking simply is assisted or enabled by language, we cannot conceive of human life apart from considering language.

After considering the theories, we'd like to suggest a middle position. That is, **language**—"a potentially self-reflexive structure system of symbols that catalogue the objects, events, and relations in the world" (DeVito, 1986, p. 176)—plays a formative role in consciousness. Language is usually thought to involve the elements suggested by DeVito's definition: self-reflexiveness, interconnected structure, and symbolic meaning. Considering these factors one by one will set the stage for later discussion.

Self-reflexiveness means that something is potentially capable of commenting on or referring to itself (Blum & McHugh, 1984, Lawson, 1985). With language we can speak about our speaking or reflect on our ability to reflect. Thus, language allows us to move to another level of experience, one level removed from direct involvement with the outer world.

When we say language has an *interconnected structure,* we mean that it has system properties. The organization of language (its grammar and syntax) cannot be separated from its collection of meanings and referents (its semantics). The French linguist Ferdinand de Saussure (1966), who established many of our modern ways of understanding language, viewed language not only as composed of the overall system of symbolic message structures, which he called *la langue,* but also as having a particular and unique property of spokenness, *la parole.* Language involves both the pattern of what can be said (la langue) and the immediate speech of communicators (la parole). Saussure's distinction is similar to the differences between structure and process, in that language has both an overall form and a particular life as it is spoken. However, you may wonder, as some critics do, whether the concepts of language structure and speech can be separated this neatly.

Language by definition involves *symbolizing.* When humans speak they enact a set of agreements that many of the sounds they utter and the marks they make on paper will be taken as substitutes for objects, relations, and experiences. Rarely is a language the product of individually negotiated agreement, however; a person is born into the stream of an already agreed-upon language. Therefore, although we have many choices of speech within a language, the language itself more or less predetermines what those alternatives will be.

Communication theorists, in tune with philosophers and linguists, usually distinguish between signals and symbols (Langer, 1951). *Signals* stand in a one-to-one unambiguous relationship to what they represent. For example, the movement of branches in a tree is safely taken as a signal that the wind is blowing, because whenever one thing happens, the other happens.

Symbolic life is different. *Symbols* suggest, rather than verify, the relations between things. For example, the red, white, and blue flag has become a visual symbol of the United States, but not all citizens think the same things when they see the flag, and they could salute other flags if they wanted to. A creative combination of shapes and colors *becomes* a flag, therefore, when persons agree that it *symbolizes* some persistent meaning that they believe to be important. In addition, we can say that the sequence of four marks *f-l-a-g* creates in English, along with the corresponding pronunciation of the letter sounds, a symbol of the red, white, and blue cloth we call the American flag. This arbitrariness is not decreed by any linguistic royalty; its symbolic origins are shrouded in living historical precedent. Although we create and change our language as we talk, it is important to remember that we are born into a society and a culture with an already existing set of linguistic rules.

the centrality of the symbol:
the language bridge to social life

The preexisting rules of language also suggest that our lives are fundamentally social, and that language can never be wholly private, even if you're thinking to yourself about what you'll say to a friend this afternoon. If you are especially interested in the nature of language and its influence on social communication, eventually you'll probably want to look more deeply into three areas of contemporary theorizing—speech act theory, semiotics, and postmodern language theory.

speech act theory.   Have you ever been tempted to say, "You're a big talker, but you never do anything about it"? Have you ever heard someone say "Talk is cheap," or "That's just empty rhetoric," or "I hear you say it, but will you do it?" Some people assume that life can be lived in one or the other of two extremes—talking about things or doing them. Talking about things, we sometimes assume, is passive, while only physical accomplishments are active. Some communication theorists challenge this distinction. Searle (1969), for example, suggests that any assumed distinction between words and actions is illusory. Although many people assume that communicators can either speak *or* act, Searle argues that by speaking we engage in significant action, a **speech act**. That is, spoken words are literally actions because they require energy and affect others. Speaking is not merely preliminary to acting or a substitute for reality—speaking is itself an act performed by one person with another or others. Through speech we can assert a truth, direct or request a listener to act in a certain way, commit ourselves to future acts, indicate psychological dispositions, or perform a symbolic accomplishment, such as saying "I do" during a marriage ceremony.

semiotics.   Symbols and signals can be considered subcategories of a larger conceptual category of messages known as signs. **Signs** are those aspects of the human environment that take on the value and function of a message because they stand for or refer to something else. **Semiotics** is the study of such signs and their arrangement into codes by which people come to understand their daily lives. Any sign takes on a particular form that comes to be understood by people in certain ways that wouldn't be predicted by that form alone. Words, as symbols, obviously, are signs. The word *panic* is not inherently more stressful to read than the word *serenity*, but has assumed such associations because of our mutual interpretations of what panic might refer to. Less obvious are how the nonverbal aspects of our lives also function as signs. How your friends or your parents set the table for dinner can indicate the kind of order expected in the communication episode we call a meal.

According to Saussure (1966), a sign exists as a relation between a *signifier* (something that calls attention to, or stands for, something else) and a *signified* (our sense of what it stands for or refers to). Although as a linguist he wasn't terribly interested in whether a sign closely resembled the reality that it presumably represented, other theorists have explored this relationship more fully (Eco, 1976; Peirce, 1931–1958). As Olson (1994) observes, "The basis of Eco's semiotics is a system for denoting the relationship that exists between the signifier and signified, their sign-function. Eco asserted that the content of a sign is not the signified itself, but a cultural conception of it . . ." (p. 72). In this sense, then, the word *panic* has as its semiotic content not the actual somatic experience of distress, but the sum of our cultural connotations for what it means to be panicked—including the associations we develop through watching movies, reading novels, and participating in other forms of popular culture—as they are interpreted by the human mind.

LINK

Semiotics, which involves studying verbal and nonverbal signs, and often their interaction, has implications for our understanding of both communication context (discussed in Chapter 3) and cultural communication (discussed in Chapter 7). Wendy Leeds-Hurwitz (1993) claims: "Just as the proper context for understanding a single sign is a code (a set of signs and rules for their use), so the proper context for understanding a single code is a culture (a set of codes and rules for their use)" (p. 155). As we saw in Box 4-1, Barthes's well-known semiotic study *Empire of Signs* (1989) places a Western reader within the unfamiliar mix of Japanese semiotic assumptions. Have you ever experienced what's commonly called "culture shock"? If so, you entered a state of semiotic slippage in which your existing assumptions about what's meaningful (which you weren't aware you were assuming) evaporate. In Barthes's book, suddenly what eating means, how people look at each other, what a smile suggests, and how furniture is arranged are all dislocated for the reader from the taken-for-granted realm to a fresh perspective.

(continued)

(continued)

Although we have chosen to discuss semiotics in terms of personal experience, equally good cases could have been made for including it in discussions of context, culture, media, and other areas in which signs are fundamental to communication.

postmodern challenges for theorizing.   In recent years, hundreds of authors have attempted to explain a shift from the assumptions of traditional modern thought to a newer set of social assumptions they call **postmodernism** (see Box 4-3). The topic is broad and difficult to summarize because scholars disagree on what postmodernism is and even whether it exists. Despite scholars' lack of agreement about definitions, the controversy is important for communication theorists and researchers to consider, especially in its implications for language study.

The term **modernism** refers to the post-Enlightenment view of rationality in Western culture, which has long been applied by science in its attempt to probe cause-effect relationships more predictably. Modernism assumes that those relationships are real and "out there" waiting to be discovered, and that they can be measured by precise research methods. Such methods lead us ever closer to the "truth," in this view, because science could be advanced by a single set of rational criteria, and society could be governed by compatible assumptions of order.

Postmodernism, in contrast, holds that, because rational order has begun to fall apart, a singular or universal understanding can no longer be applied. Lyotard (1984), a prominent postmodern theorist, contends that people no longer have faith in what he calls *metanarratives,* or grand narratives—the belief systems that once clearly defined—supposedly—how everyone was supposed to honor similar definitions of good and evil, right and wrong, and efficient and inefficient. In metanarratives, social structures were presumably explainable by a single story (if we could only agree on which story was best). In the postmodern world, though, people can't all subscribe to the same theories. The modernist grand narratives that once offered the promise of holding us together have splintered into fragmented *language games* in which different groups each develop different voices and rules for understanding. Obviously, such a philosophy resists clear definition, but a particularly helpful description of postmodernism stresses the same kind of fragmentation that Lyotard described: "Postmodernism . . . is committed to modes of thinking and representation which emphasize fragmentations, discontinuities and incommensurable aspects of a given object, from intellectual systems to architecture. . . . It prefers montage to perspective, intertextuality to referentiality, 'bits-as-bits' to unified totalities" (O'Sullivan et al., 1994, p. 234). A

BOX 4-3

ASSUMPTIONS OF POSTMODERN LANGUAGE THEORY
- Grand narratives are no longer persuasive or essential.
- The voices of different groups have been fragmented into different language games, each with its own set of rules.
- No reliable connection between meaning and either authors' intentions or external reality necessarily exists.
- Postmodern reality is based on surfaces and different layers of meaning.
- Messages are inherently unstable and unspecifiable, and cannot be locked in to singular meanings.

postmodern communication theorist would be unlikely to ask of a series of political campaign speeches, for example, "What's the basic theme here?" or "How
does all this fit together?"

The postmodernist's assumptions about language are exceptionally interesting, if not persuasive to everyone. Many postmodernists assume that ours is a
time in which signs no longer refer to things but only to other signs in infinite re-
gression. A solid sense of connecting words to reality is no longer possible, if it ever
was, because our world has become a "hyperreality" composed of words and
claims. Language becomes the new reality for the postmodern world. Therefore,
we should adapt ourselves to an existence in which meanings just can't be specified. Meanings are contingent upon other meanings, and concepts are never definable in a final sense. Postmodern critics known as *deconstructionists* (Derrida,
1982), for example, attempt to show that many messages can simultaneously mean
what they appear to mean *and* the opposite of what they appear to mean. Nor do
words necessarily mean what their speakers or writers intend for them to mean.
The postmodern theorist presumes that speaker, author, listener, reader, and
critic are all equal judges of meaning. In postmodern criticism, the *deconstruction*
of a message is a way of demonstrating its inherent ambiguity and self-
contradiction. As Rosenau (1992) describes it, the analytical method of deconstruction aims to "undo all constructions. Deconstruction tears a text apart, reveals its contradictions and assumptions; its intent, however, is not to improve,
revise, or offer a better version of the text" (p. xi). Thus, Poster (1990) believes
that to Derrida, "a reader of texts or an interpreter of culture who attempts to uncover stable, closed meanings cannot at the same time elucidate the 'textual' conditions under which alone it is possible to have meanings at all" (p. 102). To assume that language is "for" delimiting meanings, or "for" achieving complete
clarity, is to miss the essential power of language.

Deconstruction is difficult to grasp because it counters many of our commonsense assumptions about meaning. ("Do you mean that someone asking me to go
to lunch may also be asking me *not* to go to lunch?") However, in a sense, it is a
good way to remind ourselves that communication is more radically complex
than it is sometimes assumed to be. Postmodern theory emphasizes the inherently
unstable meanings of language and the complex social and personal practices
through which we attempt to communicate.

generative theory

If linguist Noam Chomsky (1957, 1975) is right, the basic rules for speaking a language aren't simply learned by children from their outside social influences such
as mothers and fathers. Chomsky theorizes that some of the rules and patterns for
developing language are inherent in the human brain, existing in what he calls
deep structures. In this view, called **generative theory**, these deep structures indicate
that language is built into human experience, and humans use these deep structures to "generate" speech and written language systems that are (at least on the
surface) apparently quite different (e.g., does German sound like English? Chinese like Spanish?). However, each language and each person's use of it is founded

on such "hard-wired" patterns. To be human is to speak, therefore, and to speak is to build on the ability to generate *transformations* of (changes to) the existing underlying structures of language. The result is a sentence—for example, "The result is a sentence." This or any other sentence is an example of a *surface structure,* or, to put it perhaps a bit simplistically, uttered speech. Chomsky and his followers see the variety of surface structures in language as important clues to the deep structures that presumably shape them. For example, "The result is a sentence" is one possible surface structure, and "A sentence is the result" is another alternative that seems to be equivalent. Both are built upon the same deep structure.

Chomsky's work revolutionized linguistics in many ways. But like most other significant research, it also generated controversy. Communication scholars should pay close attention because it presumes that we are species-ready for communication and language, and that language acquisition is basically inevitable. But Chomsky is another theorist who doesn't make commonsense assumptions. Most people unfamiliar with his theory of generative grammar would not hypothesize, as he does, that all children are born with wired-in language structures. They'd assume, if anything, that the brain was "factory installed," and that probably all our language attributes are optional accessories added on later by social learning. As a cognitive linguist, Chomsky isn't much interested in how people actually interact with each other in speech, but his work on the inherent capacity for language ultimately underscores the importance of interaction.

But what is the role of speech within a person's consciousness? How important is it in defining or sustaining conscious awareness of the outside world—or, in Bruner's terms, how does speech provide us with the "hypotheses" we need in order to perceive, and to make decisions and solve problems based on perceptions?

inner speech theory

Do you talk to yourself? Do you fear, as many people joke, that this is a sign of mental instability? Consider the possibility that self-talk is actually a hallmark of human intelligence. Feel better?

It is easy to assume that the primary purpose of language is to talk with other persons. That makes a kind of sense . . . even according to the cognitive evidence we've surveyed up to this point. But **inner speech theory** examines the talk we do with ourselves and how it helps us to think. The work of Dance (1982), Vygotsky (1962), and Bakhtin (1981) has been particularly important in developing theories of inner speech (see Box 4-4). Not only is human interaction not the sole function speech serves, but it may not even be the primary one. After synthesizing research from a variety of disciplines (Dance & Larsen, 1976), Dance (1982) concludes that *mentation* is crucial:

> The raison d'être of human communication, rather than being primarily transactional or interactional, is primarily mentation. In the earliest stages of human development, interaction may dominate mentation so that the behavioral ratio looks something like interaction/mentation. When human commu-

nication becomes fully constituted (at about the age of 7), mentation becomes and remains paramount as the primary raison d'être of human communication, and the usual behavioral ratio then looks more like mentation/interaction. This statement is not meant to slight the importance of interaction in human communication but to highlight that one of the unique aspects of human communication, as contrasted with the communication of other than human animals, is to take thought, to ratiocinate, to engage in higher mental processes. (p. 137)

With fully formed speech, then, humans not only can connect with each other more effectively (which Dance calls the *linking function*), but develop and lead increasingly more complex inner lives (which Dance and others call *interiority*). Thinking involves conceptualization, or the ability to create concepts, and rational thought, the ability to manipulate those concepts creatively, reasonably, and thoroughly.

Speech isn't only a bridge between people; it is also a bridge, or mediator, between a person's inner existence and outer impact. What good would thought and planning be without the ability to imagine through speech the likely consequences of that planning? Many communication theorists, like Dance, therefore, stress that inner speech allows us to *decenter*, or place ourselves imaginatively outside of our immediate existence. Decentering enables us to empathize or identify with others, to consider other times and places that we have not experienced directly, and to plan contingencies for an uncertain future. In a very real sense, we can be said to have developed the basis for a "world of experience" when we passed through the stage of simple vocalization in order to create spoken language. Without speech, we would have no "world."

For Dance, speech is the key to understanding human communication. Dance (1982) has created a systematic *speech theory of human communication*, and an impressive amount of evidence supports his general premise. However, the perspectives of other inner speech theorists differ somewhat. Much of the research on inner speech and its consequences was conducted by psychologists and language theorists from the former Soviet Union many years ago, and has gained acceptance in the West only in recent decades (Johnson, 1984). Luria (1961) summarized his own research as well as the research programs of Vygotsky (1962) and Sokolov (1972) when he wrote that the process of "internal speech" has been shown to be "an invariable part of the thought-process" and "characteristic of the development of almost all the higher forms of mental activity" (pp. 34–35). Most of this early research, particularly that of Vygotsky, challenged the prevailing notion that children learn language by progressing through a series of structurally similar and relatively invariant stages of development that are closely keyed to age level. In contrast, Vygotsky (1962) argues that children learn language in ways that are better predicted by social facilitation (by parents, for example), which interacts with the creative aspects of the inner voice the child tries to apply to all situations of thinking. In this sense, speech and thought are not identical processes to Vygotsky, but they are so closely related that it is not useful to consider one without the other. Therefore, because inner speech releases creative problem solving, the child's development isn't locked into stages determined by age and physiology.

L I N K

Decentering appears to be crucial in helping us to identify sensitively with others' realities. See the discussion of inclusion and empathy in Chapter 6.

More specifically, Vygotsky (1962, pp. 119–153) showed that in inner speech language is less sequential and linear than the language of interpersonal speech. He identifies four characteristics of inner speech:

1. *Abbreviation:* Inner speech presumes its "audience" (yourself) and, therefore, has no need for elaboration. (An exception occurs during those self-conscious moments when we lecture ourselves as we would another person.)
2. *Sense orientation:* Inner speech is not oriented toward precise definitions or specifications of meaning; instead, it operates in terms of what Vygotsky (1962) calls the "sense" of words—a holistic sum of whatever the words have "aroused in our consciousness" in "dynamic, fluid, complex" ways (p. 146).
3. *Semantic merger:* Vygotsky used the terms *agglutination* and *influx of sense* to describe the process by which several ideas become interassociated within a single word, almost as if they were contained by it. This process is very similar to the workings of literary metaphor.
4. *Predication:* Inner speech is oriented toward change and action and, therefore, tends to deal with "predicates" more than with "subjects." In terms of Chapter 2, inner speech is more "processual" than interpersonal speech.

A number of applied communication theorists tie Vygotsky's notions to practical concerns of teaching and learning about communication. Inner speech concepts, they argue, may be adapted to interdisciplinary programs in education and therapy that are designed to facilitate interpersonal dialogue and personal growth. Streff (1984), for instance, discusses how Vygotsky's work might be applied to the structuring of learning programs in secondary schools, while Dance (1982) notes its implications for the development of self-concept. Anderson and McClearey (1984) use Vygotsky's research to support their claim that inner speech is inherently "poetic" (i.e., human consciousness and creativity both depend on speech forms that closely resemble poetry in the world's literature).

Another Russian theorist closely associated with Vygotsky's ideas about inner speech is Mikhail Bakhtin (1981, 1986). The two never met and Vygotsky probably didn't know of Bakhtin, although Bakhtin knew of Vygotsky's research (Clark & Holquist, 1984, p. 382). Although his work was long neglected, few intellectuals of the twentieth century have become so rapidly accepted across so many disciplines. For years his research was either unknown or poorly disseminated in the West. Some of it may even have been published in the Soviet Union under the names of colleagues for political reasons; indeed, the scholarly debate over which books and articles can be credited to Bakhtin continues today. Nonetheless, contemporary cognitive psychologists, literary critics, and communication theorists (Todorov, 1984) widely apply his work in their own fields of research.

Bakhtin (1981) extends the importance of inner speech even further than Vygotsky. Inner *dialogism,* as Bakhtin termed it, complements the American symbolic interactionism, a theory that was developed independently, and which we'll

BOX 4-4

INNER SPEECH THEORISTS

- Dance: The speech theory of human communication emphasizes the *mentation* function.
- Vygotsky: Inner speaking is an *inner socialization* process that uses language in fundamentally different ways than does external speech.
- Bakhtin: Inner speaking is a *dialogism* that imports society's outer dialogue into the mind.

---

consider later in the chapter. Whereas Vygotsky conceptualized inner speech as language *usage*, Bakhtin believed that it was not simply self-to-self speech. Instead, Bakhtin's inner speech concept is an internalization of society's outer dialogue. Whenever a word is spoken (whether outer or inner), that word psychologically contains all the voices of society that have previously shaped its use. This is not a private and isolated act, however secretly it might be done. *Saying* (his translators use "utterance" more often) a word then, is social participation at its most basic level, because words are inherently dialogical.

Bakhtin's view of literature is similarly broad (see, e.g., Bakhtin, 1981; Holquist, 1990). He believed that all perception was analogous to authorship; that is, the perceiver creates a "text" in response to the world, and then proceeds to "read" and offer that text as an interpretation (to which the self or others respond). He claims that writers of poetry, short stories, and novels are simply doing at a more overt level what all of us do daily at covert levels— attempting to express our ideas about the world without overcompromising it. We will fail at this attempt, he thinks. But ultimately, inner speech helps us balance the more ordered properties of the word with the chaotic properties of the world.

With the theorists from the former Soviet Union, we can see more clearly how language in-forms personal experience. It is the medium, in fact, through which we can even *have* personal experience. Does this conclusion mean that a culture's particular language predetermines the reality that can be perceived by native speakers of that culture? If so, are speakers of a given language destined to be trapped within the categories that language creates? These are the kinds of questions that linguistic relativity theorists address.

linguistic relativity theory

In case you may hold the stereotype that all communication scholars are university professors whose research is underwritten by public and private grants, you might be interested to know that one of the most famous and influential language researchers/theorists of the century worked nearly his entire professional career as an executive for an insurance company. Benjamin Whorf started studying linguistics out of personal curiosity, but later supplemented his informal training by studying with the renowned Yale linguist Edward Sapir. Together, they are recognized for what has come to be called the *Sapir-Whorf hypothesis,* or, because Whorf became its chief spokesperson, the *Whorfian hypothesis* of **linguistic relativity theory**.

Whorf's research into different cultures, especially the Hopi culture in the U.S. Southwest, led him to wonder if language is more than a vehicle for sending and receiving information (1956). Of course, anthropologists can easily show that the language of a culture reflects the beliefs, behaviors, habits, mores, values, and feelings of the groups they study. Cultural differences and language differences appear to correspond. Each culture's unique language is sufficiently complex to handle the contingencies that arise within that culture. However, Whorf went beyond the obvious observation that human languages are distinctive to suggest a more radical hypothesis: that such language differences can create distinctive realities in the perceptual and thought processes of native speakers. Because of the nature of language, reality is relative and in some ways provisional. Thinking and perception are not only psychological phenomena but are fundamentally based on cultural factors. Language is not only capable of reacting to and describing what we see, Whorf decided, but because language places categories in our heads, it tends to determine what we're going to see.

The word *determine* became a sticky point as the theory of linguistic relativity developed. Those commenting on and writing about Whorf's hypothesis tended to overstate his ideas and turn them into a kind of linguistic determinism. Determinists tried to claim that because people spoke different languages, they could never experience a shared reality because they could never escape from the prison of their own separate language systems. This became known as the "strong version" of the Whorfian hypothesis (see Schultz, 1990, for an account of how this strong version developed). Some critics even argued that if Whorf studied the Hopi and wrote a book that he claims is accurate, then he contradicted his own thesis. If linguistic relativity is as correct as Whorf claims, they suggested, how can Whorf claim anything about his research with certainty? Therefore, because he wrote persuasively about other cultures, linguistic determinism must not be a conceptually solid theory. Critics reasoned: "If Whorf is right, how can Whorf be right? Therefore, Whorf is wrong."

Other theorists, however, have replied that Whorf never claimed the "strong version" of the theory—that language totally determines cultural reality. According to Schultz (1990), "In his clearest statements of the linguistic relativity principle, Whorf seems to be arguing that speakers of different languages do *not* all share identical forms and categories of thought simply by virtue of the fact that they are all human beings. At the same time, Whorf refrains from suggesting that all human beings possess, *within the boundaries of their native tongue,* vast resources for categorizing experience in a variety of ways" (p. 27). Whorf evidently wanted to show that each culture is linguistically rich, but in its own terms—and that other cultures with other languages will not automatically have access to the perceptual and personal experience of its people. This insight, he thought, would ultimately increase cross-cultural respect. However, from the standpoint of communication theory, his chief contribution is to spotlight language as a link: It is simultaneously the key concept of culture and the key concept of individual human thought. Thinking is not independent, but has to be accomplished within—and by—language. That language's unique rules will somehow affect the forms of thought. The study of language, Whorf (1956) writes, "shows that the forms of a person's thoughts are controlled by inexorable laws of pattern of which he is unconscious. These patterns are the unperceived intricate systematizations of his own language . . ." (p. 252).

symbolic interactionism

Another main current of thought about the influence of language on personal experience flows from George Herbert Mead, a professor at the University of Chicago from 1893 to 1931. The term **symbolic interactionism** was later coined by Herbert Blumer (1969), but it is Mead's ideas that originally defined this intellectual movement. Blumer's label stuck because it suggested the theory's reliance on language *(symbolic)* and social communication *(interaction)*.

Mead (1934) believed, as did Whorf, that persons and societies are all part of the same basic process. Both believed, too, with a number of other thinkers in the American pragmatic tradition of philosophy, that the key that unlocks this process is to study language. Human experience to Mead was a knotted but unbroken thread extending from the largest group experiences to the most private and personal ones. Although our focus in this chapter is on personal experience, many prominent communication theorists in various fields applied symbolic interactionist thought to the interpersonal (Goffman, 1959; McHugh, 1968) and mass-mediated (Duncan, 1962; Klapp, 1969, 1978) realms of communication.

Symbolic interactionists tend to believe that Mead's (1934) three-part distinction of *mind, self,* and *society* highlights the three levels of communicative force. None of the three can be defined apart from definitions of the other two. Let's start by explaining society, since individuals are born into already existing social relations. Mead defines *society* as the web of social relationships humans create and in which they engage through what he calls *acts,* which are behaviors chosen voluntarily by individuals. Society thus becomes an interlocking set of cooperative behaviors by which individuals actively adjust themselves to each other.

LINK

For more on symbolic interactionist theories, especially that of Erving Goffman, see the section on dramaturgical theory in Chapter 6.

Surely, you criticize and congratulate other people on many social occasions. But you also criticize and congratulate yourself. Suppose, for instance, you get a B on an exam. You may be satisfied with the B because it symbolizes a lot of hard work, but at the same time you may be dissatisfied with the grade because you know you could have done better. In effect, you're communicating with yourself as if you were both the subject (evaluator) and the object (evaluated) in this judgment. Although it feels normal to you to act this way, Mead believes that this deceptively simple act is one of the premier achievements of the human race.

Self becomes possible for a person as a result of noticing that, just as others can be treated as objects of action, so can he or she turn messages reflexively inward for personal notice. In addition, a person learns through social relations that others' acts are directed toward him or her. Thus, a sense of unique placement in the world develops, a sense of identity, in which language is the medium of discovery. As Anselm Strauss (1956) explains, "Mead makes action toward the self an integral facet of the act. One takes himself into account while acting toward the non-self. This self-reflexivity is dependent upon language and arises during childhood as a result of participation in groups" (p. xi). One implication of this view is that a self is neither inwardly set nor socially given; rather, it is the result of complex and ongoing transactions among persons, their actions, and the larger social structures made possible by those actions. It's only a small oversimplification to claim that you develop a self by listening to your talk with other people and inferring what kind of person would participate in such interaction.

Interaction, therefore, is inherent in your self-concept. Mead (1934) accounts for this by explaining the two types of responsiveness comprising the symbolic self: the *me* and the *I*. The *me* component is that aspect of the self that is responsive to the outside social network, the aspect that is shaped, controlled, limited, or accounted for by external forces. The *I* component is that part of the self that asserts unique points of view, responds to impulses, and creates individualized positions that may or may not be similar to those of others. While the *me* is a force for predictability and conformity, the *I* is a source of surprise and novelty.

Mind is a different level for considering the same basic processes of interaction and differentiation. Because we develop what Mead calls mind, we are able to create an interior setting for the society we see operating outside of ourselves. We can re-create intrapersonally the interpersonal "conversation of gestures" in which we participate in society. Mind, then, is *society as we internalize it*. It is the inner conversation we are able to have with ourselves as a result of language, which enables both the outer conversation and the senses of self that flow from it. In one sense, Mead presents yet another theory of inner speech. But it would be a mistake to think of mind simply as depending on self and society. Mead's thought comes full circle to remind us that a society as we know it would be impossible without the symbolic contributions of mind. Society is just as attributable to mind as mind is to society. In our brief account, we have tried to suggest this circular interdependence by reversing Mead's normal sequence of mind/self/society, but ultimately, either sequence is somewhat misleading. Society and self do not emerge developmentally from mind; nor can we start with society and then build selves and minds. (How could any group exist without its members being able to plan, symbolize, perceive, or anticipate a social future—all aspects of mind?)

Mead's contributions to symbolic interactionism do not end with his mind/self/society distinctions. He introduced a number of concepts that have helped communication theorists understand symbolic functions. Most prominent among them are:

- *Generalized other:* Over time, people develop a generalized sense of how other people react to them, and of the social expectations of these others. The individual, in developing a symbolic mind, begins to create an overall sense of how someone else thinks or feels relative to self. This creation, very influential in developing what some call a *conscience,* is Mead's *generalized other.*

✓ • *Significant symbol:* Mead's view of *symbol* was very much like that which we outlined in an earlier section of this chapter —something that comes to stand for something else at a representational level because of human agreement. Yet in society, all symbols are not equally shared or understood. Mead reserved the term *significant symbol* for those symbols that evoke basically similar meanings for communicators. A significant symbol serves as both stimulus and response for individuals within what he termed a *universe of discourse* (Mead, 1934, pp. 71, 89–90).

✓ • *Role-taking:* Mead's systematic observation of human behavior suggested a number of implications of symbolic communication. One of the most crucial of these was his view of *role-taking,* a concept similar to what we have previously discussed as decentering. Mead speculated that the extended dependency of human children on their parents and other caretakers, combined with a developing capacity for active participation in a community's symbols, allows children to play games in which they take on the roles of other people and things. That is, they symbolically remove themselves from self and *re-*place themselves in an imagined self of another person or object, thereby stimulating a recognition that reality can be seen from differing perspectives. Far from resulting in a confusion of selves, this symbolic act can be a powerful social clarification of self, resulting in increased capacities for sympathy or empathy later in life (Mead, 1934, pp. 364, ff.). (See Box 4-5.)

Without language, the symbolic interactionists claim, there would be no distinctly human experience of community or society, no "we're all in this together," no conscience or sympathy for others, no sense of who (what?) we even *are* in the first place.

Whether you agree with Mead and others that all thinking literally is speech, or whether you believe that thinking merely depends on a capacity for spoken language, it is hard to deny that personal experience (even at the most basic sensory levels) is interwoven with language concerns. Our species truly is *Homo loquens,* the "talking animal" (Fry, 1977), even when the speaking is within the self. If language is so basic to consciousness, therefore, it stands to reason that *how we talk* about an issue or a topic will strongly influence *what we can think* about it. In other words, language creates the boundaries of what is possible in human life.

BOX 4-5

MEAD AND SYMBOLIC INTERACTION

- Mead's basic distinctions: *Society, Self* ("Me"/"I"), *Mind*
- Mead's conceptual contributions and basic terms: *Generalized other, Significant symbol, Role-taking*

COGNITIVE ORGANIZATION AND PLANNING

Psychologists and communication theorists have become increasingly curious about how the human mind works. It was not always so. Researchers who identified themselves as *behaviorists* argued vigorously that knowledge about humans was developed most reliably by simply looking at people's specific actions. It was the behaviors themselves that interested such scholars, who reasoned that the human mind was a kind of *black box,* into which we would never be able to see clearly. Therefore, although behaviorists acknowledged that *something* was inside the black box, the simplest methodological approach was to define mental life out of the picture and attempt instead to compare systematically the inputs and outputs of the box. This philosophical position (for it was a specific philosophy of science that was being implemented) became for a time closely associated with social science itself. Once researchers recognized the primacy of studying behavior, they had moved toward a realm where it was considered most efficient to rely on quantitative research. The underlying philosophical assumption was that reality was both external and knowable—if we could just get our instruments and methodologies for defining it fine-tuned.

In the history of social science, debates about the merits of behaviorism have been common (e.g., Wann, 1964). However, for the moment at least, the controversy has quieted to an acceptance that we can and should know more about the cognitive processes that contribute to how we send, receive, interpret, and store messages. This acceptance carries with it a counterbalancing philosophical position: that human reality is not as much discovered as it is constructed or built by the unique perspectives of persons as they communicate. Even if we can't discover precisely how mental variables influence external behaviors, the search is worth our effort.

difference(s)

> Every child learns at school that movement is something relative, which can only be perceived in relation to a point of reference. What is not realized by everyone is that this same principle holds for virtually every perception and, therefore, for man's experience of reality. Sensory and brain research have proved conclusively that only relationships and patterns of relationships can be perceived, and these are the essence of experience. (Watzlawick, Beavin, & Jackson, 1967, p. 27)

Such a statement is dense with implications. One especially practical implication is that any object of perception cannot be perceived clearly unless it is placed in relation to another object of perception. Look at any word on this page, and look in a sustained way at only that one word. Is that word all you see? Surely not; the relation of the word to other words, of the word to the page, of the page to the book, of the book to the rest of the objects in your environment—all these relationships allow you to focus on the one word. Without the presence of other relationships, any focus on the single word would be impossible. We see relation-

LINKS

• Review the respective advantages of both quantitative and qualitative research methods in Chapter 1. In your opinion, can a behaviorist also be a humanistic, qualitative scholar? Why or why not?

• The modern/postmodern distinctions described earlier in this chapter are also relevant here. How might the behaviorist's philosophy of knowledge (his or her *epistemology*) clash with the postmodernist's diagnosis of the contemporary world?

ships between objects, not the objects themselves. We hear relationships between sounds, not literally the sounds themselves. In this sense, we can even "hear" silence.

Watzlawick et al. (1967) suggest some other examples of what happens when we attempt to eliminate relational factors: a tone that is held at a steady pitch tends to fade from conscious awareness; an unchanging gaze at any given point will yield blurrier, not clearer vision; holding your finger motionless on a surface supplies almost no information about the surface compared to moving your finger around on the surface (pp. 27–28). In each of these examples, the object's relation to other objects has been limited. Common sense might tell you that to hear a word you should concentrate hard on it. But this is not the principle on which perception seems to work. Ironically, more useful perceptual information is obtained when we are aware of differences between things, rather than concentrating on the things themselves. You can estimate how far the stop sign is from your speeding car only because you know from previous experience how large it is, and how it compares to other objects (also remembered as certain sizes) in the immediate environment. You know what to make of your friend's comment, "Nice job," only because you are able to hear it in relationship to other actual and potential comments.

Communication theorist Gregory Bateson has contributed much to our understanding of contrast and difference in conscious communication. Initial sensory input, Bateson argues, is always data about *first derivatives:* "statements about differences which exist among external objects or statements about changes which occur either in them or in our relationship to them" (Ruesch & Bateson, 1968, p. 173). The phrase "our relationship to them" suggests that a perceiver is a factor in whatever is perceived. Much of Bateson's later work (1980, 1991; M. C. Bateson, 1984) explores how people actually create a mental model of their relationship to the perceived, and subsequently experience that image of relation rather than experience the other person or object directly. Bateson reminds us that communicators cannot avoid taking a stance, which will inevitably influence both what is perceived and how it is perceived.

As an example, let's consider whether you can be said to be reading this book right now. We would suggest that you *are* reading, but what you are really reading is *your relationship to the book.* If you enjoy school and believe books are informative, you will not be reading the same book as a classmate who finds education unstimulating and books worthless. Your relation to the book will be psychologically different. You'll imagine you have a clear perception of the book's value—but remember that you are a part of the relationship of book-to-environment that makes the book meaningful.

Another theorist commonly cited across the intellectual map also comments on the perception of differences and the perceiver's relationship to the perceived. Physicist Werner Heisenberg (1958) describes scientific "indeterminacy" in advancing his *uncertainty principle* (see also Bohm, 1980). In a study of very small particles, Heisenberg and his colleagues found that the technology needed to illuminate and magnify these particles set the particles in motion. This motion would not have occurred had there been no observation. Thus, the would-be observer has two options: Don't investigate (and remain uncertain about the phenomena under study), or investigate (and still be uncertain, because no one can be sure of the precise changes introduced by the observation itself). Naturally, scientists opt for the second alternative since it provides at least some information for making educated guesses about how much change is introduced by the observation. But scientists should investigate with full recognition that the results will necessarily be indeterminate and imprecise. The relation of the perceiver to the perceived affects the perception. The looking becomes a part of the looked at.

Observers don't just relate to differences; they also create them. The uncertainty principle operates in the human sciences as well. Thus, for example, when someone says, "Go ahead and run your laps—I'll just sit here and watch" or "You know, a lot is riding on this speech because of who is in the audience," the presence of the observer changes the event in subtle and significant ways. (See Box 4-6 for a review of this section.)

social judgment theory

Perception relies on differences. But how do we respond to differences we perceive in the social sphere? How do we judge and categorize these differences, and how do we allow them to guide our attitudes and decisions?

Social judgment theory provides one set of possible answers to these questions. It has generated considerable interest and research among communication scholars over the past three decades despite its periodic falls from scholarly favor (Granberg, 1982). Although once considered nearly as important as, and as a logical successor to, the cognitive consistency theories in social psychology (Fisher, 1978), social judgment theory never engaged the sustained attention of communication theorists. However, since the 1961 publication of Sherif and Hovland's *Social Judgment*, several clear implications for communication theory have crystallized. At one level, at least, social judgment theory attempts a systematic description of some deeply influential determinants of listening style—the individual's message-processing responsibilities.

The basic concepts of what came to be called the "social judgment-involvement approach" were systematically presented first in the early 1960s (Sherif & Hovland, 1961; Sherif, Sherif, & Nebergall, 1965). This approach (its

---

BOX 4-6

DIFFERENCE AND PERCEPTION
- We perceive and organize cognitions by noting differences.
- We primarily perceive relations between things, not the things themselves.
- Attempts to perceive can introduce effects of their own, thereby changing the conditions under which perception takes place (the uncertainty principle).

primary authors, Muzafer Sherif and Carolyn Sherif, never claimed "theory" status for their work, although some others did) contends that we categorize incoming messages in terms of favorable or unfavorable judgments. Perceived stimuli are evaluated and integrated into previously developed categories of *acceptance*, *rejection*, and *noncommitment* called *latitudes*.

Only by determining the ranges of acceptable and unacceptable position statements do we glimpse an individual's relevant structure of attitude on a given topic. The marking of a single most preferred position on an attitude test, with the labeling of that choice being treated as an "attitude," is an overly simple generalization. The Sherifs thought social science should recognize that personal attitudes are more complex than that. People, they argued, are predisposed to process messages not only by comparing them to a single preferred position among many, but also by judging the acceptability of alternative statements.

A social attitude, then, cannot be summarized by a point on a scale, a single preferred stand, but rather is "a set of evaluative categorizations formed toward an object or class of objects as the individual learns, in interaction with others, about his environment, including evaluations of other persons" (Sherif et al., 1965, p. 20). Thus, social judgment theory assumes that attitudes are not mere expressions of the self but, more importantly, components of the self. The two most important features of this approach are ego involvement and assimilation and contrast effects. (See Box 4-7.)

ego involvement.   Some of the messages we encounter reflect topics that are central to maintaining our identity or that are crucial to how interpersonal well-being or survival is defined in the social environment. These messages are said to have a high level of *ego involvement*. Social judgment theorists assume that such messages are not received in the same way as messages whose topics are of more peripheral importance. The normal latitude structure for non-ego-involving topics exhibits a relatively large *latitude of acceptance*—the range of positions the person will accept (i.e., some positions are more easily accommodated because they pose little or no threat). The *latitude of noncommitment*—the range of positions in which the person does not have well-developed judgments—is large when familiarity or interest is low. But high ego involvement, which presumably evokes more self-interest and more potential threat or reward, tends to solidify attitudes differently. The range of acceptable positions diminishes, as does the latitude of noncommitment. High ego involvement tends to produce a larger group of unacceptable positions, widening the *latitude of rejection,* as the person's criteria for acceptance become more stringent.

assimilation and contrast effects.   Sherif and others have found in experiments on both physical and social judgments that a previously defined reference point—or *anchor*—in a range of more ambiguous stimuli will affect the judgment of those other stimuli (Sherif and Hovland, 1961). Stimuli close to this anchor may be perceived as being closer than actual measurement will confirm, whereas distant stimuli may appear even more distant. The clustering effect—*assimilation*—and the distortion that can be attributed to perceptual distance from the anchor—*contrast*—have especially important effects on social attitudes. The individual's own most preferred attitudinal position tends to operate as an internal anchor by which other positions are judged. This explains why some near-preferred positions are assimilated into a latitude of acceptance, and why some "discrepant" (or disagreeably different) messages that fall into a latitude of rejection produce contrast effects involving retrenchment or negative attitude change. Often, several messages of varying distance from the person's own stand—but all of which fall into the latitude of rejection—might be perceived as equally unacceptable and deserving of equally harsh interpersonal response.

the self in social judgment.   Researchers have questioned the concept of ego involvement (Kiesler, Collins, & Miller, 1969; O'Keefe, 1975; Wilmot, 1971) and its effect on latitude sizes (McCroskey & Burgoon, 1974). Individual personality characteristics or traits, for example, may have more to do with latitude of rejection than does topic involvement. McCroskey and Burgoon (1974) suggest that "... people have relatively invariant widths of latitudes of acceptance and rejection across topics and sources" (p. 425). In other words, the acceptance or rejection of new ideas, while somewhat related to a person's involvement with a topic, also tends to correlate with a person's general perceptual habits.

The Sherifs and their colleagues drew upon concepts of social norms and reference groups as well as on the psychology of intrapersonal stability to create a picture of what attitudes mean to the person. Social judgment theory provides a holistic description of attitude that respects human subjectivity. The self must be taken into central account in attitude research, these researchers thought. Their approach noted and credited the individual's phenomenal world by letting him or her personally structure and define the categories of judgment as much as possible. Thus the discovery of self-generated categories becomes in effect the operational definition of attitude itself. By attempting to explain and predict the influence of ego involvement, social judgment theory provides yet another way to study the concept of self.

BOX 4-7

SOCIAL JUDGMENT THEORY

- Social judgments shouldn't be considered as isolated marks on a researcher's scale, but as *latitudes* or ranges of possible positions on real issues.
- Social judgments are affected by the extent of the perceiver's *ego involvement* in what is being judged.
- Social judgments are adjusted by perceivers according to how they relate to a perceptual *anchor* or reference point. Judgments can be *assimilated* toward (perceived as being closer to) or *contrasted* with (perceived as being more distant from) this anchor.

constructivism

Over the past two decades or so, many communication theorists have developed a research program called **constructivism** (Delia, O'Keefe, & O'Keefe, 1982). Although its basic premises are relatively simple, the implications of constructivist thought have influenced how many researchers perceive the relationships among self, mind, and behavior.

basic assumptions.   Researchers applying a constructivist perspective make three basic assumptions about how humans communicate (see Box 4-8). First, constructivists assume that communication is an interpretive process. Therefore, communication cannot be oversimplified as a stimulus–response, cause–effect, or transmission–reception phenomenon. Messages do not bring meanings to receivers from senders; instead, messages are occasions for people to create, or *construct,* realities through their interpretations of the messages.

Second, constructivists assume that human beings can be active agents in determining how their worlds are constituted. Therefore, any conception of communication should reflect, constructivists argue, this idea of humans as choosers rather than as passive observers or victims of fate.

Third, constructivism assumes that individuals order individual choices and worldviews through complex patterns of cognitive organization. People do not collect or maintain communication data randomly, but instead use the information to create and maintain organized patterns of knowing. In this way, new situations and unique challenges can be understood in terms of the existing cognitive organization. To understand such patterns, therefore, is to understand a communication "world" as a person creates, experiences, and uses it. Understanding the patterns also provides effective clues into how a person perceives a unique self.

constructing shades of gray.   Constructivism employs a specific vocabulary for understanding communication. *Constructs,* a concept extrapolated from the work of Kelly (1963), are most simply described as "recognitions of difference." The mind, as we saw earlier in this chapter, tends to order information in terms of distinctive categories. Human consciousness is alert not only to similarity but primarily to difference as a key signal. Thus, for example, you know you have a construct for *woman* if you can perceive the difference(s) between a woman and a man. Most people can readily identify whether a piece of music is classical, rock, country, or jazz. We have immediate constructs available for these distinctions. However, some people claim that "all rock music sounds alike" or "all classical music is boring" or "all country music just sounds twangy"; these are persons for whom the constructs within that particular area of experience have not been differentiated. *Construct differentiation* occurs when increasingly specific distinctions are made and then organized hierarchically—as when a rock fan discusses an appreciation for "grunge" or "roots rock" but puts down "art rock." Other listeners who wouldn't be interested in or able to tell the differences among these categories would be said to be lower in *cognitive complexity.*

Review the section on social judgment earlier in this chapter. How might cognitive complexity research help explain the process by which latitudes of acceptance and rejection function like personality traits in some people? What implications might this have for cultural diversity in general and for multicultural awareness training in particular? (We will return to these issues in Chapter 7.)

A "So what?" question of practicality arises here. Because we can assume that people can be more or less cognitively complex at both general and specific levels of experience, then constructivism has given us a concept that helps explain why we occasionally have great trouble communicating even when we seem to be using the "same" definitions for the "same" words, and even if we grew up within the same culture. People who are more cognitively complex have more complicated category distinctions, "schemes," and "models" for the world; thus, they will perceive more gradations of meaning and more possibilities for acting within a situation. The cognitively complex person sees shades of gray where another person may see only black and white options. Good and bad are not as quickly labeled and identified; people with more sophisticated construct and interpretive schemes can begin to see potential for good in the bad, and bad within good, as well as a range of other possibilities within that continuum. Cognitively complex persons thus tend to avoid what Rokeach (1960) researched as *dogmatism* and what General Semanticists (Hayakawa, 1941) term the *two-valued orientation:* simple explanations of something as being either *this* or *that*. What constructivists call communication "strategies" will become more sophisticated and adaptable to specific problems that arise. As concept differentiation increases, cognitive complexity increases, which in turn leads to more communicative flexibility.

In a sense, constructivism is a developmental approach to human maturity. Researchers use its concepts to guide investigations of how people form impressions of others, how people engage in "perspective-taking" by assuming the roles of others, how conversations are managed, and how attitudes change.

action assembly theory

Constructivists, among other communication theorists, are interested in modeling the complexity of human cognitive structures. To do so, they look at how people use those structures to accomplish their practical everyday tasks. How someone processes and categorizes information in constructing a common reality with other persons is explained, but how that processing actually produces behaviors

---

BOX 4-8

CONSTRUCTIVISM: AN OVERVIEW

- *Constructivism* assumes that:
  Communication is interpretive.
  Humans are agents (active choosers).
  Humans organize their choices and worldviews in complex patterns that reflect how they recognize differences.
- *Constructs* are recognitions of difference.
- *Construct differentiation* and *cognitive complexity* develop as persons attempt to make subtle distinctions by organizing constructs in more complicated ways.

is left relatively unexamined. The situation is analogous to an automobile assembly plant fully tooled up for production with plenty of materials and all shifts of workers efficiently scheduled but with no instructions from the production managers on what kinds of cars actually to make. How are the instructions, the action plans, arrived at? Although this metaphor is misleading if it suggests only that communication is like manufacturing, it does point to the importance of system output. How can we develop a full understanding of inner cognitive processes without taking into account how those inner processes become externalized?

John O. Greene (1984, 1989) envisioned his **action assembly theory** to fill this need, and to answer such questions as "How do human plans become actions?" Greene (1989) suggests that there are "only two fundamental problems in understanding human communication":

> The first of these essential problems is that of meaning: How do people assign meaning to stimulus inputs such as the utterances and gestural activity of others? The second problem is that of action; that is, explicating the process(es) by which people produce the behaviors that constitute the signs and symbols of communication. A moment's reflection reveals that any substantive issue concerning human communication involves input processing, the production of responses, or a combination of the two. Thus whether one studies mass media effects, interpersonal compliance gaining, or cross-cultural nonverbal communication, the essential processes are those of input and output, meaning and action. (pp. 117–118)

Therefore, while constructivism focuses on the problem of meaning, action assembly theory tries to explain the problem of action.

Greene is much more interested in how cognition produces alternatives for actions (behavioral plans) than he is in describing either the structures of cognition or the behavior per se. Put another way, Greene seems to claim that part of the structure of cognitive life is a kind of awareness that he labels *procedural memory*—that is, our recollection of how to do things and our sense of which things typically "work" and why. Greene distinguishes this memory system from its twin system, *declarative memory,* which is our recollection of what we know. Procedural memory is of the process of producing actions ("knowledge how"), while declarative memory concerns the content of memory ("knowledge that"). Although communication obviously involves both types, Greene centers his theory on procedural memory.

Yet procedural memory itself has content, which is composed of a system of *procedural records.* Although Greene and his colleagues are conceptually quite precise in their research, for our purposes simply assume that procedural records are memories of previous communication outcomes, along with the details of actions and whatever situational factors were relevant to the outcomes. Recall the last three major purchases you made, including who was with you, what was said to you, and what you said. As you think, you are using procedural records.

But how do we know, in a given situation, how to use these procedural records or even which ones apply? Greene suggests that you use an *activation*

BOX 4-9

ACTION ASSEMBLY THEORY:

- Focuses not just on cognition or action, but on how inner plans become action.
- Basic concepts:
  Procedural memory (our "how-to" memory)
  Procedural records (content of procedural memory)
  Activation (selecting and processing records)
  Output representations (planned actions yet to be taken)

---

process to select and abstract salient or relevant records. The mind monitors the current situation in terms of the storehouse of procedural records held in memory. When a record is "activated," in essence it has matched at some level (called a *threshold*) the demands of the current situation.

In this sense, then, you compare "what's been done" and "what can work" with "what needs to happen." And in doing so you produce what Greene calls *output representations,* or planned actions that are yet to be taken. In this way the mind makes ongoing sense of the world while maintaining behavioral contact with it. As Greene (1989) explains, his approach is not simply metaphorical: "Once activated, procedural records are assembled, or integrated, to form an output representation of action-to-be-taken. It is the lower levels of this output representation that actually generate and control muscle movements" (p. 121). One simple way to remember action assembly theory's basic idea is to take the label literally. Action assembly theory views the internal assembly of actions as an inherent part of human behavior (see Box 4-9 for an overview).

T E S T I N G   T H E   C O N C E P T S

"If personal experience is really as complex as you say it is, how can I ever hope to know exactly who I am?"

Maybe none of us has enough reliable information to be able to know "exactly" who we are. We cannot use exactness as a criterion for judging our sense of identity. After all, perception is inherently inexact and filtered; conditions and relationships are subject to constant change; and inner speech is often the result of previous biases. And, if role theorists like Goffman (1959) are right, it may be more accurate to talk of our several "selves" that emerge differently as we perceive different situations, rather than a unitary "self." What we call a "self" in everyday talk is both the result of our past selective processes of perception, and the regulator of how perception operates in the present. In this way, a healthy self-concept is like a homeostatic feedback mechanism, our psychological thermostat in a sense, that keeps our perceptual systems balanced.

"Can I ever perceive myself as others perceive me?"

No, not entirely. However, the ability to decenter yourself, disengaging some-what from your own self-centered perspective, can be nurtured. With practice communicating across differences between others and yourself, you likely will become more comfortable and even more accurate imagining how you might appear and sound to others. However, as you might guess, you will create sub-tle and perhaps serious distortions as a result of perceiving their perceptions. This is analogous to what audiologists tell us about human hearing; aside from recordings, none of us is able to hear our own voice as others can because we hear our own voice partially through bone conduction, which no one else can do.

(V.R.): Undoubtedly, however, who others perceive us to be is relevant to who we have become. We observe how others treat us and, at best, infer how they perceive us. I believe I am a funny person. When others laugh at my com-ments, they are reinforcing my belief. Therefore, I make even more humorous remarks while around them. This process becomes cyclical. With other people, however, I may not make silliness a part of my routine, so they react by treat-ing me with more seriousness. I find myself acting more seriously around them. Their perception of me has affected who I think I am, but just as surely, my per-ception of myself has affected who they think I am.

"Do postmodern language theorists believe that science is worthless? That full or true understanding of communication is ultimately impossible?"

It depends on the version of postmodern thought you're consulting. Although some postmodernists vigorously challenge the merit of conventional scien-tific methods, few if any would argue that we shouldn't try to learn more about the physical world. In other words, it's not whether but *how* we conceive of science that's at issue. What kind of theorizing could we do in a different kind of science? Norman Denzin (1992), merging symbolic interactionism and postmodern theory, suggests that the postmodernist's sense of science as-sumes "there can be no science of the real, no theory of the totality, no cu-mulation of verified knowledge. There is only situated, practical activity, or-ganized and legitimated under the heading of one theory or another" (p. 159). Stated this way, a key message of postmodern theory might be: Don't squeeze fundamentally different processes into an artificial box to make them conform to a single set of explanations and definitions. Pay more attention to contexts, situated knowledge, and the ways in which meaning can leak around the edges of our explanatory boxes. Maybe, of course, our best scientists have always done this.

"Can inner speech help me cope with the world by making me more rational?"

Think of inner speech less as a tool and more as a constant process of con-sciousness. It's unlikely that you could "turn off" inner speech even if you wanted to (although some Eastern meditation disciplines aim to "clear the mind" occasionally). Through inner speech, you solve problems creatively, rehearse future actions, and imagine yourself in other people's positions in order to empathize. Therefore, inner speech does help you take the irrational in the world, process it, and thereby make better decisions.

"How do theories of cognitive organization, such as social judgment theory and constructivism, really help *my* communication?"

Theories of cognitive organization can provide you with more sophisticated ways of understanding and defining your interpersonal problems. Consider a hypothetical example: As the chairperson of a student disciplinary action board, you have been asked to explain a controversial board decision to a reporter from the campus newspaper. With your background in social judgment theory, you know to consider carefully the various audiences that might read about your comments in the paper. What kinds of ego involvement do they have in the controversy? Understanding their different levels of ego involvement leads you to predict that some of your comments will almost inevitably be considered unacceptable by readers in audience A, whose latitude of rejection is large. Even statements you consider relatively favorable to this group might stimulate negative reactions. You can predict this if you understand the psychological dynamic of contrast effects, in which some statements are perceived by listeners as being even further away from their positions than they actually are. Similarly, your understanding of cognitive complexity helps you adapt your message so that it might be understandable at the same time to both audience A (whose members' cognitive schemes seem limited to a few constructs, such as "truth" and "deception" or "right" or "wrong") and audience B (whose members, perhaps because of less ego involvement, can process information on the basis of more constructs and "shades of gray"). Being able to "map" the cognitive sophistication of listeners and readers is crucial for effective communication planning (Windahl & Signitzer, with Olson, 1992).

Y O U,   T H E   R E S E A R C H E R

1. Try a brief replication of Bruner and Goodman's 1947 study of children's perception of coin sizes. In social science research, *replication* refers to the process by which scholars attempt to "try a study again," typically by using different subjects or conditions while focusing on the same or similar variables. This strategy is important, because any number of uncontrolled factors could influence the results of a single study—yet ideally we'd like to be able to generalize findings beyond single studies. (Think of this as a "So what if it's true in San Francisco? I live in Peoria" issue.) Although some scholars seem to shy away from studies that replicate earlier ones, perhaps believing them to be less creative and interesting, replication plays an important role in social investigation.

   Begin by reviewing our discussion of Bruner and Goodman's study in this chapter (see p. 109). Then follow these steps to conduct your own research on the topic (or ask your teacher to help you adapt these instructions to a different setting):

- Arrange visits to three second-grade classes, one in a low-income area, one in a middle-income area, and one in a high-income area. You should call first, asking principals and teachers involved for their permission to visit on a certain day.
- With the teacher's permission, pass out blank sheets of 8½-by-11 paper, one per student, and tell the class you'd like them to draw from memory the shape and size of a one-dollar bill. (To make it more interesting for the students, ask them to use their creativity by coloring in the bill in any way they'd like, and by drawing anyone's picture they choose in the middle.)
- Before leaving, measure the length and width of each picture of a bill in centimeters, and determine the mean (average) area of the bill for each class. (Leave the artwork for the teacher to display, to use for teaching a lesson on money and its value, on how people's feelings get reflected in their art, or whatever other points the teacher might like to make.)
- Bruner and Goodman's results provide the basis of your research hypothesis: that the one-dollar bills depicted by students in a low-income area will tend to be larger than the bills depicted by students in middle- and high-income areas. Did this hold true in your small and admittedly simplistic replication?

2. African American writer and actor Ossie Davis (1969) asserts that "The English Language Is My Enemy." Davis noticed that English dictionaries are filled with negative connotations for "black" and "blackness" (e.g., "sullied," "foreboding," "wicked"), whereas "white" is almost always associated with more positive connotations ("purity," "innocence," "genuineness"). He claims that both black and white native speakers of the language cannot help but be affected by their immersion in the values environment of language.

- Form two small groups, one all women and the other all men. Each group should catalog as much evidence as it can for the thesis that *for women,* the English language is an enemy.
- Compare the results of your discussion with the position taken in Lakoff's (1975) critique of language and power in society, *Language and Woman's Place,* or another extended statement of feminist linguistic theory.

3. Manford Kuhn (Kuhn & McPartland, 1954; Hickman & Kuhn, 1956) was a symbolic interactionist who was especially concerned with how a "self" is subjectively experienced. He and his colleagues developed a method called the Twenty Statements Test (TST) that attempted to make

the concept of self more tangible and to make research on self more empirical.

- You can easily administer a rough form of the TST to a friend who isn't taking this course. Hand your friend a stack of twenty blank index cards. Then, simply ask him or her to answer the question "Who am I?" twenty times, each on a different card, and with whatever responses come to mind.
- Later, when you're alone, sort the cards into as many logical categories (piles of cards) as seem appropriate to you. (Examples: all of the three or four cards in one pile seem to refer to social roles the person enacts, such as "I'm a good critic of my husband's work" and "I'm an excellent student." Another pile may seem to relate to self-judgments such as "I'm confused about where I'm going with my life" and "I'm intelligent.")
- Finally, see if you can create tentative labels that characterize what makes each category of statements "hang together." As above, one pile might be labeled "roles," but with another person, there might be no cards at all that would justify this term. Still another subject's responses might justify two different piles of "role" cards, each with their own distinctive characteristics (like "family roles" and "career roles"). Two final research points are important here. First, by creating these labels you are doing a very rough and simplistic form of what empirical researchers call *factor analysis,* or the identification of a set of variables that seem to underlie or give a pattern to the data a researcher collects. Second, your research has produced a tentative *operational model* of your friend's self-concept. Remember that this will be a representation of something that is in constant flux, so you will not have pinned down who your friend is, by any means. Instead, you will have sketched an incomplete picture of how your friend's self-concept is displayed momentarily and in an artificial context. Nonetheless, communication researchers build such models in order to draw tentative generalizations.

4. The *black box* behaviorist approach to the human mind was thoroughly debated by the prominent psychologists B. F. Skinner (1953) and Carl R. Rogers (1959, 1961, 1980). Check your library for either the set of audiotapes of their 1962 debate or excerpts from the transcript that has been published in several print sources. (Although we could give specific reference citations here, regard this as a library scavenger hunt.)

- Listen or read carefully to determine which set of arguments seems most persuasive to you, and why. Which, if any, of Rogers's or Skinner's disagreements seem to be rooted in how each theorist defines terms differently? If so, which ones?

- Although some words will seem like jargon, much of the interchange is remarkably clear even for lay audiences. List terms that are new to you, and look up their meanings in a dictionary of psychology or social science in the reference section of your library.

5. Consistency theories have several distinct emphases. Compare and contrast the basic assumptions of Fritz Heider (1958), Leon Festinger (1957), and Charles Osgood (Osgood & Tannenbaum, 1955) by following these guidelines:

- Consult a survey of theories of social psychology for an overview.
- Research at least one important journal article by each scholar to discover how each characterizes the unique perspectives of his approach.

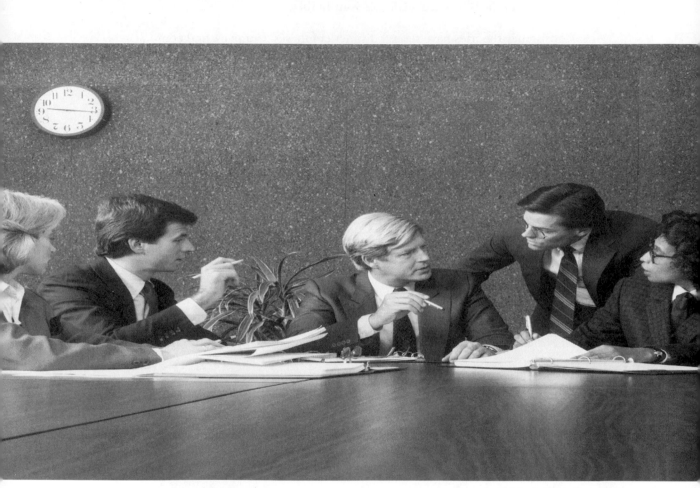

rules and the cooperation of selves

"how *do we know* how to act and what to say?"

The Source of Rules

Defining Rules
Rules in Action
Rules and Laws: Alternatives for Explaining Behavior

Coordinated Management of Meaning (CMM) Theory

Ethnomethodology: Uncovering Everyday Rules

Summary: Testing the Concepts

You, the Researcher

Rules and covering law theories make different contributions to communication theory because they are concerned with different relationships: rules theories are concerned with prescriptive relationships, whereas laws describe mechanistic relationships. Laws provide opportunity for more accurate predictions and controls, but these advantages are limited to mechanistic relationships. Symbolic interaction is dependent on rules and hence prescriptive relationships.

SUSAN B. SHIMANOFF, *COMMUNICATION RULES* (1980, P. 255)

The basic function of human communication in [an interpersonal] system is to regulate consensus . . . to adjust consensus to the need for coordination. The structure of a communication system is the set of rules which constitutes the consensus of the system at a given moment.

DONALD P. CUSHMAN AND DUDLEY D. CAHN JR., *COMMUNICATION IN INTERPERSONAL RELATIONSHIPS* (1985, P. 11)

Think about the last time you sat down with a group of friends to play a new board game or party game. Your first comment might have been, "I've never played this before—someone will have to tell me the rules."

Rules are the prerequisite to social participation. Most of us live our lives alternating between the satisfactions of spontaneity and order. Without spontaneity, we mourn our loss of freedom, creativity, and individuality. Without order, we mourn our loss of predictable social relations, belonging, and stability. In this chapter, we examine some prominent theories about the obvious and subtle social rules that allow our participation, not in formalized board games, but in the gamelike aspects of everyday life. As such, the concept of *communication rules* can be seen as analogous to procedural rules in baseball, in chess, and in filling out income tax forms. However, the analogy isn't completely accurate. Although a communication rule is rarely written down, it is no less a governor of behavior than more official organizational rules.

THE SOURCE OF RULES

Rules allow us to organize and coordinate our lives. They make order out of chaos, uncertainty, and confusion. Football, flirting, solitaire, riding on elevators, business meetings, and even friendships are guided by different sets of formal or informal rules. Imagine a committee with several members, no leader, no agenda, no note takers, and no expectations for what is to take place at meetings. When would the meeting begin? When would it end? How would the members decide what to talk about, and how to react to each other during the time they met? This would seem to be a ruleless, freeform situation. But it's not. Even in such an unstructured environment, rules of some sort will inevitably emerge if the group stays together long enough. In addition, its members enter this group with memories of how other groups in their lives developed and were coordinated. Rules-based communication theorists study how people implicitly and explicitly organize their social experiences. Rules reflect our subtle meanings and expectations for how, when, where, and how long to communicate. We know that in social situations we often adjust to accommodate each other's behavior. But how do we do so? The patterns of adjustment form the rules of the situation.

When do we begin to process information about social rules? While comprehension levels differ, most of us become aware of others' expectations during infancy. At this early stage, we explore our environment and learn from others what's acceptable or unacceptable behavior. The infant who crawls toward the basement stairs learns not to do so when a parent intervenes by picking the child up and saying, "No, away from the stairs." A young child who touches a ceramics collection on the coffee table receives a stern look and a reprimand: "Don't play with that."

As we mature, there are fewer reprimands but just as many rules. Many rules can be broken, of course, but only with consequences. The rules in social systems are rarely codified or openly discussed. Although society operates in a systematic and seemingly coordinated way most of the time, other people seldom literally instruct you how to conform. Did your parents teach you how to stand in line at a fast-food restaurant? (In the United States, most people have similar habits for lining up.) How and when to nod while another person is talking? These things happen so naturally that they seem effortless, but the extent to which these behaviors are patterned and co-orchestrated with others suggests that a very important communication process is occurring. **Rules theory** attempts to define the nature of rule patterns specifically and concretely.

DEFINING RULES

Although the chapter-opening quotations describe what rules accomplish, McLaughlin (1984) provides a more complete definition of *rules* as

> propositions, which may or may not be explicitly available to consciousness, which model our understandings of what behaviors are prescribed or prohibited in certain contexts. Rules may be stored and retrieved in a variety of linguistic forms, but the canonical rule-statement is of the form, "If situation X occurs, do (do not do) Y." Rules may be followed, or not, as the actor chooses; they are value-expressions whose truth cannot be determined. The behavior they prescribe is situation-bound. Rules are subject to alteration by consent of those whom they govern. (p. 21)

Rules, then, can be either implicit (understood at subtle levels) or explicit (obviously and consciously referred to). Consider the seating arrangements at dinnertime for a large family. The eldest sister, because of her high grades last semester, has been awarded the head-of-the-table seat according to the family's decision to reward academic achievement. Who sits where at dinner, then, is partly the result of an explicit nonverbal rule—one that has been decided on and understood by the family as a matter of course. The rule is operative within this particular family culture; however, if guests are invited, they could not be expected to know or predict this specialized formula for seating. At the same time that the explicit rule operates to govern seating patterns, several implicit rules might also be inferred by an alert observer. Although nothing else has been overtly stated about dinner seating, an observer might notice that one of the parents sits at the opposite head of the table, and that the other family members gravitate toward the same seats on the sides of the table every night. It's as though the family group has decided that this is to be expected at dinnertime: "If, during the school year, one of the children receives all As for a semester, then that child is expected (allowed) to sit at one head of the dinner table for the following few weeks." While this explicit rule clearly guides some behavioral choices, implicit rules govern other choices (such as where the other family members sit).

Some implicit rules help us interpret messages that could mean different things at a literal level than they do at the connotative or figurative level. If, for example, a member of our hypothetical family asks, "Can someone pass the salt?" the person closest to the salt shaker is likely to pick it up almost automatically and wordlessly pass it around the table . . . *instead* of responding to the question that was actually asked. Of course the person *can* (is able to) pass the salt, but the question is not interpreted literally. The question actually requests that the salt *be* passed. Similarly, if the phone rings and the caller asks the answerer, "Is Martha there?" and the answer is a simple "yes" or "no" followed by silence, the caller is likely to interpret this literal response as odd or even insulting. The caller expects either Martha to be summoned to the phone or an explanation of why she is unavailable. We thus use implicit rules to transform questions into requests, though we do this at such a natural and automatic level that no one appears to realize that something interesting has happened. It didn't seem extraordinary at all; this is ordinary, taken-for-granted talk. Most rules are just as ordinary, and they are the raw stuff from which cultures are made. Rules are learned developmentally and experientially through direct involvement in communication, not by conscious instruction.

McLaughlin (1984, pp. 18–21) identifies four additional characteristics of rules:

1. *"Rules can be followed; therefore, they can be broken."* Your circle of friends, for example, may have a rule that suggests favors are to be returned. A friend who gives you a ride to the mall thus deserves a ride from you at some later point in time. However, this does not mean that favors are always reciprocated, or that you will always remember when you owe your friend a ride. After all, rules are often broken.

LINKS

• We usually know from the physical and social contexts of communication when not to take someone's questions or comments literally. See Chapter 3 for more on this topic as well as on the other ways context can affect rule-based behavior.
• How is the salt shaker example in this chapter related to speech act theory (discussed in Chapter 4)?

2. *"Rules have no truth-value."* Rules cannot be judged against an absolute standard of authenticity or truth. Rules just exist as they are. Whether you *should* offer a return compliment to someone who's complimented you is not the same as judging whether it's right, ethical, reasonable, or "true" to do so. People often do expect to exchange compliments in most North American cultures. Rules still exist whether or not they are followed in given circumstances, because they are social creations. (Of course, if a rule—like the one for compliments—is rephrased as a description of normative behavior, then that norm could be tested empirically against reality. Thus, for example, the claim that most compliments are followed by return compliments could be researched and found to be true or false.)

3. *"Rules are conditional, but more general than the circumstances they cover."* What we consider appropriate behavior in some classes, or with some people, can be very inappropriate elsewhere. Rules often extend across situations, but cannot be understood except by a situational awareness.

4. *"Rules are 'indeterminate and negotiable.'"* Social rules change as social conditions change. But the rules change only as a result of a coordinated social process, not any individual's mandate. Many times, a new supervisor in an office or factory learns this the hard way. The new boss will have a tough time, for example, getting employees who are used to dressing casually to dress more formally if the employees and their customers are satisfied with casual attire. Persons within these conditions are both governed by, and ultimately governors of, the rules.

rules in action

shimanoff.   In perhaps the best single-volume introduction to rules theory, Shimanoff (1980) observes: "In order for communication to exist, or continue, two or more interacting individuals must share rules for using symbols. Not only must they have rules for individual symbols, but they must also agree on such matters as how to take turns at speaking, how to be polite or how to insult, to greet, and so forth. If every symbol user manipulated symbols at random, the result would be chaos rather than communication" (pp. 31–32). Shimanoff's survey of definitions and approaches in the communication literature leads her to conclude that four rules criteria are generally recognized. Rules (1) are followable, (2) are prescriptive, (3) are contextual, and (4) pertain to behavior. This last criterion assists us in distinguishing between *laws* of human interaction (relatively widespread behavioral patterns that are highly predictable) and *rules*.

First, Shimanoff (1980) specifies that rules must be *followable.* They must be understandable and accessible enough for a person to adhere to. Long ago, a high school gym teacher, who has faded into the dim memory of one of your authors, tried to establish a rule in his class that punishment for "screw-ups" (his term) would be shinning up a rope to the ceiling of the gym. His scheme, however creative and fearful it was, didn't succeed. The punishment simply wasn't possible for many of us, who were yet to develop our upper-body strength. No matter how much we may be motivated psychologically to do something, if we are unable to

L I N K

Recall, from Chapter 1, that we introduced the law/rule distinction in a different context. Later in this chapter, we will explain more about how explanations based on rules differ from those based on laws. As you might imagine, researchers focusing on rules might be interested in using different methods than laws researchers. Why? At this point, can you make an educated guess at what the basic methodological differences might be? Why?

do it the rule is not operative. As Shimanoff explains: "Communication scholars associate rules with actions rather than motions, and actions are behaviors that one may choose to perform; hence, a rule must be capable of being followed" (p. 39).

Second, rules are *prescriptive*. As such, they can be phrased as "If . . . , then . . ." statements that tell what should be done to comply with the rule or, conversely, what will happen if the rule is broken (including how the rule breaker will be held accountable). In the earlier example of the child playing with a collection of ceramic dolls without permission, more than a doll may be broken. Children learn as they mature to accept responsibility for the consequences of their actions. In the example of the ceramics collection, breaking that rule may mean breaking a doll *and* breaking some of the trust between parent and child. Obviously, many of the things we can do in life we choose not to do because of anticipated consequences. Rules, which serve as reminders of the prescriptions behind the consequences, are instruments of social order that tell us how to respond.

In a classroom situation, some kinds of rules are rarely articulated but often enforced: "If a student has a complicated question for the teacher with only two minutes left in class, that question should not be asked" (classmates will groan and ridicule the questioner); "If a student wishes to interrupt in a classroom discussion, then he or she should be careful to interrupt another student, not the professor" (though many faculty personalize class relationships and don't expect deference, students usually recognize a status gap); "If a student comes into the classroom late and in the middle of an ongoing activity, he or she will not immediately start joking with other students" (both other students and the teacher may resent the lateness and the lighthearted attitude about it).

Third, rules are *contextual*. As we discussed in Chapter 3, the interpretation of communication rules usually depends on our surroundings. Loud, raucous, boisterous behavior might be acceptable during a New Year's Eve party at a nightclub, but it would not be appropriate during many church services or public lectures. Interruptions during extended talk might be appropriate in a courtroom or even in a lunchroom, but not at all appropriate while listening to an after-dinner speech at a conference, or while interviewing your college president about the financial status of the institution. Each context sets a stage for behavior (Goffman, 1959).

Finally, rules *pertain to behavior.* Shimanoff (1980) distinguishes between cognition and behavior when she says that rules "may be utilized in making mental evaluations, inferences, judgments, and interpretations of behavior, but rules themselves do not prescribe what one must (must not) or should (should not) think" (p. 50). Because we can't read anyone else's mind, Shimanoff reasons, it is "vacuous" to believe that a system of rules can prescribe cognitions or interpretations. A researcher can observe behaviors to determine if they reflect the presence of social rules, but cannot discern directly what another person is thinking or feeling about a given rule. Only the action that is associated with the rule is visible.

ganz. Joan Ganz (1971) describes three basic ways people interact in relationship to rules: Their interaction may be (1) rule-following, (2) rule-according, or (3) rule-fulfilling.

L I N K

Later in this chapter we will examine a rules-based system called the *coordinated management of meaning.* Developed by Pearce and others (Cronen, Pearce, & Harris, 1982; Pearce, 1989; Pearce & Cronen, 1980), this theory questions whether rules must be founded on behaviors. In this view, *regulative rules,* which are concerned with behaviors, are contrasted with *constitutive rules,* or the mental constructions that guide people in "how to take" or interpret a given message. For example, in our earlier scenario of salt-passing, the basic rule at issue is that the utterance "Can you pass the salt?" should not be taken as constituting a question, but instead as constituting, in context, a request or demand. This distinction is also relevant to our discussion of *speech act theory* in Chapter 4.

Rule-following behavior exhibits a conscious and focused adherence to social rules. It reveals that the participant not only is aware of the situational requirements but also consistently follows them. This kind of chess player, to point to one concrete example, consistently monitors the rules of the game to ensure that each participant complies. This player is likely to remind an opponent of time limits and to comment on another player's humming or toe tapping as distracting. Often, relatively new or insecure players are more likely to act this way than are experienced players (unless they're involved in a tournament).

The person exhibiting *rule-according behavior* also knows the rules, but this person acts on them out of habit. The conscious or intentional acting out of a rule is not typically or necessarily present. A rule-according chess player has integrated the game so thoroughly into personal experience that consistent checking and monitoring is unnecessary. The rule-accordance behavior becomes so natural as to be un-self-conscious. Have you ever driven a long distance and, upon arriving at your destination, found that you were unable to recall many details of the trip, such as stoplights, turns, and speed adjustments? Did it seem as if you were on "automatic pilot"? Even so, you probably responded to the formal rules of driving—which side of the road to drive on, for example, and when to stop and go—without consciously doing so.

Finally, *rule-fulfilling behavior* occurs when the actor performs in ways consistent with existing social rules but without full knowledge or understanding of those rules. Instead, the rules are inferred from the behavior of other people. A passenger steps onto an elevator where three other occupants are facing the door. The conforming behavior will likely precede any conscious reflection about what the rules are in such a situation. Often, new military recruits start saluting officers simply by observing when others salute, not by conscious knowledge of when it is right or wrong to do so. Their choices are rule-fulfilling ones, even if they can't explain the rule fully.

See Box 5-1 for the major concepts employed by Shimanoff and Ganz.

rules and laws: alternatives for explaining behavior

We should note at this point in our discussion that rules theory is a relatively recent development in the communication discipline's attempt to explain human experience. A deeper and more traditional line of theorizing—*covering law theory* (see Chapter 1)—searches for more universal regularities of psychological and so-

---

BOX 5-1

RULES FUNDAMENTALS

- Shimanoff (1980) describes rules as *followable, prescriptive, contextual,* and *relevant to behavior.*
- Ganz (1971) describes how interaction, guided by rules, exhibits *rule-following, rule-according,* or *rule-fulfilling* behaviors.

---

cial processes. It asks: What factors of human life tend to apply across contexts and tend to transcend the uniqueness of individual experience? Covering law theories of communication phenomena are stimulated by the studies and methods of the natural sciences, and tend to search for consistent cause-effect relationships. If the physical "law of gravity" applies in both New York and New Delhi, laws theorists reason, then perhaps diligent social scientists may likewise discover which characteristics of human behavior might be equally applicable in the United States and India, or in 1998 and 1898. These scientists hope to discover laws that are more widely applicable than special-case rules, which they see as having limited explanatory power at best.

Unlike rules theorists, who focus on specific, changeable, and situational patterns, laws theorists tend to ask larger questions about human communication—questions about commonalities in human nature, affiliation, motivation, values, and needs. Although the dichotomy between laws and rules is sometimes a bit too neat, you might think of rules theories as stressing more of the microscopic elements in interaction and of laws theories as stressing the macroscopic. An example of one type of laws approach in communication is Berger's **uncertainty reduction theory** (Berger & Bradac, 1982; Berger & Calabrese, 1975). It suggests that a basic theme of human interaction is to develop strategies that help predict interactional outcomes by attaining additional interpersonal knowledge. Although the strategies may vary, the impetus toward reducing uncertainty will persist, Berger claims.

LINKS

• The logic of general systems theory (see Chapter 1) explains how important homeostasis, or system balance, is for complex organisms and organizations.

• We will discuss exchange theories in more detail in Chapter 6.

Similarly, other forms of human behavior have been explained by law-like generalizations. Cognitive **consistency theory** researchers, for example, study why people's tendency to maintain a state of inner balance, consistency, and congruence seems related to their communication decisions (e.g., Festinger, 1957). Another law-like generalization is found in the work of those who advocate an economic reward/cost **social exchange theory** (Gergen, 1969; Roloff, 1981). Social exchange theorists claim that interaction is guided by people's desire to maximize communication "profits" and "rewards" while minimizing their "losses" and "costs." While each individual's reward structure is somewhat unique (e.g., you might value friendship more than monetary gain), the basic assumption is that people persistently enact economic strategies and judge relationships by what they get out of them relative to what they invest in them.

Both the laws and rules approaches can be justified, and perhaps you've already sensed that both might be necessary in complex explanations. But laws and rules adherents have tended to compete with each other in social science research. In one sense, the competition is odd, because, as one theorist points out, laws may describe nothing more than the basic ways that rules develop and operate (Brown, 1973, p. 165). In another sense, the apparent competition sometimes reflects differing worldviews or explanatory goals of the researchers and theorists. Rules advocates, for instance, have suggested that their counterparts may occasionally oversimplify and overgeneralize in order to presume more commonalities in the theories than can be observed in reality. Maybe this is why Cushman (1977), a rules advocate, claims that the number of "staunch advocates of the laws perspective in the behavioral sciences [is] diminishing. . . . One reason for this decline in support has been the failure of social scientists to locate regularities which have the same degree of generality, necessity, and strong empirical support as the lawful regularities discovered in the natural sciences" (p. 30). Natural science methods and goals may create a misleading exemplar for social science researchers, he fears. Despite this skepticism, laws continue to be sought and identified in communication studies, and they still provide a conceptual alternative to the rules perspective.

Laws, rules, and systems theorists are interdependent in many ways, however. As we will see in the next section, one particular theory attempts to bridge a number of the conceptual gaps in the theoretical landscape. While it is primarily a rules-based approach, it also implies some generalizations of laws theories and the mutual coordination implied by systems theories.

COORDINATED MANAGEMENT OF MEANING (CMM) THEORY

Rules acclimate persons to each other and enable us to coordinate our behaviors. The social order is so complex that, according to some communication research perspectives, it must be constantly negotiated and renegotiated. This notion that communication is a continuous process of spontaneous on-site adjustments and calibrations is a central tenet of **coordinated management of meaning (CMM) theory** (see Box 5-2). We have already sampled its research earlier in this chapter, but we should also acknowledge the ways it differs from other rules approaches.

CMM theory, developed primarily by Pearce and Cronen (1980), integrates systems theory, symbolic interactionism, relational communication, speech act theory, and other theoretical viewpoints. As Cronen, Pearce, and Harris (1982) summarize, "CMM theory describes human actors as attempting to achieve coordination by managing the ways messages take on meaning" (p. 68). Further, the theory accounts for how *co-orientation* (the mutual recognition of an understanding) is not a necessary prerequisite for the development of coordination.

An example paraphrased and expanded from CMM theory will help explain how it differs from other rules-based theories (Cronen et al., 1982, p. 68). Explicit rules—traffic codes—are supposed to govern how people drive on city streets, and certainly implicit rules (when to honk and when not to, etc.) are in play as well. Yet when two drivers approach an intersection (say, at a four-way stop), they bring with them different interpretations of reality. One driver may be a compulsive follower of traffic codes and know them well. The other may be more of an intuitive driver who tends to respond to others' actions. Despite the differences in their knowledge of traffic codes and in their ways of defining and utilizing rules, and despite their inability to read each others' minds, they still manage to avoid hitting each other. Their safe and successful accomplishment of their different driving tasks isn't due primarily to similar definitions of the situation or its rules. Instead, it's due to their mutual and spontaneous recognition of a common situation. That is accomplished spontaneously as each driver monitors

BOX 5-2

THE CMM APPROACH TO RULES

- Assumes that people don't need the same basic understanding about their situation in order to coordinate their behavior through rules.
- Assumes that the social order is heterogeneous.
- Analyzes communication episodes by looking for *coherence, control,* and *valence.*
- Recognizes two types of rules: *constitutive* and *regulative.*
- Identifies a hierarchy of contexts extending from intrapersonal *content,* through *speech acts, contracts,* and *episodes,* to *life scripts.*

---

his or her own behavior along with the other driver's behavior, and develops new and unique rule adjustments for what behavior "means" within that situation. Meaning is thus managed in a coordinated way—and from this insight comes the label *coordinated management of meaning.* Seen in this light, communication rules don't spotlight or dictate what people should do as much as they spotlight how people decide what to do. This difference is significant in CMM theory.

Most other rules-based theories assume that society basically exhibits a *homogeneous social order,* or one that is similar across contexts. In this social order, people generally share the same assumptions about what is right and wrong, appropriate and inappropriate, expected and prohibited in communication situations. In contrast, CMM theory holds that this assumption of homogeneity is suspect because it doesn't account for the myriad times when, for example, students from New York must talk with professors from Wisconsin or when an Oklahoma patient is treated by a doctor new to the United States. Instead, we have a *heterogeneous social order,* which, within some general similarities, is composed of many different tastes, styles, assumptions, language habits, and expectations. CMM theory takes into account both commonalities and differences. Therefore, it becomes especially useful for understanding communication in conflicts, in cross-cultural contexts of high ambiguity, and in ethical quandaries.

Three questions are central in CMM scholars' study of communication *episodes,* which are speech occasions in which communicators can identify beginnings and endings: (1) "What is the coherence?" (2) "What is the control?" and (3) "What is the valence?" *Coherence* is the extent to which actors within situations make sense of the communicative episode. It does not have to be the same for each party, and, in fact, is likely not to be the same. *Control* is the extent to which actors are able to influence what happens in the episode. *Valence* is the extent to which the actors like or dislike the episode that develops.

Obviously, CMM theorists define rules in a somewhat different way than other rules theorists. In CMM theory, rules exist within the cognitive powers of individuals. In this sense, CMM theorists take a more psychological approach to rules, as compared with the more sociological orientation of most other rules theories, such as those surveyed by Shimanoff (1980). However, CMM theory does not ignore larger social and cultural patterns. Rules in CMM theory are for sense-making (achieving coherence), for mutually oriented control (the management dimension), and for organizing patterns of affect (the valence of perceived interaction).

Two types of rules manage meanings in communication: constitutive rules and regulative rules. *Constitutive rules* "organize actors' hierarchies of meaning. They specify how meanings at one level of abstraction may count as meaningful at another level of abstraction. For example, 'You are beautiful' counts as compliment" (Cronen et al., 1982, pp. 73–74). These rules are called constitutive because they "constitute" or make up people's inner senses of meaning. They also account for why the comment "You are beautiful" might "count as" an insult if it was voiced sarcastically in a given context. *Regulative rules* organize the constitutive rules into guidelines for behavior. What kinds of actions emerge from the interpretations of the actors?

Years before the development of CMM theory, Ruesch and Bateson (1968) asserted that "a social situation is established when people have entered into communication; the state of communication is determined by the fact that a person perceives that his perception has been noted by others . . ."(p. 28). Clearly, social situations are held together by the coordination of rules: "Any social situation is governed by explicit or implicit rules; these rules may be created on the spur of the moment for a particular situation, or they may be the result of centuries of tradition. In the context of communication, rules can be viewed as directives which govern the flow of messages from one person to another. . . . Rules can be viewed as devices which either stabilize or disrupt a given communication system, and they provide directives for all eventualities" (Ruesch & Bateson, 1968, pp. 27–28). CMM research focuses on the immediate episodes in which rules are created and employed to manage meanings. However, it does not deny the existence of more persistent, socially based rules.

Remember that Ruesch and Bateson's model of communication contexts emphasized the number of communicators involved at each level. As you might expect, the CMM hierarchy of contexts emphasizes somewhat different factors that relate to the interpersonal meanings for relationships. Phillipsen (1995) notes that although CMM theorists present varying versions of its hierarchy in different publications, the levels can be summarized as: Level 1 (*content* of personal experience, such as perceptions or cognitions); Level 2 (*speech act*, such as whether an utterance counts as a question, a threat, or other functional category); Level 3 (*contract*, the system of mutual "understandings" that characterize any specific interpersonal relationship); Level 4 (*episode*, a series of speech acts that appear to participants to have an identifiable beginning and end); and Level 5 (*life script*, how a person uses many episodes to create an identifiable style of managing meanings with others. Obviously, the higher levels of context are in many ways more powerful in influencing how communicators choose to coordinate their communicative acts.

Rules are present in any social situation. But remember that people in social settings assume roles that are affected by their adherence to, rejection of, or willingness to coordinate relevant rules. Most people who attend church services know the basic expectations: In many churches they are to enter quietly, take a seat in the pew, maintain silence, participate at the appointed times, and so forth. These factors, taken together, might define in part the role of worshiper as it would be seen from the outside, if we assume that all worshipers are fundamentally similar (the ho-

L I N K

See Chapter 3 for a discussion of Ruesch and Bateson's (1968) influential model of social context in communication.

mogeneous social order assumption applied to churches). But what counts as worshiping in the interpretations of the various people in the church if we adopt instead the heterogeneous assumption that differences abound even within seemingly similar groups? These rules are in the interpretations of the communicators, not merely in their behavior patterns. Using these rules, then, communicators might achieve a coherent social interaction, even if someone in the fourth pew thinks a teenager's style of clothing constitutes irreverent behavior and is annoyed by it.

ETHNOMETHODOLOGY: UNCOVERING EVERYDAY RULES

Ethnomethodology, pioneered by sociologist Harold Garfinkel (1967), is an intensive microscopic look at the common and ordinary ways people employ their concepts of the world. Based on a phenomenological and experiential approach to symbolic interaction (Rogers, 1983), an ethnomethodologist's task, according to Garfinkel (1967), involves learning how people in everyday settings, without realizing they're doing anything remarkable, make practical sense of their complex social experience and translate that "common sense" into action. Ethnomethodology, which literally means "the people's methods," tries to uncover "the formal properties of commonplace, practical common sense actions, 'from within' actual settings, as ongoing accomplishments of those settings" (p. viii).

The reason the "folk communication" approaches of Garfinkel are examples of *phenomenology*, a term that sounds intimidating and distant for many beginning students, is that phenomenologists are philosophers and social researchers who "study situations in the everyday world from the viewpoint of the experiencing person. This experiential view helps phenomenologists understand people and human life so that they can work effectively with them" (Becker, 1992, p. 7). This brief definition does not indicate the richness of phenomenological research, but it does clarify why many rules theorists believe that understanding communication involves studying real people's attempts to make everyday experience meaningful.

Garfinkel and other ethnomethodologists who followed him (e.g., Sudnow, 1978) try to show how the most ordinary aspects of our daily lives are amazing accomplishments of coordination. Instead of using the "taken-for-granted" assumptions (Schutz, 1967) that most of us use, Garfinkel seems to ask, "What if we regard these acts as 'problematic'; that is, as a series of coordinated solutions to quite complex problems?" In this way, ethnomethodology studies the most mundane and trivial events of our lives (such as expressing agreement with others or walking into a room) in order to find the fundamental significance within them. Because many of these actions are so mundane that social actors forget about them, Garfinkel's methods are designed to get people to unearth these buried and invisible assumptions. In one exercise, for instance, he asked students to engage in ordinary conversations with friends outside of class, but with one important difference: "without indicating that what the experimenter was asking was in any way unusual, to insist that the person clarify the sense of his commonplace remarks" (1967, p. 42). Here's an excerpt from one case example:

The victim waved his hand cheerily.

(S) How are you?

(E) How am I in regard to what? My health, my finances, my school work, my peace of mind, my . . . ?

(S) (Red in the face and suddenly out of control.) Look! I was just trying to be polite. Frankly, I don't give a damn how you are. (Garfinkel, 1967, p. 44)

Only by interfering with normal rules and assumptions, Garfinkel argues, do we expose those rules for study. Otherwise, they simply blend into our cultural context as subtle, nearly invisible accompaniments to everyday life. Garfinkel's research revealed what CMM researchers also found, that implicit rules prohibit taking literally the questions in some greetings, because to do so is to complicate interaction unnecessarily. The meaning of the interchange could not be inferred from the words alone; knowledge of the rules that manage everyday talk is also required. Although this may sound trivial, it's actually a very practical reminder to travelers in different cultures, for example, who carry their handy little phrasebooks or hand-held computer translators and expect these tools to be enough to get them by.

Mitchell (1978) suggests that Garfinkel's ethnomethodology "would maintain that since no situation is completely covered by rules for 'communicative interchanges' . . . all members in all situations employ documentary methods for practical theorizing to ferret out and to communicate the sense of what is going on" (p. 153). Ordinary people in everyday situations, in other words, behave very much like social scientists. When it comes to communication, we are all theorists, practitioners, and researchers.

> **L I N K**
>
> Review in Chapter 1 the discussion of theorizing as an everyday occurrence. Are there any dangers of over-theorizing or overanalyzing in everyday life?

T E S T I N G   T H E   C O N C E P T S

"Do different cultures inevitably have different rules?"

Not inevitably, but they're often different enough that you're likely to be surprised constantly. You should expect when traveling or communicating cross-culturally that you're likely to behave in some ways that are quite "natural," "normal," and "reasonable" to you, but that an observer from the other culture will consider ridiculous, thoughtless, or even insulting. Communication thus depends to a large extent on the implicit expectations that each culture builds into its everyday interaction styles—thereby enacting its "rules." Because many such rules regulate nonverbal communication, they tend to be subtle, contextually diverse, and difficult to control. At the same time, they define relationships powerfully. Perhaps the best "rules" for cross-cultural communicators to follow are (1) expect to be surprised and (2) become a good ethnomethodologist.

"You claim that as communicators, 'we are all theorists, practitioners, and researchers.' I understand that I have to theorize, but when am I necessarily researching communication in everyday life?"

In your own way, each day, you theorize about better ways of doing things or of thinking about particular subjects. For example, you suspect that a different style of shooting a basketball would help you hit more free throws, or that studying with your friend would improve your grades in history. To develop the theories, however, you must first have a need to change particular behaviors (you want to hit more free throws or you want to improve your grades to get a scholarship). Perhaps you solicit the advice of friends ("Do you study better alone or in a group?") or note how specialists solve problems similar to yours (by observing the free-throw shooting styles of professional NBA players). When you do so, you are conducting research.

Therefore, think of research as the active link that narrows the gap between what you are able to do now and what you would like to be able to do. Similarly, rules theorists attempt to illuminate how humans act together to get things done. If the rules are functional (if the methods "work"), then teachers, trainers, students, and others will be better able to adjust their own behaviors accordingly.

"At my college, there are many rules that students have to follow. The administration calls them 'traditions.' What's the difference?"

Traditions are customs, ways of talking, or behaviors that are handed down from generation to generation. They are discussed and experienced mutually in a particular community or culture, and in many ways they define that community or culture. Communicative rules are often based on traditions. Rules that are based on strongly held traditions may pass from implicit understandings ("People usually go to church on Wednesdays on campus") to explicit prescriptions ("Everyone must attend chapel on Wednesday or submit a doctor's note to be excused").

Y O U,   T H E   R E S E A R C H E R

1. As a result of being an alert observer of your communication theory class, describe the regulative rules that seem to guide when students ask questions or make comments in class. How do such rules help predict when students engage in or avoid class participation? How are the rules governing content, context, timing, tone, turn taking, and topic relevance displayed in the classroom? List as many regulatory rules as you can think of, and describe each one as an "If . . . , then . . ." statement.

2. Locate two articles in communication journals, one that supports rules theory as a viable approach to explaining interpersonal communication, and one that criticizes or questions the merits of rules theory. Hint: The National Communication Association (formerly the Speech Communication Association) publishes an index to articles in communication journals (Matlon, 1992), and a number of other indices and databases are also available to help you avoid the legwork and time-consuming (but often interesting!) browsing in the stacks. Discuss your findings in class.

3. Ethnomethodologists often study familiar communication encounters by actually interfering with participants' normal routines. They want to discover what happens when expectations that are taken for granted are violated. They learn interesting things about the familiar by making it "strange." Try conducting an informal ethnomethodological study of your own:

- During the course of one or more days, make a point of asking family members and friends with whom you talk to clarify comments that they expect you to understand without clarification (e.g., "You know what I mean" or "I bombed out on that test"). Avoid indicating that what you're doing is unusual. Present your inquiries as neutral, sincere requests for more information (e.g., "What do you mean, you 'bombed out' on the test?" or "What do you mean by 'I'm having a good time tonight'?"). You might even choose to question the most mundane or trivial assumptions: if someone asks "How are you?", answer something like, "How am I? Compared to what?"
- Immediately after each conversation, take notes on the other person's verbal and nonverbal reactions to your questioning. Also describe how the person expressed frustration with the interference you caused in the flow of the conversation.
- Examine the data you have collected. What conclusions can you draw about people's expectations for the *ease* of conversation? For the *accuracy* of communication? What conversational rules are at work here? Discuss your findings in class. Consult Garfinkel's book, *Studies in Ethnomethodology* (1967), for some entertaining examples of how people demonstrate their underlying expectations when those expectations are violated.

communicative
interdependence
"is autonomy overrated?"

"Ensnared" in Narcissism?

What Do People Need as Communicators?
X Social Exchange Theory: Rewards
   American Pragmatism: Social Contact
X FIRO Theory: Inclusion, Control, and Affection

Relational/Interactional Theory
   Axiom 1: "The Impossibility of Not Communicating"
   Axiom 2: "The Content and Relationship Levels of Communication"
   Axiom 3: "The Punctuation of the Sequence of Events"
   Axiom 4: "Digital and Analogic Communication"
   Axiom 5: "Symmetrical and Complementary Interaction"

Interpersonal Perception Theory

Dialectical Theory

Dialogic Theory
   Buber: Dialogic Meeting
   Rogers: The Person-Centered Approach
   Gadamer: Hermeneutics and Productive Communication

Dramaturgical Theory
   The Theatrical Metaphor
   Burke: The New Rhetoric of Identification
   Goffman: Impression Management
   Bormann: Symbolic Convergence

Summary: Testing the Concepts

You, the Researcher

Our uniqueness is not *in* us. It is something which comes to be as we respond to what is not ourselves. This sort of love, this sort of relationship takes place *between* persons and cannot be counted on as a social technique at our disposal.

MAURICE S. FRIEDMAN, *TOUCHSTONES OF REALITY* (1974, p. 262)

Recently, a student we'll call Mary enrolled in an interpersonal communication class. Her contributions to class discussions and her papers were excellent. She took readily to the concepts of communication and understood them well. She came to believe that the course material was intensely relevant to her daily life and began to apply the concepts to her most important relationships, those within her immediate family.

So far, so good. Every teacher probably hopes to encourage just this kind of practical spirit in students. For such students, class is not just for memorizing distantly formed sets of facts, but an opportunity to try things out, to experiment with what works in daily life.

But Mary had a few problems. Although she found that her communication skills did improve, her goal of taking these improvements home with her was more difficult to accomplish than she'd initially thought. She became discouraged with the members of her family. They seemed to become even more annoying to her as the course went on. She learned how to improve her listening but became more upset than ever when her husband and children listened poorly to her. She tried out the listening "techniques" from the textbook, but the family just thought she was talking weird, and accused her of playing games with them. She tried "assertiveness" and "self-disclosure," as the text suggested, but found that her husband longed for the predictability of their former roles and wished she wasn't taking those stupid university classes after all.

What went wrong? Were the theories and skills stressed in class wrong? Was the teacher wrong for encouraging real-life applications and for stressing practical implications of the theories? Was the family wrong in impeding Mary's personal growth and development? Was Mary wrong, or just not effective enough in trying out these skills? Did she (or her teacher) misunderstand what the theories really say? All of these are relevant questions, and they strike at the very heart of justifying communication study in the first place.

As we've seen in earlier chapters, people often assume that communication is an activity that you can train yourself to accomplish: "I communicated that to him, but he evidently wasn't listening" or "She's an excellent communicator—I know she'll do well in her job interview." This assumption is also reflected in how communication programs are often assessed: The individual's behaviors or behavioral potentials are measured in order to determine "communication competence." Although the ability to recall information, prepare a well-organized five-minute talk, or phrase a focused question are all obviously *related* to communication, the sum of individual skills will never equal communicative competence (Spitzberg & Cupach, 1984). People communicate within systems of relations that establish their own constraints.

We might ask, then: Was Mary necessarily a better communicator by having taken the class? Maybe not. Possibly, if the class encouraged her to think individualistically, to search for increased autonomy and independence from others' messages and expectations, and perhaps even to hope for more self-actualization and self-respect (as if these qualities could be quantified), then Mary's communication with others could have deteriorated in quality, even while her self-confidence was strengthened in the short run. Maybe the class didn't encourage this outcome at all but simply gave Mary the tools with which to lead herself in this individualized direction. Teachers, researchers, and theorists alike have become increasingly suspicious of communication measures that presume participants to be autonomous bundles of behaviors and skills. A person may develop better *skills* in speaking and listening, but these skills do not necessarily translate into *communicative competence*. As Maurice Friedman (1974) reminds us in the chapter-opening quotation, competence in communication finds its wellsprings in interdependence, not in techniques.

"ENSNARED" IN NARCISSISM?

Despite Friedman's suspicion of technique, much of American popular culture encourages a self-orientation. One recent sociological survey points to several dominant social trends, including a concern for managing others competitively and a desire to seek personal fulfillment therapeutically (Bellah, Madsen, Sullivan, Swidler, & Tipton, 1986). Both trends emphasize an autonomous self as the perceived avenue to success and as the most valid style of communication. Lasch (1979), although he seems to exaggerate often for effect, captures much of this trend in American culture when he describes our "culture of narcissism." Communication researchers motivated by such concerns (Vangelisti, Knapp, & Daly, 1990) have investigated what is called _conversational narcissism,_ a construct they trace in part to the work of sociologist Charles Derber (1979). A conversational narcissist works to shift attention to the self and away from other persons or a shared problem orientation.

In discussing how traditional societies can only survive through a tradition of interdependence, Derber (1979) critiques American cultural trends: "America is developing . . . not toward greater community or cooperation, but toward an intensification of the entrenched individualism. The continuing decline of the family, the neighborhood, and other 'community' institutions along with the strengthening of capitalist values and institutions suggests the yet further ensnarement of the individual" in individualistic conditions. Moreover, Derber fears that social relations will be even more dehumanized as people become "preoccupied with . . . personal growth" and "increasingly incapable of transcending a highly complex but intensified egocentricity" (pp. 93–94).

Derber did not make a complex theoretical point, but he was suggesting something more complicated than that Americans are selfish. He sketched the backdrop for the kind of theoretical discussions we need to have more often in the communication field. If communication is seen simply as what an individual can

LINK

Both the individual and community perspectives are important standards for making ethical judgments. We suggest some ethical implications of Derber's point about individualism precluding community in Chapter 10, where we look at *communitarian* theorizing in communication ethics. Other theorists of ethics, as you'll see in that chapter, are more concerned with protecting individual rights and the freedom of communicative choice.

will through skills, we reinforce the "ensnarement" (to use his term) of people within individualistic assumptions. Such assumptions are embedded in the culture. But despite them, communication is not something *I* do; communication is a *we* process. The result (and, therefore, the criterion) of communication competence is not autonomy but interdependence.

Mary wasn't being selfish by trying out her newly found communication skills in her family life. She had every right to believe that she was better equipped to help establish effective communication. Studying communication is highly practical. But it isn't ultimately dependent on building skills if the appreciation of interdependence doesn't accompany them.

If you agree that autonomy is overrated and overemphasized, maybe you are curious about which theories of interpersonal life are most helpful in addressing this imbalance. These may turn out to be the most practical theories of all for you.

In this chapter, we ask some basic questions about communication interdependence. We begin by discussing what needs people attempt to satisfy through communication. Next, we survey several different approaches to the fundamentally mutual and social nature of interpersonal communication: the relational/interactional theory of the "Palo Alto" group; the interpersonal perception theory of Laing; the dialectical theory of Baxter and others; the dialogical theories as developed and applied in various ways by Buber, Rogers, and Gadamer; and the dramaturgical theories of Burke, Goffman, and Bormann.

WHAT DO PEOPLE NEED AS COMMUNICATORS?

To anthropologist Ashley Montagu (1962), "the individual is a myth. There are no individuals. There are many persons, however, who try to be individuals, who endeavor to live their lives separate and apart from their fellow human beings" (p. 61). Are they successful in this attempt? Or do they need more? One group of theorists suggests that communicators use relationships to obtain the individual rewards they think they need. However, other theorists reply that motives for communication are more complicated, and that people need social contact itself, for its own sake. The answers to these questions are especially revealing when we consider whether there is such a thing as a particularly *human* nature.

social exchange theory: rewards

Recently you may have said, or heard someone say, something like this: "Why don't you drop him? What are you getting out of that relationship, anyway? He's just exploiting you." Such statements are common enough to suggest that we typically reflect on the quality of our communication and try to evaluate the cost of our relationships relative to their rewards. "Is it worth it?" we ask.

One possible answer to the question "What do communicators need?" comes from *social exchange theory* (see Box 6-1). Researchers and commentators from this tradition (Blau, 1964; Homans, 1961; Thibaut & Kelley, 1959) tend to answer the question in a relatively individualistic way. Despite the fact that most exchange theorists have taken a sociological approach to studying communication, they conceptualize dyadic communication as the individual's primary means for attaining desired rewards and reinforcements. However, their individualistic tone is tempered by a relational requirement. The viability of social exchange rests on the assumption that human beings recognize each other's life situations, notice each other's needs, and in some ways are likely to engage in *reciprocity*—a condition in which a response is correlated to the worth of the original message (Gouldner, 1960). In other words, humans act with other humans in full recognition that their acts will be noticed and in some way reciprocated (i.e., that they will receive a return on their communicative investment).

According to Blau (1963), this economic analogy is at the core of social exchange theory: "The distinctive character of a social exchange is that one person furnishes a service to another and, while there is a general expectation of some future return, there is no advance stipulation of the precise nature of the return" (p. 139). Thus, Blau continues, "social exchanges . . . entail services that create unspecified obligations in the future and therefore exert a pervasive influence on social relations" (p. 140). *Rewards* are constantly being compared to *costs*. It's not just the individual motive to get rewarded that is important here, Blau explains, but beyond that, the establishment of an economic base for the relationship in which the partner feels a "requirement to reciprocate in order to receive further benefits" (p. 140). What an individual feels rewarded by, of course, will vary from person to person. Accompanying a roommate to a play may function as a reward for some people and as a frustrating cost for others.

Persons in relationships naturally compare their rewards versus their costs, in an attempt to achieve a form of communication "profit." Thibaut and Kelley (1959) conceptualize this phenomenon in terms of the *comparison level (CL)* phenomenon. A CL, simply stated, is an inner standard set by the individual that indicates an acceptable level of satisfaction in a relationship or situation, on the basis of various forms of social judgment and past experience. In effect, this means that persons symbolically model how their needs should be met and create expectations below which they will not feel satisfied. For example, a classmate whose company you enjoy but who consistently forgets about you when she's promised to come over and share chemistry notes, probably wouldn't meet your CL for friendship. The enjoyable and rewarding conversation you share is more than counterbalanced by a cost—the annoying inconvenience of waiting around for her all the time. However, does not achieving this CL standard mean that you'll end your relationship with her? Not necessarily. To answer this question, Thibaut and Kelley would theorize that you also generate another standard—a *comparison level for alternatives* (written as CL_{alt}). This means that you compare the rewards and costs of your existing relationship to the anticipated rewards and costs that you would receive if you ended the relationship. If the CL_{alt} is low, you might be willing to put up with her annoying and unpredictable behavior (if, for example, as a new student on campus you hadn't made many friends yet, you might imagine that without this classmate you'd have no one to talk with at school). Your relationship with her is below your CL for such relations (i.e., it is far from ideal), but it is above

BOX 6-1

SOCIAL EXCHANGE THEORY:

- Presumes that people communicate by trying to achieve relational "profit" by producing more *rewards* than *costs*.
- Depends on an expectation of *reciprocity* in maintaining relationships.
- Assumes that people evaluate relationships for their exchange potential by employing *comparison levels* and *comparison levels for alternatives*.

---

your CL_{alt} (i.e., it is better than you currently expect to be able to establish with other classmates).

Social exchange theory encourages an image of human interaction as a calculation and, to some extent, of human beings as interpersonal accountants. In suggesting that we monitor ourselves and each other in this manner, theorists seem vulnerable to charges that they demean or dehumanize communication. They might even be seen as contributing to the conversational narcissism we discussed earlier. Although social exchange concepts are individualistic in some ways, you shouldn't forget that the basis for exchange in the first place is an expectation of reciprocity. Humans ultimately are not individualized and isolated schemers; rather, they cooperate with, rely on, and need each other in a variety of subtle ways.

Before examining the nature of relationships more completely, let's look briefly at two other views on what communicators need, one derived from philosophy and the other from psychology.

american pragmatism: social contact

Although the human mind is capable of considering itself a separate and independent unit, studies of culture and socialization demonstrate just how dependent individuals are on interaction with others, even for their sense of self. As persons become more and more individualized (increasingly unique in personality and in the experiences that differentiate them from others), they become less and less individualistic and more and more socialized (Montagu, 1962). Their interwoven connections with others make this inevitable.

Whether you like it or not, then, you are never totally separate from the interests, attitudes, actions, and, most importantly, the influence of others. This doesn't mean that you can't make your own decisions or try to gain more control over your actions than you had, say, last month. Our point is not that you are buffeted around in a sea of social forces and pressures, where waves take you in unpredictable and uncontrollable directions. Language gives you the potential to establish a personal direction. But interpersonal contact is the foundation for the differentiation that's possible with language. Without interpersonal contact, you could not think of yourself as a separate being. Yet with that contact, you realize that you can never be truly separable.

One of the most influential social philosophies in twentieth-century American thought has been *pragmatism* (Dewey, 1927, 1934). Scholars in this tradition tried to test the findings of the natural and social sciences against the experienced effects of ideas, and they taught that the essential meaning of any concept or idea is in the effects it is observed to initiate. Philosopher Cornel West (1993) claims that the best characterization of pragmatism is that of C. I. Lewis: "Pragmatism could be characterized as the doctrine that all problems are at bottom problems of conduct, that all judgments are, implicitly, judgments of value, and that, as there can be ultimately no valid distinction of theoretical and practical, so there can be no final separation of questions of truth of any kind from questions of the justifiable ends of action" (quoted in West, 1993, p. 109).

Pragmatists, therefore, including philosopher John Dewey (1927), psychologist William James (1896), and language theorist C. S. Peirce (1931–1958), look at the ways social effects are integrated into individual experience. Dewey's work is very much associated with the symbolic interactionist ideas we surveyed in Chapter 4. Although much American philosophy has taken an individualistic turn, Dewey maintains a balanced view of the link between person and society. Consistent with the ideas of George Herbert Mead (1934), Dewey (1927) thought that selves and social forces define each other: "Any human being is in one respect an association, consisting of a multitude of cells each living its own life. And as the activity of each cell is conditioned and directed by those with which it interacts, so the human being whom we fasten upon as individual *par excellence* is moved and regulated by his associations with others; what he does and what the consequences of his behavior are, what his experience consists of, cannot be described, much less accounted for, in isolation" (p. 188).

firo theory: inclusion, control, and affection

Psychologist William Schutz (1966), researching his *FIRO (fundamental interpersonal relations orientation) theory*, identifies three basic interpersonal needs: *inclusion*, *control*, and *affection* (see Box 6-2). Although he believes that persons seek ways to fulfill these three needs, his system does not presume that all persons are equally motivated by them or that the needs can predict human behavior precisely in any given circumstance.

Inclusion, as Schutz (1966) uses the term, is similar to the idea of interpersonal contact. It refers to people's need to be recognized as participants in human interaction. People generally need to associate with others and to have their associations noted. Although people also value privacy and aloneness on many occasions, they seem at the same time to have lingering fears of being abandoned, ignored, or renounced by others. An absence of inclusion, suggests one medical researcher (Lynch, 1977), can be fatal, because the human body and mind are linked in this need for interpersonal connection.

If feeling included is a baseline condition for healthy human existence, then the need to make a difference—*control*—is the next logical level. Schutz here is not referring to a desire to have one's own way all the time or to manipulate others

LINKS

• One common theme in this chapter's theories is that humans seek out and "need" social contact in order to become psychologically whole and mature. As noted in Chapter 4, symbolic interactionists argue that it is only through such contact that we become and remain distinct individuals. For an effective blend of symbolic interactionist cultural theory with pragmatism, see Norman Denzin's *Symbolic Interactionism and Cultural Studies* (1992).

• The social contact we need must have a practical impact. William James, a prominent thinker in the tradition of American pragmatism, offers an interesting perspective (originally appearing in a 1907 newspaper interview) on our discussion of the relationship between theory and practice in Chapter 1:

Reality as such is not truth, and the mind as such is not a mere mirror. Mind *engenders* truth *upon* reality; and as our systems of truth are themselves part of reality (and indeed for us its most important parts), we may say that reality in its largest sense does grow by human thinking. Hence arises the idea that our minds are not here simply to copy a reality that is already complete. They are here to complete it, to add to its importance by their own remodeling of it, to decant its contents over, so to speak, into a more significant shape.

In point of fact, the *use* of most of our thinking is to help us to *change* the world. We must for this know definitely *what* we have to change; and thus theoretic truth must at all times come before practical application. But the pragmatist writers have shown that what we here call theoretic truth is itself full of human contradictions. It will be as irrelevant unless it fits the momentary purpose in hand, as our ideas will be irrelevant when they do not fit the reality—the two factors must fit each other. . . . Thus we seem set free to use our theoretical as well as our practical faculties—practical here in the narrower sense—to get the world into a better shape, and all with a good conscience. (James, 1982, p. 133)

In Chapter 8 you'll read about the questions raised by theorists of persuasion. What does Schutz's work suggest about why people might feel impelled to try to persuade others to change their beliefs, attitudes, or actions?

in a bossy manner. These aggressive desires have been studied elsewhere in the communication literature; for example, *Machiavellianism* (named for the sixteenth-century Italian author of *The Prince*) is the interpersonal willingness to manipulate others for personal gain. Schutz's use of the term *control* is more neutral, referring to people's desires to make a difference in their social environments and to have some say over what happens. If there is no such sense of control, persons feel they are at the mercy of others or vulnerable to the whims of fate. They are less likely to attempt significant projects or to initiate interaction with others. They become, in other words, spectators and not participants in living.

Finally, according to Schutz (1966), people need *affection;* that is, they seek a sense of interpersonal warmth or of being liked or loved. Friendship and other intimate relations often serve this function, of course, and the absence of such relationships is a source of much of the alienation we feel from time to time. Even though someone might be noticed consistently, and even have a measure of power over others, existence still might seem empty. In this dimension of interpersonal need, as with the other two, people's behaviors and desires vary widely. Obviously, people don't just *have* (or not have) affection (or inclusion or control)—they *experience* it to some degree in relation to its opposite or its absence.

RELATIONAL/INTERACTIONAL THEORY

A touchstone of modern communication theory is Watzlawick, Beavin (now Bavelas), and Jackson's *Pragmatics of Human Communication* (1967). Its authors, therapists and researchers at the Mental Research Institute in Palo Alto, California, are collectively referred to, along with other colleagues, as the Palo Alto group. They thought that a unified theoretical synthesis was needed to explain the everyday conflicts that surprise and frustrate people in their families and workplaces. Although they discovered part of that synthesis from their mentor, Gregory Bateson, they wanted to explore an even wider landscape of contemporary thought in the social sciences, mathematics, literature, and philosophy. As they write early in the book, " . . . a phenomenon remains unexplainable as long as the range of observation is not wide enough to include the context in which the phenomenon occurs" (pp. 20–21). The relationship between what is studied (whether it is a person, a behavior, an object, or something else) and its environment is where scientists must concentrate their attention. Although this insight had already taken hold in the natural sciences by the mid-1960s, the social sciences, they thought, were still searching for the "properties," "characteristics," or "traits" that were assumed to make people more or less social, more or less communicative. This stress on *relationship function* as a representation of communication, in contrast to the message transmission and reception model, is the most significant contribution of the Palo Alto group. As the researchers explain: "The observer of human behavior . . . turns from an inferential study of the mind to the study of the observable manifestations of relationship" and "the vehicle of these manifestations is communication" (Watzlawick et al., 1967, p. 21).

Pragmatics of Human Communication is not a work of pop psychology. The authors wrote for professionals and translated and applied many of the trends of the day from general systems theory, information theory, existential thought, the philosophy of paradox, and their own "home base" of psychological and psychiatric research. Gradually, they drew from and inspired an even wider range of colleagues and research (Watzlawick & Weakland, 1977; Watzlawick, Weakland, & Fisch, 1974).

Despite the technical, occasionally dense prose of *Pragmatics*, the book is surprisingly readable. The authors, for the most part, provide clear definitions of terms and apply their theoretical insights to both the daily dilemmas of real people and examples from the literary world. An extended analysis of Edward Albee's play *Who's Afraid of Virginia Woolf?* shows how systems analysis can be applied to interpersonal relationships. Although the authors were modest about the completeness of their book (p. 13), there can be no doubt about the extent of its ambition. In many ways, the book is a model of interdisciplinary synthesis in the social sciences. If we had to choose one professional book to recommend to communication undergraduates, both for its historical and conceptual values, this would be it. Don't be put off by the age of the book. Much of the literature in interpersonal communication over the past thirty years can't be understood apart from its connection to this reorienting work. Further, much of the current debate over how to define communication can be traced to the 1967 Watzlawick, Beavin, and Jackson position.

Although the discussions of psychotherapeutic implications and applications to family therapy are fascinating in this and other works by the Palo Alto group, our focus here is on the five influential "axioms" of the theory.

L I N K

Disagreements about how to define communication will probably always characterize the discipline, and much of this disagreement is healthy. See Chapter 2 for more on this controversy.

axiom 1: "the impossibility of not communicating"

As mental health professionals, these authors were just as curious about the sources of misunderstanding as they were in the achievement of understanding. Obviously, these aren't different concepts, but the same issue approached from different perspectives. Yet the different perspectives can yield different questions as well as different answers. If behavioral researchers assume, as most did before the publication of *Pragmatics,* that communication is only the receiver's achievement of the sender's understanding, then they will tend to study those acts that attempt to produce congruent understanding in senders and receivers. Some of those behaviors will be found to be communicative (i.e., "successful"), while others will not.

Pragmatics turns this perspective on its head. Watzlawick, Beavin, and Jackson note that because "full" understanding is not achievable (that would be mind reading), it is practical to think of any behavior that leads to an understanding of the relations between people as having message value. "Behavior has no opposite," they claim. It's impossible for silence or absence, for example, not to be perceived as messages by others who notice them, whether or not they were specifically intended as messages by the actors. (Are you avoiding communication by skipping class or by not turning in a paper, or are you just substituting new messages that you and your teacher might interpret in the relationship?) In recent years, some communication scholars have questioned axiom 1 by stressing intention in message formation. But the axiom reminds us that listeners and receivers may, as a part of *their* intention, attach communicative significance to any behavior.

axiom 2: "the content and relationship levels of communication"

Whenever persons speak, they perform dual functions. Each communicator provides information (or "content") for the other, and each suggests (directly or indirectly) the type of relationship they share. Bateson (see Ruesch & Bateson,

1951) calls these functions the *report dimension* (content) and the *command dimension* (relationship). These are simultaneously present in communication, according to the Palo Alto group. For example, take the simple statement, "Loan me your car this afternoon." On the surface, the statement refers to a car and when it's needed for transportation. This is its *content level* of communication. The message is about a car. But what else is it "about?" Is there another level of description that would help communicators understand more thoroughly what is going on here?

The Palo Alto theorists would say that in this example, the content of the statement is basically equivalent to, say, "I'd like to borrow your car this afternoon." But the two statements are experientially quite different at the *relationship level* of communication. The first one ("Loan me your car . . .) implies that the speaker has developed within the relationship a right to demand a loan of the car and, therefore, is in some ways more powerful than the listener. This message level can hardly be more important, for it is the way people often signal put-downs and even compliments without coming right out and identifying such messages as negative or positive. The relationship level is experienced as important, but it can be denied overtly by communicators if challenged or if it's convenient to do so. ("You were offended by what I said? Aren't you being a bit insecure?")

While the content level contains the appropriate "data" of communication, the *rules* by which we guide our interactions are often found at the relationship level. As noted in Chapter 3, the mechanism by which this happens is termed *metacommunication*. In the metacommunicative functions of interaction, therefore, persons clue each other in on "how to take" the more obvious content messages. For example, you've probably had the experience of a good friend kidding you incessantly about a personal problem or fault. Yet you realize that this kidding isn't meant as insulting or degrading. Another person, maybe a rival of yours on the basketball court or in the office, would not be able to say the same things without you feeling insulted or degraded. But what's different? At the relational level, you and your friend have learned the metacommunication signals, many of them nonverbal, that allow you to distinguish between positive and negative tones. Watzlawick, Beavin, and Jackson, too, later point out that in pathological family patterns, people can even compliment loved ones with words and nonverbal cues that ultimately can signal relational animosity. Then they can deny the hostile intention, pointing instead to the overt content of the talk.

axiom 3: "the punctuation of the sequence of events"

Just as punctuation marks in sentences indicate starts, stops, and pauses, similar clues regulate relationships. In the study of communication, **punctuation** is a process of perception through which people organize their ongoing interactions into recognizable openings, closings, causes, and effects. The events themselves, viewed externally, may appear to be seamless. It's often unclear what "caused" what, but it's usually very clear what happened and in what order. However, people confronted with such experiences want to understand some things as responses to others and to organize the whys and wherefores of communication. "You started it!" and "No I didn't—*you* did!" exemplify different punctuations of

LINK

Metacommunication is perceived in social talk because of how we use *constitutive rules.* See Chapter 5 for more information about how CMM theorists explain this process.

an argument between two children (or adults). Sports coaches and managers sometimes discuss a "turning point" in a game after which the momentum changes significantly. Group leaders and consultants in the same way are alert to "critical incidents" such as arguments or emotional breakthroughs that, according to their punctuation, change the tenor of subsequent talk in the group.

axiom 4: "digital and analogic communication"

Watzlawick, Beavin, and Jackson (1967) claim that human communication messages take one of two forms:

> They can either be represented by a likeness, such as a drawing, or they can be referred to by a name. Thus, in the written sentence "The cat has caught a mouse" the nouns could be replaced by pictures; if the sentence were spoken, the actual cat and the mouse could be pointed to. Needless to say, this would be an unusual way of communicating, and normally the written or spoken "name," that is, the word, is used. These two types of communication—the one by a self-explanatory likeness, the other by a word—are . . . equivalent to the concepts of the analogic and the digital respectively. Whenever a word is used to *name* something it is obvious that the relation between the name and the thing named is an arbitrarily established one. Words are arbitrary signs that are manipulated according to the logical matrix of language. . . . In analogic communication, on the other hand, there *is* something particularly "thing-like" in what is used to express the thing. (pp. 61–62)

LINKS

• Considering the subtlety of rules (see Chapter 5) and the complexity of cultures (see Chapter 7), how difficult do you think it is to learn how to metacommunicate in a new culture? Students who study in a new country or culture face this task every day.
• Recall our discussion of punctuation in Chapter 2, when we developed the concept of *process*.

Digital communication, then, depends on arbitrary agreements like the all-or-none unambiguous digit-based system of computers. A digit, such as the number *1,* can stand for one person, one fork, one desk . . . or it can simply stand for an option other than zero. It is the agreement between persons that makes a digital message stand for anything they want it to, even for objects that are fantasized or not physically present. Through digital messages we may free ourselves from a now world, a prison of the present, in order to talk about events long past or about people we are yet to meet. Because of digital message agreements, we can plan for the future. This kind of understanding is the basis for our entire system of language—it is like a code that we try *not* to keep secret. It is essential to human communication.

Analogic communication is also essential but in a different way. Analogic messages are connected more fundamentally to the actualities that are being communicated, and therefore, they are said to be more immediate than digital messages. If someone says, "I'm shaking your hand" without actually shaking a hand, the statement is digital. *Actually shaking the hand* is analogic. Because analogic messages are clearly related to nonverbal communication, and are clearly immediate in character, it should come as no surprise that they are crucial in the development of metacommunicational meaning. Analogic messages, in fact, are indicators *of* relationship, the Palo Alto group authors assert, and are not statements *about* relationships. This explains why people, when faced with *mixed messages* (contradictions between the verbal/digital and the nonverbal/analogic types of communication) almost invariably believe the latter.

axiom 5: "symmetrical and complementary interaction"

Theorists of the Palo Alto group researched two basic patterns of interaction. Symmetry in art and architecture implies an obvious balance among elements. Similarly, in *symmetrical interaction* each of the two parties essentially seeks to match or mirror the behavior of the other. For example, one person's shyness will be met by shy reactions from the other, or an angry tirade triggers an angry response. Symmetrical interaction may not be orderly or harmonious. It may result in competition, in which each message contribution is met by the other side with a corresponding attempt to keep up the prevailing pattern. Thus, an insult often begets an insult, sulking might create more sulking, and you're more likely to receive Christmas cards from those to whom you send cards. Similar to the exchange theorist's *norm of reciprocity,* symmetrical interaction behavior can often be observed to generate its own reflection.

Complementary interaction is the behavioral opposite of symmetrical interaction. It, too, characterizes many human relationships and also can be destructive. Suppose, for example, you have an argument with a friend. Your friend yells at you during the argument, but instead of yelling back in a mutually escalating way (or a symmetrical pattern), you react by withdrawing. What you've done is adapt your reaction not by matching the friend's behavior, but by fitting your response to the behavior. In effect, you've accepted the friend's behavior relationally and adapted to it by producing its logical opposite behavior. In a complementary pattern, yelling may be met with silence or whispering, passivity with aggression, attempts to persuade with willing receptivity, dominance with submission, giving with taking, and so forth. Although complementary relations do not usually develop a sense of competition (although there may be other conflicts within the pattern), the long-term consequences of this type of relationship are interesting to conflict researchers. It could produce *schismogenesis,* a condition in which the two complementary positions become progressively farther apart, each as a result of the other (Watzlawick et al., 1967, p. 68). For example, a demanding husband who persistently criticizes an accepting, passive wife (or vice versa) may find that the more he criticizes, the more passive she becomes. This response is not satisfying to him, however, and he feels a desire to criticize more often and more sharply. Her submission then deepens. In effect, their behavioral patterns diverge.

Symmetrical patterns, therefore, are based on relatively equal status and relatively similar behaviors, whereas complementary ones are based on status differences and divergent behaviors. In all likelihood, everyone's communication lives are composed of mixtures of each of these types of interaction, and they are not necessarily destructive. Problems arise when symmetrical relations escalate out of control or when complementary relations become more and more rigid.

In the preceding discussion, we've assumed that each partner in the relationship is aware of the other. That is almost true by definition: How can there be

L I N K

Consider the highly verbal and digitized environment of computer e-mail, in which discerning mixed messages clearly is harder. What significant problems could be created by this context? What are the implications for developing online communities and friendships? Will future technologies restore more of the opportunity to perceive mixed messages? In considering these questions, you may want to review the discussion of online communication context in Chapter 3.

a relationship between people without their mutual recognition? Still, relations can weaken to the extent that people reduce their awareness (or their willingness to show their awareness) of the partner's definition of self. Relational/interactional theorists accept Martin Buber's (1965a) view that *confirmation*, the capacity to be noticed and perceived in both actuality and potentiality, is a distinguishing feature of mature, healthy communication. Conflict can result when one person rejects the other's definition of self, but that rejection still indicates an awareness of who the other person is. However, what happens when one partner communicates as if the other doesn't exist?

This condition, called *disconfirmation,* can be psychologically damaging, especially for people who are otherwise vulnerable due to their relative absence of power, their age, or their mental condition. Psychiatrist R. D. Laing (1969), whose early work in this area is often cited by the Palo Alto group, quoted the psychologist and philosopher William James: "No more fiendish punishment could be devised, even were such a thing physically possible, than that one should be turned loose in society and remain absolutely unnoticed by all the members thereof" (pp. 98–99). Laing examined families in which children were not "subject to outright neglect or even to obvious trauma," but instead received "subtle but persistent disconfirmation, usually unwittingly" (p. 100).

Overall, the Palo Alto group's premise is simple: A communication relationship is crucial in determining message meanings. However, a relationship is not just two people directing messages at each other from their separate home bases. We'll only understand communication by studying relations between persons, rather than analyzing the persons themselves. Persons' perceptions of relationship become their primary clues for developing relational strategies as well as their primary evidence for drawing conclusions about others. As we will see in the next section, Laing has been an important contributor to our understanding of relational perception.

INTERPERSONAL PERCEPTION THEORY

R. D. Laing (1969) wanted to focus on relationship, but was interested at the same time in how people accomplish the complex psychological process of perception. Only when people can match or coordinate their perceptions (of each other, of the relationship, of the other's view of the relationship, and so forth) can there be what Laing (1969) calls a "genuine relationship":

> Interpersonal life is conducted in a nexus of persons, in which each person is guessing, assuming, inferring, believing, trusting, or suspecting, generally being happy or tormented by his phantasy of the others' experience, motives, and intentions. And one has phantasies not only about what the other himself experiences and intends, but also about his phantasies about one's own experience and intentions, and about his phantasies about one's phantasies about his phantasies about one's experience, etc. There could be no greater mistake than to suppose that these issues are mere "theoretical" complexities, of little

L I N K

For more thorough discussions of Buber's concepts, see the section on dialogic theory later in this chapter and the section on dialogic ethics in Chapter 10.

practical relevance. . . . Family interactions are often dominated by these issues. (p. 174)

As an example of interpersonal perception analysis, let's consider a hypothetical relationship involving a father and daughter. The father sees his fifteen-year-old daughter, Carla, as an intelligent and independent young person. But he wonders if his persistent reminders about not drinking will boomerang: Will they be heard as nagging? As sincere expressions of concern? As indicators that Carla is untrustworthy? In order to decide, the father will, without planning to do so, use what Laing, Phillipson, and Lee (1966) call *metaperspectives,* or perspectives about perspectives. He will consider how he sees himself (maybe as a diligent parent), how he sees Carla (maybe as not only intelligent and independent, but also as vulnerable to peer pressure), and how he thinks Carla sees Carla (maybe as bright and mature). In Laing's (1969) notation procedure, how a person sees self is noted as $[p \rightarrow p]$; how that person sees another is $[p \rightarrow o]$; and how the person sees someone else's view of the other's self is $[p \rightarrow (o \rightarrow o)]$ (pp. 174 ff.).

Therefore, Carla's dad, if he is normally perceptive about his relationship with his daughter, can generate even more relational data through metaperspectives. He develops a judgment about how Carla believes he sees their relationship: "I think Carla understands that I love her and want her to be independent, so my concern for her will more likely be seen as love than as meddling." This could be identified in a complex but reasonably clear notation: $[p \rightarrow (o \rightarrow (p \rightarrow o))]$.

Using the metaperspectival approach, and assuming that each person's experience is all they can access directly as evidence in making their own relational decisions, Laing, Phillipson, and Lee (1966) developed the *Interpersonal Perception Method* questionnaire to explore how people in **dyads** (two-person relationships) perceive and define their interactions differently. Each person is asked to respond (on a scale of "very true" to "very untrue") to a series of questions. Here are a few sample questions from the instrument given to one member of a relational dyad:

A. How true do you think the following are?
   1. She takes me seriously.
   2. I take her seriously.
   3. She takes herself seriously.
   4. I take myself seriously.
B. How would *she* answer the following?
   1. "I take him seriously."
   2. "He takes me seriously."
   3. "I take myself seriously."
   4. "He takes himself seriously."
C. How would *she* think you have answered the following set?
   1. She takes me seriously.
   2. I take her seriously.
   3. She takes herself seriously.
   4. I take myself seriously.
      (Laing, Phillipson, & Lee, 1966)

With both persons' responses, the researcher has a reasonably thorough map of the perspectives and metaperspectives with which they approach the relationship. Using this data, a counselor or therapist can focus on the areas in which the partners' metaperspectives are most inconsistent or incongruent (i.e., on those areas where each partner inaccurately perceives the perspectives and metaperspectives of the other).

One outcome of interpersonal perception research is a clearer picture of the roles people begin to define in relationships. A *role* is that set of behaviors expected of a certain person ("John's role in the group is to keep things light," we might say) or a certain position ("It's part of the role of a leader to keep our discussion on track"). Husbands and wives, job applicants and interviewers, young and old, and many other social groups may find themselves in predictably different roles if their ways of developing and using metaperspectives differ. In many roles, a person's social behavior might be analyzed almost as if it's a theatrical performance, with the criterion for effectiveness being dramatic impact. Later in this chapter, we examine a set of theoretical perspectives that use the metaphors of drama to illuminate the communication process.

DIALECTICAL THEORY

Relational/interactional theory and interpersonal perception theory set the stage for a group of theorists associated with the more recently developed **dialectical theory** of personal relationships (Baxter, 1988, 1990; Baxter & Montgomery, 1996; Cissna, Cox, & Bochner, 1990; Rawlins, 1992). To conceive of communication as *dialectical* means that relationships result from the interplay of perceived opposite forces or contradictions, and from how relational partners negotiate these ever-changing processes.

Dialectical theory thus explains communicative behavior by avoiding several simplistic assumptions that many people tend to make about relationships. For example, at times communicators want to think that they can have a relationship that is fully open and disclosive ("I wish I had the kind of friendship where I could tell my deepest secrets to him, any time I wanted"). Or they'd like one with complete freedom ("I want a relationship with no strings attached"), or one with automatic feelings of safety ("I know I can always count on her to be there for me; I never have to doubt that"). Interestingly, some communicators want the freedom of total openness only sometimes; at other times, they expect to have their privacy respected. Many of us want to avoid being dependent on other people—until we need their help, of course, at which time dependence doesn't seem so bad.

However, these situations suggest only a handful of the many tensions of interpersonal life that concern dialectical theorists. To understand the nuances of communication, they argue, we should realize that relationships often develop from persons' negotiation of contradictory states, values, and desires. Baxter and Montgomery (1996) assume that relationships are organized around the dynamic interplay of opposing tendencies as they are enacted in interaction. . . . The ongoing interplay between oppositional features is what enables a relationship to exist as a dynamic social entity. A healthy relationship is not one in which the interplay of opposites has been extinguished or resolved, because these opposing features are inherent in the very fabric of relating. Instead, a healthy relationship is one in which the parties manage to satisfy both oppositional demands, that is, relational well-being is marked by the capacity to achieve "both/and" status. (p. 6)

What are some dialectical contradictions that mature communicators must reconcile in healthy relationships? In her work, Baxter (1988, 1990) suggests several primary ones: autonomy/connection, openness/closedness, and predictability/novelty. She studies how such seemingly oppositional pairs must be defined in terms of each other, and how they rely on each other in communication. For example, you probably value autonomy in the sense of being thought of as "your own person." But if you always define desirable behavior as "being your own person no matter what," you undercut the very notion of a relationship with another person. Partners in long-term marriages know that this process is more subtle than what's normally considered "compromise." It is a negotiation of a constantly shifting balance—unique for each couple—between autonomy (as self-regulation) and connection (as system adjustment). Not all scholars in this area claim theory status for their work. However, dialectical theory has carved its own distinct niche in the realm of interpersonal concepts and theories.

DIALOGIC THEORY

So-called commonsense notions of communication tempt people to concentrate on the individual's psychological perspective, as we've noted earlier. But if relational and dialectical theorists are on the right track, and if symbolic interactionist concepts are accepted, a person does not and cannot develop an identity except through communication with other social beings. Now, consider another group of theorists who claim "the fundamental fact of human existence is neither the individual as such nor the aggregate as such" (Buber, 1965a, pp. 202–203). Fundamental human reality, to theorists of **dialogue**, can only be observed during those occasions when people meet each other (Anderson, Cissna, & Arnett, 1994). The work of theorists Martin Buber, Carl Rogers, and Hans-Georg Gadamer represents this line of research (see Box 6-3).

buber: dialogic meeting

Identity, language, and communication reside in what philosopher and theologian Martin Buber (1965a) calls "the between," the region of human existence that links self and others. It is not possessed by individuals, although we sometimes

LINKS

- See Chapter 10 for a discussion of Taoist philosophy, which holds that life's essential processes have to be defined by referring to their opposites. Thus, strength can't be known in isolation, but only by understanding and acknowledging weakness. Strength and weakness, though evidently contradictory terms, are mutually dependent because each depends on the other for its very existence. Taoists suggest that although such "oppositions" appear to be separate, they are essentially parts of the same process. Dialectical theorists who work in a Western context seem to apply this insight from Eastern thought.
- In the most recent book-length exposition of dialectical theory, Baxter and Montgomery (1996) stress the importance of dialogue in explaining interactional dialectics. In addition to our discussion of dialogic theory in this chapter, we examine dialogue in several other places in the book: See Chapter 4 for a discussion of Bakhtin and inner speech, and Chapter 10 for an elaboration of the dialogic ethic.

speak as if individuals "have" selves, as if an identity or self-concept could be possessed in a psychological, inner sense. Selves and relationships emerge from *between* people, not from within them. To Buber (1957, 1958, 1965a, 1965b) life is not at all a matter of inner experience, but rather could only be lived authentically through *meeting* others.

In a wide-ranging series of books on religion, philosophy, literature, theater, and culture (1957, 1958, 1965a, 1965b), Buber developed his *philosophical anthropology.* By this he meant that he wanted to uncover the potentialities of human existence by investigating culture and human nature as if he were encountering them fresh. Although we will meet Buber again in Chapter 10's discussion of ethical perspectives, we'll introduce the foundation of his philosophy here. Buber's ideas are increasingly practical, we believe, in a world of cultural conflict. Dialogue, to Buber, is not only attainable, but can become a concrete presence in daily life.

Buber's (1958) most famous insight is his distinction between the basic human attitudes of *I-Thou* and *I-It.* He describes the "I-Thou" attitude (or, as some scholars believe to be more accurate as a translation, the "I-You" attitude) as one that invites and allows dialogue; in it, the person sees and responds to the other as the unique person that he or she is, not as a representative figure, a stereotype, or an extension of one's own personality. In contrast, a person with an "I-It" attitude treats the other person as an object, as something that can be concisely described, measured, manipulated, and accounted for. With the "I-It" frame of reference, a communicator might easily justify generalizing another person into a stereotypical category or assuming the other is a predictable representative of a category. Buber does not criticize the existence of "I-It" relations in human life, given that many daily relationships necessarily involve surface contact with others, and in fact, the object world is important to human existence. However, he does show that an "I-It" orientation can preclude "genuine dialogue" when it dominates a relationship.

By *genuine dialogue,* Buber (1965a) means "spoken or silent" communication "where each of the participants really has in mind the other or others in their present and particular being and turns to them with the intention of establishing a living mutual relation between himself and them" (p. 19). This contrasts with two other conditions: *technical dialogue,* which appears to have a give-and-take quality but is actually designed only to achieve a specified end through objective communication, and *monologue,* which is a dominant voice divorced from the expectation of response.

Critics (e.g., see the discussion in Glatzer, 1966) sometimes portray Buber as a mystic whose philosophy is practical only for people who already agree with each other or who already share the same humanistic principles of dialogue, respect, and authenticity—but that it is impractical for communicators who disagree vehemently with each other. Yet Buber (1965a) meant his ideas to apply, if anything, *more* to what he called "the conversation with the opponent" in a concrete encounter; the basis of that conversation is not the "demand" but the persistent refusal to withhold one's self from the dialogue (pp. 34 ff.). Buber believed that our habit of withholding ourselves from response precludes genuine communication in our time.

LINK

How might politicians and leaders of social movements apply Buber's ideas about dialogic meeting? What does his philosophy suggest about how persuasion is managed in public? We'll consider related questions about attitude change, media, and ethics in Chapters 8, 9, and 10.

Communication scholars have adopted the dialogic perspective primarily as a philosophical system that justifies the importance of speech, but not as an overall model of the communication process. In his review of the contributions of Buber and others to our understanding of dialogue, Stewart (1978) distinguishes four characteristics that many communication-based studies of dialogue seem to share. First, such studies stress that communication is a context-dependent and transactional process (rather than a message-centered or effect-centered process). Second, the studies stress *experientialism*, or the idea that dialogue depends on immersion in the concrete details of everyday life in order for learning to be significant. In other words, we learn more about dialogue when we engage in it directly than when we hear or read descriptions of it. Third, Stewart identifies a "focus on self and subjectivity" in studies of dialogic thought in the 1970s (although later studies tend to be more aligned with Stewart's first characteristic, emphasizing relational and "between" factors). Finally, dialogic studies in communication focus on *holism*—"the conviction that speech communication research and teaching which is based on a unidimensional perspective should be replaced by a point of view which embraces a multitude of interdependent cognitive, affective, behavioral, and contextual variables" (Stewart, 1978, p. 185).

rogers: the person-centered approach

One professional communicator who tried to make dialogue practical in a variety of contexts is psychotherapist Carl Rogers (1959, 1961, 1980). For students interested in studying the professional implications of dialogic philosophy, Rogers's work is an appropriate place to begin. Across the world, Rogers is regarded as one of the most influential psychologists of the twentieth century. Although his later writings are very much influenced by Buber's dialogic insights, Rogers's early works also illustrate many dialogic principles. In essence, Rogers suggests that individuals are not automatically "persons," but instead they *become* persons through their contacts with others. Or, in other words, "persons" are fluid processes shaped through interaction with other persons.

Although some critics represent Rogers as a proponent of individualistic selfishness in the "Do your own thing" vein (Geller, 1982; Schultz, 1977), Rogers attempted to build a systematic theory of dialogic human interaction. He derived his theoretical principles primarily from his counseling practice and his practical experience in facilitating groups, often in settings of intercultural conflict.

Rogers worked diligently to build theory (1959), but interestingly enough, believed that within the process of interaction, while meeting the other, a communicator needs to be "atheoretical." By this he meant that theory should guide what we do and what we know about communication, but that we should not conform slavishly to principles, skills, and concepts. Theory, ironically, can deflect us from the immediacy of face-to-face communication. To the extent that Rogers tried consciously to practice "Rogerian" principles in therapeutic talk, he found that communication was doomed to be of low quality. Instead, his theory of effective therapy emerged from analyzing countless hours of recorded sessions of himself and other counselors and therapists interacting spontaneously with clients with diverse problems. To Rogers, the conditions of effective communication in therapy are more broadly applicable to nontherapeutic interpersonal communication. Therfore, he altered the designation for his overall perspective from *client-centered therapy* (a term still in wide use) to the more inclusive *person-centered approach* (Bozarth & Brodley, 1986; Levant & Shlien, 1984).

Beyond recognizing the need for social contact in the way we discussed earlier (1959, p. 207), Rogers's theory identifies three essential conditions that can "free" interaction to become effective dialogue: congruence, positive regard, and empathy.

congruence.   Rogers (1959) found that communicators more easily facilitate understanding if they can achieve *congruence*—or a matching of their inner experience (to the extent that persons are aware of it) with their outer behavior. That is, if a teacher is bored with a particular topic but attempts to hide that feeling (producing incongruence), the quality of classroom communication will likely suffer as the students notice the verbal and nonverbal dissonance experienced by the teacher. Although critics argue that some humanistic psychologists advocate almost indiscriminate and "expressivist" self-disclosure by stressing congruence (Hart & Burks, 1972), a closer reading of Rogers's work clarifies that he favors disclosure that is relevant, is appropriately timed, and fits the roles and contexts in which communicators find themselves (Cissna & Anderson, 1990, pp. 134–135).

positive regard.   The condition of *positive regard* is variously called "acceptance," "regard," "respect," and, consistent with Buber's work, "confirmation." Rogers (1959) notes that when communicators do not attach conditions on their acceptance of others, their relationships produce more effective understanding. The positive regard in Rogers's system attaches to the person, not necessarily to the person's behavior. This is an important point to remember, because many reactions to Rogers's label have focused on such questions as, "How can I have positive regard for a neighbor who has cheated me out of my property rights? Or for someone who beats people up?" You do not need to like the other person in order to regard his or her personhood and human potential positively. To disqualify someone automatically for something they've done (or someone they're assumed to be) is to create a gulf across which understanding is unlikely to develop. A research tradition within interpersonal communication, *confirmation theory,* probes such concepts as Rogers's *positive regard,* Buber's *confirmation,* and Laing's *metaperspectives* (Cissna & Sieburg, 1981).

empathy.   *Empathy* has a long and varied history in the disciplines of communication, psychology, and philosophy (Katz, 1963). Some scholars identify it with a mode of knowledge in which a person mystically transports his or her perception into the mind of another in order to "know" the other's subjective feelings. Buber and scholars who associate themselves with his philosophy have preferred Buber's term *inclusion* and the closely related concept *imagining the real*—conditions in which communicators learn to accept as realistic both their own perspective and (without leaving their own personal ground of being) the

L I N K

How are empathy and inclusion similar to, different from, or dependent on the mental adjustment of decentering described in Chapter 4?

perspective of others. The key here is the relational basis of reality. A person should neither believe the self to be the center of a communication universe, nor believe the self should be abandoned in an attempt to glide into another's experience. Although some scholars regard empathy as comparable to imaginative mind reading, Rogers (1959) is not among them. As he explains: "A state of empathy . . . is to perceive the internal frame of reference of another with accuracy and with the emotional components and meanings which pertain thereto as if one were the person, but without ever losing the 'as if' condition. Thus it means to sense the hurt or the pleasure of another as he senses it and to perceive the causes thereof as he perceives them, but without ever losing the recognition that it is *as if* I were hurt or pleased and so forth" (pp. 210–211). The implications for practical interpersonal communication are inescapable. Can one person ever truly say, then, "I know exactly what you're going through after your father's death. My father died last year, too"? Rogers's definition of empathy suggests that you can't know another's experience with certainty because the other person couldn't have had exactly the same relationship with a parent as you had with yours. Therefore, empathy is basically a process of imagining tentative clues, not one of gaining precise knowledge. Further, attempts at empathy serve as positive relational messages, because they advertise our willingness to grant full credence to another's uniquely different experience. This advantage is lost, of course, if you consider empathy to be a full identification with the exact feelings and thoughts of the other person.

Rogers developed his theory of interpersonal dialogue from years of personal experience in his own therapeutic practice. He uses that practical data to refine the theory. His work demonstrates a merging of the concerns of theory and practice into what has been called a **praxis**—or the conception of theory as practical, and practice as theoretically informed (Cissna & Anderson, 1990; Williams, 1976, p. 268). Theory and practice are not opposites in Rogers's system; the two converge in a praxis of communication.

gadamer: hermeneutics and productive communication

The relational/interactional, interpersonal perception, and dialogic theories place their primary attention on the relationship between communicators, and thus they tend to downplay the mechanics of the message-interchange process. However, some communication analysts, as we've seen, are more concerned with communication as a mechanistic process. They implicitly assume that a major function of communication is to convey information accurately from one person to another.

Good communication in this conduit-like view consists of a message that is "encoded" for an identifiable purpose by a speaker and then received (accurately, adequately, or appropriately) by a listener. In many instances, such a view adequately identifies problems in communication that might need repair or additional attention. However, scholars don't assume that this is the most reasonable way to conceptualize the process. Seeing communication as interdependence, in fact, suggests that the misunderstandings might be as important as accurate understanding in the long run.

L I N K

In discussing the definitions of communication in Chapter 2, we analyze this tendency toward mechanistic explanation as an example of the *conduit metaphor*. Recall that it views communication as analogous to a speaker placing meanings in containers (words) and delivering them through a conduit directly to a listener, who in turn receives and notes (more or less accurately) the intended meanings "carried by the word containers."

Hermeneutics, a branch of philosophy and, originally, of theology, studies how interpretations are developed out of people's encounters with written and oral "texts." It has produced an alternative communication theory of meaning, as Deetz (1982) describes:

> Most researchers have assumed a representational view of understanding. The listener is assumed to have understood when s/he can recreate what the speaker meant. The desire to avoid misunderstanding is central in this view. Modern hermeneutics demonstrates the possibility of a more productive view. The interest here in interpersonal interaction is with the development and unfolding of meaning which is not yet available to either interactant, rather than in a comparison of the speaker's psychological intentions with those of the listener. The nature of dialogue is to open that which is out of reach and beyond comprehension. (p. 8)

Deetz's last sentence is especially instructive. When dialogue develops, the consequences are essentially spontaneous and unanticipated. The interpretations emerge from the moment of interpretation itself, and not from prior intentions of the speakers or from any special capacity of language to carry meanings. Thus, for the hermeneutical theorist, the real value of communication is in how it uses all the resources of human experience (including misunderstanding and prejudice) to produce meaning creatively, meaning that was not present before the communication occurred. This is why Deetz argues for a view that is not merely reproductive but for one that is *productive*—that is, one that produces fresh and new meaning.

A persuasive representative of the hermeneutical approach to communication is contemporary German philosopher Hans-Georg Gadamer (1982; Warnke, 1987). "Reaching an understanding in conversation," Gadamer (1982) writes, "presupposes that both partners are ready for it and are trying to recognise the full value of what is alien and opposed to them. If this happens mutually, and each of the partners, while simultaneously holding on to his own arguments, weighs the counter-arguments, it is finally possible to achieve an imperceptible but not arbitrary reciprocal translation of the other's position (we call this an exchange of views), a common language and a common statement" (p. 348). When Gadamer mentions "the full realization of conversation," he means that something has been expressed "that is not only mine or my author's, but common" (p. 350).

Although Gadamer's concern with dialogue and his respect for the other's position echo in some ways Buber's philosophy and Rogers's concern with empathy, it would be misleading to suggest that this is all he is saying. Out of every dialogic encounter, Gadamer stresses, some new understanding develops, and *should* develop. The new understanding happens through the text (message), however fixed it might seem, "questioning" the interpreter while the interpreter questions the text. To Gadamer, questions are genuine and dialogue is possible *only when the answers are not already known* (such as when a young student asks about a teacher's feelings about the Vietnam War, or when a lost traveler asks directions of a native resident). The opposite of dialogue is an argument in which both parties become so entrenched in their positions that their only questions to

BOX 6-3

DIALOGIC THEORY

- Buber's *philosophical anthropology* emphasizes *"the between"* and *"I-Thou"* relations.
- Rogers's *person-centered approach* emphasizes *congruence, positive regard,* and *empathy.*
- Gadamer's *philosophical hermeneutics* emphasizes *productive meaning* (rather than reproductive), *genuine questioning,* and *linguisticality.*

---

the other are ones designed to disclose flaws in the opposing argument. We can see this anti-dialogue clearly at work in the American judicial system. Attorneys are taught in law school never to ask a question of a witness to which they do not already know the answer. The last thing a trial attorney wants in most cases is a surprise disclosure from a cross-examined witness.

Gadamer (1982) has some surprising challenges in store for communication students. Students learn from some textbooks that "meanings are in people, not in words," and that "language is a system of signs that are used arbitrarily to refer to things." But Gadamer asserts that people do not use language to accomplish their ends; it would make as much sense to think of language using people to achieve its ends. Language is a living historical presence from which human beings cannot escape even if they wanted to. If language was only a set of tools, Gadamer claims, people could choose to use or not use it. Instead, people have no such choice, having been born into a preexisting linguistic world. The meanings available to language are the ways available to people to live in the world. According to Gadamer, then, people don't have experiences first, then decide how to express them. Instead, the experiences themselves are already influenced by the language into which we're born. He challenges students of language to assume that in a very real sense words do have meanings independent of any one person's use of them. Language has a historical quality of "ongoingness" and *human beings belong to language.* Gadamer calls this phenomenon *linguisticality.*

The concept of linguisticality suggests interesting implications when we consider communicative interdependence. Earlier in this chapter we stressed that communicators are not autonomous, but fundamentally interdependent with other communicators. Gadamer extends this concept significantly. Communicators, because of their necessary immersion in language and particular historical contexts, are also interdependent with language itself. In other words, we are shaped by language, just as we help to shape language for future generations.

 LINKS

- Note how Gadamer's idea of linguisticality assumes that all language is an integral part of our cultural context. It's not just a way of "in-forming" personal cognitive experience, as discussed in Chapter 4, but more broadly forms the fundamentally human aspects of all experience.
- Another prominent dialogic theorist, Mikhail Bakhtin, is discussed in Chapter 4.

DRAMATURGICAL THEORY

the theatrical metaphor

Think back to the last time you attended a play. Sitting in the theater, you probably understood that you were watching a performance of a written text that had been presented many times before by different actors, directors, and technicians. You understood intellectually that the actors' comments and conversations, however spontaneous they sounded, were in fact a kind of illusion of immediate reality. In one sense, the actors' lines were said in the immediate moment, but the words were not spontaneous, nor were the actors free to be "themselves." Your mind's analytical side led you to this conclusion. Yet when the theatrical experience works, the illusion becomes its own reality and the boundaries blur between what is scripted and what is immediate. You experience what is true, and that drama is immediate and, in its own way, real.

Communication scholars who label themselves "dramaturgical theorists" don't imply that society is a completely predetermined presentation in which persons simply mouth someone else's scripts. Instead, **dramaturgical theory** explores how spontaneous social action relies on the same bases as theatrical performance. In interaction, social actors try to (1) coordinate their behaviors convincingly, in order to (2) give audiences the impression that reality is present within the boundaries of the interaction. In this regard, the concept of *role* is central. Our roles are composed of the behavioral expectations that people associate with who we are and with what positions we enact.

Sociologist Elizabeth Burns (1972) concludes that the theatrical metaphor may be more practical than people might assume, especially in diagnosing communication effects:

> In ordinary life each person is engaged in a constant endeavour to mark out his own role, his setting, his course of action and to distinguish between those who are to be fellow actors and those who are to be spectators. . . . In their most highly valued relationships and preoccupations people like to think of themselves as free of all the attributes of an actor. It is, however, possible to preserve the necessary sense of authenticity if "theatricality" is seen not as a mode of behaviour but as a mode of recognition. It belongs to the critical, judging, assessing "I" that stands aside from the self—as conscience or "ego." But its function is enriched by theatrical awareness and theatrical insights that take into account the self as a social being. (p. 232)

Dramaturgical theory, therefore, is useful as a metaphor to help us understand how we coordinate our lives. Just as actors on a stage cannot create their lines and lives autonomously without creating problems for their fellow actors, so do we in everyday life sacrifice personal control over our "lines" in order to produce a convincing ensemble performance. The roles must be meshed.

Following Shakespeare ("All the world's a stage"), some communication theorists have extended the theatrical metaphor. In this section we consider the contributions of three scholars: Kenneth Burke, Erving Goffman, and Ernest Bormann (see Box 6-4).

burke: the new rhetoric of identification

The twentieth century has known only a few Renaissance persons whose knowledge and understanding cut across almost all traditional disciplinary boundaries in the human sciences. Kenneth Burke is one of them. Is he a literary critic or a sociologist? A psychologist or a communication theorist? A poet or a historian? He is all of these.

Several of Burke's many contributions have deeply influenced rhetorical and communication theorists. One is his distinction between what he calls the *old rhetoric* and an emerging *new rhetoric.* The old way of studying rhetoric was based on *persuasion,* the ability to affect others' attitudes and behaviors through "deliberate design" (Burke, 1967, p. 63). But with the advent of such disciplines as anthropology, psychology, and sociology, investigators came to realize, Burke claims, that a better way to approach rhetoric is through identification. In *identification,* the object of communication is not to change another's attitude but to set up the conditions in which persons can find commonality with each other's experience. This too can be deliberately designed, yet it goes much further in accounting for the unconscious and transcendent motives of persons in their symbolic environments.

For example, advertisements for Benetton, a worldwide corporation that markets clothing, have shown no clothing whatsoever and have included no verbal inducements to buy clothing. Instead, the campaign focuses on a controversial and colorful series of visual images called "the united colors of Benetton." While a few ads include surprisingly direct sexual images (of multicolored condoms, of a nun and priest kissing) that have shocked some people, most of the ads simply feature persons of different races and backgrounds juxtaposed graphically. Communication across differences is therefore foregrounded. The "old rhetoric," a rhetoric of telling, would have given us reasons to buy the clothes. The "new rhetoric" provides no such reasons, and might even attempt the opposite by being unreasoning and arational. Instead of telling us about the clothing for sale, the rhetoric aims to *show* an identification with the company itself. In this way, the ad campaign functions more like a dramatic play. Arthur Miller's *Death of a Salesman,* for example, doesn't tell us what to believe and change about modern society. Instead, the play *shows* those effects and trusts our identification with the acts, agents, scenes, agencies, and purposes of the theater.

These major notions of dramatic identification have been elaborated by Burke (1969) to explain essential elements in the wide range of human communication outside of strictly theatrical events. Burke refers to them collectively as the *dramatistic* **pentad:**

> *Act*—the behaviors; what is accomplished. (What happened?)
> *Agent*—the person(s) performing dramatically. (Who initiated the action?)
> *Scene*—the situation in which the action occurs. (Where and when did it happen?)
> *Agency*—the means used by the agent(s) to accomplish communicative goals. (How did it happen?)
> *Purpose*—the motivating reason behind the rhetoric. (Why did it develop as it did?)

These five elements help explain how we identify, or fail to identify, with each other in social situations. The first and most crucial concept for Burke is the act.

L I N K

Chapter 8, which describes other theories of rhetoric and attitude change, will define persuasion in more detail.

To act implies that we make a specific choice to behave in a certain way. An act is based on humans' symbolic capacity, which grants us this freedom to choose. *Action,* to Burke (1969), can be distinguished from *motion:* Action follows from choices, but motion is caused by outside or external forces. Baseball players act (or choose a direction for their communicative behavior), but a baseball can't act; it must wait to be put into motion. This distinction seems obvious and even trivial until you consider the number of times you've heard someone claim, "She *made* me angry" or "His insult *forced* me to retaliate." These conclusions are not true in a literal sense, but they can objectify human experience unnecessarily and perhaps justify the manipulation of others.

The elements of Burke's pentad are interactive; they cannot be isolated conceptually from each other, as if they operate separately. Therefore, Burke suggests that analysts of rhetoric look for consistencies and inconsistencies among the elements of the pentad. For example, are there times in which the behavior of a dramatic performance (act) is inconsistent with the setting (scene) in which it occurs? You might ironically call a close friend by the nickname "Killer" because you know he has a gentle disposition, but an introduction of this same man in a professional setting would more appropriately include his real name and perhaps even a formal title. Nothing is inherently wrong with either the official or the informal name. It's the potential combination of a name and a situation that could be labeled "wrong." Burke calls this kind of analysis the consideration of *ratios,* and suggests that we look to such interactions as an *act–scene ratio* (as in the example of when to use nicknames) or *agent–scene ratio* problems (such as befell 1988 presidential candidate Michael Dukakis when he evidently looked silly to a large number of voters when caught by journalists in a "photo opportunity" wearing a combat helmet and driving a tank).

goffman: impression management

Since the 1950s, Erving Goffman has observed and analyzed how ordinary people use complex strategies to achieve their conversational goals. Through an impressive series of works (1959, 1974, 1981), he has charted the means by which we accomplish *impression management.* His most influential book was his first, *The Presentation of Self in Everyday Life* (1959), in which he develops elaborate metaphors from the theater and supports them with a multitude of examples from daily living.

Goffman believes that people engage in *role enactment.* Have you ever accused someone of being phony or of pretending to be someone he or she is not? Certainly that person may have been a deceiver. But Goffman uses a series of role-oriented questions about communication to show that we are all phony in some ways, that we all play inauthentic roles to some extent, and that we are inclined by our nature to pretend at times in our communication with others. Sometimes, what seems like pretending is simply a process of playing out our identities. Another communication theorist within sociology describes Goffman's views in this way: "People are not, originally and in some factlike way, 'mothers,' 'surgeons,' or 'crazy.' Instead, they are cast into these roles by themselves and by others. Moreover, the actor always retains the possibility of a certain distance from the role" (Brown, 1977, p. 199). There are different ways mothers can raise children and different ways surgeons can perform operations. But with too much divergence or distance from the role, people risk being socially redefined in ways they don't like: "My education professor isn't really a teacher—he's more of a babysitter in class."

Goffman (1959) believes that humans almost always behave strategically with each other, although much of this strategy results from role enactment at very subtle levels. For example, although you might believe you are simply asking a question of your department manager, to Goffman you are engaged in *face work*, or maintaining an appropriate image or impression. Although you believe you are simply stopping your commentary briefly in order to change the topic, Goffman would say that by sustaining that otherwise silent moment with an "Ummm . . ." you are actually maintaining the *floor*, or your socially sanctioned permission to speak to others. And though some critics suggest that Goffman believes human existence is little more than a con job we pull off on each other, his unique contribution is to spotlight the intricate importance of the mundane. Often the larger significance of human life is best seen in the seemingly trivial patterns of small talk.

— Critique

Goffman's view of human nature is very direct and role related: Our symbolic capacity blurs the line between "real" and "deceptive" behaviors. How can we tell who is genuine and who is phony in a world where people can behave in almost completely different ways at work and at home? As Cuzzort and King (1989) note, ". . . Goffman probes deeply enough to make us see that what we consider a 'real' performance has elements identical to those involved in the phony performance. This requires us to think in new ways about the essential nature of humanity" (p. 284).

Although *role enactment* is a central concept to Goffman, several other concepts are also important aspects of his approach to impression management.

personal front.   Goffman observes that we attempt to foster particular impressions we want others to have of us. When we act in strategic ways to encourage these impressions, we are said to be maintaining a *personal front*. We do this through some relatively fixed biological factors as well as through more immediate tactical expressions, including "insignia of office or rank; clothing; sex, age, and racial characteristics; size and looks; posture, speech patterns; facial expressions; bodily gestures; and the like" (Goffman, 1959, p. 34).

expressions "given" and "given off."   We can distinguish between those impressions we intend (those *"given"*) and those over which we're not in control and which our audience builds as a result of its interpretations of unintended cues (those *"given off"*) (Goffman, 1959). Normally, the cues "given" (you wear a suit for a job interview) are considered to be part of your personal front, and those "given off" (your voice quavers in the interview) might be analyzed as unintended deviations or slips from your strategic front.

footing.   When two communicators seem to interact on the basis of different statuses or different assumptions about who has power, they are said to have

LINK

Does Goffman's point about the blurred line between real and phony performances suggest something important about the ethics of communication? How can we say it's more ethical to be "real" (or honest or true to a principle) when there are countless ways we try to convince people otherwise (e.g., that we're confident when we're not, that we appreciate a meal when we don't, and that we loved that verbal jab from the boss when we didn't)? See Chapter 10 for how several prominent ethical theorists grapple with such problems.

different *footing* (Goffman, 1981). It's an interesting metaphor, suggesting a more solid conversational ground for some interactants than for others. That is, some people's roles in a given situation (e.g., parent, teacher, or minister) grant them a freedom to speak and act that distinguishes them from others. Chances are, your doctor calls you by your first name, whatever your age or status. But do you say, "Thanks, Melvin" or "See you next week, Marcella" when you leave the doctor's office? The difference is in the subtle operation of footing.

regions.   Goffman notes in his studies that people behave differently not only in terms of who they are with but also as a result of where they are. Most often, these two factors are merged: When someone is "on" in a *front region,* the audience for a personal front sees a relatively official performance designed for it; in a *back region,* or *backstage,* the front is dropped in favor of less guarded behavior. The American fascination for understanding this distinction can be seen in the desire to know what Madonna, Michael Jackson, or Hillary Rodham Clinton are "really" like. (The movie *Madonna: Truth or Dare* presumably shows a private side of Madonna, but Goffman might be suspicious of how "backstage" a performer's behavior really is when a camcorder is present.)

teamwork.   Goffman (1959) finds that persons often depend on *teamwork,* on each other, to present a coherent social performance. But this dependence does not always result from friendships or open collusion. In a small-group discussion among the members of a committee, for example, Connie may notice that Marsha persistently wants every member's opinion before ending a discussion. Thus, Connie remains silent until asked specifically about her opinion. She therefore gains the floor in an uninterrupted and special way—and with greater impact—than would have been possible had she volunteered her ideas earlier in the discussion. Connie and Marsha have cooperated in a teamlike way to define a situation.

frame.   Goffman (1974), as well as other symbolic interactionists (McHugh, 1968) and linguists (Tannen, 1989, 1990), examines how communicators define their situation(s). A *frame* is a definition or an interpretation of what a situation means, and framing, therefore, is the act of asserting such a definition. For example, do you always know when you're having an argument? If we were to present a transcript of a husband and wife talking about their budget for the coming year and ask you for a description of what the two people were doing, you might respond that they are "arguing," while others might say that they are "planning," "analyzing," "discussing," or "criticizing each other's spending habits"—or they might offer a variety of other attributions. But there is a significant difference emotionally between planning and arguing. These two different definitions could have drastically different consequences for the couple conversing, as well. If the husband (or wife) frames the conversation as a planning session, he (or she) will be ready primarily to discuss in analytical terms the overdrafts and spending habits of the family. If the wife (or husband), on the other hand, frames the discussion as an argument with a series of criticisms being traded, emotional defensiveness is more likely.

LINKS

• Goffman's point about how regions influence communication is yet another demonstration of the importance of context, discussed in more detail in Chapter 3.
• Postmodern theorists (see Chapter 4) would find the ambiguities of what's "front" vs. what's "back" region behavior especially interesting, and might argue that the distinction will continue to blur in our increasingly mediated society.

Goffman's work, as highly specific and idiosyncratic as it sometimes is, has influenced a wide variety of scholars in conversation and discourse analysis (Nofsinger, 1991; Stubbs, 1983), in symbolic public leadership (Klapp, 1969), and in mass-mediated communication theory (Meyrowitz, 1985). When Goffman assumes that we play roles as if performing for others, he does not see this as negating our humanity. Instead, his brand of symbolic interactionism locates humanity precisely in our abilities to be flexible in roles and to adjust our behaviors in order to take others into account.

bormann: symbolic convergence

Building on the foundation established by symbolic interactionists, Ernest Bormann's (1972, 1983, 1989) **symbolic convergence theory** is based on his earlier *fantasy theme analysis* of rhetoric. In his dramatistic approach, Bormann (1989) suggests that the "central focus of the symbolic convergence perspective is upon the communicative processes by which human beings converge their individual fantasies, dreams, and meanings into shared symbol systems" (pp. 188–189). Bormann also assumes that communication cannot be understood without transcending the individual as a unit of analysis. He is primarily interested in how people communicating together develop shared stories that give meaning to individual experiences so that those experiences "converge" into something larger and more coherent than isolated feelings, thoughts, or explanations. Persons dramatize their interpretations of individual meanings in terms of group symbols— thus, he arrives at the term *symbolic convergence.*

Bormann uses a number of specialized concepts in developing his theory:

fantasy theme.   *Fantasy themes* are those topics that groups and communities construct as shared explanations for their communication. The focus of a fantasy theme is not so much on the here and now as on the remembered (and concocted) past and an imagined future. As Bormann (1989) explains:

> Fantasy theme analysis studies the way communicators discuss fictitious and nonfictitious events in the past or in the future or at some other place than the here-and-now of the immediate communication episode. The ongoing flow of experience may seem chaotic or confusing; immediate behavior may seem impulsive; occurrences may seem accidental. The speaker who recounts such experiences (after the fact) places the events into narrative form and provides an explanatory structure for them. The narrative form implies or attributes motivations to the personae and may provide an explanation based on lawfulness or the will of a supreme being rather than on chance or accident. The same is true of an account set in the future. The group may come to share a dream of what they want to achieve in the future by means of dramatic portrayals of characters in that future scene. Such dreams of the future are also structured interpretations of events. (p. 190)

Therefore, fantasy themes are the ways groups order their experience by talking about it. One year baseball's Pittsburgh Pirates adopted the slogan and

L I N K

See Chapter 9 for Joshua Meyrowitz's (1985) theorizing about how the electronic media change our expectations for regions, frames, and teamwork. He employs some of Goffman's concepts to develop a theory of mediated place.

song "We Are Family" to create a different rhetorical tone for the season. A basketball team that considers itself a "team of destiny" and another team that considers itself "snake-bit" are each in the process of developing a group fantasy. Bear in mind that to Bormann, the term *fantasy* does not have a negative connotation. It simply refers to a consistent organizing explanation that arises from the group's own talk and in which the group believes.

fantasy type.   Persons in a group with fantasy themes often interact with others to extract common substory meanings from those larger narratives. This phenomenon is the creation of *fantasy types*. Thus the "Old West" in the United States includes the fantasy types of "mountain man," "homesteader," "outlaw," and "noble savage," among others. Klapp's (1962) analysis of dramatic types in sociology—heroes, villains, and fools—draws from a similar source.

chaining.   When a group forms a fantasy that guides it dramatically in its relation to other groups, that fantasy becomes a basis for the talk of the group. When symbolic convergence theorists discuss *"chaining out"* fantasies, or the process of fantasy "chains," they are referring to the actual conversational dynamics involved in extending the fantasies. One element of a group's collective dramatic narrative is built upon a previous contribution, then that one stimulates another, and so on. Enthusiasm (or discouragement) may build as different comments link together to shape the story. Fantasies do not emerge spontaneously; rather, their implications are constructed and construed through communication itself.

script.   Bormann's theory is more content-oriented than other dramatistic accounts, such as Goffman's. In the symbolic convergence process, the content that comes to be accepted and not debated is referred to as *script*. Individual scripts may be acted out in rolelike behaviors, or group scripts may illustrate the status of a developing collective consciousness.

rhetorical vision.   "When sufficient fantasies have been shared," Bormann (1983) claims, "and the members develop enough fantasy types they may begin to shape them into a unified symbolic system which portrays a broad and consistent view of much or a portion of their social and material reality. The result is a *rhetorical vision*" (p. 75; emphasis added). Such a broad-based narrative is what guides the American Dream, the New World Order, and many other ideologies. Religious denominations also develop their own rhetorical visions.

However, it would be a mistake to assume that a rhetorical vision always regulates individual behavior. It doesn't—Catholics might still obtain abortions and Zen Buddhists might succumb to materialistic longing. What a rhetorical vision accomplishes, however, is to give meaning to individual behavior and symbolically integrate individuals into a larger community consciousness. A valuable function is served even when a rhetorical vision does not drive all the actions of the group members. Bormann's explanation of a complex and often ephemeral process is a unique contribution to communication theory.

BOX 6-4

DRAMATURGICAL THEORY

- Burke's *new rhetoric* emphasizes *identification* over persuasion, and the explanatory potential of the dramatistic *pentad*.
- Goffman's *impression management* approach emphasizes *role enactment*.
- Bormann's *symbolic convergence theory* emphasizes the analysis of *fantasy themes* and how they form larger *rhetorical visions*.

TESTING THE CONCEPTS

"How can I keep from becoming a Mary?"

(R. A.): Mary, who is actually a composite of quite a few students (both male and female) in my classes over the years, represents an excellent student, one who takes learning seriously. Maybe all teachers would like to have such "problems"—Mary not only does all her assignments, but persistently applies course ideas to her daily life. She takes the course so seriously, in fact, that she becomes a "true believer." I think I recognize part of myself in her, too, and ache with her at the problems she encounters. True believers not only believe in something; they desperately want others to believe in it, too. They have trouble understanding why someone else would make a different choice.

Students who intend to become specialists in communication will ultimately realize, we think, that the new information they're learning is not a cure-all for relational problems, and that it should never be forced in this way on others in their lives. Husbands, wives, children, friends, and "significant others" have not been sitting in on the classes, and they already have their own ways of communicating that probably make sense to them. They will not always see better communication students as better family members, for example—although ideally this is what could happen. In addition, if communicators find themselves in unhealthy and dysfunctional family systems, even "good" methods will not produce good results. Be careful not to invest too much faith in methods, techniques, and information. Because all of us have the potential to act like Mary, we should know that our excitement about studying communication should be tempered by a recognition that effective communication in everyday life is not something we can impose on other people.

"How do I know if I'm genuine or if I'm behaving like a scripted 'actor' with the people in my life?"

(V. R.): For over ten years I worked with the elder members of my church, affectionately known as the "Keenagers." I drove the church van and took them to various meetings and special events. When I met them in the church hallway or on the street, they'd hug me, pinch my cheek, or give me a kiss. Some years ago (long before beginning college and majoring in communication), while shopping with my husband, several of the "Keenagers" crossed the street just to talk with me and give me a hug. After they left, my husband responded, "Boy, do you have them snowed! You're really quite an actor." I was astonished by his remark and a little hurt.

After studying communication theory, especially Goffman's work, I learned that possibly I *was* acting with people, in ways that they expected me to act when I was around them. My mother and father see me differently than my children do. While I was a student (admittedly a "mature" one), my classmates often viewed me as funny, outgoing, and the comedian of the group; now, however, the same kind of students tell me I'm "much too serious." We are flexible human beings who adapt to specific situations. Possibly we should not regard acting as a negative concept, but as a necessary series of adjustments we must make with people to be as "real" as we can in each specific relationship at specific moments in time.

Y O U,   T H E   R E S E A R C H E R

1. Assume you are interested in discerning whether people in your hometown are "narcissistic" in the communication sense described at the start of this chapter. Further, assume that you have a million-dollar grant allocated for a thorough study of this phenomenon, and that you have unlimited time and a flexible schedule for conducting it.

   • Create an operational definition of narcissism that will guide your research. An *operational definition,* as we indicated in Chapter 4, seeks to define something by recognizing how it works in actual practice. For example, one operational definition of the concept, "potential for success in graduate school," is the achievement of a certain score on the Graduate Record Examination combined with a certain level of undergraduate success measured by grade point average. In other words, an operational definition answers the question, "How will I know it when I see it?"

   • Describe in detail four different research approaches you could use to explore this issue. What distinct purposes will each approach serve? What are its unique advantages and limitations? Perhaps most importantly, how will the four approaches you've chosen work together to provide a more coherent picture of conversational narcissism in your hometown, and more generally, in contemporary American culture?

2. Do you believe that feeling included and being recognized in social interaction are bases for our physiological health, and that the opposite communicative conditions can lead to disease? What is the evidence for your opinion? Interview an experienced health-care practitioner (doctor, nurse, psychiatrist, social worker) to get her or his assessment of this issue. What evidence does this professional cite to support opinions?

Compare what you believe and what you learn from the interview with Dr. James Lynch's evidence in his books of medical research, *The Broken Heart: The Medical Consequences of Loneliness* (1977) and *The Language of the Heart: The Human Body in Dialogue* (1985).

3. As you saw in this chapter, Watzlawick et al. (1967) analyzed Edward Albee's play *Who's Afraid of Virginia Woolf?* to show how systems principles can have practical applications in relational communication. For a similar analysis of your own, choose any short story, novel, or play you've read recently (perhaps for a literature class), and write a five-part essay illustrating your understanding of how the five axioms developed by the Palo Alto group theorists can be observed within the work. (If you need help choosing a literary work, you might seek out several contemporary authors who specialize in probing the mysteries of interpersonal relationships. Look for the short stories of Ursula LeGuin or Raymond Carver, or novels by Anne Tyler, Barbara Kingsolver, or David Carkeet. Your teacher and others in class may have additional suggestions.)

4. Obviously, as a philosopher, Martin Buber (1958) can theorize about the effects of the "I-Thou" relationship. But how can "I-Thou" dialogue be researched if its meaning generally resides in "the between" of the relationship, as Buber says, rather than in the psychological experience of the persons communicating? Examine the current issues of the journals *Human Communication Research* and *Journal of Applied Communication Research;* which article—if any—comes closest to focusing on "the between" as Buber would recommend?

5. Gadamer is one of several prominent European philosophers who claim to represent hermeneutics in studying the relation of interpreter to text. We do not have the space in a book like this to compare and contrast all the varieties of hermeneutics, but if you are interested in the area, you might want to investigate the differences between Gadamer's position and that of critics like Derrida (1982), and between Gadamerian thought and other strains of hermeneutical scholarship represented by Habermas (1979), Ricoeur (1981), and others (Hollinger, 1985).

Hazel Hankin/Stock, Boston

living
across
cultural borders

"what should we know about
cultural understanding
and misunderstanding?"

7

In a novel of Africa, Ajofia, a leader of Umuofia, speaks through an interpreter to the new missionary: "Tell the white man that we will not do him any harm," he said to the interpreter. "Tell him to go back to his house and leave us alone. We liked his brother who was with us before. He was foolish, but we liked him, and for his sake we shall not harm his brother. But this shrine which he built must be destroyed. We shall no longer allow it in our midst. It has bred untold abominations and we have come to put an end to it." He turned to his comrades. "Fathers of Umuofia, I salute you"; and they replied with one gutteral voice. He turned again to the missionary. "You can stay with us if you like our ways. You can worship your own god. It is good that a man should worship the gods and the spirits of his fathers. Go back to your house so that you may not be hurt. Our anger is great but we have held it down so that we can talk to you."

Mr. Smith said to his interpreter: "Tell them to go away from here. This is the house of God and I will not live to see it desecrated."

Okeke interpreted wisely to the spirits and leaders of Umuofia: "The white man says he is happy you have come to him with your grievances, like friends. He will be happy if you leave the matter in his hands."

"We cannot leave the matter in his hands because he does not understand our customs, just as we do not understand his. We say he is foolish because he does not know our ways, and perhaps he says we are foolish because we do not know his. Let him go away."

CHINUA ACHEBE, *THINGS FALL APART* (1959/1969, p. 175)

Most people have no difficulty with cultural differences in the abstract. Most of us, in fact, believe we're reasonably open minded, sensitive, and accepting of others—when *they* act reasonably.

We begin to have trouble at those points of encounter—such as the one Achebe describes in his novel—when each side believes it is as open minded as it can possibly be, given the perceived narrow-mindedness of the stranger. As you've learned in earlier chapters, much of your communication behavior is based on an undercurrent of expectations, values, and premises about which you're barely aware, if you even think about them at all. This often invisible layer of experience is what you'll consider in more detail in this chapter.

DEFINING CULTURE

Understanding another culture is not the same thing as understanding someone else's subjective, emotional, or cognitive experience. People do "carry" fragments of culture in their heads, to use a loose metaphor, but they also enact culture through their behaviors, artifacts, governments, religions, media choices, and systems of economic exchange. Culture is not primarily what people think about or believe as much as it is what they assume they *don't have to think about* in order to accomplish their daily business. Therefore, understanding culture involves both psychological (mental and cognitive) aspects and communicational (interactional, relational, and social) aspects. It is reflected in very tangible objects as well as in the intangibles of expectations, values, and attitudes.

For example, it's significant that the missionary in Achebe's (1959/1969) book brought to Africa physical artifacts of his religion, and that even in an alien (to him) environment, the church building and the land on which it stood possessed a sacredness that could be "desecrated" by people who had lived on that same land with their own culture all their lives. One culture looked at a building and saw merely an unfamiliar structure it might be able to tolerate, while the other culture saw a symbol of the basic goodness of heaven and earth. Thus, the dynamic of the missionary's culture was not just in his mind but also could be observed in his relation to objects—that is, to objects he expected to possess power even for people unfamiliar with the objects' importance to him.

Our language contains so many different connotations and potential definitions of **culture** that critic Raymond Williams (1976) calls it "one of the two or three most complicated words in the English language" (p. 76). However, Harry Triandis (1994), a cross-cultural researcher born in Greece, attempts to synthesize the divergent definitions into a single starting point: "Culture is a set of human-made objective and subjective elements that in the past have increased the probability of survival and resulted in satisfactions for the participants in an ecological niche, and thus become shared among those who could communicate with each other because they had a common language and they lived in the same time and place" (p. 22). For communication scholars, one of the most interesting implications of Triandis's definition is that it demonstrates why and how cultures perform valuable functions for their members.

People in groups develop what we call a culture because it simplifies their communicative tasks in several ways. First, culture creates a better chance of survival; similar people banding together for physical or psychological protection is an age-old communication strategy. Second, people find interaction within their own culture satisfying because to some extent it helps them to avoid uncertainties and to experience fewer interpersonal surprises that may lead to problems. Third, because culture is ecological, its shared attitudes, values, and customs provide a sense of identity for its participants. Culture can be understood best, according to Triandis (1994), as a "superorganic" phenomenon; that is, one into which individuals are born, and one that will outlive those individuals. This isn't to say that people don't influence culture by their actions, but that culture is not under the conscious control of individual leaders, no matter how powerful others may believe them to be.

As anthropologist Clifford Geertz (1983) reminds us, cultures are so super-organic that people forget that their definitions aren't really universal. For example, the notion of an individual *person* is itself a cultural construction that is common in only *some* cultures. "The Western conception of the person," Geertz (1983) writes, "as a bounded, unique, more or less integrated motivational and cognitive universe, a dynamic center of awareness, emotion, judgment, and action organized into a distinctive whole and set contrastively both against other such wholes and against its social and natural background, is, however incorrigible it may seem to us, a rather peculiar idea within the context of the world's cultures" (p. 59). Although American students typically assume that one of the highest values of humanity is for an individual to be a separate communicator responsible primarily to the self, this goal wouldn't even cross the minds of most people in some non-Western cultures. As you can imagine, communicating across such assumptions presents problems of a fundamentally different order than you'd encounter waiting on customers at a fast-food eatery in Omaha.

Serious students seem to us to have three particular kinds of questions when encountering cultural communication problems for the first time. Therefore, we have organized this chapter around these questions:

1. What kinds of terms and concepts help communicators understand the importance of studying this rapidly growing area of cultural research?
2. What kinds of cultural theories best explain the public tensions that can develop across gender, ethnic, race, and class lines?
3. How can cultural communication theories be applied practically to help resolve cross-cultural misunderstandings?

As with earlier chapters, however, you should remember that our brief survey cannot represent the whole range of scholarly research in cultural communication theory. For each theory or position we stress here, several others could have been chosen.

✳ CULTURE: BASIC THEORETICAL CONCEPTS AND APPROACHES

cultural syndromes

Triandis (1994) classifies cultures according to patterns that are observable in one form or another in all cultures. A **cultural syndrome**, he writes, is a "pattern of beliefs, attitudes, self-definitions, norms, and values that are organized around some theme that can be identified in a society" (p. 2). While the patterns themselves are useful (see Box 7-1 for descriptions), perhaps it's even more important to think of cultures literally as patterns, probabilities, or systems of human experience and action, rather than as a series of immutable laws or inevitable occurrences. A culture doesn't *make* people behave in certain ways, but it does embed behavioral patterns in its worldview so that it usually doesn't occur to people to act otherwise.

Four Cultural Syndromes

Think of *cultural syndromes* as the tendencies or patterns that cultures develop to organize communicators' behavior along certain dimensions. Although any one culture inevitably will be a mixture of patterns, each dimension may be considered a continuum.

- *The complexity syndrome:* Some cultures rely on a great number of distinctions and complex relationships among different persons and groups (such as extended families and diverse occupations), whereas other cultures are comparatively simpler.
- *The individualism syndrome:* Cultures grant greater or lesser primacy to the relatively independent rights and goals of individual actors.
- *The collectivism syndrome:* Cultures grant greater or lesser primacy to conformity with larger social groups; this tendency can either take a *horizontal* form of high interdependence and cooperation with the group, or a *vertical* form that emphasizes service or conformity on the basis of authority, structure, and tradition.
- *The tightness syndrome:* Cultures differ in the extent they implicitly regulate behaviors by norms and roles. Tighter cultures prescribe relatively narrow norms of behavior and strict sanctions for deviating from them, whereas looser cultures tolerate or accept a range of conflicting or pluralistic norms. According to research in this area, tightness appears to correlate with homogeneity—that is, the more similar a group's members might be, the tighter the norms of behavior are likely to be.

Source: Triandis, 1994 (pp. 144–180).

With these reservations in mind, Triandis (1994) summarizes research showing how cultures can be categorized in four different ways. There are cultures that can be typified (1) as more or less complex in the social distinctions they invoke (the *complexity syndrome*), (2) as more or less individualistic in the ways they attach importance to a single human being (the *individualism syndrome*), (3) as more or less interested in conformity based on interdependence and tradition (the *collectivism syndrome*), and (4) as more or less reliant on strict norms and roles for regulating behavior (the *tightness syndrome*).

borderlands and border crossings

Some of the research summarized in the preceding section might suggest that it is relatively simple to measure or categorize cultures. You might also be tempted to jump to the conclusion that because such measures have been developed, higher scores on certain criteria might indicate that some cultures are "better" or more admirable than others, or that cultural differences present insurmountable problems for communicators.

See Chapter 5 for more information about the communication rules that govern how these patterns develop distinctively in different cultures.

However, cultural differences may not be as isolating or as disabling as some people assume. In one sense, it's intuitively obvious that cultural comparisons, such as comparing people's expectations for appropriate behavior in Russia and Rio de Janeiro, will involve differences. But does this mean that everything is different? Clearly not. We live in an age of media involvement that cuts across historical national and cultural boundaries. Many people, if not most, live at the intersections of a variety of cultural traditions and become competent at a variety of cultural vocabularies. Albert Murray (1970) observes that blacks and whites in the United States have evolved traditions that differ from each other, but they have also co-created such traditions as jazz and forms of everyday talk that thoroughly interfuse blacks and whites with each other. Murray believes that African Americans and whites, despite their many differences, are culturally more similar to each other than either is similar to any other cultural group in the world.

When cultural practices mix vigorously, we can expect extraordinary communication. Literary theorist Mikhail Bakhtin (1986) believes that cultural boundaries are especially important for understanding what motivates writers. He thinks that critics "have not taken into account that the most intense and productive life of culture takes place on the boundaries of its individual areas and not in places where these areas have become enclosed in their own specificity" (p. 2). The same reminder applies to theorists.

A similar concept, **borderlands** (Anzaldúa, 1987, 1988; Rosaldo, 1989), helps us understand not only important differences but also the overlaps and profound interpersonal challenges of cross-cultural living (see Box 7-2). Gloria Anzaldúa (1987) suggests that to discuss "borders" (as opposed to "borderlands") is to "define the places that are safe and unsafe, to distinguish *us* from *them*. A border is a dividing line, a narrow strip along a steep edge" (p. 3). However, Anzaldúa (1987) uses the term *borderlands* to refer to the places where people live who are affected by the different sides of the border; that is, people who find their identities defined exclusively by neither side of the border, but defined simultaneously by the contradictions and tensions of both sides. The borderlands concept means that our future will not be in the hands of people whose identities are culturally insulated or pure-bred, but will be defined increasingly by "a new space: a new field of identity" (Sanchez-Tranquilino & Tagg, 1992, p. 560). This new kind of vigorous if often tense cultural environment will place a premium on flexible communicators—those able to switch freely between cultural codes of language and behavior, and live with ambiguity and contradiction. The borderlands concept thus invites students of culture to imagine how people exist and live not just within but also across older definitions of cultural borders.

Renato Rosaldo (1989) reinforces Anzaldúa's insight:

In rejecting the classic "authenticity" of cultural purity, she seeks out the many-stranded possibilities of the borderlands. By sorting through and weaving together its overlapping strands, Anzaldúa's identity becomes ever stronger, not diffused. She argues that because Chicanos have so long prac-

BOX 7-2

THE BORDERLANDS CONCEPT

- Reminds theorists not to assume that cultural differences are pure or contained within borders, but that most people live in the vicinity of various borders and are inevitably affected by simultaneous cultural influences.
- Reminds theorists that cultural differences cannot be measured precisely because social actors always absorb a variety of cultural influences within a pluralistic society.
- Reminds theorists that most persons live in many different borderlands, and that people will be increasingly challenged to negotiate competing demands on their communicative energy.
- Reminds theorists to take a process perspective on communication, one that emphasizes change, adjustment, ambiguity, and flexibility over static definitions of what a culture "is."
- Reminds theorists that a new kind of cultural identity can emerge from the tensions of blending different codes and cultural patterns.

---

ticed the art of cultural blending, "we" now stand in a position to become leaders in developing new forms of polyglot cultural creativity. . . .

A renewed concept of culture thus refers less to a unified entity ("a culture") than to the mundane practices of everyday life. . . . Ethnographers look less for homogeneous communities than for the border zones within and between them. Such cultural border zones are always in motion, not frozen for inspection. (pp. 216–217)

In other words, you should temper your understanding of Triandis's (1994) cultural syndromes with an understanding of how difficult it is to assess cultural differences with precision.

high- and low-context cultures

Although the borderlands concept warns us not to overgeneralize the importance of a culture's borders, researchers remain interested in how patterns of verbal and nonverbal communication vary among cultural groups. Remember that verbal and nonverbal messages cannot be considered separately, because each message code operates as the context for the other code. Thus, for example, a comment expressing your confidence about an upcoming exam will always be interpreted in the context of some nonverbal message, such as a furrowed brow that suggests to the listener you're worried about the exam. Similarly, the nonverbal message of a handshake is usually embedded in a sequence of talk that lets an observer know how to "take" the handshake.

Edward T. Hall (1992), an anthropologist whose work has influenced generations of diplomats, travelers, and scholars, has devoted his professional life to a form of scholarly *empathy*. He attempts to place himself within the standpoints of non-Western cultures in order to make their everyday habits and interpretations seem less "strange" and more accessible to the European and North American mind.

Among his other contributions, Hall (1977) has popularized the distinction between **high-context (HC) cultures** and **low-context (LC) cultures**:

> A high-context (HC) communication or message is one in which most of the information is either in the physical context or internalized in the person, while very little is in the coded, explicit, transmitted part of the message. A low-context (LC) communication is just the opposite; i.e., the mass of the information is invested in the explicit code. Twins who have grown up together can and do communicate more economically (HC) than two lawyers in a courtroom during a trial (LC), a mathematician programming a computer, two politicians drafting legislation, two administrators writing a regulation, or a child trying to explain to his mother why he got into a fight. (p. 91)

Notice how Hall's context distinction depends on understanding the relationship between verbal and nonverbal message systems. What a person says to a listener to a large extent is based on what the speaker presumes the listener knows or is able to figure out from the context, and therefore what doesn't need to be specified overtly. Cultures differ in the extent to which their actors depend on nonverbal messages to clarify verbal messages. Some cultures (HC) rely heavily on such nonverbal messages as object language, tone of voice (a form of paralinguistics), and timing (chronemics) to alert listeners to what needn't be said in order to presume understanding. But other cultures (LC) socialize speakers to approach talk in a more explicit and elaborated way; low-context cultures expect listeners to supply fewer elements of context as essential message features. (See Box 7-3.)

Hall's distinction between HC and LC cultures extends the linguistic research (Bernstein, 1960) that distinguishes between *elaborated codes* and *restricted codes* (see Box 7-4). People speaking in an **elaborated code** supply a great deal of verbal explanation and information because they are expected to do so. Receivers cannot be expected in elaborated code situations to make connections easily or to have a storehouse of concepts with which to contextualize the new message. Let's consider an appropriate and very immediate example: In writing this textbook for students of communication, as authors we must use a relatively elaborated code. Even though some readers might be comfortable with less explanation, we would risk not reaching other readers who might have less background in the field if we used a less elaborated code. The classroom, therefore, is often an elaborated code situation, analogous to Hall's idea of a low-context culture. In other words, teachers can't assume too much about what students will under-

L I N K

Review the basic concepts of Chapter 3, "The Context of Communication," in order to understand more fully how cultures and cultural differences reflect how people manage contexts differently.

BOX 7-3

THE CULTURAL IMPACT OF CONTEXTING

Hall's theoretical distinctions suggest a highly practical interpersonal skill he calls "contexting":

> Japanese, Arab, and Mediterranean peoples who have extensive information networks among family, friends, colleagues, and clients, and who are involved in close personal relationships, are "high-context" (HC). As a result, for most normal transactions in daily life they do not require, nor do they expect, much in-depth background information. This is because it is their nature to keep themselves informed about everything having to do with the people who are important in their lives. Low-context people include the Americans and the Germans, Swiss, Scandinavians, and other northern Europeans. Within each culture, of course, there are specific individual differences in the need for contexting—that is, the process of filling in background data—but it is helpful to know whether or not the culture of a particular country falls on the high or low side of the scale. . . .
>
> HC people are apt to become impatient and irritated when LC people insist on giving them information they don't need. Conversely, low-context people are at a loss when high-context people do not provide enough information. One of the great communications challenges in life is to find the appropriate level of contexting which is customary both at home and abroad. Too much information frequently leads people to feel they are being talked down to; too little information can mystify them or make them feel left out.

Source: Hall and Hall, 1987 (pp. 8, 11).

stand through context without verbal elaboration, because they aren't sure of all the different experiential contexts of their listeners.

A **restricted code,** in contrast, might characterize the talk of sorority sisters, for example, if they have lived together for an extended period. Over time, persons who interact often with each other develop special streamlined speech forms that are highly context-dependent, in Hall's terms. In such relationships, less needs to be verbalized in order for others to understand and identify with a speaker. Twins, to use another fairly obvious example, may know each other well enough to be able to finish each other's sentences accurately; they share a restricted code.

Anthropologist Mary Douglas believes that all language depends to some extent on unspoken assumptions, but that it takes a sophisticated understanding of communication to be able to study what's *not* said as well as what *is* said. This is why

BOX 7-4

HALL'S CONTEXT DISTINCTIONS
FOR CULTURES

- *High-context cultures* rely more on context to help communicators understand the intended meanings of messages. These communication systems depend more on *restricted codes* of language.
- *Low-context cultures* rely more on verbal description to help communicators understand the intended meanings of messages. These communication systems depend more on *elaborated codes* of language.

Source: Hall, 1977.

she titles one of her books *Implicit Meanings* (1975). Researchers such as Bernstein (1960) and herself, Douglas writes, are "interested in the dark side of the moon, in the meanings that are conveyed without being spoken" (1975, p. 173). Studying culture means explaining how people decide on mixing the spoken with the unspoken, which is another way of stating that "culture is communication" (Hall, 1959).

THEORIZING ABOUT CULTURAL DILEMMAS

Some people assume that the role of theories is to aid in the description of the world. Through theories, the assumption goes, we discover more and more about how complex processes work, which, in turn, better enables us to know what we want to do about them. This assumption certainly describes a major function of theorizing, and most social scientists are guided by it. Surely most of the theorists discussed in *Questions of Communication* have been motivated by this goal of discovery.

the role of theoretical critique

Some theorists, however, also recognize that theories themselves are potent social forces. Sometimes, in fact, our theories are so interwoven into our lives that we lose sight of them as theories and act as if they *are* the realities they supposedly represent. Recall from Chapter 1 that a theory can never be value free; instead, it always involves the value assumptions of the theorist. Remember, too, that once a theory becomes widely discussed and acceptable (if not also fully accepted), it can create blinders for researchers and analysts who might find the theory so persuasive that they're unable to think outside of its suggested parameters.

Whether such blinders are big or small problems often depends on who you ask. Some theorists, especially in the broad field of cultural communication and criticism, approach theory not as a method of empirical discovery, but as an ideological playing field. To them, some practices become widespread not just because they illuminate some truth, but also because they are politically comfortable or beneficial to groups in power. These theorists ask unsettling questions, such as: Who profits from the belief that large-scale studies of men can be generalized to include women's behavior? Who profits from the belief that the essential standards for assessing world civilizations seem to have been developed in the European context of ancient Greek and Roman civilization? Thus, some very intriguing theorizing in communication and other social sciences focuses on where the interpersonal dimensions of culture meet the interpersonal implications of cultural politics.

Communication students who are curious about social practices generally will want to understand some basic vocabulary of the vigorous dialogue about multiculturalism now taking place in the intellectual world. A look through communication journals in recent years should convince you that our discipline is immersed in such a dialogue, yet the controversy rages widely across disciplinary boundaries. Some theorists seek to uncover hidden assumptions in so-called neutral or scientific or observational theorizing, and want to call attention to the far-from-neutral political consequences of communication theories. In other words, their theories critique the ideologies and hidden assumptions of both other theorists and of the social science disciplines.

We suggest that students learn about theories of cultural critique in order to become better informed participants in this important social conversation, and not because we want to push our own agenda. For example, we believe you should learn how Molefi Kete Asante develops his theoretical perspective of Afrocentrism because his ideas are discussed by many other theorists and political figures, and not necessarily because we're convinced that you should become an advocate of Asante's position yourself. We need informed participants in a cultural dialogue of theories, communicators who are knowledgeable enough to be fair both to positions that are personally near and positions that are, culturally speaking, more distant.

In this section, you'll learn about three theoretical positions that respond to somewhat different yet interconnected cultural dilemmas. Despite their differences, you'll note similarities in how the theorists create their arguments and develop their conceptual systems. All of the authors, for example, agree that the issues of power and domination of certain groups over others should be central concerns in cultural theorizing. They also believe that cultural critique can be a valid part of theorizing, in that valid evidence can come from synthesizing historical and critical sources, as well as from the more traditional methods of social science research. We explore how articulation theory responds to dilemmas of class and social distinction, how feminist theorizing and muted group theory responds to certain dilemmas of contemporary gender relations, and how Afrocentric theory responds to the dilemma of race.

the dilemma of power: articulation theory

Cultural studies has developed over the past two or three decades as a cross-disciplinary look at how communicative power is identified with broad social and

L I N K

Chapter 8 presents theories about how attitudes are changed in public settings. For now, imagine the challenges of "contexting" that confront such cross-cultural persuaders as international marketing executives and diplomatic representatives.

cultural patterns of understanding (Carey, 1989; Grossberg, Nelson, & Treichler, 1992). Sociologists, political scientists, psychologists, literary critics, philosophers, and communication scholars from a wide range of traditions have been attracted to cultural studies approaches, but most of their works are characterized by an intense interest in media influence and interpersonal communication. Cultural studies scholars tend not to be quantitatively oriented in their methods (some may even ignore or renounce surveys and experimental designs for gathering communication data). Instead, they prefer qualitative methods of critical analysis and diagnosis. "Theory" to them means a slightly different enterprise than it does to quantitative social scientists. As Slack (1996) explains:

> "Theory" is a term that often connotes an objective, formal tool, or even a "value-free" heuristic device. Cultural studies resists thinking in terms of the "application" of theory in this sense. . . . In place of that conception of theory, cultural studies works with the notion of theory as a "detour" to help ground our engagement with what newly confronts us and to let that engagement provide the ground for retheorizing. Theory is thus a practice in a double sense: it is a formal conceptual tool as well as a practising or "trying out" of a way of theorizing. . . . Successful theorizing is not measured by exact theoretical fit but by the ability to work with our always inadequate theories to help us move understanding "a little further on down the road." (p. 113)

The theorist Slack has in mind when discussing this approach is perhaps the most influential representative of contemporary cultural studies, the British intellectual Stuart Hall.

Among Stuart Hall's (1989, 1992, 1996) many enduring contributions to this area of research is his application of **articulation theory**. Cultural studies theorists use articulation theory to explain power relations as *communication phenomena,* not as mere exercises in overt manipulation or coercion. We discuss Hall's approach to articulation theory first because it provides a useful context for the other more specific gender and racial approaches, as you will see later in this section.

By *articulation,* Hall (1996) refers to the process by which ideas and cultural concepts—that may or may not otherwise be closely related—are linked through public discussion into complex clusters that then appear to be unified and whole. His use of the word *articulation* implies two meanings: (1) The more obvious sense of something related to talk (e.g., people are said to "articulate" well if they talk plainly and to be "articulate" if they speak intelligently), and (2) the less common sense of how things can become connected, attached, or adjusted together (e.g., in a company, the research and development department has to be "articulated" with the marketing department in order for its products to be successful). Hall (1996, p. 141) points out that in Britain, an "articulated lorry" (a truck) is what people in the United States would call a trailer; the front cab of the truck is connectable to any number and kinds of trailer loads, depending on the choice of the company or client.

Articulation, then, is a rich metaphor for ideas. Political and advertising campaigns can be articulated—hooked, in a sense—to a wide range of discursive

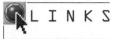

LINKS

• Does Stuart Hall's articulation theory remind you in some ways of the general systems theory, discussed in Chapter 1? Both theories discuss the relation of wholes to their parts. After reviewing systems assumptions in Chapter 1, and after reading this chapter's section on articulation theory, decide for yourself what their similarities and differences might be. For example, what interest does Hall seem to have in describing the interdependence of the various components linked or articulated together in cultural conversations? How might GST theorists deal with hierarchies and power relations?

• Does articulation theory also remind you of some of the problems associated with the social context of communication, discussed in Chapter 3? How might the articulated whole become the context through which its linked parts must be interpreted? Review Chapter 3 for clues to this interesting question.

appeals based on different cultural values. In the 1988 presidential election, for instance, it was a process of articulation by which Vice President Bush's campaign sought to identify Governor Dukakis with the label of "liberal" and with the American Civil Liberties Union (ACLU). This method of encoding messages relied on a complicated set of power relations, including the credibility of a sitting administration, the target audience's image of liberals as "soft on crime," and the electorate's association of the ACLU with minority and crime issues. Similarly, in the 1996 presidential election, President Clinton's campaigners used a strategy of articulation when their ads implemented the "Dolegingrich" strategy, attacking Bob Dole and the then much less popular Speaker of the House Newt Gingrich as a team, though Gingrich did *not* run as Dole's vice presidential candidate.

Although articulation theory has not always been applied in precise ways in cultural studies (see Hall, 1996; Moffitt, 1993; O'Sullivan, Hartley, Saunders, Montgomery, & Fiske, 1994, pp. 17–18; Slack, 1989, 1996), it is especially useful in analyzing cultural problems in contexts where there are competing interests with different investments of power and domination. As Stuart Hall and other theorists apply the concept of articulation, it appears to have the following characteristics (see also Box 7-5):

1. *Articulations are shifting, temporary phenomena, constantly in flux.* An articulation that once served a cultural purpose may be rearticulated when power bases and group goals change. In the 1960s, for example, Jews were the minority most closely aligned with the black civil rights movement in the U.S. South; in the 1990s, many African Americans have sought different cultural alliances.

2. *Articulations are arbitrary features of discourse; they are not necessary or inherent in the phenomena being described.* In other words, articulations are not the properties of unified wholes but are characteristics of how we talk about phenomena we consider whole. Consider, as an example, a train that travels between Philadelphia and New York. "It" has a number and a schedule, and regular travelers are used to saying that "it" is later or earlier today than "it" was yesterday. However, in terms of its actual components, today's train may be composed of a very different set of cars, coupled (articulated) in a very different way, than yesterday's train. But the

---

BOX 7-5

ARTICULATIONS:

- Are links or connections between phenomena or groups that produce the structure of cultural events, groups, or texts.
- Are shifting and temporary.
- Are arbitrary constructions that can be observed in the discourse about events, groups, and texts.
- Are dependent on social hierarchies and distributions of power.
- Are links forged between dissimilar, as well as between similar, elements.

travelers are convinced that, even though the *physical* identity of the train's components may be quite different, the *essential* identity of the train remains the same. Of course, the *potential* identities of a number of trains are highly variable, depending on the articulations decided on by those with the power to determine the trains' couplings. The Republican Party identifies itself as the party of Abraham Lincoln, which appeals to minority voters, while the ACLU identifies itself as an organization that protects both conservative and liberal free speech. Both organizations want to be perceived as unified wholes, but articulation theory suggests that they—and all groups and ideologies—are formed by articulated links among shifting components. Such theorists and critics analyze the articulations through which today's "train" might be differently coupled than yesterday's train.

3. *Articulations are dependent on hierarchical relationships.* Articulation theorists note that although a truck's trailer may be larger and heavier than the truck's cab, its movement depends on decisions directed from the front. Therefore, articulation theory asks such power-based questions as these: Who *gets* to define the relationship between two ideas? Who relies on whom for assent or acquiescence? How do groups come to understand that their voices have more or less impact than the voices of other groups? Not surprisingly, many articulation theorists are motivated by Marxist social analyses, in which ideology is an important concept. An **ideology** is a set of ideas that is so thoroughly accepted by its believers that they do not question its existence or importance. Some would argue that American individualism is an ideology within the social sphere, and that American capitalism is an ideology within the economic sphere. According to Slack (1989), ideology "is the mechanism that organizes the multiplicity of connections into a temporarily essentialized system of representation within which we live out those connections as real. Ideology is . . . of particular importance, for it is within ideology that relations of power are presented, represented, contested, and rearticulated" (p. 333).

4. *Articulations potentially tie together both similarity and difference,* allowing theorists to describe how cultural phenomena are often composed of both unity and distinctiveness, the harmony of sameness and the tension of difference. Hall (1996) cites singer Bruce Springsteen's appeal as one that "can be read, with equal conviction, in at least two diametrically opposed ways. [Springsteen's] audiences seem to be made up of people from 5 to 50, busily reading him in different ways. The symbols are deeply American—populist in their ambiguity; he's both in the White House and On The Road. In the 1960s, you had to be one or the other. Springsteen is somehow both at the same time" (p. 138). The concept of articulation thus allows us to think of a complex cultural phenomenon as *both* a unified whole and composed of different parts, perhaps even inconsistent or contradictory parts. Once you begin to sense how common articulations are, it is logical to ask who in society has the power to disseminate their articulations of events and how they put that power into play.

Articulation theory, then, gives students of communication a useful vocabulary for describing how communicative power is expressed and perceived—or, as Hall puts it, how that power is "read."

the dilemma of gender: feminist theorizing and muted group theory

"The modern women's movement," writes linguist Robin Lakoff (1990), "now has behind it some twenty years of theoretical thinking about the many aspects of 'the woman question,' one of the most important and agonizingly insoluble issues among them being language. From early on, women have recognized the need to take back the language, reclaim it or parts of it, get a right to decide about how to speak and be spoken of and to" (p. 198).

One approach to understanding culture is to understand how it structures language and nonverbal practices between and among its various subgroups. A related issue of great cultural significance is how cultures make meaningful (or even validate) the differences between women's and men's communication habits. In some cultures, reports Lakoff (1990, pp. 200–201), anthropologists have found that men and women claim to have developed separate languages that are unintelligible to each other. Lakoff, however, suggests that at most, such men and women have decided to pretend that they *can't* understand each other when in fact they actually *can*. In a predominantly Western model of gender, though, they often *don't* understand each other well, although they pretend they *do*. Lakoff (1990) notices that "there are deep and subtle differences that lead to more serious kinds of misunderstanding: both sexes use the same words in the same constructions, but understand them differently. This misunderstanding is serious: we think we understand and have been understood, when we really don't and haven't. The differences lie in areas that are not explicitly available for inspection, that require metacommunication to be fully examined. And . . . metacommunication is not something this culture (like most) values or is comfortable doing" (p. 201). Women and men who grow up speaking English are likely to believe that certain differences in female and male communication are natural. Men and women may speak somewhat differently, use different strategies in their speech styles, choose different adjectives in certain situations, have different communicative goals and motives, establish different nonverbal patterns, and be talked about by others differently (Frank & Anshen, 1983; Kalbfleisch & Cody, 1995; Kramerae, 1981; Kramerae & Treichler, 1990; Wood, 1996).

Are these differences between women and men natural? Research in gender roles suggests that many of the differences can be attributed to conditions of power and powerlessness. That is, while some women's speech has been found to include more hesitations, qualifiers, and tag questions than men's speech, Frank and Anshen (1983) summarize research that suggests these features are also characteristic of the speech of other power-diminished groups: "The use of the stereotypically women's language features is correlated more with social powerlessness than with sex" (p. 46). But answering this question raises another: How do the differences in power develop?

L I N K

Lakoff's (1990) mention of metacommunication should ring a bell for you. Review Chapter 6 for more on metacommunication, and on how communicators' meanings for each other are clarified by communicating about communication. Metacommunication can be a relatively simple outcome of the interaction of verbal and nonverbal codes, as it usually is (a wink tells you not to take an insult seriously), or it can be an elaborate strategy to talk about someone's talk (as in a therapist's conversation with a client). Lakoff refers to conscious attempts to metacommunicate, to take the covert assumptions of communicative interaction and unfold them overtly.

LINK

Muted group theorists, whose approach could be adapted to understanding communication styles of any subordinated social group, relate the feminist critique of language to a basic assumption of *linguistic relativity*, discussed in Chapter 4. The given view of reality that a language system presumes makes it difficult to see the system's effects and even more difficult at times to see an escape. See Chapter 4 for a fuller discussion of linguistic relativity and its critics.

Feminist theory points to sexist distinctions inherent in the English language, a phenomenon that children growing up in families and schools cannot avoid. Remember that language structures personal experience, as we have stressed in this book. Language is our agency of socialization and the prime criterion by which progress in the school system is judged. As male and female children become proficient in language, they become attuned to the power differences that distinguish the sexes. Although we do not have the space in this book to summarize the full argument, feminists theorize that subtle and not-so-subtle linguistic features, such as the use of *he* and *mankind* to refer to women as well as men, and the tendency to call professional women by their first names while using titles for their male counterparts, all support the presumption of power inequality between the genders (see Pearson, Turner, & Todd-Mancillas, 1991, pp. 79–102).

Theorists and researchers distinguish between gender and sex, although most people in everyday life do not. *Sex* is a biological and physiological condition into which a person is born, and **gender** is a cultural and social construction created by how people talk about different kinds of male and female behavior. As Wood (1996) observes: "Biological sex is transformed into culturally constructed gender as we interact with social structures and practices that express, uphold, and encourage individuals to embody prevailing views of women and men" (p. 4).

Therefore, women and men tend to internalize different power patterns, to speak with predictably different linguistic patterns called *genderlects* (which are analogous to dialects), and to reinforce different social stereotypes. One particularly focused approach that attempts to account for these differences is **muted group theory**, originally developed in the writings of anthropologists (Ardener, 1978) and well summarized in the communication field by Cheris Kramerae (1981). Kramerae argues that women's language is often effectively silenced or redirected relative to the power of men's language. Muted group theorists assume that the differently socialized gender experiences of men and women create different perceptions of how the world works. Further, they assume, in Kramerae's account, that the "political dominance" of men's perceptions translates into the linguistic habits of individual speakers, "impeding the free expression of women's alternative models of the world," and that women are implicitly required to alter their models to reflect male communication patterns or to become "mute" or inarticulate (p. 3). Men then use women's muteness or inarticulateness in such situations to support the existing structure of interpersonal politics.

In a review of muted group theorizing and associated research on women's talk, Kramerae (1981) notes that the theory also suggests the following hypotheses:

- Females are more likely to have difficulty expressing themselves fluently within dominant (public) modes of expression.
- Males have more difficulty than females in understanding what members of the other gender mean.
- Females are likely to find ways to express themselves outside the dominant public modes of expression used by males.
- Females are more likely to state dissatisfaction with the dominant public modes of expression.

- Women refusing to live by the ideas of social organization held by the dominant group . . . will change dominant public modes of expression as they consciously and verbally reject those ideas.
- Females are not as likely to coin the words that become widely recognized and used by both men and women.
- Females' sense of humor—what relationships between persons, places, and things they consider incongruous—will differ from males' sense of humor. (p. 4)

Recall, from the Introduction to this book, our discussion of Belenky and colleagues' *Women's Ways of Knowing* (1986) study. Although they do not test muted group theory directly, their extensive interviews reinforce Kramerae's point. Belenky et al. (1986) note that silence is a position that characterizes many women's reaction to public life, at least at the beginning of their involvement in it. The researchers also describe a "continued injunction against articulating needs, feelings, and experiences" among women, an expectation that women should "curtail their voice," and a "tendency to allocate speaking to men and listening to women" (p. 167). One interviewee, a successful professional woman, made these revealing comments: "You know, the older I get the more I realize that I'm willing to talk about things I care about only if I know the other person is really listening. If I don't feel that, I find myself falling into a silence, even when I'm at work or in the middle of a professional meeting" (p. 147).

the dilemma of race: afrocentric theory

In 1995 and 1997, the U.S. media audience became engrossed in the O. J. Simpson trials. Simpson, the actor and former football star accused of murdering his ex-wife and her friend, was found not guilty after a long and complex criminal trial, in which both the defense and the prosecution were said to have "played the race card." That is, they supposedly made race-based appeals to the jury and, secondarily, to the public, based on Simpson's status as an African American. His acquittal sparked different emotional reactions, largely along racial lines; blacks generally celebrated and whites generally protested. In 1997, a second trial based on a lawsuit, this time in civil court, reconsidered these issues and found Simpson liable.

Throughout the Simpson controversy, lawyers, commentators, and everyday observers discussed race as though the term clearly denoted a consistent and clear meaning for various publics. Most people, in fact, believe that race is a biological or scientific label for a set of clearly defined characteristics that differentiate human groups. Even though everyday speakers usually aren't sure of the science behind the word *race,* we continue to use the term as though we, and all our listeners, know exactly what we're talking about. However, as a number of commentators argue (see Box 7-6), race has largely lost its status as a precise biological concept, and instead may have become one of our most prominent social myths. **Race**, in effect, has become a shorthand way of referring to differences in our cultural patterns of communication, as they are linked (rightly or wrongly) to visible physical features such as skin color.

L I N K S

- Belenky et al.'s (1986) research on "women's ways of knowing," reviewed in the Introduction to this book, indicates that an immersion in silence, a position that some women take, is relatively rare. Nevertheless, it "is an important anchoring point for our epistemological scheme, representing an extreme in denial of self and in dependence on external authority for direction" (p. 24). The women interviewed, however, repeatedly used the metaphor of "gaining a voice" to describe their learning, personal growth, and development, suggesting that the fear of being silenced may be a common experience for women.
- Some feminists (Collins, 1991) have identified themselves specifically as black feminist theorists. One prominent feature of this approach is its consistent reliance on dialogic principles. See the related discussions of interdependence in Chapter 6 and of dialogic ethics in Chapter 10.

BOX 7-6

WHAT IS RACE?
BACKGROUND FOR COMMUNICATION THEORISTS

- Race is "a social category of people who are supposedly distinguished by inherited and invariable characteristics. Whereas race can at first glance be viewed as an innocent description of what certain people look like, it carries a hidden agenda about their 'nature,' how they behave and are expected to behave." Further, "ultimately we have to identify an unofficial package of ideas and assumptions that go with race: that a racial group has historical legacies associated with a geographically defined area and culture of origin, and that usually such groups can be identified by skin colour. The stage is therefore set for xenophobia and bigotry . . ." (O'Sullivan et al., 1994, pp. 255, 256).

- " 'Race' as a meaningful criterion within the biological sciences has long been recognized to be a fiction. When we speak of the 'white race' or the 'black race,' the 'Jewish race' or the 'Aryan race,' we speak in misnomers, biologically, and in metaphors, more generally. Nevertheless, our conversations are replete with usages of race which have their sources in the dubious pseudo-science of the eighteenth and nineteenth centuries" (Gates, 1992, p. 48).

- "The term 'race' itself has become suspect in scientific circles. Nevertheless, in popular parlance . . . 'race' . . . continue[s] to be widely used" (Montagu & Matson, 1979, p. 175).

- "There is no doubt that all human beings descend from an original population (probably, as it happens, in Africa), and from there people radiated out to cover the habitable globe. . . . In a sense, trying to classify people into a few races is like trying to classify books in a library: you may use a single property—size, say—but you will get a useless classification, or you may use a more complex system of interconnected criteria, and then you will get a good deal of arbitrariness. No one—not even the most compulsive librarian!—thinks that book classifications reflect deep facts about books" (Appiah, 1992, pp. 37, 38).

We are not suggesting that people should stop using the word *race*. We only suggest that you remember how the term is used in contemporary discussions of race; that is, to refer to very rough generalizations about different groups' cultural patterns of communication. If you're interested in a challenging summary of recent discoveries about what we term *race*, see Kwame Appiah's (1992, pp. 28–46) essay, "Illusions of Race."

Clearly, different groups develop different cultures, and the rules and expectations of those cultures color their perceptions of the world. What is less clear is how communicators might try to avoid using their own culture's pattern as the standard for how all people should communicate. Molefi Kete Asante, writing as

Arthur L. Smith, published one of the first books in the field of communication on interracial interaction, *Transracial Communication* (1973). In recent years, he's become a foremost critic of *Eurocentrism*, the tendency to explain and judge all cultural phenomena in terms of standards developed within traditional European art, science, literature, and philosophy.

For example, a public speech considered by most teachers in the United States to be organized, rational, well supported, and effective tends to conform to rhetorical standards developed in ancient Greece and Rome by Aristotle, Cicero, Quintillian, and other classical teachers. In addition, the European world tends to regard a speech as the speaker's uninterrupted possession, undertaken while a passive audience attends to the speaker's message. Asante does not argue that these standards are wrong; rather, he points out that they are not universal. Thus, his argument is not with the application of European theories of communication and science to many people and situations, but with aggressive attempts to impose those standards on all people and all cultures equally. There is no single right way to give a speech, but many ways that will lead to different kinds of effectiveness depending on the cultural context. To extend the speech example, Eurocentric analysts have a difficult time understanding a shared-responsibility speech situation, where an audience actively cooperates verbally with the speaker (as in the African American call-and-response tradition; its enthusiastic audience responses often sound like interruptions to Europeans and others outside the tradition).

Similarly, Asante (1987) contends, European thinking should not be the presumed benchmark for all questions of science, politics, religion, and social policy. Thus, because we stressed in Chapter 1 that theories involve the values and assumptions of the theorists and researchers who develop them, Eurocentrism has implications not only for the theorizing done by scholars, but also for the theorizing we are able to imagine doing in the future (see Box 7-7).

Asante (1980, 1987) responds to Eurocentrism with the theoretical counterposition of **Afrocentricity,** which is based on the alignment of African Americans and others in the world with African cultural origins. (Following Asante's reasoning, Asians [see Cheng, 1987; Kincaid, 1987b], Arabs [see Hasnain, 1988; Said, 1978, 1981, 1993; Tehranian, 1988], and others in the world may find themselves in unique rhetorical and cultural situations not easily couched in terms of Euro-

---

BOX 7-7

WHERE DOES SOCIAL SCIENCE DO ITS RESEARCH?

"Social psychology is a product of Europe and North America. Almost all that we know systematically about social behavior was derived by studying individuals and groups from those regions of the world. However, 70 percent of the earth's population lives outside Europe and North America; in cultures that are quite different from those of the 'West.' "

Source: Triandis, 1994 (p. xv).

pean ideals.) Asante's theoretical position involves "placing African ideals at the center of any analysis that involves African culture and behavior" (1987, p. 6). Note that in response to what Asante perceives as the Eurocentric tendency to place European thinking at the center of all cultural understanding, he does not assume that we should substitute African thinking to bump Eurocentrism from that center. Asante's historical and critical synthesis of evidence suggests, that people of African descent will never find an authentic cultural existence while denying the influence of African cultural experience. Empathy, not domination, appears to be Asante's (1987) essential motivation: "Ascertaining the view of the other is important in understanding human phenomena. African responses and actions, however, have too often been examined from Eurocentric perspectives. The misunderstandings between Europeans and others have provoked in me an interest in alternative perspectives" (p. 11). Although some theorists who label themselves Afrocentric are more politically oriented, and some Afrocentric historical summaries have been criticized (Coughlin, 1996), Asante tries not to substitute one form of overgeneralization for another. He simply wants to get beyond what he terms the intellectual colonialism of Europe.

Many concepts are important in Afrocentric theory, and each seems to be related closely to the others. In one of his touchstone works, *The Afrocentric Idea* (1987), Asante stresses these communication concepts:

1. *Rhetorical condition.* Asante suggests that we should pay less attention to what is said in various situations and more to the conditions in which talk (and the designation of who is able to talk) is governed by power and dominance relationships. A theorist understands communication and social rhetoric not just by listening to the content of words, but also by focusing on the structural assumptions of power that govern any cultural situation.

2. *Orature.* This term refers to "the sum total of oral tradition [in African-based culture], which includes vocality, drumming, storytelling, praise singing, and naming" (Asante, 1987, p. 60). Even though there is an important historical legacy of literature in Africa, the Afrocentric perspective fundamentally values talk over writing. The spontaneity, immediacy, and narrative base of the spoken word reigns over the sequential, linear, writing-oriented rationality of European cultural standards. An oral tradition values a wider range of rhetorical effectiveness than the narrow persuasive ideals of traditional rationality; it also invests the audience with much of the rhetorical power that European systems attribute to the individual speaker. Further, Afrocentric theory tends to presume—contrary to the European perspective—that arguments don't themselves have power apart from how they're said and by whom.

3. *Nommo.* A powerful aspect of Afrocentric orature is a kind of reverence for the spoken word as an instrument of *nommo,* which Asante (1987) describes as "the generative and productive power of the spoken word" (p. 17). When speakers are immersed in *nommo,* Asante says, they understand that "all magic is word magic" (p. 49). It involves not only what

LINK

In Chapter 8, we discuss the European rhetorical tradition in more detail. Aristotle, an ancient Greek philosopher, defined rhetoric as the art of finding the available means of persuasion in a situation. European styles of teaching rhetoric emphasize the desire to change someone else's mind. In contrast, Asante (1987) defines an Afrocentric sense of rhetoric as "the productive thrust of language into the unknown in an attempt to create harmony and balance in the midst of disharmony and indecision" (p. 35). Do the two positions on rhetoric suggest different ethical premises? Keep this question in mind when reading Chapter 10, "Theories of Communication Ethics."

words mean, but also how they're said through "intonation and tonal styling," which are *substantive* parts of most African American oratory" (p. 48). We can hear *nommo* in action in rap music and in how African American disk jockeys present the music. McPhail (1994) believes that *nommo* is a form of rhetoric that "offers some important theoretical directions for a discussion of race based upon parallel conceptions of communicative action" (p. 106). The Afrocentric assumption is that the word is never conceptually static but always changing, acting as a stimulus to further meaning, and in no sense a package or object of meaning whose force can be predetermined.

APPLICATIONS AND EXTENSIONS OF CULTURAL COMMUNICATION THEORIES

Clearly, many cultural theorists are interested in clarifying basic communication concepts and in developing critiques of the power structures of class, gender, and race. Students should understand that communication theorists are active participants in the wider intellectual dialogue about culture—a dialogue that sometimes gets so heated that some have termed it the "culture wars." Nevertheless, communication theorists go beyond merely developing concepts or taking critical positions. Historically, the study of intercultural communication also has involved the highly pragmatic task of adapting communicators from one culture to the demands of others (see Leeds-Hurwitz, 1990; Moon, 1996).

Whether theorists want their theories to change society or not, individuals still must develop skill in cross-cultural communication and understanding. We have chosen one major theory to represent how powerful this kind of question of communication can be: Kim's (1988, 1991) cross-cultural adaptation theory. Many other theories could serve the same function, but we find Kim's wide-ranging and rich theory particularly useful in showing how many communication factors are involved in understanding culture. You'll also see again, in the context of this theory, how practical a solid theoretical perspective can be.

an example: cross-cultural adaptation theory

Imagine that a young Japanese woman named Yuko is about to come to the United States to study at a prominent Midwestern university. Although she has taken English throughout most of her schooling in Japan and has thoroughly investigated U.S. culture, she is quite nervous. She has heard stories of other Asian students who were equally talented, but who had bad experiences in America. They got homesick, felt awkward and disconnected, and found that they could barely concentrate on their schoolwork. Although Yuko is happy to have the opportunity to study overseas, she almost wishes she'd never applied for the program that supports her studies. She knows she'll be challenged in ways she can't even begin to imagine (see Box 7-8).

L I N K

Contrast the notion of *nommo* with the assumptions of the *conduit metaphor* discussed in Chapter 2. Recall that the conduit metaphor and its linear way of depicting communication is supposed to be an inherent part of the structure of the English language. It assumes, contrary to Asante's views and contrary to contemporary theories emphasizing *process*, that we act as if words are packages of meaning that can be delivered to receivers. Do you think Afrocentric theory is, in this way, similar to the process-centered view of communication described in Chapter 2? Do you believe Asante is suggesting that African Americans use the language differently? Why or why not?

BOX 7-8

SOME POSSIBLE DISORIENTATIONS
FOR JAPANESE TRAVELERS IN THE UNITED STATES,
AS DESCRIBED BY A CROSS-CULTURAL RESEARCHER

"The Japanese are likely to be startled at the ease with which Americans approach and enter into intense conversations with people they scarcely know. Americans' lack of sensitivity to protocol and to status differences, or their deliberate efforts to undermine them, may appear naive or downright insulting. Their constant questions and revealing disclosure may seem intrusive and overbearing, forcing the Japanese to discuss matters they regard as private. The extent to which Americans recount their experiences, failures, and successes may sound self-centered and pompous. Their informality and impulsiveness may deprive social occasions of their congenial predictability. The pace at which Americans move and talk, their verbal and physical flamboyance, may be unnerving. Their eagerness to contradict, even to argue bluntly, disturbs the harmony that should prevail. Equally astonishing is their ability to engage in such conflicts without it impairing their feeling for each other. Their endless analyzing, insistence on verbal precision, and binding agreements reveal an incredible trust in words over people. They are prone to error because they are always in such a hurry."

Source: Barnlund, 1989 (pp. 190–191).

Young Yun Kim (1988, 1991; Gudykunst & Kim, 1984) has applied her interest in cultural issues to the specific practical question that worries Yuko: How can someone adapt successfully to a new cultural situation? Research in cultural communication, Kim believes, must examine more than the differences between cultures; it should also try to illuminate the practical human problems of what it takes to move from a set of comfortable cultural assumptions—an experience of feeling essentially "at home"—into new cultural assumptions that are experienced as alien and challenging. How does this shift happen for strangers, immigrants, refugees, sojourners, and travelers? Kim, in other words, is not just fascinated by cultures but by developing a **cross-cultural adaptation theory**—the systematic explanation of how individuals learn to reorient their communication assumptions in new cultural contexts.

In an increasingly interdependent world, networked with rapid transportation and communication systems, every person becomes a potential cross-cultural visitor, often unexpectedly. For example, one recent study (Ross, 1996) reports that an increasing number of global firms send executives to other countries to gain competence in cross-culturally ambiguous situations and add to their knowledge about other cultural systems. Many more firms now also bring foreign nationals to the home country to gain the same kind of experience. To understand the cultural disorientation that these managers will face, or that Yuko will face in her student experience, demands a multidisciplinary integration of research ranging from individualistic psychological constructs to large-scale anthropological research (see Box 7-9). Kim (1984, 1988, 1991) suggests that it is not enough simply to believe that the stranger learns culture in a linear way by adding information to previous information, or that adaptation primarily depends on people being tolerant of, or friendly to, each other. Instead, Kim's theory is "integrative." Yuko's kind of question won't be answered by using the individual person as a unit of analysis. A broader theoretical base is needed—the "creative integration" of a systems approach (Kim, 1984).

Kim's theoretical base has several important features, which we have abstracted from a more complex description in her book (1988).

assumptions. Individuals within cultures are "open systems" who inherently seek an internal homeostasis or balance in order to avoid stress. As "open systems," people make decisions about how to act in terms of a continual interchange of information with their environments. They thus develop cultural identities by developing competent communication and information interchanges with that environment. When the environment changes, however, people—as living systems—seek to grow and adapt to those changes. For example, if you have had the experience of studying in another country or culture, you know it was not easy to study while adapting to a new culture, but improvement in studying probably came along with an improvement in your cultural competence. Yet you weren't wholly in charge of your own level of cultural competence, because you had to depend on others in the environment to know how to react. No one can bring into a new environment all the resources necessary for adaptation. Yuko is right to be worried.

Kim uses the terms "stranger," "host," and "ethnic" in ways that may seem unfamiliar at first. A *stranger* is her overall term for someone who comes into an immersive cultural situation without much background for understanding that culture; strangers can be immigrants, travelers, diplomats, or exchange students. *Host* refers generally to the new cultural experience for the stranger—its people, its practices, and its media—taken, for the most part, as a whole. Just as *stranger* doesn't have negative connotations to Kim (as it sometimes does in everyday English), the concept of *host* doesn't necessarily have positive connotations. *Ethnic* refers to the cultural origin of the stranger and, to the extent that there are traces of that origin in the host culture, to the intracultural support groups and neighborhoods that are part of the adaptation process for many people. For example, Yuko, our hypothetical Japanese student, flies into Chicago to begin her year-long adventure as a Northwestern University student. Although she knows English well, she feels like a *stranger* at first, and is considered one in Kim's terms. Gradually, as Yuko encounters the *host* environment more and more deeply (campus, city, national television networks, and so on), she begins to notice more diversity in the host culture, whereas at first she saw primarily how different she was from a uniform culture in which everyone else seemed competent. She is aided in the transition by *ethnic* communities of Japanese students on campus in Evanston and Japanese Americans she meets in the city.

L I N K

Review the principles of general systems theory in Chapter 1 to aid your understanding of Kim's cross-cultural adaptation theory.

dimensions.   Kim develops her theory in terms of six basic dimensions. Although they can be distinguished for purposes of analysis, remember that in a systems approach, each dimension (and its subprocesses) can be related in a variety of ways to all other dimensions. Remember, in other words, that these dimensions are *not* separate categories (see Box 7-9 for an overview).

1. *Personal communication.* In this dimension Kim presents research describing the many factors that influence whether a stranger will be competent in knowing the basic communication expectations of the host system. This aspect of her theory draws on general communication competence literature in order to show how competence (knowing how to communicate effectively) depends on *cognitive* (mental), *affective* (emotional), and *behavioral* (action) factors. Updating Kim's concerns about intercultural communication competence, Chen and Starosta (1996) have recently synthesized the cultural communication literature into three similar categories: *intercultural sensitivity, cognitive process,* and *behavioral process.*

Yuko, having talked with a variety of former international students from Japan, begins to believe she is intellectually well prepared to come to the United States. She reads and writes English as fluently as any of her peers. She has studied with an English tutor who has helped her role-play different conversational situations, such as an advisement appointment in which she chooses classes. However, she is concerned about her emotional readiness and fears she'll feel off-balance at the boldness of American students. Although she knows she is linguistically competent, she feels awkward.

2. *Host social communication.* Much of the cross-cultural adaptation research Kim summarizes describes the extent to which successful adapters participate directly in the social communication processes of the host culture. This includes

---

BOX 7-9

THE BASIC DIMENSIONS OF CROSS-CULTURAL ADAPTATION
- *Personal communication:* how competent the stranger is in the expectations and behaviors of the host system
- *Host social communication:* how the stranger becomes tied to host system relationships and mass-communication content
- *Ethnic social communication:* how the stranger remains tied with representatives and messages of the stranger's own ethnic group
- *Host environment:* how receptive the host environment is to strangers, and how much pressure for conformity it exerts
- *Predisposition:* what the stranger brings as "baggage"—background, preparation for change, openness, and resilience
- *Adaptation outcomes:* how successful adapters achieve functional fitness, psychological health, and an intercultural identity that creates a third-culture perspective

Source: Kim, 1988.

both *interpersonal communication processes* (often researched in terms of the number and strength of host relational ties, such as friendships and close working relationships) and *mass communication processes* (strangers who watch, listen to, and read a great deal of media content may find themselves better adapted to the host culture, thereby increasing their media involvement). The mass communication involvement seems to be especially important as a mediating factor of adaptation in the early stages of cultural transition, before the stranger has had a chance to establish interpersonal ties. Kim's (1988) metaphor helps us understand the crucial importance of social communication: "The process of migration from society to society can be compared to the up-rooting and re-rooting of transplantation. All migrants are removed from most, if not all, of the long-standing friends, family, relatives and co-workers with whom they participated in interpersonal communication activities. In the new society, they are faced with the task of constructing a new set of relationships that is critical to meeting their personal and social needs: making a living, learning the new language, seeking companionship and emotional security, or finding a new social identity" (pp. 105–106). The transplanting metaphor suggests the importance of culture to defining the quality of our lives. Most strangers, immigrants, and other travelers adapting to new cultures have moved from a sense of comfort to one of disorientation, even trauma. They face challenges that they were unprepared to anticipate before entering the new culture. However, participation in host-based social communication can provide some of the information necessary to meet those challenges.

Yuko consciously decides not to eat by herself in the dorm, even though she knows no one. Although it takes enormous courage for her, over the first few days she notices several women who appear ready to eat alone; Yuko asks if they'd like to eat with her. They are curious about her motivations for studying at Northwestern, and ready to introduce her to Chicago. Already familiar with some strains of American popular culture (rap music, jazz, Bruce Willis films), she sets out to explore other kinds of radio and television programs.

3. *Ethnic social communication.* Many strangers in a new host environment are helped by groups who have already experienced varying degrees of adaptation to the new culture. The stranger's interest in finding and joining such groups may be explained by a human tendency to reduce uncertainty in interaction. However, researchers are divided about whether this is a negative factor that inhibits cultural adaptation or a positive factor that helps to maintain ethnic identity for the stranger during the difficult transition period. (See Kim, 1988, pp. 118–119 for a summary.) Kim's (1988) systems theory, however, suggests that strangers' social communication within ethnic communities "can *both* promote *and* impede their adaptation process depending on the extent that it replaces their host communication activities over time" (p. 119). In the short term, ethnic communication appears to promote adaptation, but over longer periods of time it maintains previous cultural ties which, if they're with other inadequately adapted strangers, hurts the adaptive goals of the stranger.

Yuko is approached by representatives from the Asian Student Association, and appreciates their invitation to join. Although she was warned before leaving Japan about relying too much on other Japanese students, she is grateful for conversations with people who've faced the same dilemmas she is facing. Their support becomes important for her, but she resolves not to narrow her own experiences too much. She accepts several invitations for dinner with friendly Japanese families in the community, but makes sure she attends soccer and volleyball matches with a circle of American friends.

4. *Host environment.* Adaptation is also influenced by many factors reflecting the kind of environment the stranger encounters. Kim's theory accounts for this with predictions based on two aspects of the host culture, receptivity and conformity pressure. *Receptivity* refers to the extent to which cultures welcome and communicate readily with the cultural "other." *Conformity pressures* within host communication patterns describe the expectations that strangers should rapidly adapt and understand the locally accepted ways of doing things. Kim (1988) notes that some societies value and readily accept cultural diversity, but others are more homogeneous and controlled (p. 130); this appears to be roughly the same phenomenon described by Triandis (1994) as the *tightness syndrome* (discussed earlier in this chapter). Kim's theory suggests that receptivity is often perceived in the social practices of a society, such as in the integration or segregation of its housing patterns, while conformity pressure is often reflected in language practices (1988, pp. 129–130).

At first, Yuko senses that some of her instructors and classmates are not excited about having her in their classes. In her public speaking course, for example, the teacher has repeatedly asked her to look at others directly, eye-to-eye, when speaking, to increase the volume of her voice and use more vocal inflection, and to move around more when using visual aids. But these instructions don't seem to fit her personality. Still, Yuko gamely tries to comply. She also notices several students in the back row who, instead of listening closely to her speeches, read the student newspaper and whisper to each other as she speaks.

5. *Predisposition.* Not only do strangers encounter a new context in the host culture, but they also carry along some "baggage" from their home culture. More specifically, strangers bring with them to the new culture several predispositions that can help or hinder their adaptation to the new cultural demands. Two are straightforward: *cultural/racial background* may be relatively similar (or dissimilar) to the requirements of the host culture, and what Kim calls *preparedness for change,* which formal or informal education may help foster.

More complex is the problem of *personality attributes.* The adapting individuals are successful to the extent that their personalities exhibit the qualities of openness and resilience. *Openness* means that strangers honestly and accurately assess the feedback they receive in response to their attempts to adapt. The successfully adaptive stranger avoids the extremes of closed defensiveness about the new challenges on the one hand, and an unreflective acceptance or acquiescence about the new culture on the other. *Resilience* refers to the inner strength that strangers need to accept cultural misunderstandings and defeats, and still bounce back. Kim (1988) is quick to note that resilience should not be equated with "stubbornness and tenseness," but with a relaxed, persistent flexibility when encountering difficulty: "Without openness and resilience, [strangers] are less capable of absorbing culture shocks and withstanding challenges of the adaptation

L I N K

Kim's cross-cultural adaptation theory underscores the crucial importance of understanding the physical and social contexts of communication discussed in Chapter 3, in both the nonverbal and verbal realms. In addition, the theory begins to account for how individuals internalize such features of context in their thought processes (see Chapter 4).

process, just as a building without give in its structure will easily collapse in a storm" (p. 135).

Yuko is upset at the rudeness of some students in her public speaking class, and the unwillingness of the teacher to adapt the speaking assignments to the needs of her cultural group. However, after thinking long and hard about her problem, she tells herself that although this treatment seems unfair, she does not have to be demoralized by it. She decides to experiment a bit with her speaking style in the ways recommended by the teacher, just to see what happens. During a long-distance phone conversation with her parents, Yuko reports that some of her classmates seem selfish, but that they don't seem to be doing as well in the class as the ones who are more friendly toward her. She agrees with her parents that these rude students shouldn't be able to affect her negatively.

6. *Adaptation outcomes.* Kim (1988, pp. 139–146) identifies three primary outcomes of successful adaptation: increased *functional fitness, psychological health,* and *intercultural identity.* As strangers become more functionally fit, they may find that their inner resources become more congruent with the demands of outer reality in the host environment. However, the converse can also be true. An increasingly good fit between stranger and host system can help to change the system, too—the effects go in both directions. At the same time, adapters tend to experience more psychological balance or homeostasis and to avoid the high-stress experience of *culture shock,* in which individuals begin to isolate themselves out of feelings of despair.

Although not all strangers adapt this effectively, those that do build a new *intercultural identity,* what Kim also calls, a *third-culture perspective,* which is "an inclusive viewpoint that represents more than one cultural perspective—either the home culture or the host culture, but, at the same time, transcends both groups" (Kim, 1988, pp. 144–145). This does not mean that strangers give up their original ethnic identity, but that they gain a wider perspective or intercultural identity that includes elements of the home and host cultures' perspectives. This broader perspective is similar to the borderlands concept discussed earlier in the chapter. This third-culture position is neither a simple maintenance of the old ethnic perspective nor an assimilation into the new host perspective. Instead, third-culture communicators hold elements of both, and they do so by *articulating* (in Stuart Hall's terms) their perspectives in new ways.

Yuko finds her confidence increasing as the semester progresses, and she even decides to join several other organizations. She's still frustrated by how easily some students assume that she's unintelligent just because her competence in English doesn't match theirs. Occasionally, she suspects that some people avoid her because they've prejudged her culture. Although she still experiences conflicts, her initial feelings of queasiness and culture shock have diminished, and she believes she belongs at Northwestern now. She rarely feels lonely, even when she misses her family and friends back home. Although her grades could be improved, Yuko knows she's gaining an even more valuable kind of education than most of her classmates. Now she has transcended a Japanese experience without giving it up, *and* has achieved a midwestern U.S. cultural experience without being limited to it. Although most of her peers settle for a single cultural life, she has managed to build a multicultural life. Yuko doesn't have to choose between keeping her Asian identity *or* submerging herself to become something completely "American." She is both Japanese and knowledgeable within a U.S. cultural setting—and more. Yuko has developed an intercultural identity, in Kim's terms a *third-perspective*. She has adapted cross-culturally.

extensions of the culture concept

The notion of culture has caught on in the communication discipline for several reasons. E. Hall (1959) is on the right track when he equates culture and communication, and Birdwhistell (1970) is insightful when he notes that communication and culture "are terms which represent two different viewpoints or methods of representation of patterned and structured human interconnectedness. As 'culture' the focus is upon structure; as 'communication,' it is upon process" (p. 251).

Communication theorists and researchers thus find it useful to apply the concepts of culture to a wide variety of relationships. They use culture as a metaphor or they apply it literally to suggest that cultural assumptions are formed in all types of communication encounters, not just in interethnic or international ones. Two such attempts to apply culture have focused on the areas of relational culture and organizational culture.

Relational culture is Julia Wood's (1982, 1995) term for describing how individuals in close dyadic relationships create culture-like patterns that guide their interaction. In other words, without planning to do so, people in dyads informally and collaboratively build a social structure of expectations, rules, and standpoints with which they govern their communication with each other and with the outside world. What works in one relationship, therefore, will not necessarily work in another. In effect, each relationship becomes its own unique culture because its partners tend to socialize each other with their messages and interpretations. Over time, they build a structure of "patterned . . . interconnectedness," as Birdwhistell calls it (1970, p. 251). However, Wood is careful to point out that dyadic relationships, like cultural systems, can never be static; as processes, they are in a state of constant fluidity. While we could say that people "create" relationships, Wood's notion suggests that people are also *created by* their relationships in a dialectical exchange.

Organizational communication researchers note that people working on common tasks also tend to develop cultures. Eisenberg and Goodall (1993, pp. 136–140), in pointing out the importance of cultural approaches to organizational theory, claim that the primary goal of **organizational culture** research is to probe how each organization resolves the unique dilemmas of its environment. Although it might be tempting to assume that research into organizations explains organizational communication generally, organizational culture research warns against such an easy explanation. Instead, it portrays the organization as a site of many shared assumptions unique to that organization, but also as a site of conflicting messages, multiple interpretations, and contested meanings (similar to the borderlands concept discussed earlier in this chapter). Organizational researchers inter-

L I N K

You may have noticed many similarities between Wood's relational culture approach and the dialectical theories of interpersonal communication developed by Leslie Baxter and others. See Chapter 6 for more on dialectical theory and interpersonal interdependence.

ested in culture, therefore, see organizations as places that both maintain cultural boundaries of their own and—because of workers' external relations—necessarily bring into contact many other kinds of overlapping boundaries (Pacanowsky & O'Donnell-Trujillo, 1983; Putnam & Pacanowsky, 1983).

The study of organizational cultures raises a problem of practicality that we should address here, at the conclusion of this chapter on culture and communication. Many organizations, especially in the private sector, are interested in bottom-line issues. Some communication theorists, therefore, have wondered about the extent to which their theories and studies might be co-opted by managers attempting to manipulate their organization's culture. Should theorists conduct studies that might ironically make management's attempts to increase worker efficiency more efficient? What began as a "bottom–up" series of studies describing how organizations differ could be turned into a "top–down" strategy for manipulating employees. However, as Eisenberg and Goodall (1993, p. 150) point out, controlling or managing organizational cultures is not as easy to accomplish as some executives assume, though a systematic approach to managing cultural dialogue within an organization is usually advisable. Remember that culture is a constantly shifting process that depends on many shared and partly shared meanings; it changes, but it also actively resists manipulation.

In this resistance lies humans' basic frustration with cultural interaction; but in this also lies our basic fascination with it.

TESTING THE CONCEPTS

"Is what we call American culture a part of the 'borderland'?"

If you think of "America" as a country (some people do not because there are many countries in the Americas), then there are many pockets of protected group identities that seem not to have much to do with different cultural groups—some rural areas, gated subdivisions, and segregated neighborhoods come to mind. To call American culture a "borderland" in the sense of this chapter's theorists might be a bit misleading.

On the other hand, American culture, when considered more broadly, seems to be in the forefront of an emerging borderlands mentality, both in the United States and across the world. Although Americans often segregate themselves into neighborhoods and locales that think and behave similarly, the lines are blurring and each unique cultural identity must now increasingly confront a broader context of integrated culture as well as other cultural groups. Further, in an era of international business, frequent and relatively inexpensive travel, and the availability of virtually instant global communication, the ambiguities and merged identities of the borderlands experience are expanding. So are the challenges. Barnett Pearce (1989) advocates what he calls *cosmopolitan communication,* which "enables coordination among groups with different, even incommensurate, social realities" (p. 169). He believes this approach allows us to respect differences while also finding ways to coordinate our communication practices across those differences.

"What is the difference between race and culture?"

The term *race* is currently being contested by a variety of theorists, almost as if it's the ground or terrain on which groups can fight their verbal battles. It's safe to say that today race is no longer the precise scientific concept it was thought to be in the early part of the twentieth century (see the definitions in this chapter). Then, it was assumed that races "had" certain biological characteristics and potentials that did not characterize other races. Now, when people refer to race, they are usually referring to a mix of ambiguously defined biological characteristics and a wide range of cultural cues and communication styles generally associated with certain groups. What we call race is a kind of verbal and conceptual shortcut to discussing culture. Still, as we stress in the text, race and racism are real because people talk about and experience their reality.

"Yuko chose to come to the United States and attend college. Why didn't she see what she was getting herself into?"

Yuko did all she felt necessary to prepare for the culture shock she would experience in the United States. Usually, that is not enough to guarantee feeling comfortable, however, because discomfort naturally comes with any venture into new territory. The best and most thorough way to understand a different culture is to immerse yourself in that culture. It was impossible for Yuko to grasp the *entire* new experience ahead of time because any culture involves not only a recorded history, a language with grammar, syntax, and vocabulary, and a set of artifacts (all of which Yuko could study ahead of time), but also involves patterns of subtle and usually implicit interpersonal relations (which she couldn't anticipate precisely before she arrived). Kim's (1988) research demonstrates how disorienting a stranger's experience can be, as well as how successful adaptation to a new culture can occur.

YOU, THE RESEARCHER

1. On your own campus, interview three students or faculty members (not from your communication class) who represent three different cultural backgrounds. For example, you may know of a physics professor from Jamaica who has just been hired, or a student from Pakistan who's also studied in London. Ask the interviewees to describe how cultural assumptions did or did not help prepare them to face power issues (concerning gender, race, and ethnicity) on campus. Here are some other suggestions for doing this research:

   - Approach this project as if you are a journalist preparing to write a human-interest story. Carefully prepare a set of four or five basic questions that will guide your interviews, but beware of the tendency to channel the interview only along these lines. Your interviewees may want to take you in equally good, but different, directions. Take careful notes or, with the others' permission, tape the interviews.

- Remember that your task is just to discover the persons' perspectives, not to persuade them that they're victims, members of dominant classes, or stereotypical representatives of cultural groups.
- Look for similarities and differences in your subjects' comments. Does your interview data reflect any of the concepts described in this chapter? Discuss your findings in class.
- Consider the possibility that you could turn your research into a feature story for your campus or local newspaper, perhaps by collaborating with one or more classmates. If you do write such an article, you could use your three interviewees as focal points for the story, but you'll probably want to add extra information, too.

2. For one week, watch several television news programs carefully. Record in a notebook how the programs portray cultural differences in their coverage of the news. For example, apart from the weather report, how many stories comprise a nightly local newscast? Of these, how many concern themselves with confrontations or collaborations between gays and straights, between blacks and whites, between representatives of ethnic neighborhoods and wealthy areas, or other cultural issues? Then, view five half-hour sitcoms to see how these programs portray cultural encounters and the identities of the people involved. Compare and contrast how the television news and situation comedies portray cultural differences. Discuss your findings in class.

3. Visit a local video store or library and select several movies produced in countries, and in languages, other than your own. While viewing each one, look especially for portrayals of female/male role differences and their effects. You don't have to assume that the writers, directors, producers, and actors intended to present these differences in the way you interpret. Discuss with other students how much of what you see in the films represents the unspoken assumptions of the cultures in which they were filmed, and how much of each portrayal comes from the unique vision or agenda of the filmmakers. For example, a Japanese film from 1960 might cast women in roles subservient to men, but a 1990s Japanese filmmaker might consider the tension between women and men in the workplace to be dramatically interesting and might consciously try to advance a personal agenda different from the overall culture.

Billy E. Barnes/PhotoEdit

changing minds

"how does rhetoric persuade us?"

Being the product of conditioning and being free to change do not war with each other. Both are true. They coexist, grow together in an upward spiral, and the growth of one furthers the growth of the other. The more cogently we prove ourselves to have been shaped by causes, the more opportunities we create for changing. The more we change, the more possible it becomes to see how determined we were in that which we have just ceased to be.

ALLEN WHEELIS, *HOW PEOPLE CHANGE* (1976, PP. 87-88)

C. P. Ellis changed his mind. Ellis is one of many ordinary Americans profiled in Studs Terkel's book, *American Dreams: Lost and Found* (1981, pp. 221–233). All of Terkel's subjects are noteworthy, but Ellis stands out because his story clearly demonstrates the power of public and interpersonal persuasion in a country that says it values free speech.

Born and raised in Durham, North Carolina's textile culture, Ellis tried a variety of working-class jobs in search of the American Dream, but never found it. Instead, he found bitterness and disillusionment while working in the mills, on a bread route, at a gas station, and on the maintenance staff at Duke University. But he still didn't have enough money at one time even to fill the fuel oil tank at his family's house. This wasn't the way America was supposed to be at midcentury if a person went to church, worked hard, and felt patriotic. Something was wrong; someone had to be blamed. Ellis's father, a member of the Ku Klux Klan, blamed blacks, Jews, and Catholics. The younger Ellis found his niche there, too, and with the habit of blaming others came an entire worldview. Klan members eventually respected him enough to select him as president of the Durham chapter.

In a series of interracial civic meetings, Ellis was exceptionally open about his negative feelings toward blacks—so much so that he was admired by both sides for his honesty. He was asked to coordinate policies with a black activist woman he'd learned to hate. As co-chairs of a human relations committee, each was criticized for being willing to work with the other. The Klan members couldn't believe their man was doing this: "C. P., what the hell is wrong with you? You're sellin' out the white race" (Terkel, 1981, p. 229). At the same time, "Ann was gettin' the same response from blacks: 'what are you doin' messin' with that Klansman?" (p. 230). Eventually, each discovered that their children were being harassed by other children at school, and each began to notice the other's reaction to their parental agony. They had much in common after all.

Ellis still didn't favor integration, but he supported the resolutions that the integrated committee came up with. When the all-white school board refused to take the resolutions seriously, Ellis decided to run for the board himself. The Klan had turned against Ellis, as did many low-income whites. Blacks and liberals were suspicious, but Ellis shook a lot of hands and met a lot of everyday people. He lost the school board election, but not by much. In losing, however, he seemed to gain the enthusiasm he needed to return to high school through an alternative program and graduate.

Ellis, now an ex-Klansman, saw more possibilities for change. At work, he ran for president of the union, even though he thought he had no chance of winning the election. His opponent was black, as was 75 percent of the membership. Moreover, the company executives didn't like Ellis, and they advertised his racist past by posting signs and flyers. In response, Ellis called a mass meeting:

> I invited some of my old black friends. I said: "Brother Joe, Brother Howard, be honest now and tell these people how you feel about me." They done it. (Laughs.) Howard Clements kidded me a little bit. He said: "I don't know what I'm doin' here, supportin' an ex-Klansman." (Laughs.) He said: "I know what C. P. Ellis come from. I knew him when he was. I knew him as he grew, and growed with him. I'm tellin' you now: follow, follow this Klansman." (He pauses, swallows hard.) "Any questions?" "No," the black ladies said. "Let's get on with the meeting, we need Ellis." (He laughs and weeps.) . . . It makes you feel good to go into a plant and butt heads with professional union busters. You see black people and white people join hands to defeat the racist issues they use against people. . . . Can you imagine a guy who's got an adult high school diploma runnin' into professional college graduates. . . ? I gotta compete with 'em.
>
> They say the older you get, the harder it is for you to change. That's not necessarily true. Since I changed, I've set down and listened to tapes of Martin Luther King. I listen to it and tears come to my eyes 'cause I know what he's sayin' now. I know what's happenin'. (Terkel, 1981, pp. 232–233)

C. P. Ellis changed his mind. And his life. Not all of us make changes that are this dramatic, but the basic dynamics of attitude change are similar in most people's lives. What are those dynamics? How are people persuaded through others' rhetoric? These are the central questions we address in this chapter. As we do, remember C. P. Ellis. We'll return to him occasionally to illustrate the practicality of rhetorical concepts.

In this chapter you won't receive a comprehensive catalog of contemporary research on attitude change. That has been done well elsewhere (see, e.g., O'Keefe, 1990). Our goal in this chapter is to pique your interest in theorizing about this important subfield of communication. You'll discover the place of persuasion in the overall development of communication theory. As the chapter-opening quotation from psychotherapist Allen Wheelis suggests, humans are simultaneously free and determined, and studying persuasive communication messages illustrates how this is true. We will develop this notion in three additional sections. First, we'll examine the relationship between mind and persuasion. Second, we'll begin our conceptual survey with the rhetorical tradition of persuasion, focusing on the contributions of such ancient theorists as Plato and Aristotle. In this survey, you will see how classical rhetorical theory has influenced what we define as persuasion theory today. Finally, we'll attempt to show how persuasion theory has

L I N K

Persuasion and attitude change are discussed repeatedly in this book because the study of them draws on many other conceptual areas. Cognitive and social psychological principles of persuasion, such as cognitive complexity, consistency principles, and social judgment theory, are reviewed in Chapter 4 on personal experience. Aspects of interpersonal persuasion are discussed in Chapter 6 on communicative interdependence. Social exchange research, in particular, forms much of the basis for interpersonal compliance-gaining theory. Chapter 9 evaluates the so-called media threat of powerful propaganda, which people once feared could sway the masses. Chapter 10 on theories of communication ethics presents the ethical and moral dimensions of manipulation, power, control, choice, and self-determination.

practical implications in everyday life. We'll consider examples from the field of medicine in which persuasion can best be understood as a "helping relationship."

CHANGING MINDS AND MINDING PERSUASION

mind

The human *mind* is often discussed as if it were the cockpit, central processing unit, or control center of the body. When everything seems to be working predictably, we say people are "minding their manners." Mind also is invoked if things go badly. If we want others to stop doing something, we might say we "mind" their actions. Children who don't comply with family rules are described as "not minding their parents." When your friend won't accede in an argument, you might say he or she "has a mindset." People who are excessively worried and express it in unconventional ways are said colloquially to have "lost their minds." Our society tends to value people who can "make up their minds."

So—what's a *mind?* Is it a synonym for *brain,* or is it something more? (See Box 8-1.) Recall from Chapter 4 George Herbert Mead's (1934) claim that language lets us imagine internally the shape and complexity of our external society—and this, to him, is the basic phenomenon of mind. In effect, mind allows us to plan and decide, even to try things out imaginatively, before we engage in overt behaviors. For summaries of current research in discursive, language-linked theories of mind, see recent books by Harre and Gillett (1994) and Wertsch (1991).

Biologist J. Z. Young takes a slightly different, but consistent, perspective in his influential book, *Programs of the Brain* (1978). His central analogy—the idea of a *program*—is not derived primarily from computer programs but from the pre-Victorian sense of an organized plan for accomplishing a particular end. According to Young (1978), scientific researchers have found that "the brain operates in certain organized ways that may be described as programs, and the actions of these programs constitute the entity that we call the mind of a person" (p. 8). Some researchers in communication and psychology (see, e.g., Goss, 1989, pp. 133–137) use the term *schema* to refer to an organizing concept similar to Young's use of *program*. The concepts of mind, program, and schema, therefore, are teleologically important; they refer to the ability of the conscious organism to ac-

---

BOX 8-1

THE MIND:

- Uses language to help persons re-create internally the complexity of society (Mead).
- Is the disciplined set of *programs* or *schemata* (plural of *schema*) by which persons organize their plans for action (Young).

complish its objectives and goals. In fact, without this symbolic capacity, it's hard even to imagine having or setting objectives in anything other than a mechanical sense.

We could say that C. P. Ellis's *mind* changed when his *program* for deciding how to organize his actions changed. Or we could say that his *program* changed when his *mind* did. Mind and action are intimately connected; each helps to construct the other. This is why it's useless to try to explain a person's behavior by saying, for instance, "I know why he's not getting A's in school anymore—he changed his mind about the importance of studying," as though the changed mind *caused* the changed behavior. In fact, from Young's (1978) program-oriented standpoint, the changed behavior and the changed mind are two facets of the *same* phenomenon. That phenomenon, consciousness, is language-based and communication-based: " . . . Life is guided by programs and . . . programs are written in languages," Young writes; and "indeed our thesis is that the faculty of communication pervades all of living" (p. 9).

persuasion

Herbert Simons (1976) defines **persuasion** as "human communication designed to influence others by modifying their beliefs, values, or attitudes" (p. 21). Although this definition seems to refer more to messages than to communication as an overall process, it emphasizes that persuasion implies a kind of intentional behavior with reference to a plan or goal, at least on the part of a speaker. However, Burgoon and Miller (1990), drawing on Langer's (1978) work on *mindfulness,* suggest that not all persuasive attempts are mindful, rational acts orchestrated by a knowing persuader. They admit that some level of intention is required in any definition of persuasion, but they find it fallacious to overemphasize highly rational elements in the definition. According to Burgoon and Miller (1990), scholars shouldn't assume "that persuaders are constantly in the highly mindful state of making rational choices, deliberating about alternatives, and rehearsing strategies." Instead, we should more often consider "the everyday world of persuasive discourse where many attempts at change, or reinforcement, consist of relatively mindless acts. Habituated behavior, whether successful or not, is the symbolic staple of would-be persuaders in many, if not most, daily persuasive encounters" (p. 157).

Every four years a national presidential election reminds us of the variety of possible avenues for gaining influence, or at least for securing our acquiescence (Edelman, 1964). Many of these avenues have not changed significantly over the past two thousand years. However, in the twentieth century, the means and media for conveying influential messages have changed radically. Political candidates, for example, no longer advertise themselves from a tree stump, the back of a wagon, or the bunting-laden caboose of a train on a whistle-stop campaign. Television and other electronic media supplement the print media in providing more news and more advertising than audiences could ever hope to assimilate. As technology advances, so apparently does the public's reliance on it. The modern audience seems to be an inviting and fertile ground in which persuasive messages can take root.

L I N K

How might Greene's action assembly theory, discussed in Chapter 4, contribute to the study of mind? To our understanding of how people change their minds?

Political campaigns might also remind us of how much persuasion already exists in our everyday relationships. It's not just senators and governors who want to be "elected." All of us might be considered informal politicians as we go through each day trying to be tactful to some people, confrontive with others, and strategic toward still others. You may hope to persuade a job interviewer that you're the best potential employee among the applicants. Your teacher may hope to persuade you that the reading assignments are helpful and necessary. Parents may hope to convince teenagers that drugs and alcohol are dangerous. You may hope that your statistics on smoke alarms will be believed in your speech for Public Speaking class.

CONCEPTS FROM THE
RHETORICAL TRADITION OF PERSUASION

Communication theories have focused for centuries on the problem of persuasion. Therefore, the classical rhetorical tradition in Western civilization has had a long and influential history in the education of communicators (see Box 8-2, p. 232). The advice and analyses of such early theorists as Aristotle, Plato, Isocrates, and others have been so persuasive that they are still studied intensively by scholars and students today. (Some excellent summary sources include Harper, 1978; Hauser, 1986; Kennedy, 1963; and Kinneavy, 1980.)

rhetoric

Rhetoric, defined by Aristotle (384–322 B.C.) as the faculty or ability of finding "the available means of persuasion" in a situation (1954, p. 24), was accorded a central role in ancient Greek civilization. Although some contemporary treatments of rhetoric emphasize its functions in constructing social reality, in helping people make sense of others' behaviors, and in coordinating social action, Aristotle's concern with the impulse for influence persists in rhetorical theory today. Because each male citizen in Aristotle's Greece was expected to be able to argue his case in the public forum, rhetoric became an essential discipline in the education of that time. Rhetoric is still considered a specialized study of communication, one that emphasizes humanity's symbolic capacity to plan messages for practical ends.

By now you probably understand that we do *not* use the term *rhetoric* with its modern pejorative connotations. If a contemporary politician says, "My opponent is engaging in mere rhetoric" or "Enough rhetoric! Let's talk real issues here!" the implication is that rhetoric is empty talk unsupported by solid reasoning or evidence. This negative or superficial usage is not what we mean by rhetoric. Like Aristotle, contemporary rhetorical theorists have the utmost respect for the study of intentional talk—talk that is expected to help people respond to ideas.

One ancient rhetorician, however, was more skeptical about the potential power of a skilled *rhetor* (one who uses rhetoric). Plato (c. 428–348 B.C.), a Greek philosopher and one of Aristotle's teachers, was suspicious of the *Sophists,* itinerant teachers who specialized in teaching people the practical everyday applications of rhetoric. Even to this day, Sophists have "bad press"; our politicians often accuse each other of "sophistry," which has come to imply the deceptive and biased use of rhetoric. In his dialogue *The Gorgias,* Plato pointedly criticized how rhetoric was commonly misused. He said that it wasn't a genuine area of study as much as it was a simple knack for impressing or fooling other people. This knack for rhetoric, Plato argued, was not much more complicated than the knack for cooking. Although he later adjusted his philosophy to advocate a more comprehensive approach to human communication based on dialogue and the testing of ideas, his warning about an uncritical faith in rhetoric remains appropriate today.

A contemporary of Plato, Athenian orator Isocrates (436–338 B.C.), took rhetoric more into the political realm in his teachings. Isocrates helped to educate the political decision makers of his day, stressing that only through rhetoric could a society maintain social order or a group maintain cooperation among its members. In this sense, then, rhetoric is the glue that holds the political process together, not a threat to that process (as Plato asserted in *The Gorgias*). In the program for training rhetors described in his *Antidosis,* Isocrates claimed that rhetoric could be found in the thought processes, in the intrapersonal realm, of communicators. Therefore, in this view, we use language not just to influence others but also to conduct internal dialogues for the purpose of solving problems. Our thoughts and our rhetoric are interdependent.

Isocrates and Plato sketched the outline of a body of thought, and Aristotle filled in much of that outline. Many of our basic concepts of rhetoric thus emerged from the Greek and Roman classical rhetorical tradition.

occasions for rhetoric

Three basic types of occasions call for rhetoric, according to classic rhetorical theory. *Deliberative rhetoric* is seen in discussions of public policy in legislative groups; it basically concerns itself with questions such as "What do we do about . . . ?" and similar inquiries. *Forensic rhetoric* occurs in courtrooms and other places where the facts and interpretations of individual cases are argued. This term persists today in the organized competitive speech activities known on many campuses as "forensics programs." *Epideictic rhetoric* refers to the ceremonial speaking in public forums that praises or blames individuals for their virtues or vices. Epideictic speaking can be expected at funerals, weddings, and other special occasions where people gather to honor or celebrate a person, group, or event.

When we consider these occasions for rhetoric in the context of contemporary persuasion, they hardly seem stale. For example, although we sometimes like to think of political campaigns as opportunities for deliberative rhetoric, they often shift rapidly toward epideictic rhetoric when an opponent's character is being discussed as much as content. Similarly, when ex-Klansman C. P. Ellis called a meeting of his union during his campaign for union president, he himself brought up the charges the company had made against him and invited the members to consider and debate the truth or falsity of the charges. He also enlisted the

L I N K

Consider this interesting connection between classical rhetorical theory and inner speech theory, surveyed in Chapter 4: To what extent do you think persuaders have a responsibility to be introspective about their interior dialogues? In other words, should rhetors become more *mindful?*

L I N K

Because of the type of education in which Aristotle was most interested, he saw the occasions for rhetoric as being mostly in the public realm. Yet, as you know from Chapters 5 and 6, many of our most important occasions are interpersonal and relatively private. How does persuasion work within interpersonal occasions where the influence is not unidirectional but transactional (see Chapter 2)?

Consider persuasion in the dyadic context or level that we described in Chapter 3. Miller and Boster (1988) discuss how most persuasion research has focused upon one-to-many situations that do not consider the uniqueness of what researchers call *compliance-gaining* in personal relations. (Garko, 1990; Marwell & Schmitt, 1967;) Miller and Boster highlight three uniquely important characteristics of personal occasions for persuasion: the existence of a relational history, the opportunities for interaction, and the concern for relational outcomes. In other words, when we try to persuade each other within our interpersonal relationships, we more readily take into account details from our past encounters with the other person; we can more easily adjust our approaches while we're applying them, because we're aware in an ongoing way of the other's reactions; and finally, rhetors in personal relationships attempt to influence the other while being fully aware of how much the attempt could change the relationship itself. All of these factors mean that interpersonal and public persuaders communicate in contexts with somewhat different ground rules.

aid of several black colleagues to testify to his open-mindedness and honesty. He invited debate at the meeting about what kind of leadership the members wanted. Ellis constructed, in other words, a situation that melded all three types of rhetorical occasion—people examined and evaluated his character, debated their different interpretations (forensic), and attempted to coordinate their views through rhetorical deliberation (deliberative).

inartistic and artistic persuasive appeals

Classical rhetorical theorists distinguish between inartistic and artistic persuasive appeals. They consider *inartistic means of persuasion* as the less interesting and effective of the two, because inartistic approaches emphasize the discovery of the facts of a given case that are largely external to the choices of the individuals concerned. Inartistic methods of proving a case are simply "found" in the situation or in the external inducements (Aristotle mentioned oaths and torture as examples); they are not the result of the creativity or imagination of the communicator. For example, has a professor "persuaded" students to study in a required class when everyone knows that grades will be recorded on student transcripts and may be important in future job searches? A professor's reference to grades can be an inartistic means of persuasion because grades are situational threats that aren't primarily based on the professor's own rhetorical skill. Of course, many professors do motivate students creatively to study, apart from the threat of grades. On what does their persuasiveness depend?

Artistic means of persuasion are characterized by creativity and genuine persuasion. Although the facts of a case are important, they don't (as we sometimes wish) "speak for themselves." Facts must be interpreted and presented creatively in order for them to have influence on an audience. The distinction can be seen in a perhaps apocryphal story told about the famous defense lawyer, Clarence Darrow. Asked to describe how he chose reasons for acquittal to include in his summation to a jury, Darrow replied that he didn't try to give a jury any reasons to free his client. Instead, he made the jury want to free his client, and trusted that the jury would find its own reasons. Darrow's approach, in other words, relied on the artistic rhetoric of interpretive appeal that he helped to construct with the jury, not on the naive assumption that the inartistic factual and rational proofs of the case could be persuasive in their own right. Television viewers of the 1996 O. J. Simpson trial (whatever their convictions about his guilt or innocence) undoubtedly noticed a similar reliance on artistic means of persuasion by Simpson's lawyer, Johnnie Cochran. In his summation, for example, Cochran vividly described not only the facts and proofs of the case but also the possibilities, thereby inviting the jurors to form their own interpretations of "reasonable doubt."

For Darrow, Cochran, and Aristotle, persuasion develops from how listeners use artistic messages to change their minds and behaviors. Similarly, C. P. Ellis's persuasive power didn't come from coercing others to see things his way or from the obvious power of the facts he espoused. Instead, to put it in an unusual but appropriate way, he spoke his life in the public arena and relied on his knowledge of how his audience made their decisions. In much the same way, no one influenced Ellis to change his mind in a simple cause-and-effect manner. He persuaded himself, slowly building a new worldview from the messages that others (intentionally and unintentionally) provided.

types of artistic proofs

Aristotle described three general types of artistic proofs, which were for him the different choices rhetors make when they seek to persuade others. They can rely on *ethos, pathos,* and *logos.*

ethos. As Aristotle observed, the force of a message's content is often not enough to sway an audience. The audience hears arguments and messages in the context of who is proposing them. A person of high prestige and reputation might be believed sooner and more deeply than someone who is not seen as credible by an audience. *Ethos,* meaning "personal proof" or "ethical proof," is tied to the character of speakers, who simultaneously offer themselves to audiences alongside the words they speak. Indeed, a vital part of the Roman tradition of classical rhetoric was an extension of this notion. Quintillian and Cicero, among others, thought virtue should be assumed in the definition of a rhetor, that a skillful Roman rhetor was—we note, with apologies to skillful female rhetors—a "good man, speaking well." It was not enough, merely to speak well.

The classical theorists thus created a foundation for what modern theorists describe as *credibility.* The speaker's reputation, experiences, and knowledge are taken into consideration by audiences, as is how much the rhetor can be trusted in a given situation. Although modern studies differ somewhat in how they define credibility (see Andersen & Clevenger, 1963; Delia, 1976; Infante, Parker, Clarke, Wilson, & Nathu, 1983), two issues usually emerge as most important: *expertise* and *trustworthiness.* Generally, these labels ask the implicit questions, "Does the speaker know what he or she is talking about?" and "Can the speaker be trusted to be honest, accurate, and unbiased in the rhetoric?" A third factor often discovered in credibility studies, *dynamism,* suggests that many auditors admire rhetors who have enthusiastic and animated presentation styles.

Three reminders are important in considering the dynamics of personal proof. First, because audiences often don't make credibility assessments rationally, a speaker's physical appearance, clothing, ethnicity, group associations, and body type may affect his or her *ethos.* Second, remember that *ethos* or credibility is basically an audience-based phenomenon. We may often talk colloquially about a speaker "possessing" a high degree of credibility or even charisma, but this kind of reference is conceptually misleading. It's actually the audience that develops and sustains a rhetor's *ethos.* High *ethos* remains as long as the audience sustains its belief in the rhetor's expertise, trustworthiness, and dynamism. Finally, remember that *ethos,* like all communication, is a situational issue. While C. P. Ellis attained a high degree of credibility with some (but not all) audiences when speaking about race relations in Durham in the 1960s and 1970s, this does not necessarily mean that he'd maintain that credibility in other situations (e.g., at a KKK meeting, a National Organization of Women seminar, a convention of aca-

LINK

Chapter 5 examines theoretical concepts associated with communication rules. What rules, in your opinion, govern how speakers can talk about their own credibility in public, without seeming to brag or to be excessively arrogant? Consider public self-references to credibility in such situations as political campaigning, job interviews, and teaching Sunday school. Which rules seem to apply in each of these situations?

demic sociologists studying inner-city problems) or even with the same audience types in the 1990s. Credibility, therefore, depends much more on the audience and situation than on the speaker's dynamic style or sincerity.

pathos.   Discussions of rhetoric prior to Aristotle probably emphasized emotionally based persuasion (Harper, 1978, p. 38), explaining, perhaps, why Aristotle sought to create a more balanced view of this mode of proof. It is neither the type of appeal that necessarily should be a rhetor's first choice, nor the type that necessarily will produce results with all audiences. *Pathos* refers to the rhetorical use of messages that appeal to an audience's emotions and passions. C. P. Ellis became a willing convert to the Klan because he felt bitter about what he perceived as the dismissal of white people's concerns. He wanted to blame someone in order to feel better, and the Klan's rhetoric gave him that outlet. Similarly, in changing his mind, it was his sadness about the common economic plight of many blacks and whites that became the soil in which his new and more generous rhetorical assumptions were planted.

Advertisers use emotional appeals to promote their products, and political campaigners usually presume that the public's emotional involvement with a topic should be factored into the overall campaign strategy. The 1988 presidential campaign provides an excellent example. In a commercial referring to Massachusetts Governor Dukakis's policy of furloughing criminals from overcrowded jails, the Bush campaigners showed a photograph of a criminal who had benefitted from such a furlough, and who later murdered a person. The photograph of Willie Horton, an African American, was a typical "mug shot," probably taken while he was angry. He looked, according to many liberals and conservatives, menacing at best. Would the photo have been shown if it was, instead, a smiling white male? Democrats also charged that Horton's race and his expression in the photo were calculated to appeal not only to the meanest stereotypes of racist whites but to the fears of middle-class whites who might otherwise be attracted to Dukakis. Republicans countered that the photo was not intended as a racist ploy to play only on an audience's fears, but as an accurate portrayal of their concern with crime as an issue in the campaign.

All significant issues, the argument goes, involve emotions. In Chapter 10 we'll discuss ethical criteria for communication. At this point, though, you might consider whether you find the Bush campaign's commercial and its appeal to emotions ethical or unethical. Is it the emotional appeal itself that's ethical or unethical, or is it the situation or context in which the appeal is made? Many persuaders attempt to appeal to our needs to be first, best, part of a group, and so on. Muscular dystrophy telethons appeal to our emotions, too. Are they unethical? Television viewers are familiar with photographs and videos of starving children across the world with their distended stomachs and emaciated faces looking longingly toward the camera. Promoters of many causes—good and bad, necessary and trivial—have understood Aristotle's concern with appealing rhetorically to audience emotions.

Hauser (1986, pp. 110 ff.) points to two common misconceptions about the role of emotions in persuasive communication. First, emotions, he writes, are not

L I N K

When reading Chapter 10 on communication ethics, consider which theories of ethics best help you sort out the issues of emotionality and negative advertising in political campaigns.

"things" that can be stored up (like "pent-up" feelings, or "repressed anger") or expended like commodities. They are better understood as judgments and interpretations, unique to each individual, that develop as a result of a complex interplay of psychological and physiological factors. This insight leads to the other misconception: that many people believe emotions come largely from outside the self. Hauser (1986) believes it is more productive to see emotions as specific and pointed toward referents: "We don't feel love in general. We love Dad, we love Kirsten, we love our dear friends who have shared so many rich experiences with us" (p. 111). Emotions are inner interpretations affectively tied to outer experiences. Just as some philosophers believe that there is no such thing as "consciousness" in general, but that consciousness must always be "consciousness-of-something" (they call this the concept of *intentionality*), Hauser is saying that emotions must be of and about referents.

logos. Aristotle understood that persuasion ideally should be based on the logical arguments and reasons that a rhetor can present to an audience. Information that is presented in a precise order and accompanied by statistical support, examples, and relevant testimony encourages listeners to arrive at a specific conclusion recommended by the rhetor. This kind of "logical proof," called *logos*, makes sense and is rational. But is it always possible or practical?

In the Aristotelian theory of communication, humans often use shortcut versions of rational processes. For example, a *syllogism* is a form of logical reasoning that moves from *major premise* through *minor premise* to *conclusion*. Therefore, regardless of the actual truth of the claims of the premises, one could at least trust the reasoning mechanism. A parent might reason with a child (validly): All cats are going to die (major premise); Rascal is a cat (minor premise); therefore, Rascal is going to die someday (conclusion). Or a parent might reason (with suspicious validity): All religious persons are narrow-minded; Sister Margaret is a religious person; therefore, Sister Margaret is narrow-minded (and we shouldn't trust her). Maybe the world would be a better place if everyone reasoned with each other carefully and precisely; then again, maybe it wouldn't. Careful reasoning doesn't guarantee good results if rhetors aren't knowledgeable. As Aristotle noted, the world isn't a place where everyone reasons syllogistically with accurate information. Folks in everyday life tend to be persuaded more by their own reasoning than by logically "correct" reasoning imposed from outside their own experience. In this imperfect world, we often assume that there are some things in communication that we don't need to say or prove.

Realizing the alogical character of much human communication, Aristotle proposed that people typically engage others with examples and enthymemes. The rationale behind producing *rhetorical examples* is similar to the inductive assumptions of qualitative social scientists, who study human interaction using an accumulation of case studies or ethnographic methods of observation (see Chapter 1). *Enthymemes* are similar to syllogisms, except that one of the two premises is implicit. Because the rhetor will tend to assume that a listener can fill in some of the assumptions, all the dimensions of the appeal don't need to be made explicit. For example, in C. P. Ellis's case, the company executives decided that all they needed to do to block his

BOX 8-2

CLASSICAL RHETORICAL THEORY:

- Defines the study of *rhetoric* as finding "the available means of persuasion" (Aristotle).
- Analyzes *deliberative, forensic,* and *epideictic* contexts for rhetoric.
- Elevates *artistic* over *inartistic* means of persuasion.
- Distinguishes among different types of proof: *ethos, pathos,* and *logos.*

---

election was to let the predominantly black union membership know of Ellis's past ties with the KKK. The rhetorical reasoning went something like this: "C. P. Ellis is a white man who once led an anti-black group; therefore, you would not want him representing you." A premise, a step in the reasoning, has been omitted here. The company executives expected this message to be persuasive because it more or less created a psychological "space" into which audience members could insert their own assumptions, fears, suspicions, and, perhaps, hate. However, the company's message didn't mention fear or hate directly. Further, although this example might seem to imply that persuasion by enthymemes involves poor reasoning, this is not necessarily the case. In fact, this form of *logos* is most common in human affairs, and not necessarily negative. "We need to practice more so we can win the big game Saturday night" is enthymemic reasoning, too.

Probably the most important contribution of Aristotle's theory in this regard is that it takes audiences very much into account. The validity of an enthymeme isn't in its logical form (as with a syllogism); rather, validity resides in the shared social meanings, interpretations, and assumptions by which people together make decisions. In this sense, persuasion is not primarily a psychological process but a process of social communication.

RHETORICAL THEORY APPLIED: SOME EVERYDAY EXAMPLES

Thoughtful students in any field of study should persistently ask themselves this question: How does what I've learned in class relate to real-life problems and situations? We firmly believe that the whole world is a classroom, and that you don't stop learning after you've earned your college degree. If learning is only directed toward achieving a grade or a degree, then that insight is likely to fade after the end of the semester or after graduation. How can communication theory, or more specifically, persuasion theory, guide how you address the practical problems that complicate human life?

the health context: persuasion and a hero's new role

Some years ago, one of the most famous and popular celebrities in the world, Earvin "Magic" Johnson of the National Basketball Association's Los Angeles Lakers, announced that he had tested positive for the HIV virus. One of the most feared and mysterious medical dilemmas of the modern era, AIDS remains a disease about which researchers know too little. Public education and public communication programs have been in some cases confused and contradictory. Although the disease had already created horrible suffering in the lives of millions of private and public persons, Johnson's announcement that he was retiring from the NBA galvanized public opinion and sensitized many people to the immediate need for open communication about AIDS. Johnson decided to become an advocate for AIDS education and research, in order to mobilize and humanize public concern. Since his announcement, he has done much (including coming out of retirement briefly to resume his career) to demystify the disease.

Johnson's experience spotlights the relationship between medical professionals and their public. To what extent should doctors and public health officials also go beyond their traditional roles of treating and informing the public, given their constraints of time, energy, and financial support? Should they become active persuaders? And if so, how should the public react? Should the public continue to be guided by the traditional medical model that implies physicians are experts who consider the complaints brought to them by patients and then prescribe treatments with which patients should comply? This implies a linear, one-way model of communication that may be seriously outmoded. Maybe we can never go back to that way of thinking about medical problems. Maybe we're now too interconnected in our society.

The medical dilemmas of the late twentieth century illustrate the extent to which persuasion must be approached as a "helping relationship." Linear assumptions of persuasion no longer apply, if they ever did. We must marshal public and private resources in order to communicate *with* people, not *at* them. The most effective and lasting persuasive messages give people a voice in their own fates and encourage them to use that voice. Effective rhetoric thus encourages response and reality testing, not unthinking compliance or acquiescence. Interestingly, though, in the rubric under which a great deal of interpersonal influence is now researched—*compliance-gaining theory*—some persuaders known as "agents" attempt to change a "target's" behavior in the direction the agent wishes. Kelman's (1966) discussion of compliance as a form of social influence is instructive. He believes *compliance* occurs when someone does what someone else wants done "to achieve a favorable reaction from the other. He may be interested in attaining certain specific rewards or in avoiding certain specific punishments that the influencing agent controls" (p. 152). Clearly, then, compliance is conceptually linked to the presence of the agent as well as to the agent's ability to provide rewards or punishments. The changed behavior is exhibited, Kelman believes, only under the "surveillance" of the agent (p. 160), and it is unlikely to be internalized. Garko (1990) critiques how closely researchers have linked compliance-gaining to theories of exchange and power, and how reliant their theories have become on unidirectional influence. He suggests that theories of interpersonal influence should become more transactional and mutualized.

In an increasingly complex contemporary culture, where social problems, medical problems, political problems, scientific problems, and issues of personal morality cannot be realistically separated, only an interpersonally responsible persuasion seems appropriate for energizing public policy. Society must have persuasion, but it must become, in a sense, mutualized.

the doctor-patient relationship as mutual persuasion

Communication theorists Smith and Pettegrew (1986), writing in the journal *Theoretical Medicine,* explore the differences between the traditional medical model of doctor-patient talk and a rhetorically based model they call *mutual persuasion.* They point out that although the doctor role tends to be quite caring, concerned, and well meaning, a *medical model* of doctor-patient persuasion assumes the doctor will emphasize diagnosis, prognosis, and directives aimed at a relatively passive patient whose role, in turn, is to comply with the prescribed treatment. Compliance refers to the extent to which the patient does what he or she is told by the physician, regardless of the patient's own attitudes, beliefs, or values. In fact, the medical field even publishes a journal, *The Journal of Compliance in Health,* which reports on research into how doctors, nurses, and other health professionals can attain higher degrees of compliance from their patients. However, as Smith and Pettegrew (1986) note, only about half the time do patients comply with "doctors' orders." "From an ethical perspective," they write, "this may be good news. We can applaud patients' resistance to the undermining of their own autonomy. From an efficiency perspective, the news is bad" (p. 130). Noncompliance could result in deteriorated health.

If health-care professionals rely on the medical model's directives and prescriptions to enforce compliance, they do have some support that persuasion theory would predict: the patient's faith in the doctor's authority and the personal respect he or she tends to hold as a result of public admiration for the profession. In rhetorical terms, the physician brings to the relationship a degree of *ethos,* which causes some patients to accept the doctor's orders unquestioningly. After all, doctors often have something akin to an information monopoly concerning health care in general and the medical histories of their patients. In the traditional medical model, the doctor controls the questions that elicit the patient's medical history, then controls the information that is to be applied toward a diagnosis. Finally, the information is presented to an acquiescent patient in a digestible form designed to justify the doctor's assigned treatment. Bear in mind that Smith and Pettegrew (1986) are not critical of physicians' motives or personalities here; they only mean to describe the accepted medical practice that has evolved over the years in most Western cultures.

The doctor serves as a benevolent but thoroughly rational persuader who objectively "knows the appropriate values and acts [in] patients' best interests" (Smith & Pettegrew, 1986, p. 131). In fact, much medical theory encourages this approach to avoid the possibility that doctors could lapse from rational decision making into subjective manipulation, and thereby undermining a patient's "informed consent." According to law, patients must understand enough about their treatments and illnesses to agree in an informed way to what physicians might prescribe. Some authorities, including a presidential commission, have urged doctors to adopt a totally neutral, affectless style of presenting information to patients, so as not to influence the patients' choices too much. Thus, in this setting, a generalized medical model of communication puts doctors in an untenable situation: They must inform and direct patients, yet the patients must have a say in the treatment; doctors must be caring, yet they must be careful not to let their treatment preferences be communicated by subtle manipulation, such as through tone of voice or gestures (Smith & Pettegrew, 1986, p. 135).

Notice how the medical model described here resembles Aristotle's description of inartistic bases for communication. Either the older form of the medical model is used, in which physicians are granted the presumed power to manipulate, or the newer form of the model is advocated by some reformers, in which manipulation is supposedly avoided by physicians who simply present the alternative treatments and their probable outcomes for patients. The assumptions of the reformed medical model are (1) that the facts should speak for themselves and (2) that the inherent logic in certain treatments should be clear to patients as a result of doctors' dispassionate presentation of the information. If artistic persuasion is present, it is primarily in the forms of *ethos* and *logos*. According to Smith and Pettegrew (1986), the guidelines of the President's Commission for the Study of Ethical Problems in Medicine and Biomedical and Behavioral Research suggest that "no tone of voice, word choice, or nuance which could influence the patient is to be used lest the communication fall short of rational persuasion and become manipulation" (p. 135). However, this stipulation is obviously futile, if not silly, knowing what you now do about the conditions of human interaction. As many concepts discussed in this book demonstrate, humans cannot help but influence each other verbally and nonverbally during their communication. Even the absence of certain facial expressions will be interpreted in some way by the conversational partners.

Smith and Pettegrew (1986), therefore, build a case for *mutual persuasion* as an alternative model for doctor-patient communication. In this model, both parties are expected to make influence attempts, and both parties will recognize that influence is an inevitable result of interpersonal communication. The authors base their reasoning not on contemporary attitude change research or compliance-gaining theory, but on the oldest Western tradition of rhetoric, whose theorists "attempted to describe how the citizenry could arrive at decisions in the absence of certainty and where the assent of a number of individuals was required" (p. 138). The mutuality model must assume choice on the part of both parties. In fact, as we've seen in our account of classical rhetorical theory, the role of the audience is crucial even in the definition of rhetoric. If an audience doesn't hear and respond freely to a speaker, then what we're talking about is not rhetoric but coercion.

The mutuality model also assumes that people involved in genuine conversation are not able to make, nor are they interested in making, clear-cut distinctions between reason and emotion. Therefore, doctors and patients alike are active symbol users, speakers, and listeners; neither is controlled by the other. It is only under these circumstances, Smith and Pettegrew argue, that the medical field can hope to gain a higher rate of patients who follow through in response to agreed-upon treatments. This isn't mere patient compliance but the coordi-

L I N K

You might use the doctor-patient interpersonal relationship as a source for examples and applications when you study ethical theories in Chapter 10.

nated actions of doctors and patients. In the mutual persuasion approach, the patient responds not just to a doctor's orders, but also to an agreement in which both parties have a personal investment. In a sense, this is not compliance as Kelman (1966) defines it, but behavior that is consistent with a personal decision. As C. P. Ellis discovered in a different setting, ultimately we all persuade ourselves or we're not persuaded at all.

T E S T I N G   T H E   C O N C E P T S

"Why the emphasis on ancient rhetorical theory? Haven't we learned anything more about persuasion since ancient times?"

Obviously, we have progressed very far in our ability to predict communication effects, and many modern theories are far more sophisticated than Aristotelian theories. Yet most students who read Aristotle are surprised at the quality of his insight into the human predicament. He wrote in a very different era and in a very different culture, with communication rules that undoubtedly contradict many in the contemporary United States (e.g., Aristotle did not question slavery or the second-class status of women in ancient Greece). At the same time, however, few communication theorists in the history of the world have been as persuasive as Aristotle.

"Is it good that *ethos* or credibility can be so persuasive? After all, don't we already put too much emphasis on image politics?"

This would be an especially good question for classroom discussion. Whether or not we like modern methods of media campaigning, the phenomenon of personal credibility will persist. It's not so much an issue of good or bad as it is a question of emphasis. If so-called ethical proofs (the appeal of who a speaker is) are effective, and even differently effective with various audiences and across various situations, communication theorists need to account for these variables.

"How can I get my friend to quit smoking (or overeating, or gambling)?"

You probably can't. That is, you probably can't create the perfect message that will change your friend's mind about smoking. The main messages in this chapter's treatment of public and interpersonal rhetoric, however, are that persuasion is a mutual process and that both parties are active participants in that process. Rhetors can supply reasons, resources, and possibilities, and should do so if they feel strongly about a social issue (such as smoking), but they cannot cause others to change in a linear way.

Y O U,   T H E   R E S E A R C H E R

1. We sometimes refer to a speaker's *credibility* or *ethos* as though it were a possession. However, most communication research focuses on credibility as an audience-based process. That is, no leader can be thought of as

having uniformly high or low credibility across all situations; rather, she or he is more or less credible depending on the audience, topic, and context. Conduct a brief study of credibility on your own:

- List three national figures or celebrities who are regarded by you and your friends (an implied audience for the celebrities) as highly credible in their respective fields.
- For each high-credibility figure you selected, identify an audience, a topic, and a context where you would predict the person's credibility to be quite *low*. Explain why you chose the audience, topic, and context for each person.
- Using basic methods of communication research, how could you determine if your reasoning is accurate in these instances? Discuss your proposed studies in class.

2. Interview three persons in helping professions, such as counselors, doctors, nurses, and social workers.

- Ask them to describe how much they think their clients and patients change attitudes and behaviors as a result of communication with the "helper."
- Ask them to what extent such attitude change in others is specifically intended by the professional. In other words, are the effects of helping outcomes of the relationship or of a persuasive strategy consciously employed by the professional?
- The medical profession studies the effectiveness of intentional persuasion, which it calls "patient compliance." Research is conducted on how health-care providers can more effectively persuade patients to follow through with treatment directives. How could the model of mutual persuasion be researched, given its different assumptions about causality?

3. Research the conditions of Greek culture in Aristotle's time. How did men and women regard each other? Were all people regarded as equal? Did some people not have the same rights as others? What power inequalities and elitist assumptions existed in Aristotle's time? Consider whether the culture in which Aristotle wrote affects your opinion of his theory of rhetoric. Why, or why not?

4. At your campus library, trace a public-information campaign about the effects of smoking. Analyze advertisements, interviews, and news releases. Explain where you see the following phenomena at work:

Ethos	Enthymemes
Pathos	Rhetorical examples
Logos	Mutual persuasion (or a lack of it)

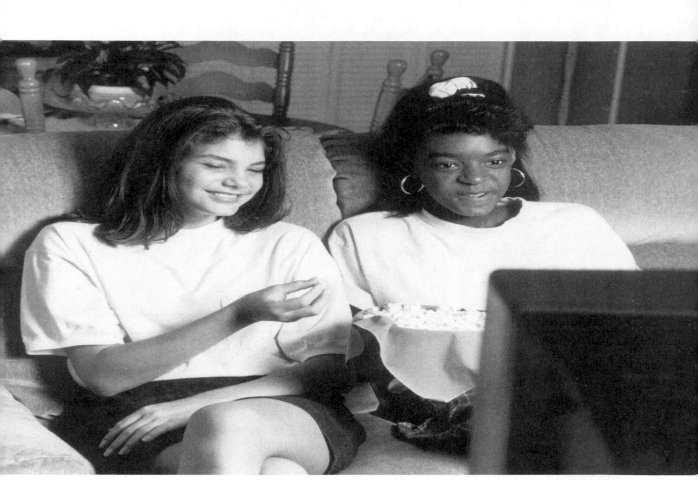

the influence of the media world

"do we get what *we* deserve?"

Super media are sounds we wake to from a clock radio. They ride with us in the car. In office and classroom, they are the sources of information. They occupy our home as an electronic window and printed page. Super media bring us the news, scare us, relax us, and at times inspire us. We cannot live without them, and we sometimes fear we cannot live with them.

MICHAEL R. REAL, *SUPER MEDIA* (1989, P. 7)

Media are not fixed natural objects; they have no natural edges. They are constructed complexes of habits, beliefs, and procedures embedded in elaborate cultural codes of communication. The history of media is never more or less than the history of their uses, which always lead us away from them to the social practices and conflicts they illuminate. New media, broadly understood to include the use of new communications technology for old or new purposes, new ways of using old technologies, and, in principle, all other possibilities for the exchange of social meaning, are always introduced into a pattern of tension created by the coexistence of old and new, which is far richer than any single medium that becomes a focus of interest because it is novel. New media embody the possibility that accustomed orders are in jeopardy, since communication is a peculiar kind of interaction that actively seeks variety.

CAROLYN MARVIN, *WHEN OLD TECHNOLOGIES WERE NEW* (1988, P. 8)

Media communication—for us, by us, and about us—seems to surround us in contemporary culture. Theorists try to understand how the media might change the entire social fabric, and individuals in daily life often wonder how the media might affect them personally. Parents worry that violent television shows might affect their children in negative ways. Will children who watch such shows grow up to become violent adults? If a situation comedy portrays a racist (even a bumbling and foolish one) as a protagonist, will viewers understand the satire, or instead get the idea that racism isn't a terribly serious issue? Can modern advertising techniques manipulate people into buying products or candidates they wouldn't otherwise choose? What about the values and beliefs we bring to our media exposure? How successfully can we separate the effects of watching television, for instance, from the effects of talking about television with friends and neighbors? Have our own communication habits as media audiences helped to create the kind of media system we sometimes criticize? Could audiences have more power than we realize? Do we, in other words, sometimes get the media environment we "deserve"?

Such questions are difficult to answer because we don't have a clear lens with which to observe the mediated world. Because we exist only in that environment, we can't observe it in comparison with other environments. As communication theorists often say, you have to remove yourself from a given frame or system in order to perceive it more clearly. Yet the media seem to occupy a nearly all-encompassing frame.

Our everyday lives are immersed in media messages. People wake up to alarm clocks that are tuned to their favorite radio stations; the night before, they fell asleep watching David Letterman. They read morning newspapers to scan more news than they could possibly assimilate. While traveling to work they strain to listen to radio traffic reports, more news, and entertainment programs. Over lunch, people talk about films, television series, and the insults of outrageous radio personalities. They also talk about distant world leaders, usually on the basis of forty-five-second news "bites" chosen by distant anonymous network producers and directors. How could modern executives manage without telephones and fax machines? Computer access to information is now taken for granted, not just in businesses but also in many homes throughout society's strata.

Entertainment options continually expand through the media. Cable television and satellite dishes supplement local stations in most areas of the country. Global access is assured, even if global contact isn't. A media consciousness shapes the kinds of futures people can imagine and the kinds of planning they can attempt (Brand, 1988; Negroponte, 1995; Taylor & Saarinen, 1994). An anthropology of modern society, then, must include media. Without taking media influence into account, an analyst would miss the most pervasive aspects of everyday experience.

Yet within this media environment, individuals often feel small and insignificant: "What can I do? I'm just one person." Some critics claim that the technology of the media de-personalizes people, making us less humane, less connected to each other, and more dependent on the decisions of powerful people we haven't even met and who haven't met us (Berger, Berger, & Kellner, 1974; Ellul, 1964, 1985; Ferrarotti, 1988). Some people feel as if they are at the mercy of a media-controlled coalition that conspires to shape how its audience thinks. Or, in an anthropomorphic way, people assume that the media have an independent and malevolent existence, that technology is somehow inherently evil, and the most dangerous technologies are those that disseminate information.

Theorists analyzing mass media provide surprising insights for those of us in mass audiences who are willing to pay attention. The information media become more powerful in an age that treats information as a commodity. Audiences expect media to have that power, and so it exists. To some extent, however, familiarity with the theories of mass communication and other mediated systems can allay some of the fears associated with the idea that the modern media engage in manipulation. To some extent also, familiarity with media theories can provide a survival kit for making decisions in a culture that is overseen by *super media* (Real, 1989), media that pervade an entire culture.

Before continuing, we should define what we mean by manipulation, and compare it to some other processes of social communication. Obviously, communicators affect each other, often deeply so. You may have been profoundly influenced by a special teacher, by a member of the clergy, or by role models in public and private life. Such influences are natural and normal. While people should admit that they can be influenced, we should also admit the constant potential for influencing others. Even the tiniest conversational pebble we toss creates ripples. Thus, *influence* could be unplanned or accidental. So we shouldn't be surprised that people in families, organizations, and societies make differences in each others' lives; it is impossible to *avoid* having an effect. Human beings constantly adjust to the actions of others. Persuasion happens when people voluntarily change their ways of thinking and feeling (usually intentionally) as a result of the (usually intentional) messages of others. The distinction between *influence* and *persuasion* is somewhat fuzzy in the communication literature. But what about the persistent fear of some people that they're being taken advantage of or manipulated by others' communication? What, if anything, do they fear beyond the suspicion that their attitudes, values, and beliefs are subject to change?

The word *manipulation* is derived from the Latin *manus*, "the hand." In human affairs, it has come to refer to a process of taking control over someone's or something's fate—as in picking up an inert object and placing it elsewhere, at your will. Manipulation, then, is a situation where one person or group expects automatic reactions from another person or group. Realistic choice seems removed or reduced. No wonder people became frightened when they heard of the "mind control" and "brainwashing" techniques that were supposed to have been so effective in the mid-twentieth century (Brown, 1963). The public began to wonder if a powerful system of mass media (newspaper and magazine empires, then radio, then television) could systematically undermine its ability to make personal choices. Although modern societies wanted more sophisticated and direct means to communicate with diverse groups, they also feared that the systems they wanted could manipulate people directly through propaganda and thought-control methods. This concern with manipulation led, in the 1940s and 1950s, to what is retrospectively called the *magic bullet theory* of media effects, which we discuss in detail later in this chapter.

Although this simplistic "hit the target" analogy is no longer influential, the concern about media manipulation continues to fuel many media reform efforts in the 1990s. How far should advertisers be allowed to go in promoting their products before they cross an ethical line into manipulation? Is it possible for subliminal communication messages to cause us to buy certain products? Are society's power relationships (haves/have-nots, male/female, majority/minority, and so on) inherently reflected in the corporate nature of media conglomerates, reducing our choices and thereby manipulating our social and political preferences? Although this chapter can't answer these questions definitively, it will introduce you to many of the theorists who are grappling with them. Using their concepts and propositions, you will become a better decision maker about the effects of the media, and a media theorist yourself.

In this chapter, we will look at three issues of media theory. First, we summarize how people make sense of media messages—that is, how they receive, process, and use such messages in their daily lives. Second, we examine some emerging theories of how media become cultural agencies. Because the media both shape and are shaped by the general culture in which they exist, understanding the media may provide the best clues to understanding contemporary life. People are socialized and acculturized in part by attending to the media. Third, we examine in more detail those theories that help us relate interpersonal communication to mass communication problems. The connections among the different levels of communication study are important. Yet they are often neglected, because individual researchers might focus solely on either interpersonal or mass communication. This dichotomy, in fact, is often reflected in the splitting of academic communication departments on college and university campuses.

HAVE MEDIA CHANGED HOW WE MAKE PSYCHOLOGICAL SENSE?

> Each medium, if its bias is properly exploited, reveals and communicates a unique aspect of reality, of truth. Each offers a different perspective, a way of seeing an otherwise hidden dimension of reality. It's not a question of one reality being true, the others distortions. One allows us to see from here, another from there, a third from still another perspective; taken together they give us a more complete whole, a greater truth. New essentials are brought to the fore, including those made invisible by the "blinders" of old languages. (Carpenter, 1960, pp. 173–174)

A number of theories go beyond the claim that the public's attitudes and beliefs are changed by media messages. These theories suggest instead that something more fundamental occurs, that how persons perceive and make sense of the world is affected by the introduction of different media into human experience. (See Box 9-1 on p. 249.) Stated somewhat differently, it's not just the power of the messages to change *what we think* (a content issue) that must be analyzed, but we should also recognize the power of the media themselves to change *how we perceive* (a process issue). As Edmund Carpenter claims in the preceding quotation, the media we invent to help us communicate become similar to new "languages" that structure our experience. The media, therefore, can't be understood as simple pipelines carrying the same messages to different people.

mcluhan: media extend and change our senses

A landmark of twentieth-century communication theory is Marshall McLuhan's *Understanding Media* (1964). His basic idea, developed in earlier work as well (1962), is that media restructure the human consciousness in surprising ways. If European and American cultures revere linear and sequential analysis, we can trace this, according to McLuhan, to the invention of movable type and the institutionalization of writing. The *media*, says McLuhan, are nothing more than extensions of human senses. For example, clothing is a medium extending the skin,

LINK

You have probably become more interested in how teachers and scholars are shaping the discipline as they also shape its fundamental theories. See Chapter 11 for more on the structure of communication as a discipline or interdiscipline.

and radio and television extend the reach of hearing and vision (simultaneously, in the latter case). Drawing in part on the earlier work of his Canadian country-man, Harold Innis (1951; Carey, 1989, pp. 142–172), McLuhan (1962) asserts that ". . . if a new technology extends one or more of our senses outside us into the social world, then new ratios among all of our senses will occur in that particular culture. It is comparable to what happens when a new note is added to a melody. And when the sense ratios alter in any culture then what had appeared lucid before may suddenly be opaque, and what had been vague or opaque will become translucent" (p. 41). DeFleur and Ball-Rokeach (1982), in their summary of Innis's notions (as elaborated by McLuhan), call this an issue of "technological determinism." The "nature of the media technology prevailing in a society at a given point in time greatly influences how the members of that society think and behave" (p. 184). Perhaps the word "determinism" is an overstatement, just as most commentators on communication recently have claimed that McLuhan's thesis—"the medium is the message"—exaggerates the importance of the media and underplays the importance of media messages.

But McLuhan and Innis were on to something. Indeed, without their insights, theorists might not have paid as much attention to the message value of the different media themselves. For example, television *shows* can be "about" crime, or cartoons, or news. But, McLuhan asks, what is *television itself* "about"? Does the existence of television encourage us to think about and evaluate things more in some ways than in others? McLuhan (1964) reminds us that "the 'content' of a medium is like the juicy piece of meat carried by the burglar to distract the watchdog of the mind" (p. 32). To think of content as the most important meaning of media is to mislead yourself, McLuhan thought.

McLuhan's *Understanding Media* (1964) builds on this basic idea that the media *are* messages. It also integrates tremendously diverse sources from history, literature, and social criticism to demonstrate how the electronic media affect modern sensibilities. Although some of McLuhan's distinctions no longer motivate researchers and creative theorists, they remain historically interesting, and in their time, they were exciting and heuristic ideas. McLuhan became a pop culture "hero," as his ideas were debated on talk shows and in the popular press; he even appeared in a cameo role—as himself—in a Woody Allen movie. In addition to his central thesis, McLuhan's ideas about hot and cool media and the global village have been highly influential.

Hot media, to McLuhan, are those that demand relatively little of audiences; they supply or attempt to supply a great deal of information while leaving little for the listener, viewer, or reader to "fill in." Hot media are highly definitional and intense. In a sense, they tell the audience much of what it needs to know in a situation, and leave little to the imagination or participation of the audience. Compared to the English language, Asian alphabets that are pictographic define meanings less precisely for readers, "spelling fewer things out," and thus are, in McLuhan's sense, not so "hot." (Books tend to be "hotter" media than radio or television, since print seeks to "tell" readers more definitive detail than they literally need for purposes of interpretation. And textbooks tend to be hotter than novels.) Those media that require (or invite) more audience participation in creating meaning are said to be *cool media*.

L I N K

Compare McLuhan's "hot" and "cool" media distinctions to the discussion in Chapter 7 of elaborated and restricted content codes. Are the concepts similar? Analogous? What are the important differences?

How can McLuhan's concepts of hot and cool media help people understand today's culture? Most of the modern electronic media seem to be moving in "cooler" directions, with interesting implications. The cooler media climate invites an ambiguity of style that we can see at work in the political arena. A politician who defines issues too precisely may be seen as logical, but not in tune with the thought patterns that the electorate has come to expect. People feel more included by the cool media, more likely to want to feel a part of what's going on. Their expectations change, sometimes subtly, for what defines public discourse. Other implications McLuhan attributes to the emerging cool media are the modern concerns with total effects, rather than isolated meanings, and the concern with processes rather than products.

According to McLuhan (1964), an outgrowth of this emerging "coolness" in the media is the interwebbing of the entire world into a *global village*. Making strong and individualized statements is appropriate to a "hot" medium, but a different rhetoric better fits a world increasingly linked by computers ("extensions of our central nervous systems") and other electronic mass media (McLuhan & Fiore, 1968). Whereas in the first oral cultures, villages were places of immediacy and interdependence, the innovation of the printing press and other industrial sophistication made it possible for people in faraway places to trade messages with each other. McLuhan (1964) believes that the new electronic media have returned the communication environment to a state of immediacy once more:

> The immediate prospect for literate, fragmented Western man encountering the electric implosion within his own culture is his steady and rapid transformation into a complex and depth-structured person emotionally aware of his total interdependence with the rest of human society. Representatives of the older Western individualism are even now assuming the appearance, for good or ill, of Al Capp's General Bull Moose or of the John Birchers, tribally dedicated to opposing the tribal. Fragmented, literate, and visual individualism is not possible in an electrically patterned and imploded society. So what is to be done? Do we dare to confront such facts at the conscious level, or is it best to becloud and repress such matters until some violence releases us from the entire burden? For the fate of implosion and interdependence is more terrible for Western man than the fate of explosion and independence for tribal man. (p. 59).

Obviously, McLuhan comes down on the side of confronting the implications of our interdependence, since it was our own invention of certain types of media that led us to our retribalized "village"-like state of consciousness, changing us forever. McLuhan, in effect, argues that we cannot return to a primarily linear, sequential, "literate" consciousness because we've become holized. Instead of scholars analyzing *parts* more efficiently, McLuhan wanted theorists to understand wholes more effectively.

ong: the human "sensorium"

McLuhan's early interests made him a scholarly role model for one of his students, Fr. Walter J. Ong, who has assumed significant intellectual stature in his own right.

LINKS

- Review the discussion of immediacy in Chapter 3. How might Mehrabian, for example, predict the differences between the immediacy of face-to-face interaction and the immediacy of electronically linked communication in e-mail or online chat rooms? Theorists are now trying to grapple with describing the differences between face-to-face and digital forms of presence (Anderson, 1994, 1997; Gozzi & Haynes, 1992; Jones, 1994; Walther, 1993, 1996).
- Was McLuhan a postmodern theorist? Reread his statement in the context of Chapter 4's discussion of the postmodern challenge for theorizing.

In a manner somewhat similar to McLuhan's, Ong attempts to synthesize literature, history, the arts, and social science to discover larger patterns. Some of his work on print culture in Western thought was published early enough to influence McLuhan's *The Gutenberg Galaxy* (1962). In two of his most admired books, *The Presence of the Word* (1967) and *Orality and Literacy* (1982), Ong effectively uses McLuhan's themes as foils or touchstones for his own creative thought.

Ong (1967) describes what he calls the human *sensorium:* "the entire sensory apparatus as an operational complex" (p. 6), or the network of habits by which people employ their senses of sound, sight, touch, smell, and taste. The relationships of the senses to each other (whether a given group, for example, emphasizes sound over touch in its way of prioritizing experience), to a large extent define human cultures. Ong (1967) believed humankind has experienced three stages of language transformation: (1) the *oral*, (or *oral/aural*) *stage;* (2) the *script stage*, including the inventions of the alphabet and typography; and (3) the *electronic stage* (pp. 17–110).

The *oral stage* consisted of using language not as records or packages of meaning, but as immediate experience. Language was not used to "keep" knowledge exactly, because even the storytellers and singers of earlier cultures—whose responsibility it was to maintain the group's culture—typically "retold" stories inexactly. Instead, the word was seen as a celebration of life, not a tool for its manipulation. The *script stage* changed that somewhat. With the alphabet came a switchover in human consciousness. Humans gained more control over sound by representing it visually, as well as achieving more control over time. The order in human affairs that resulted changed human consciousness because it changed the sensorium. "It appears no accident that formal logic was invented in an alphabetic culture," writes Ong (1967, p. 45). Typography increased people's reliance on visualization in the sensorium, but it did not create this reliance, because earlier peoples also had to be keen observers. Instead, typography married visualization with the word. Statements and representations could be repeated exactly. This made the word more believable, increasing people's trust in "the isolated thinker, the man with the book, and downgraded the network of personal loyalties which oral cultures favor as matrices of communication and as principles of social unity" (Ong, 1967, p. 54).

Ong questions McLuhan's belief that media in the *electronic stage* have created the equivalent of a retribalized and orally centered global village. The current electronic involvement with the word has features of the oral stage, of course; it makes communication less reliant on formal literacy. But modern people cannot, will not, and should not forget literacy. The new electronic culture extends people's senses of being "present" for each other by merging print and orality into human consciousness. We are now in an age of *secondary orality,* Ong believes, which differs considerably from our earlier dependence on orality. It is a new consciousness with a different set of ground rules:

> . . . before writing, oral folk were group-minded because no feasible alternative had presented itself. In our age of secondary orality, we are group-minded self-consciously and programmatically. The individual feels that he or she, as

an individual, must be socially sensitive. Unlike members of a primary oral culture, who are turned outward because they have had little occasion to turn inward, we are turned outward because we have turned inward. In a like vein, where primary orality promotes spontaneity because the analytic reflectiveness implemented by writing is unavailable, secondary orality promotes spontaneity because through analytic reflection we have decided that spontaneity is a good thing. We plan our happenings carefully to be sure that they are thoroughly spontaneous. (1982, pp. 136–137)

Ong illustrates both his similarity to and his disagreement with McLuhan. At the same time, his last several sentences eloquently suggest the paradoxes of modern living.

Ong has been increasingly influential in the current intellectual community (Dance, 1989; Gronbeck, Farrell, & Soukup, 1991; Havelock, 1986). He undoubtedly influenced the prominent contemporary media theorist Neil Postman, whose recent work explores television's new emphasis on visual presence to the exclusion of analytic thinking. Postman (1985) does not attempt to show, as do Ong, McLuhan, and others, that perception and modes of consciousness themselves are changed by technology; rather, he claims that each new technology changes the "structure of discourse" that people believe to be appropriate. Yet he also believes that there is a relationship between technological advances in the media and human consciousness (p. 27).

Postman (1985) provides an interesting example that is relevant to students and teachers. If you agree with his reasoning, the example demonstrates a shift in the modern consciousness—from print-oriented to television-oriented thinking. In print-oriented thinking, according to Postman, a reader or other message recipient usually assumes that the message should be internally consistent and without contradiction, because the context of the communication is assumed to be singular. In other words, "where the author is coming from" is assumed by the typographic mind to be one place. Postman (1985) often points out to his younger students that what they write in one part of an essay is inconsistent with other parts: " 'I know,' they will say, 'but that is there and this is here' " (p. 110). The teacher assumes that students are writing from one coherent and cohesive point of view, connected by threads of meaning, which is a very print-oriented way of thinking.

However, Postman points out that television has changed the styles of modern discourse, so that the contexts for any opinion now seems "discontinuous" and constantly shifting. Yesterday cannot be compared with today because a person's stance or opinion could shift at any minute. Postman's students, raised in the age of television more than he was, have incorporated an expectation for discontinuous thought. Television moves abruptly from violent tragedy to giggly comedy with almost no transition, and nothing is perceived as wrong or amiss; after all, the network is not assumed to be advancing a singular position. As Postman (1985) notes, ". . . in a world of discontinuities, contradiction is useless as a test of truth or merit, because contradiction does not exist" (p. 110). Perhaps, he speculates, this is why the American public seemed relatively unconcerned when President

LINK

The new tolerance for inconsistency and contradiction that Postman (1985) describes may help explain the theoretical appeal of contemporary postmodern thought. In Chapter 4, we discuss the scholarly debate over postmodern theoretical assumptions about language. You may find it interesting to reconsider postmodern theory in light of media theory. Poster's *The Mode of Information* (1990) and Taylor and Saarinen's *Imagologies* (1994) are two books that examine media contributions to a changing postmodern world. McLuhan, Ong, and Postman all range widely over the intellectual terrain in drawing connections between mediated communication and the basic ways we construct perceptual worlds. Do you believe the electronic media and the new online culture will continue to erode the older linear rationality of modernism? Why or why not?

Reagan repeatedly made public statements that were seemingly mutually exclusive or inconsistent.

HAVE MEDIA CONTROLLED OUR CULTURAL AND SOCIAL BEHAVIORS?

To this point in the chapter, we've discussed theories of how the media alter how we think and, therefore, how we talk. Media do not function as neutral conductors of messages from sources to receivers, in other words. They are, instead, an inescapable part of our social environment. Beyond that, the medium with which we choose to communicate a message inevitably becomes a part of the message itself. In systems theory terms, the medium is a component of the whole communication system, one that bears a relationship to all other components.

If we hope to answer, even tentatively, the question heading this chapter— "Do we get what we deserve?"—we need first to acknowledge that the media are perceptually influential, and then to consider the consequences of that influence on human affairs. Since it's impossible in a brief book to survey all the theories that attempt to account for media impact, in this chapter we'll summarize representative theories that indicate the range of historical, conceptual, and political concerns in this growing area of communication research.

shot with a "magic bullet"?

As the twentieth century became more technologically sophisticated, observers of the mass media became increasingly worried. They feared that the public would be highly vulnerable individually to persuasive messages that would emanate from powerful media sources. In the introduction to this chapter we referred to this as the **magic bullet theory** of mass-mediated communication, although it has also been called the **hypodermic needle approach**, as well. Listeners, viewers, and readers were seen as targets of the media "bullets" (messages), which, if accurately sent, could produce certain desired results. Or, in the second analogy, the audience is conceptualized as a patient who receives an inoculation of persuasion from the media, which, in turn, hold the audience's fate in their hands.

The magic bullet approach is based on a number of assumptions. Although the theory may at first seem simplistic, it was highly believable in the post–World War I age of unsettled international and interpersonal relations:

1. People in major industrialized societies (in which the mass media were developing) experienced feelings of disconnection and *anomie* (a sociological term that describes the breakup and confusion of values within a society) (Theodorson & Theodorson, 1969, p. 12). Traditional societies, with their strong bonds based on families and community affiliation were changing rapidly after the First World War, and members of newly massmediated societies were in many ways presumed to be disoriented and psychologically isolated from each other.

BOX 9-1

MEDIA CHANGE OUR PERCEPTION AND SENSE MAKING

- Innis and McLuhan: Media radically *extend our senses,* becoming messages that transcend the importance of the content they are presumed to carry; the electronic media help to create a new *global village.*
- Ong: Media adjust the human *sensorium,* changing the relationship of senses to each other; this is seen in stages of *orality* (primary orality), *script* (literacy), and *electronic* (secondary orality) experience.

2. Although people in different groups of a society varied widely in their beliefs, attitudes, and values, they were thought by communication researchers to respond to significant messages in largely similar and predictable ways.
3. People were considered very persuasible, and their attitudes easily changed to quite different positions. This assumption, as well as the previous one, were thought to have been established by the success of international propaganda campaigns during World War I.
4. Cause-effect thinking—and its manifestation in the social sciences of the day, the stimulus-response assumption—tended to assign each effect to a specific and identifiable cause. In the case of media effects, the cause or stimulus was media content, and the effect or response was attitude (and often behavioral) change.

The presumption that audiences were fundamentally vulnerable to media power motivated many communication researchers for years, although, interestingly, many sociologists and other social scientists evidently understood that the mass media did not have the kind of direct and immediate influence sometimes attributed to them (Delia, 1987). Gradually, communication researchers in the areas of voting and marketing behavior began to notice effects that were not attributable to the impact of campaign messages on isolated voters.

the two-step (and multi-step) flow of influence

Using voting and marketing data, some theorists began to speculate that the media audience was not as atomized—that is, not as spread out and isolated—as they'd previously thought. Nor were they as malleable. Theorists began to talk of "the obstinate audience" (Bauer, 1964) and of how interpersonal variables intervened between sources and receivers of media messages. It became clear that everyday face-to-face talk about mass communication sources was a vital part of the communication system.

opinion leaders in personal relations. The most influential scholarly attempt to revise the magic bullet theory was the book *Personal Influence* by Katz and

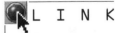

L I N K

More attention to rhetorical theories, discussed in Chapter 8, might have helped early theorists predict that audience effects of media messages were less automatic, and audiences were more active and "obstinate" than critics initially presumed. Rhetorical and social science theories clearly complement each other.

Lazarsfeld (1955), although an earlier book laid its conceptual groundwork (Lazarsfeld, Berelson, & Gaudet, 1948). Basically, these authors argue that we cannot understand the media system either by looking to media content for its inherent effects, or by looking to media audiences for their vulnerability. Instead, a third major variable, interpersonal relations, must be factored into this seemingly simple equation. Their research suggested that the most significant media effects are not directly caused, but instead come from relationships with influential persons in an audience member's own everyday experience.

Katz and Lazarsfeld (1955) call these persuasive agents *influentials* or *opinion leaders*. Most audience members are not directly addressed or changed by media messages, but their discussions of the media with others subsequently form or change their opinions. Moreover, certain people in this interpersonal system become influential because their opinions are listened to and heeded carefully by others. Opinion leaders also tend to be more exposed to the mass media than other people, and they specialize in specific areas of media coverage to which they have paid particularly close attention (e.g., someone might be an opinion leader in politics but not in fashion). Only rarely is an opinion leader found to be influential across the board.

The **two-step flow theory** thus takes mass communication beyond a simple stimulus–response model, in which the process was seen as a simple one-step or linear injection of attitude. Rather, it looks at mass communication from the point of view of a single audience member, and media messages are seen as filtered through an intermediate step, in which influential others monitor and interpret media content and then disseminate that content interpersonally.

Ironically, the researchers of personal influence in media systems were really demonstrating that many of the most important effects of the mass media are not mass effects at all, but a complex and subtle web of interpersonal effects. They showed that part of our understanding of any level of communication must be based on understanding the other levels. But what does this mean in practical everyday terms? It means, for example, that your reaction to *Murphy Brown* or *Good Morning America* is not attributable solely to the show, or to you, or to a straightforward interaction of the show and your attitudes. Rather, your reaction to a television show or other type of media content has to be considered in terms of your interpersonal relationships; your friends and acquaintances, whether they know it or not, are probably exerting some type of opinion leadership.

Subsequent theorists, considering the two-step flow model of mass communication too simple, developed *multi-step flow theories*. Although the basic philosophy is similar, interpersonal influences are seen as more intricate and multilayered than in the two-step flow theory. In addition, mass communication content depends on many other factors of interpersonal influence for its effects. This can be seen in practical terms by a simple hypothetical example: Think about your experience with an innovative or controversial television show, such as *Politically Incorrect, Third Rock from the Sun, Married with Children*, or, from several years ago, *In Living Color*. Did you happen to discover the show by chance and watch it before any of your acquaintances did? Or did you hear about the show from one of them? "Hey, did you see that strange new show on Fox network last night?" or "I know you're interested in medical shows; you ought to watch the new one on Monday nights," or "Can you believe something that obnoxious got on the air?" For whatever reason, you decide to tune it in. Aside from the personal preferences and values that you brought to the occasion, and aside from the actual content of the show and the intentions of its producers, directors, actors, and network executives, several other facts are already relevant for any theory of the media system:

1. Interpersonal factors probably influenced your decision to watch the show (e.g., "I like Tamara, and I'd like to have more to talk with her about. I think I'll watch *Third Rock,* too").

2. While watching the show, your friend's recommendation, warning, or enticement about it probably affected your reactions. To the extent that your friend had high or low credibility for you, your judgment was influenced in a positive or negative direction by associating the (impersonal) television program with that (personal) direct experience (e.g., "I don't get it. This seems so stupid. But Tamara thought it was sophisticated and deep. She's probably seeing all the humorous twists more clearly than I could. Come to think of it, I do like this show more than I thought I would").

3. While watching the show, you will be formulating and perhaps rehearsing the reactions you'll share with the person who suggested your viewing choice, and might be anticipating further communication with others about the show, as well. This doesn't need to be a conscious process. Overtly or covertly, all healthy persons process personal experience in the context of anticipated future social interaction. ("I think I'll tell Tamara how fascinating the show was, and how I'm planning to watch it next week, too. I'm really looking forward to it. Maybe Jim would like to know about it, too; I'll call him.")

4. After watching the show, your talk about it with others becomes a part of the mass communication system. Advertisers, celebrities, and public relations specialists are well aware of the value of "word-of-mouth" information, and the multistep flow model is more or less a theoretical form of this process (e.g., "Simone, have you seen *Third Rock?* It's weird, but funny. I think you'd like it." . . . "Thanks. I've already heard about it from people at the office").

Therefore, what may seem to be a simple process of receiving messages directly from media sources is clarified to be what it actually is—a complex web of interpersonal processes operating within the context of media topics and choices. Causes and effects are difficult to pinpoint in this multi-step web of influences. One model of communication that attempts to take interim influences into account is based on the gatekeeping role of the media.

gatekeepers in the media system Westley and MacLean's (1957) model of gatekeeping helps to clarify the concept of interim decision makers, or gatekeepers, in combined mass communication and interpersonal communication systems. *Gatekeepers* are those persons, groups, or roles that control the kind and amount of information receivers can receive, supplementing an audience's direct knowledge of its communication environment. Officially or unofficially, gatekeepers monitor the range of messages that might be relevant to a given audience, select and abstract the portion of that range they believe will fit the audience needs, and relay only those messages to the audience. Gatekeeping is relevant to what media researchers call the **agenda-setting theory** of the media (McCombs & Shaw, 1972). In brief, this approach suggests that media sources don't force us to believe certain things, but instead by the nature of the profession they must give us a selective, limited set of options to think about. No news medium, for example, can report all of what happens in a given day. Certain stories make the newscast or the paper, and some don't. Media gatekeepers therefore set the agenda for social and political life without necessarily being manipulative in doing so. Gatekeepers, whether we like it or not, are an inevitable influence on what we know, or on what we think we know.

Informal opinion leaders who communicate interpersonally at the office, in the factory, or at school can also be gatekeepers, as Katz and Lazarsfeld (1955) suggest. Or gatekeepers can have more official roles within the mass media: The producer of *NBC Nightly News,* the managing editor of the *New York Times,* and the manager of your campus radio station can all decide what information gets reported and what information doesn't get reported, based on their interpretations of the relative importance of that information.

Westley and MacLean's (1957) model of gatekeeping is illustrated in Figure 9-1. Although the diagram may look confusing at first, it illustrates a basic process: the intentional attempt of person *A* to create with person *B* a certain communication relationship with a certain symbolic content. This is not the kind of transactional model we discussed in earlier chapters, but it does indicate some of the directional factors that people have in mind when they try to create a certain ef-

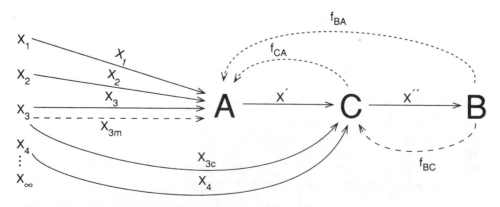

Figure 9-1   Westley and MacLean's Model of Gatekeeping

Source: "A Conceptual Model for Mass Communication Research," by B. H. Westley and M. S. MacLean, Jr. In *Journalism Quarterly,* vol. 34 (pp. 31–38). Copyright © 1957. Reproduced with permission of the Association for Education in Journalism and Mass Communication.

fect with their messages (as shown by the arrows in the figure). Further, the *X*s at the left of the figure designate what the authors call *objects of orientation,* or the infinite range of available objects and events capable of being transformed into symbolic messages and stimuli. Both person *A* and person *B,* of course, can select from this experiential environment of *X*s those objects of orientation they want to attend to; but no two persons will select the same *X*s, nor will they make their selections for the same reasons. Person *A*'s selection of certain objects of orientation forms the basis for his or her message to person *B.*

So far, the model is very straightforward. But Westley and MacLean point out that there is often another communication role fulfilled by a person or group whose purpose is to expand the message environment of the audience (*B*). *B*s can't successfully monitor the incredible diversity of the media world, and thus won't be able to process successfully much of what *A* is creating. Enter the gatekeeper role, *C,* which operates much like *B*'s (unappointed) agent in selecting information about objects and relationships. Much of the world's information potential (*X*s), and influence potential (*A*s and the *AX* relations) are thus filtered through this gatekeeper (*C*) to an audience.

A few examples will illustrate the importance of the gatekeeper's role in a society dominated by the mass media:

1. Your friend living in Milwaukee is keeping you abreast of neighborhood gossip that it would be very hard for you, living in Chicago, say, or Walla Walla, to collect. But your friend, as your gatekeeper, is inevitably leaving out some things, and probably overemphasizing others.

2. This textbook is a message that operates within a mass medium—the publishing industry. If you can imagine that Westley and MacLean occupy the *A* role and you as a reader occupy the *B* role (in that they have a particular point of view they'd like you to understand), then we, as this text's authors, occupy the *C* role. Whether an audience's interest is communication or internal medicine, most audiences can't check independently on everything they read or hear, so they end up trusting strangers who claim to abstract and present this other message faithfully and helpfully. Therefore, you as a reader are our audience, and even though we think we are well informed, we will undoubtedly select different features of the model to explain than other authors would choose. We will also emphasize certain issues more than others would. Remember, then, when analyzing mass communication systems, that gatekeepers are everywhere, and no one can avoid them.

3. During the Persian Gulf War, newspapers served as gatekeepers for the public, military briefers served as gatekeepers for the press, generals and the commander-in-chief served as gatekeepers for the briefers, and the intelligence-gathering community served as gatekeepers for the generals and president.

4. TV personalities, such as Oprah Winfrey, Dan Rather, Diane Sawyer, and Geraldo Rivera, also mind the public's gate, promoting some informational and entertainment trends in American culture while blocking others.

As persons who attend to the mass media, therefore, we should strive for a realistic understanding of who our opinion leaders and gatekeepers are in the media and of how gatekeepers influence the persuasive impact of media messages. It's not enough for informed citizens to know what we believe; we should be more attuned to *how we come to believe* what we do, and how our beliefs are constantly shifting in response to mediated communication messages.

You've probably noticed that the media theories discussed thus far tend to look at effects from the standpoint of the media, which initiate messages for and have effects on audiences. This tendency is perhaps natural. But now, let's reposition our theoretical stance to consider the media system more from the vantage point of its audiences.

uses and gratifications theorizing

Probably the most prominent of the recent advances in media theory has come from research in the **uses and gratifications approach**, which examines what audiences have in mind when they expose themselves to the media (Blumler & Katz, 1974; Palmgreen, 1984). In other words, to what *uses* do audience members put media messages as they see, hear, or read them? And what personalized or social *gratifications* do audience members attempt to gain from their use of media messages?

The emphasis of uses and gratifications research is on what audiences attempt to do with media messages, not on the effects of the media on audiences. This distinction is important. Unlike some other media theories, uses and gratifications theory does not assume that media audiences are basically passive. Media audiences are conceived as active agents in control of their own destinies. Let's consider a simple example: Imagine that a younger brother, who seems generally healthy and happy, has a habit of attending films that you believe are too violent and gory. Naturally, you're worried about the outcome of his interest in such movies. Will he be psychologically affected by them? Is he in danger of becoming more violent himself, or of condoning casual violence in society? Some media-centered theorists would examine such questions by looking for the effects of the movies on persons like your brother. They might perform short-range studies, administering attitude test instruments before and after people's exposure to violent films. Or they might seek to discover longer-range effects through *longitudinal studies,* which follow a group of subjects over a specified period of time and chart (through focused interviews, journals, and similar methods) their media choices and changed attitudes, beliefs, values, and behaviors.

A uses and gratifications theorist, however, would take a very different approach to examining the same issue. Although these theorists have diverse ideas, they tend to assume that it's more important, conceptually and analytically, to start any analysis with the audience. Before we can know whether media messages are harmful, they claim, it's necessary to know what the audience members are "doing with" the messages. Is your brother watching the films as indications of the way society should solve problems, essentially using the story line on screen or video as a training film? Are his gratifications those of personal esteem, perhaps by identifying with killers and asocial law-and-order types? Or is your brother using the films as mechanisms for escapism and fantasy, understanding full well that they bear no necessary resemblance to healthy social existence? Are his gratifications basically social ones, perhaps simply wanting to be able to talk about the films knowledgeably with friends at school? In such a case, he wouldn't be identifying with the film's characters; he'd be using the film's characters to identify, perhaps in healthy ways, with people in his immediate interpersonal environment. He might even watch violent heroes in order to make fun of them, and therefore fit in with a clique of friends.

Among the most important assumptions of uses and gratifications research are the following (adapted from Palmgreen et al., 1985):

- Audiences are active and goal-directed.
- Audiences want personal needs satisfied and approach media with that goal in mind.
- Media compete with other sources for people's need satisfaction.
- Media content and structure can't by themselves predict how audiences will develop patterns of gratifications.
- Gratifications "can have their origins in media content, exposure in and of itself, and/or the social situation in which exposure takes place." (p. 14)

These assumptions remind us of several important aspects of uses and gratifications theory. For one thing, even though theorists emphasize to different areas of the theory, they generally do not claim that psychological factors almost solely influence media impact or that the media are themselves powerless (Blumler, 1985). Instead, media content (i.e., what the media "says") has to be considered along with media characteristics and structures (i.e., how each medium "packages" and presents its messages) and in the context of audience activity.

Palmgreen et al.'s (1985) general media gratifications model, illustrated in Figure 9-2, shows the various factors that the gratifications theorist must consider as well as the relationships among them. The single-direction arrows, of course, indicate effects and influences; double-direction arrows indicate mutual effects. Although a full description of this model is beyond our purpose here, you should consider three important ideas illustrated in Figure 9-2: (1) "Society" and "Individuals" (shown in boxes 1 and 11) are far from separate concepts; (2) "Effects" (in box 10) are not directly influenced by "Media Content" (box 3) *nor* do effects directly influence media content; and (3) "Gratifications Sought" (box 8) can be affected not only by individuals and their attitudes but also by "Beliefs and Expectations about Media and Alternatives" (box 5).

Thus, one question we might ask in media analysis is: "To what extent does the mediated environment change an audience's notions and evaluations of what to expect in daily life?" This is the central question addressed by cultivation theory.

cultivation theorizing

Cultivation analysis, largely identified with the work of George Gerbner (1970) and his "cultural indicators" research into television's role in society, recognizes

L I N K

Recall our discussion of Schutz's FIRO theory of interpersonal needs in Chapter 6. Do inclusion, affection, and control also apply in mediated situations? Why or why not? Uses and gratifications theorists try to understand human motivation at its most basic levels. How might this important point represent a connection between psychological and media studies?

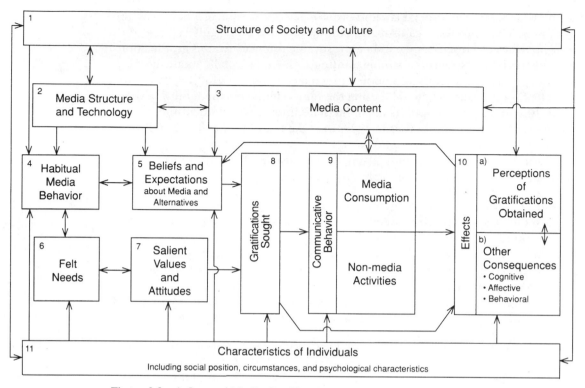

Figure 9-2   A General Media Gratifications Model

Source: "Uses and Gratifications Research: The Past Ten Years," by P. Palmgreen, L. A. Wenner, and K. E. Rosengren. In K. E. Rosengren, L. A. Wenner, and P. Palmgreen (Eds.), *Media Gratifications Research: Current Perspectives* (p. 17). Beverly Hills, CA: Sage Publications. Copyright © 1985. Used with permission.

that media do not necessarily have a direct "magic bullet" effect on audiences; even so, the media can still be powerful agencies of modern life. Cultivation analysis rests on the basic notion that the media don't change people as much as they change the ground rules by which people define reality. That is, the media change our social expectations. The metaphor implies that media content, like a farmer in the field, cultivates, readies, and assists some developments while discouraging others. The farmer doesn't literally make seed crops grow, or even literally keep individual weeds, should they pop up, from draining nutrients away from crops the farmer wants to grow. The farmer simply creates the conditions in which one set of outcomes is much more likely to occur than others. In much the same way, media structure and content "cultivate" modern audiences with particular expectations and definitions of reality.

The questions of cultivation theorizing maintain a dual focus on media and the people who utilize them. According to Signorielli and Morgan (1990), cultivation researchers ask:

1. What are the processes, pressures, and constraints that influence and underlie the production of mass-media content?

2. What are the dominant aggregate patterns of images, messages, facts, values, and lessons expressed in media messages?
3. What is the independent contribution of these messages to audiences' conceptions of social reality? (p. 9)

A researcher engaged in a cultivation analysis of television might compare media content with the viewing habits of heavy viewers and light viewers to see if heavy viewers are more likely to reflect, in their own views of "real life," the patterns of reality presumed and presented on television. For instance, does the fact that televised entertainment programs disproportionately feature violence encourage violent behaviors among viewers? Cultivation research (Gerbner, Gross, Morgan, & Signorielli, 1980) tends to show that instead of this kind of overt effect, the media "cultivate" and viewers develop a view that the world is "mean," "dangerous," and difficult to understand. The prime outcome, then, is that people who are heavy viewers tend to feel defensive, mistrustful, alienated, frustrated, and often uncooperative. Does the television medium cause this? Not exactly, but it is an accomplice.

Gerbner (1990, p. 257) refers to two types of cultivation. *First-order cultivation* refers to the literal beliefs people hold about the world. Some people, for example, may think that because they see more Hyundai ads this year, this suggests that Hyundai must be establishing a foothold in the American automobile market. *Second-order cultivation* has a symbolic dimension, and more far-reaching implications. Gerbner's (1990) explanation of a specific example is extremely relevant for modern society. Second-order cultivation involves:

> the symbolic transformations . . . that exhibit the special power of symbolic life over and above verisimilitude. That is the special characteristic of terms of discourse to shift from specific cases to general classes and to be understood symbolically rather than literally. For example, in the television world, men outnumber women at least three to one. Taken literally, this would suggest that heavy viewers would underestimate the number or proportion of women in the world, which is not the case. Relative underrepresentation in the fairly rigidly structured symbolic world, however, is not only a question of numbers. It translates into differential "quotas" of life chances, ranges of activity, stereotyped portrayals, and levels of occupations. Questions dealing with these symbolic transformations of numerical deviations from statistical norms tap dimensions most relevant to cultivation. (p. 257)

Therefore, the fact that a child viewing television regularly would see fewer women on television, would easily be counterbalanced in the first-order realm by his or her direct experience with approximately equal numbers of men and women in everyday life. But at the symbolic (second-order) level, however, the media cultivate a set of cultural expectations about the diminished importance, prominence, and centrality of women's contributions. This is disturbing because the symbolic level, almost by definition, is harder to recognize, analyze, and change. The child may internalize these shadow distinctions that have been cultivated, and build behavioral patterns that reflect them into her or his life.

L I N K

Cultivation analysis and cultural studies are relevant to multicultural and intercultural communication, discussed in Chapter 7. For example, cultivation research might provide evidence that feminist theorists could apply within their framework. Critical theorists often focus on the social centrality of media in critiquing culture.

Some theorists and philosophers of communication focus on the power relations that have become institutionalized by such distinctions among social groups. They suggest that their mission is primarily a "critical" one: to critique the power relationships within the media system.

cultural studies, critical theory, and critical theorizing

A currently influential strain of work in media theory can be traced to the Centre for Contemporary Cultural Studies, located at the University of Birmingham in England (Grossberg, 1984; S. Hall, 1989; Hoggart, 1972; Williams, 1981). Although known generally as the *cultural studies* approach, it is less a unified method for analyzing social processes than it is a broadly defined interdisciplinary stance adopted by some theorists commenting on the modern media.

Cultural studies approaches to media theorizing usually are characterized by the following:

1. They tend to deny that "communication" or "mass communication" should be considered as discrete fields or disciplines of study that can be analyzed apart from other aspects of culture. Studying culture as a total system of life is necessary for these scholars. Cultural studies proponents, therefore, tend to believe that too much of twentieth-century communication theorizing and research uses a somewhat restrictive "transmissional" definition of communication (Carey, 1989).

2. Despite a broad cultural conception of communication that could potentially analyze nonverbal messages and artifacts, cultural studies theorists recently have stressed the historical role of language in forming both culture and its human institutions (Williams, 1981).

3. Cultural studies approaches tend to take value positions into account in theoretical explanations of social power. This is another way of saying that they often take the form of *critical theory*. This doesn't mean that they are negative, though critical theorists are often oppositional in their approaches and may take certain positions to point out or counter established institutional meanings and methods.

4. Many cultural studies theorists, especially those who consider themselves critical theorists, tend to be Marxist in political orientation and, therefore, focus on power, class, and economic distinctions in social life. Critical theorists are likely to analyze society in such terms as *ideology* (a set of widely held beliefs whose validity is not questioned) and *hegemony* (the usually institutionalized and in-place distribution of power that makes one social group dominant over another or others, often with the implied acquiescence of the dominated). For example, if it's impossible almost by definition for poor or middle-class people to own newspapers and television stations, then doesn't this fact influence the rhetoric—news, advertising, programming—that characterizes those institutions? Doesn't the extent to which the language and concerns of the "community" get rep-

resented, then, become more a matter of guesswork or condescension than anyone's direct responsibility, duty, or influence?

5. Cultural studies theorists tend to focus on creative explanation in social science, rather than on precise prediction. Cultural studies thus seems quite different than many other theoretical perspectives when it's first encountered. These works read more like communication commentary or social criticism than what some people would identify as "theorizing." As Carey (1989) writes, "cultural studies does not attempt to predict human behavior; rather, it attempts to diagnose human meanings. It is, more positively, an attempt to bypass the rather abstracted empiricism of behavioral studies and the ethereal apparatus of formal theories and to descend deeper into the empirical world" (p. 56).

L I N K

Cultural studies communication theorists blend theorizing with social criticism in order to reveal the often-hidden distinctions in our power relations. Theorists who specialize in probing race, class, and gender distinctions thus often build on the contributions of critical theorists operating within the cultural studies tradition. See Chapter 7 for a discussion of theory as cultural critique.

who's controlling (and who's dependent on) whom? a recap with dependency theory

We need to return briefly to our central question in this section: To what extent might the mass media control people's behaviors and everyday experience? No survey textbook can give enough detail about the various theories to allow you to answer the question fully. Although it isn't exactly a case of "you pay your money and take your choice," much of the answer depends on the credence you invest in the various types of research, in various models of human motivation, and in what you believe is essential to human nature. Our job is not to argue for or against particular theories, but to introduce them realistically to you and summarize the current state of theorizing (see Box 9-2).

BOX 9-2

A BRIEF OVERVIEW OF
TWENTIETH-CENTURY VIEWS
ON MEDIA POWER

- *Magic bullet theories* focus on the power of sources or messages to influence individuals directly.
- *Two-step and multi-step flow theories* focus on the influence of everyday opinion leaders in creating media effects within audiences.
- *Overtly audience-based and culture-based theories* focus on how audience needs and cultural values contribute to the nature of media effects. Examples include *uses and gratifications theory, cultivation analysis, cultural studies, critical theory,* and *dependency theory.*
- *Reintegration of the interpersonal in audience theories* focuses on how media audiences make mass media content and interpersonal communication interdependent. Examples include *para-social interaction, play theory, spiral of silence theory,* and the *theory of mediated place.*

Early on, the magic bullet assumptions suggested that the mass communication media had basically direct and powerful effects on individuals. Because society was assumed to be a weak force on individual behavior, persons were considered as relatively isolated individuals with few resources for combatting propaganda and advertising campaigns. However, people aren't this vulnerable, argued multi-step flow theorists. Instead, they argued that media effects were filtered through a social network of influential opinion leaders. Interpersonal communication was itself a mediating influence, theorists began to believe, and therefore it might not be as necessary to worry about the manipulative power of radio, television, and publishing conglomerates.

More recently, uses and gratifications theorists have suggested that the media have only those controls over an audience that the audience itself enables through trying to meet its own psychological and social needs. That is, persons in the audience seek out and use media messages to meet their own goals in life. Some uses and gratifications advocates say this is a transactional process of audiences and media sources simultaneously shaping messages (Wenner, 1985), but taken to its logical conclusion, most gratifications research appears to place responsibility for media content and structure on the audience. The media, in this view, are responsive to various publics. Media specialists ascertain who we audience members are, what we want, how we process information in order to seek gratifications for ourselves, and they usually try to give us what we want or what we seem to want. The media may be no more dangerous than is the public itself, concludes the uses and gratifications theorist. But, on reflection, that may still be pretty dangerous.

Cultivation theorists answer the question about audience control in a somewhat more subtle way: The media become dangerous because they are capable of shaping the public's expectations about what constitutes reality. We don't have as much to worry about in terms of direct persuasion, because the media can't manipulate us to vote for one candidate when we favor another. But they can and do cultivate preferences and stereotypes that influence what choices we consider to be reasonable. Because many people believe that the mass media represent the way the world really is (rather than a characterization or caricature of it), this subtle influence is powerful in part *because* of its subtlety.

Cultural studies and critical theorists argue that analysts don't need to look that far beneath the surface. Simply understanding what comprises a culture can tell us that the message systems of the media are an integral component of culture. Recognizing that power readily becomes institutionalized in this kind of media environment, critical theorists contend that the division of societies into dominant and subordinate groups should come as no surprise. The media, after all, have become a symbol of power in modern society and, therefore, represent the institutionalization of information control. In a mass society, only the mass media can disseminate information, preferences, opportunities, and the viability of political choices. Only the mass media can be culture's lens through which we view who holds power: men, whites, heterosexuals, the wealthy, and the healthy, according to critical theorists.

Throughout much of the history of media theory, then, theorists have attempted to identify the kinds of influence that the media exert on audiences and vice versa. The "vice versa" is an important reminder. One attempt to synthesize the various theories and hypotheses has resulted in a **dependency theory** of the media (DeFleur & Ball-Rokeach, 1982). It stresses the interdependent relationships among the media, audiences, and society's structures. As we begin to understand more about how these factors may depend on each other, we'll be able to develop a clearer picture of mass communication systems.

People depend on the media for cognitive, affective, and behavioral reasons. *Cognitive dependencies*—those related to human thought processes—include *ambiguity resolution* ("What will happen to the stock market next week?"), *attitude formation* about objects of concern (toothpaste, the Chicago Cubs, Cher), *agenda-setting* ("Will personality and negative campaigning become a prominent issue in the next mayoral race?"), *enlargement* (a PBS series on the Civil War enlarged the historical belief systems of millions of Americans), and *values articulation* (some television series, such as *Chicago Hope* and *Law and Order*, deliberately create moral dilemmas that challenge viewers to formulate their own positions). *Affective dependencies*—those related to emotion—include *desensitization* ("I used to be uncomfortable watching people get killed in movies, but now it just seems natural"), *fear and anxiety* ("Let's not go out tonight—there've been too many muggings downtown"), and *morale/alienation factors* ("Our neighborhood got profiled on Channel 5 again"). Finally, *behavioral dependencies* include *activation* ("Let's write a letter to the editor about the school bond vote") and *deactivation* ("We wrote a letter to the editor last year and what good did that do? Don't waste your time") (DeFleur & Ball-Rokeach, 1982).

Obviously, much of mass communication theory depends on an understanding of how people process information both intrapersonally and interpersonally. In the final section of this chapter, we'll describe a number of additional theories that attempt to account for the interdependence of interpersonal and mass communication.

ARE MASS COMMUNICATION AND INTERPERSONAL COMMUNICATION DIFFERENT PROCESSES?

Remember that the two-step flow and multi-step flow of information concepts are based on systems of interpersonal influence. When describing them, we contended that it is impossible to understand media effects without taking personal relationships into account. Indeed, *Personal Influence* is the title of Katz and Lazarsfeld's (1955) groundbreaking book in media theory. But what other theories and concepts can bring this interpersonal dimension more into focus? Although many could be discussed, we'll highlight para-social interaction, play theory, spiral of silence theory, and the theory of mediated place. These contributions help us understand the so-called "new media" of electronic technology—including interactive video systems, computer-mediated communication, teleconferencing, and others (see Brand, 1988; Chesebro & Bonsall, 1989; Hawkins, Wiemann, & Pingree, 1988; Kaplan, 1990; Rice & Williams, 1984; Walther, 1996).

Theorist Michael Real (1989) describes what he calls the *super media* (1989). He doesn't intend to evoke trivial comic book images, but instead wants to suggest

L I N K

Think about dependency theory in the context of the transactional theory of communication discussed in Chapter 2. A transactional approach assumes a relationship in which the presence of each element shapes, and is shaped by, the basic definition of other elements. For example, by definition you can't analyze teaching quality without analyzing someone's learning, because teaching and learning exist in a transactional relationship with each other within schools. There's no such thing as a teacher apart from the learning of students. Do you believe this same process applies to media sources and their audiences? If not, why not? If so: What, if any, would be the exceptions?

the root sense of "super," the sense of something covering or including other things. To Real (1989), the electronic media in modern society have become an encompassing and overriding environment for all communication, interpersonal and mass. McLuhan (1964) and Ong (1982), of course, would not argue with Real's conclusion.

para-social interaction

Television executives understand that dropping a major character from a popular television series is a risky decision, one that could spark a firestorm of viewer protest. Viewers might react with anguish just as though they've lost a relative or friend. Indeed, they have.

Horton and Wohl (1956) describe how media audiences project feelings of friendship and affiliation onto media personalities. In effect, audiences listening to radio or watching television form psychic relationships, engaging in **para-social interaction**, with soap opera actors or news anchorpersons. These relations are strikingly similar in emotional tone and psychological consequences to face-to-face relationships with "real" people. Of course, the media figures, even if fictitious, *become* real to audiences as soon as they are considered to be real. As sociologists have long suggested, in some situations it doesn't matter if what someone believes to be real actually matches with some objective "reality"; if it's acted on as if it were real, it becomes real in its consequences. It isn't pathological and rare, but normal and common, to form such para-social relations, even if it's a one-way process.

Of course, it's not normal or healthy to become obsessed with media figures, losing track of one's own life. An extreme case of para-social interaction took place in the early 1980s, when a young man became obsessed with actress Jody Foster and sought to gain her attention by attempting a presidential assassination. Similarly, the film *The King of Comedy* explores a para-social relationship that is unhealthy for a psychologically unstable man.

play theory

William Stephenson (1967) uses his **play theory** to explain how people react subjectively to the media. Even in reading the news in a newspaper or magazine, Stephenson contends, a citizen is largely motivated by a desire to engage in what he calls *subjective play,* fantasy, and personal myth-making (p. 3). Later in his book, Stephenson contrasts subjective play that leads to *communication-pleasure,* with the *communication-work* assumptions of those who advocate persuasion and social control theories of media.

"Play," Stephenson (1967) writes, is what people do when feeling "self-sufficient" and relatively free. "Work is not disinterested, is not an interlude in the day for most people. It produces goods, services, or ideas . . . by application of effort for a purpose" (p. 193). Stephenson considers it obvious that few people in a mass audience use media for "communication-work." Instead, they try to use mass media messages (as Horton & Wohl [1956], coming from a psychiatric perspective, would agree) for "sociability and self-existence" purposes (Stephenson, 1967, p. 194). Although some communication trends in the 1990s have made the home more of a viable workplace with the introduction of such "new media" options as e-mail, voice mail, fax capabilities, and access to the Internet, Stephenson's supposition probably holds true even today.

The most basic media effects come from media structures and messages that encourage *convergent selectivity*. "Selectivity" implies that, psychologically speaking, individuals can roam freely and select, frame, and toy with messages, and "convergent" implies that such choices will converge around their distinct or idiosyncratic emotional needs. According to Stephenson (1967), people don't play to attain conscious rewards but to entertain themselves, enhance their self-concept, and exercise their freedom of inner choice. Thus, what sometimes can seem to be the most superficial aspects of mass communication are potentially the most important:

> Reaching the truth is a matter for science, technology, reason, and *work*. Charisma, imagery, and fiction are characteristic of convergencies.

> But this is not to be despised. On the contrary, reality is so complex that its symbolical representation is essential to give it meanings that ordinary people can appreciate. Politics is conversation about freedom, liberty, fundamental rights, and the like—issues which need bear little relation to ongoing real conditions or legislative actions. But all these can be good fun, that is, good communication-pleasure. (Stephenson, 1967, p. 195)

Small wonder, then, that normal viewers might identify psychologically through para-social interaction with media figures and feel a real sense of personal loss, perhaps, when Connie Chung gets nudged from a job, George Bush loses an election, or *Cheers* stops producing new shows.

spiral of silence theory

German researcher Elisabeth Noelle-Neumann (1984) has explored what happens when people are asked to give their opinions on public issues. Not surprisingly, she discovered that people do not express their opinions as if they issue directly from some inner true self. Instead, as we've seen, people psychologically evaluate and identify with others' positions, and then consider the social and interpersonal consequences of voicing their own opinions publicly. Persons who believe themselves in a majority are more likely to feel bolstered by numbers, are more likely both to speak up in the first place, and are more likely to speak assertively about the beliefs and values behind the opinions.

Noelle-Neumann's work asks us to consider what happens when the media polls and news accounts publicize public opinion so effectively that they make it clear (perhaps clearer than it "really" is) which side of a controversial issue is in the majority and which is in the minority. Her **spiral of silence theory** describes the phenomenon that develops: People who perceive themselves in a minority inhibit their communication, and those who perceive themselves in the majority are more motivated to speak. Thus, those in the minority, who speak less, will be relatively underrepresented in the media and audiences will tend to underestimate their impact or influence—leading to a downward spiral of less and less assertiveness from such groups. Conversely, once a group believes its side is ascending, it becomes bolder, more likely both to communicate openly and to over-estimate its own influence.

An interpersonal tendency to save face in effect interacts with a media tendency to stifle dialogue. The gap between the "haves" and the "have-nots" potentially widens as the latter group wonders, "What's the use of speaking out? We've already lost." The implications of Noelle-Neumann's theory are obvious for presidential election polling and large-scale social issues such as public sentiment for or against a war. Less obviously, the theory also applies to a group in a small town that might wish to take a stand on library censorship, but believes it is in a tiny minority. The local paper and radio station may have editorialized emphatically for the banning of Mark Twain. But if the group speaks out in spite of its estimation of failure, breaking the spiral of silence, the members might discover they have more allies than they thought, allies who also had been silenced. Noelle-Neumann justifiably questions the compatibility of mass communication systems with some aspects of democratic theory.

Some recent commentators, while acknowledging the impact of her work, have questioned why Noelle-Neumann, a journalist during the Nazi regime in Germany, largely neglects perhaps the most obvious example of the spiral of silence—the silence of German mass assent to Hitler's policies (see, e.g., Simpson, 1996).

the theory of mediated place

The research on television has been severely limited to the extent that it views electronic media merely as new links among pre-existing environments. That is, such research ignores the possibility that, once widely used, electronic media may create new social environments that reshape behavior in ways that go beyond the specific products delivered. (Meyrowitz, 1985, p. 15)

One of the most exciting and innovative recent media analyses is Joshua Meyrowitz's *No Sense of Place: The Impact of Electronic Media on Social Behavior* (1985). In what we might call a **theory of mediated place**, Meyrowitz blends and extends the work of McLuhan (1964) and Goffman (1959) to show how a new *media matrix* (the whole system of individual media acting interdependently) has changed our expectations for what constitutes a "place" or a "social situation."

People used to define places in physical terms. You and I were in the same "place" if we could talk with each other directly and with maximum sensory involvement. We weren't in the same "place" if one or both of us moved our location in physical space. But what of media that create new extended informational settings that are also extended "places?" To use Meyrowitz's analogy, it is as if modern technology has torn down some walls that we once used as demarcation of separate places—this is "family life," that is "work life," there is "politics," here is "personal decision making," and so forth. In some other instances, the media have erected new walls. Since the media matrix extends access to information and extends it simultaneously, the lines are now blurred between the public and private spheres of life.

Consider, for example, the recent social preoccupations with the private lives of politicians, with the undermining of authority, with the blurring of distinctions between parental and children's roles in families, with openness in discussing sex and personal problems publicly, and with people's increased willingness to discuss empowerment in gender, social class, and ethnicity issues. All such changes have become possible, at least in part, because media, to Meyrowitz (1985), have "combined previously distinct social settings, moving the dividing line between private and public behavior toward the private, and weakened the relationship between social situations and physical places. The logic underlying situational patterns of behavior in a print-oriented society, therefore, has been radically subverted. Many Americans may no longer seem to 'know their place' because the traditionally interlocking components of 'place' have been split apart by electronic media. Wherever one is now—at home, at work, or in a car—one may be in touch and tuned in" (p. 308). Television makes it harder for an aristocracy or a repressive regime to maintain itself in power. When people no longer "know their place" in physical terms, they also no longer "know their place" in terms of social position. The electronic media matrix makes information about each social reward and each social danger much more equally available across the spectrum of social differences. The matrix also makes it possible for the public to worry in new ways about whether to elect a president who has cheated on his or her spouse or to approve a judge who's smoked marijuana. Who would have known enough to care, before the new technology? Their place, "over there," has become our place, "over here."

Meyrowitz's theory is a suitable place to wrap up our discussion of mass communication theorizing. He draws on almost all the themes we've surveyed. He assumes that the media become messages in their own right, and that these messages affect human perception. He believes that social class and power relations in society are traceable to a mediated environment, as well as to the individual actions of political and social figures. He understands why interpersonal behaviors and mass media phenomena must be studied as different aspects of the same process. Perhaps most important, he shows how the whole fabric of a society is influenced by communication. Communication is not just one component of a society, but the basis of constituting a society in the first place.

LINK

How does Meyrowitz's view of nonphysical place change your understanding of communication ecology, discussed in Chapter 3? For example, in terms of his *media matrix*, what would constitute "crowding"?

T E S T I N G   T H E   C O N C E P T S

"I still don't know if the media primarily influence me and the rest of their mass audience, or if I primarily influence the media. Which is it?"

This doesn't seem to be an *either-or* issue. The answers, we're finding, are more complicated. You can assume with some assurance that the media do not have the power to manipulate people directly, as was feared in the early decades of the twentieth century. Because people both select and subsequently talk about media content in their own ways (in order to achieve their own "gratifications"), audiences are powerful influences on the media. Perhaps the most powerful influence the media have on your life is in the subtle adjustments they make in your perception. But if you accept the hypotheses of Ong, McLuhan, and Meyrowitz, for example, it's not only what you perceive that should be considered, but also the bases on which you claim to perceive at all.

"Isn't McLuhan's theory just a cultural fad from the '60s?"

Contemporary communication theorists are in something of a dilemma when considering McLuhan's work. On the one hand, some of it seems dispensable as an artifact of an earlier time. Although he was no "flower child," his kind of intellectual adventure seems more congenial to that era, and his kind of hyperbole seemed more acceptable in the late '60s. McLuhan's wilder claims were not always taken seriously, and "McLuhanisms" were controversial even then. But on the other hand, he replied that his mission was as an "opener" or intellectual stimulant—that his statements and books were "probes" designed to liberate other people's thought. He wasn't as concerned with being right as he was concerned with being stimulating. We usually get our most creative innovations not from people who are concerned with being right or playing it safe, but from people like McLuhan who are willing to be wrong in creative and expansive ways. Even though many of McLuhan's ideas are not widely revered today, his probes led us to new and important territories of understanding. This is a crucial role of any theory, one that jostles other researchers' interest in previously unexplored ideas. Interestingly, current theorists of digital culture have rediscovered the relevance of McLuhan's work: ". . . in recent years, the explosion of new media—particularly the Web—has caused new anxieties. Or to put a more McLuhanesque spin on it, the advent of new digital media has brought the conditions of the old technologies into sharper relief, and made us suddenly conscious of our media environment. In the confusion of the digital revolution, McLuhan is relevant again" (Wolf, 1996, p. 124). (See also Press, 1995.)

YOU, THE RESEARCHER

1. Chart your media usage for a week. Every four or five hours, update an informal log to show the minutes you spend:

   - Reading: books_____   newspapers and magazines_____
   - Watching: films_____   rented videos_____   TV networks and cable systems_____   video games_____
   - Listening: to radio_____   to audio systems_____
   - Talking interpersonally about: media programs, films, and characters_____   media accounts of political and social issues_____
   - Communicating with others, using: telephone_____   fax_____   mail service_____
   - Working individually with computers: on individual creative tasks_____   on "bulletin board systems," "chat rooms," or "e-mail"_____   using online databases or searching the Internet_____

   Compare the media distribution and investment of your time with that of other students. Are some of your different habits rooted in family traditions? In job responsibilities? In personal preferences? What do the class logs suggest about the pervasiveness of media influences in modern society?

2. Media theorist Arthur Asa Berger (1982) warns that "the danger for the Marxist media analysts is that they know the answers before they ask the questions" (p. 64). This is another way of suggesting that at least some critical theory research has an ideological agenda of its own, and a point of view it is ready to project and defend. In your college library, locate the Spring 1993 issue of the *Western Journal of Communication* that examines this issue of ideology from a variety of angles. Read the articles by Condit (1993), Wood and Cox (1993), and several other contributors. Then, based on your reading, consider whether you think Berger's criticism is fair or unfair. How might the researcher in this tradition best maintain both an open mind and an ideological commitment simultaneously? Or, conversely, why might this task be impossible, unrealistic, or unnecessary? Explain your reasoning.

3. Confront the para-social interaction phenomenon by introspection. Among television personalities, such as interview journalists like Cokie Roberts, sitcom characters like Frasier, and talk show hosts like Oprah Winfrey, which ones seem to be your "friends?" Your "enemies?" Confidants or allies? A secondary question: What personal needs do you fulfill by such psychological identification with these people you don't know and probably will never meet? What do your answers tell you about the relationship between para-social interaction and uses and gratifications theories of the media? Would a large-scale research study of such personal introspections be helpful in deepening our theoretical understanding of everyday media use? Why or why not?

4. Use Westley and MacLean's model of gatekeeping, shown in Figure 9-1, to illustrate the process of an evening newscast. For each component of the model, identify the corresponding person(s), group(s), or message(s) in the newscast.

5. Explore how advertisers promote products in the new medium of cyberspace. On the Internet, find some advertisements via a search engine or on nationally based homepages. (What, for you, counts as an advertisement, and why?) Look at how the products are advertised—their association with their sites, their graphic design, and the different types of appeal they seem to make. Also consider these questions: To whom do the advertisers appeal? Why are the ads placed in certain locations? How might this new advertising on the Internet affect our perception of the media in general? McLuhan (1964) argues that certain types of advertising are best suited to the print and electronic media: "The continuous pressure is to create ads more and more in the image of audience motives and desires," "the need is to make the ad include the audience experience," and "the steady trend in advertising is to manifest the product as an integral part of large social purposes and processes" (p. 201). Do you think his conclusions hold true for online advertising? Explain your reasoning.

Bill Bachman/Photo Researchers

theories of communication ethics

"when *is the* effective choice the ethical choice?"

Entire new professions are now being trained to use . . . methods for probing or concealing secrets. Government surveillance and information-gathering ha[ve] reached unprecedented dimensions throughout the world; so have infiltration by social scientists for scholarly or commercial purposes, undercover journalism in search of exposés, investigation by private agents and underworld sources, and industrial surveillance and espionage. These practices invite imitation and retaliation, and thus in turn generate a need for still more effective and more secret prying.

The new techniques and the changes they make possible join with the long-standing personal and professional conflicts over secrecy to raise practical moral problems for us all. Yet these problems are often postponed or explained away or dismissed altogether. . . .

SISSELA BOK, *SECRETS* (1983, P. XVII)

I f the discipline of communication can be said to have a personality, it is definitely a complex one. At times, the reputation of a department of communication on a campus is of a group of professionals primarily interested in the applied aspects of human behavior—teaching and learning about how persons can put into practice "better" or "more competent" or "more effective" strategies for communicating. This takes many forms: Classes in public speaking, reporting, interviewing, listening, small group communication, broadcast management, public relations, and others all display this ongoing interest in "what works" in human communication behavior. The pragmatic personality of the communication discipline has been one of our strongest and most-needed contributions to academic life, because it counterbalances the "ivory tower" or "egghead" image with which some social critics dismiss professors and their classes.

THE "WHETHER" QUESTION

At other times, however, the field of communication studies is challenged to show another side of its personality. Scholars recognize that any discipline of study must be based on more than an understanding of everyday practical effectiveness. People who are genuinely interested in learning about communication, then, are not just interested in implementing strategies to accomplish goals in particular instances. They are also concerned with why those strategies work. As we discussed in Chapter 1, a body of knowledge about any area of study has to be buttressed by a body of theory that can explain why and how specific learnings can be generalized and transferred to new situations. This foundation for practical application goes beyond that "what works" question to another issue: "Why does it work?" We've written *Questions of Communication* for students who have, or who are on the road to having, this type of deep curiosity about communication. An education without either practical application or theory would be fragmented at best.

However, yet another facet of the discipline's personality remains to be considered. In some ways, it is simply an additional area of theorizing. But in another sense, it is a separate question, substantially different from the "What works?" and "Why does it work?" questions. A comprehensive communicator should also be able to ask what we call the *"whether"* question. When we know something about what works and why it works, people still need to ask *whether* to behave in the indicated ways: Is it right? Is it fair? Is it restrictive or deceptive to others? As Bok points out in the chapter-opening quotation, such questions, especially when they are considered in the context of new techniques for invading privacy and violating freedoms, define the domain of ethics. In their examination of ethical problems in the mass media, Christians, Rotzoll, & Fackler (1991) define *ethics* "as the liberal arts discipline that appraises voluntary human conduct insofar as it can be judged right or wrong in reference to determinative principles" (p. xvii). Their emphasis on "voluntary human conduct" is pivotal. Arnett (1991), in reviewing communication scholarship in ethics, points out that the concepts of *choice* and *choice making* seem to be the distinguishing features of a communicational approach to ethics.

This chapter begins with a survey of the general theoretical and philosophical foundations on which ethical communication decisions may be built. It then discusses in more detail some specific ethical systems that are especially relevant to communication in our increasingly complex society, one in which we are simultaneously expected to be able to affect others' behavior and maintain our own psychological health.

In a massive study of American character directed by Bellah, Madsen, Sullivan, Swidler, and Tipton (1986), the researchers found that many U.S. citizens are primarily willing to discuss communication only in terms of its "managerial" dimension (how can someone use communication techniques to gain the cooperation or compliance of others?) or its "therapeutic" dimension (how can someone enhance her or his "self"?). Both dimensions potentially could ignore the ethical dilemmas of what to do as a communicator when self-interests and community interests are—or ought to be—balanced. Kenneth E. Andersen (1991), working from an ethical perspective, has surveyed the literature of communication theorists, finding that "individual theorists . . . rarely address ethical issues directly in terms of the role and function of communication in a society and for individuals" (p. 6). Even for a clearly ethics-related concept such as a speaker's credibility, he notes that "the emphasis is more typically on the impact of the credibility of the source in terms of outcomes, rather than the impact or ethical quality of a particular choice or practice," and that "pragmatic questions of effect, rather than ethical quality, are the usual concern" (p. 6).

Thus, researching the pragmatics of communication effects does not necessarily lead to an awareness of the ethical implications of such communication.

Though it would be encouraging to think that behavior and ethics go hand-in-hand, *what happens* on the one hand and *whether it should happen* on the other are usually divorced issues in communication studies. A number of ethicists, however, have attempted to develop coherent theories for analyzing ethical concerns in tandem with pragmatic effects.

As teachers and authors, we do not believe the study of communication is an amoral or ethically neutral activity. But neither are we ready to assume only one moral and ethical stance and teach it as the necessarily correct one. Instead, we intend in this chapter to set the table for you, introducing some of the enduring traditions of ethical decision making that have engaged communication scholars. We describe their similarities and differences and (if we're successful) confront you with some difficult personal choices. If you feel uncomfortable or even squirm a bit while reading this chapter, then we've done our job as authors. You may be forced to rethink some recent choices. As ethicist Michael Josephson once said in an interview, "I want to make you uncomfortable, because growth will only come out of a little level of discomfort" (quoted in Moyers, 1989, p. 17). Do you feel uncomfortable, for example, knowing a recent study found that 61 percent of high school students and 32 percent of college students admitted cheating on an exam within the past year, that more than 33 percent of students said they would lie, if they had to, to get a job, and that 21 percent of college students reported they would falsify an organizational report in order to keep a job ("Ethics of Young," 1992)? At times, ethical discussion is difficult because we are uncertain about what to do. Ironically, discussion is sometimes difficult because we feel certain that our own positions are justified, correct, or necessary under the circumstances, and that no alternatives are reasonable.

Few thoughtful people who have read widely in ethics give themselves the luxury of certainty, as though they could be absolutely convinced that one system is invariably correct while all others are misguided. An argument can be made for each system. In any case, ethical theory is fascinating because it is the area of communication studies that helps us to integrate the "what works," the "why it works," and the "whether it should happen" questions.

THEORETICAL AND PHILOSOPHICAL FOUNDATIONS FOR ETHICAL COMMUNICATION DECISIONS

In the film *Do the Right Thing*, writer, director, and actor Spike Lee explores the inner turmoil of an urban neighborhood and the people who live there. Against the backdrop of community and racial violence, Lee projects a story of simmering tensions—tensions that eventually boil over. Whites and blacks, angry for different reasons, are both confronted with the question implied by the film's title: What is "the right thing" to do? How should we talk to each other? How tolerant and accepting should we be in the face of oppression? Although sensitivity, acceptance, and openness are nice, when might intransigence, standing one's ground, or even attack also be justifiable as communication behaviors? Lee is smart enough not to deliver final answers to us. He is content to frame the questions eloquently.

In fact, the ambiguity of Lee's title in some ways mirrors our lives. We often talk about the "right" (or "wrong") things to do as though we are able to match our decisions to an absolute standard or to have our choices judged by an impartial moral tribunal. Although religious and spiritual dogma might serve this function for some people, the supposedly clear-cut lines of right and wrong that are proclaimed by adherents often blur. Increasingly, even intradenominational church conventions are places of questioning, argument, and contention.

Are there foundations or guidelines for coming closer to the "right thing" in human communication? While a number of guidelines have been offered, they are not literally theories of communication ethics. However, they do apply equally well to interpersonal communication, social policy, politics, and other realms of human interaction.

deontological approaches

You are enrolled in a course taught by a professor whom you admire and like personally. The professor has advised, encouraged, and guided you through the course as well as through the maze of university requirements. But you've just accidentally discovered that a classmate has purchased an already-prepared term paper from a "research company" near your university, which the student intends to turn in as the final assignment for the course. You know that other students also engage in this sort of activity. You also know that your classmate's grade is unlikely to influence your own grade. What should you do?

Deontological ethics, also called *deontology*, is that branch of ethical study that asserts that ethical choices arise from personal allegiance to principles that are relatively unchanging and ongoing. In the preceding scenario, then, to the extent that you're guided by an appropriate principle, your decision will be ethically based, whatever you ultimately decide. A deontological approach to your dilemma might mean that you'd rely on the principle of truth-telling, for example. Further, you'd probably assume (as an informal deontologist) that all students should be subject to the same rules and should have equal chances to obtain high grades based on their intelligence and effort, not on their checking accounts or on their willingness to cheat. Your allegiance to this principle might lead you to make the ethical decision to report the student's intentions to the professor. (Of course, your allegiance might be to an entirely different principle, like "Never turn in your peers," and you'd still be reasoning deontologically.)

Many social groups organize themselves around the deontological concept that right and wrong are based on a higher moral authority. Right and wrong, when determined prior to behavioral dilemmas, can be used as moral benchmarks for personal decision making. Society itself, deontologists believe, is founded on the rational assumption that humans will recognize the need to submit to principle. Only then will social communication be both fair and reasonably coherent. This is the basis, for example, of the service academies' reliance on an "honor code" in which a cadet violator must be reported by innocent observers, or else the witnesses have also violated the code.

Probably the most famous of the deontological theorists is the eighteenth-century German philosopher Immanuel Kant, whose principle of the *categorical imperative* has guided countless decision makers. Kantian theory suggests that a fundamental decision made about one member of a group ought to be "universalizable"—that is, to apply equally to all members. Any deviations from this application of principle would need to be established as exceptions. Further, he extended his imperative to claim that people should not be treated merely as means to an end, nor should people decide moral questions on the bases of convenience or self-interest. Instead, Kantians hold that moral laws are often internalized in the conscience of humans, providing access to ethical principles.

teleological approaches

Teleological ethics, or *teleology,* is the philosophical study of how goals and outcomes can shape human behavior. Therefore, according to Flew (1984), ". . . characteristically, certain phenomena seem to be best explained not by means of prior causes, but by *ends* or aims, intentions or purposes. Teleological explanation seems typical of living or organic things—plants, animals, people. Thus an animal's behaviour is sometimes best described in terms of its goal (food seeking, for example); a chess player's activity can be understood in terms of his purpose—to win" (p. 350). An analyst taking a teleological position believes that people are proactive, not just reactive, in accomplishing their goals. That is, people are aware not only of what influences them at any given point in time, but also are aware of wanting their acts to influence a changeable future.

Obviously, teleological ethics is a future-oriented explanation, and therefore it is often called a *consequentialist ethic.* Consequences, rather than motivations, principles, or causes, are paramount. How might teleological ethics help you make the decision about whether to report the student in our earlier example? In a consequentialist approach, you would probably assess what would likely happen as a result of your action (reporting the student, staying silent, or finding another option). Then you would compare that consequence to its alternatives to determine what good would come from each. No principle can tell you this reliably; you must become immersed in the dynamics of each social situation.

The most notable teleological position, *utilitarianism,* is associated with the work of nineteenth-century British philosopher John Stuart Mill. In this view, the most ethical human actions are those that produce "good" consequences for the greatest number of people. You can see how Mill's approach and Kant's approach—both reasonable in their own ways—might easily produce contradictory advice about how to address your term paper predicament, however. As a duty-directed deontologist, you could suggest that the principle of truth should be maintained as a first ethical criterion, and you would probably tell the truth about the other student's cheating. However, as a utilitarian, you wouldn't necessarily be convinced that telling the truth is the most ethical action. Who would ultimately be helped by the informing? Who would be hurt? It's possible for you to reason teleologically that it is ethical to report the cheater so that everyone else's grade in the class would remain relatively higher (a fair or good consequence for a greater number of people). Or you might reason that reporting the cheater would result in a severe penalty for that student, but no one else would really gain much from it. In this last interpretation, failing to report the student's cheating would be seen either as ethically sound behavior or, at worst, as not unethical.

Presumably, *Washington Post* reporters Bob Woodward and Carl Bernstein acted from a teleological ethic when they used deceptive interviewing practices to break the Watergate story about political espionage in the early 1970s. Some informants were told that their statements were not the primary investigative breakthroughs, but were instead secondary corroborations of accounts the reporters had already received. Under this false understanding, the sources talked more freely. In fact, however, their stories formed the informational structure of the entire narrative—the basic argument that persuaded other interviewees to talk. The magnitude of the Watergate story and the degree to which the facts were submerged, combined with the assumption that "the greatest good for the greatest number of people" would be served by publicizing the wrongdoing, led Woodward and Bernstein to a consequentialist criterion of ethical communication.

egalitarian approaches

Combining some aspects of both duty-based ethics and utilitarian ethics, **egalitarian ethics**, or *egalitarianism,* attempts to evaluate communication by the criterion of equality. The central question usually becomes: Have the conditions produced by the communication enhanced or hindered equal treatment for the persons affected by it?

Egalitarian ethicists sometimes discuss their position in contrast to a kind of ethics occasionally treated as a separate category—*egoistic ethics*. An egoistic ethic basically asks if the outcome is good (or positive, or helpful, or gratifying) for the person doing the evaluating, quite apart from human issues of altruism (Singer, 1986). To return to our example, if you ponder whether to report your classmate's cheating on the basis of egoistic ethics, you would primarily wonder if doing so would improve your own status in the class; if so, then the message will be treated as a reasonable and ethical thing to do. Ironically, the cheating student evidently reasoned egoistically also.

Since humans don't live or even think in isolation, however, egalitarians wonder if it is ethical to encourage people to act as if they each were isolated from society or from the social consequences of actions. Each of us is constantly affected by the others who we constantly affect, even if that connection is only dimly seen in a given context. Instead of the unquestioning acceptance of external duty advocated by deontologists, or the social calculation urged by the consequentialist ethic, or the selfishness of the egoistic ethic, egalitarians theorize that human affairs are better served by an ethic that prevents the weaker or less protected members of society from being taken advantage of by the stronger members. Only in this way, egalitarian theorists argue, can all of us have equal access to the communication information, channels, and interpretations that keep a society viable.

The most famous proponent of this position is contemporary philosopher John Rawls. In *A Theory of Justice* (1971), Rawls develops a *veil of ignorance* criterion, with which communicators can evaluate their social acts. When considering how to act or speak toward others, Rawls's theory of justice requires individuals who are self-interested in a particular social outcome to place their acts on one side of a metaphorical curtain, and all possibly affected persons on the other side (including themselves), regardless of race, class, gender, power, or other distinctions. Rawls suggests that ethical communicators about to make a decision should remove themselves mentally from their actual circumstances in order to enter a hypothetical reality (behind the "veil") from which they are as likely to emerge weak and dependent as powerful and independent. Decisions made on one side of the "veil of ignorance," therefore, could not take such distinctions or the biases arising from them into account. Subsequent communication decisions would potentially influence all persons equally and fairly, and justice would be the theoretical result.

For example, in our student cheating incident, would it be any more or less ethical to report it to the professor if the student was your personal friend? As a Rawlsian egalitarian, you'd have to place that friendship on the other side of the "veil" and make the ethical decision on how to communicate without recourse to either the fact of the friendship or to your egoistic desire to maintain it. The social fact of friendship would have no fundamental relevance to the ethical decision. Rawls's metaphor of the veil of ignorance would remind you of this by stipulating that the cheater would be as likely to emerge from behind the veil as a stranger as to emerge as the friend he or she "really" is. The "right thing" has more to do with maintaining a just or fair social community than it does with maintaining special privileges or special information such as who are friends and who aren't. Such distinctions should not be critical in ethical decision making in this view. Through such egalitarian reasoning, democratic governments justify legal systems protecting the rights of the accused, even if the accused in a particular case represents a social or economic group often unfairly associated with crime. Opponents of capital punishment also appear to use a "veil of ignorance" ethic in their reasoning: "That person in prison could be you or me. Wrongful accusations can victimize *anyone*. What policy best guarantees a process of justice, regardless of our knowledge about someone's past criminal record, socioeconomic class, ethnicity, or other factors that may not be relevant to this case?"

Although the deontological, teleological, and egalitarian theories of ethics are only generalizations summarizing complex systems of philosophical thought in ethics, they provide a background for our survey of ethical systems with more specific application to communication theory.

LINK

What could be the consequences of applying Rawls's veil of ignorance criterion to your decisions about communicating ethically across cultural boundaries? Given what we know about how cultures shape people's values of right and wrong, can we agree on a cross-cultural ethic? See Chapter 7 for clues on addressing these difficult questions. We'll return to them in our discussion of Taoist thought later in this chapter.

BEYOND "WHAT WORKS": SPECIFIC THEORIES OF COMMUNICATION ETHICS

Students of philosophy and students of communication theory have much in common, probably more than they (or some of their professors) may realize.

BOX 10-1

PHILOSOPHICAL QUESTIONS
FOR ETHICAL COMMUNICATORS

- To what extent should ethics be *deontological,* or based on following relatively unchanging principles?
- To what extent should ethics be *teleological,* or based on analyzing the consequences of messages?
- To what extent should ethics be *egalitarian,* or based on maintaining equality and justice among communicators?

After all, what is philosophy but an attempt to systematize our overall but tentative wisdom concerning how people communicate their ideas and feelings in various contexts? Philosopher Abraham Kaplan (1961) stated well the connection between philosophy and everyday communication (although he did so in an era when the importance of gender-neutral language was not yet recognized):

> A philosophy which speaks, even indirectly, only to philosophers is no philosophy at all; and I think the same is true if it speaks only to scientists, or only to jurists, or priests, or any other special class. For the business of philosophy, as I see it, always was—and remains—to articulate the principles by which a man can live: not just as a scientist, citizen, religionist, or whatever, but as the whole man that he is. To describe a man's philosophy is to say how he orients himself to the world of his experience, what meanings he finds in events, what values he aspires to, what standards guide his choices in all he does. (p. 4)

Communication studies and philosophy are thus cohorts in the human "orientation to the world of . . . experience" and in the discovery of "meanings" in the everyday world of communication events and choices.

We do not mean to suggest that philosophers and theorists of communication ethics are unconcerned with "what works," but that they tend to go beyond that level of analysis or questioning to ask the "whether" questions we discussed earlier. They want to go further in order to unearth other dimensions in the communicative endeavor, such as whether some possible actions might accomplish one's ends, yet at the same time be undesirable or harmful within the communicative matrix of society. Such an overview of communication effects is barely different from the transactional perspective we discussed in Chapter 2. An analyst may discover quite a bit about *behavior* by researching individual people, but might miss the importance of *communication* by doing so. Communication focuses on relationships (and vice versa). As such, it has multiple dimensions, only one of which is pragmatic in the technical sense. The other major dimension is, and must continue to be, ethical. Even if we know how to act in order to achieve a desired objective, we're still left with choices about whether it's right or appropriate to act in that manner. In other words, then, to learn about communication is simultaneously a study of actions and reasons. It is important not to lose sight of this distinction. As you will see, one important classical treatment of rhetoric emphasizes the unity of acts and reasons (Aristotle, 1954). Others we'll summarize will stress a dynamic ecology of values (Taoist ethics), the importance of avoiding manipulation and objectification (dialogic ethics), the openness to ideas (marketplace of ideas ethics), and the place of stories in informing our ethical decisions (narrative and communitarian ethics).

virtue ethics

Aristotle's famous definition of the scope of rhetoric—"the faculty of observing in any given case the available means of persuasion"—shows his intense interest in "what works" in communication (1954). Indeed, his *Rhetoric* served in some ways as a manual of persuasion for communicators in ancient Greek civilization. As Solmsen (1954) writes in the introduction to a translation of *Rhetoric and Poetics*, "Aristotle certainly visualizes a speech not as composed for the admiration of literary connoisseurs through all time but as designed for a specific, practical end, as delivered before an audience, as calculated to prove and to convince" (p. xii).

Yet Aristotle also generally recommends that communicators relate to each other in nonmanipulative ways. In a discussion of **virtue ethics**, he defines his central term, *virtue,* as the way people create and preserve "good things; or a faculty of conferring many great benefits . . ." (Aristotle, 1954, p. 57). Common virtues are justice, courage, temperance, magnificence, magnanimity, liberality, gentleness, prudence, and wisdom. But Aristotle goes on to show that "virtue"—which sounds so much like a trait or a series of principles—is in some ways a relational term: "If virtue is a faculty of beneficence, the highest kinds of it must be those which are most useful to others" (p. 57). Further, "justice" can be defined only through the development of an interpersonal ethic: "Justice is the virtue through which everybody enjoys his own possessions in accordance with the law; its opposite is injustice, through which men enjoy the possessions of others in defiance of the law" (p. 57).

Aristotle's position on moral virtue in situations involving ethical choices falls somewhere between the extremes of action. Referred to by contemporary scholars as the **principle of the golden mean**, it suggests that when people are faced with ethical choices in a situation, the most ethical action is often the one at a midpoint between two extremes; for example, between being foolhardy and rash on the one hand, and totally passive on the other. According to Aristotle in *Nichomachean Ethics* (1947), "virtue . . . is a state of character concerned with choice, lying in a mean, i.e. the mean relative to us, this being determined by a rational principle, and by that principle by which the man of practical wisdom would determine it. Now it is a mean between two vices, that which depends on excess and that which depends on defect; and again it is a mean because the vices respectively fall short of or exceed what is right in both passions and actions, while virtue both finds and chooses that which is intermediate" (p. 340). Under the principle of the golden mean, then, total commitment to extremes of one side or another in a controversy indicates an ethically suspect lack of discernment. Aristotle discusses extremes in terms of excess and deficiency. Communicators concerned with ethics might reassess their positions to see if a middle ground might be more appropriate. Although meeting in the middle may not result in total agreement, it is a hallmark of the rational society and a sign of ethical communication.

taoist ethics

Much older than Aristotle's ethical guidelines, though not nearly as influential in Western civilization, is *Taoism* (pronounced as if it were a *D*). This ancient Chinese philosophical system is largely based on two works: Lao Tzu's *Tao te Ching,* over two thousand years old, and the *Chuang Tzu,* a book that's come to be known by the name of its author. The *Tao* ("Tao" is often translated by Western scholars as "The Way," despite Taoism's mistrust of language's ability to capture reality) is thoroughly culture-specific in its Eastern origin. However, its applications to Western thought have been noted consistently (Bynner, 1962; Cooper, 1972; Zhang, 1988). In addition, references to Taoist concepts have been increasingly prominent in contemporary Western communication and rhetorical theories (Jensen, 1987; Kincaid, 1987a; Oliver, 1962).

Taoist philosophy is suspicious not only of language as a mirror of reality but also of any system of "shoulds" that purports to tell people how to behave. Although this may seem to make Taoism an unlikely source of an ethic for communication, its rich thought is actually quite similar in many ways to some of the basic insights of contemporary communication theory. As such, Taoism offers the student of communication an array of fresh insights that seem also somehow familiar.

The basic assumption of **Taoist ethics** is that life is an organic whole with its own dynamic ecology. Within this holistic system, no individual person or thing exists except in relation to others; thus, no action can be taken egoistically. In contrast to a deontologically defined principle or duty that guides an individual's decision making, harmony with the whole is the criterion by which a Taoist begins to generate communicative decisions. This does not mean, in the words of the "me generation," that one must always "go with the flow" or never confront another, but that a person must always take into account the ways individual action may be counterproductive when considered holistically. Thus, *yin* (the passive and receptive elements of living) and *yang* (the active and forceful elements) exist interdependently and dialectically.

In other words, *yin* and *yang* each come into being along with and because of the other. That neither is definable without reference to the other seems to be the basis of Taoists' skepticism about language. Logically, if no thing can be truly specified without references to the "not-things," then how can language capture reality? How can words ever encompass enough? Obviously, the ancient Taoist *yin* and *yang* philosophy of interdefinition predates Dewey and Bentley's (1949) twentieth-century transactional view of human experience. Alan Watts translates this transactional dynamic as "mutual arising" (1975, pp. 43, 53). The *Chuang Tzu* takes an interpersonal perspective on this concept: "If there were not [the views of] another, I should not have mine; if there were not I [with my views], his

LINKS

• Taoist philosophy supports the dialectical theory of relational development discussed in Chapter 6.
• Review the section in Chapter 2 on transactional (as opposed to self actional or interactional) relations. Taoist ethical guidelines emerge from a transactional perception of reality.

would be uncalled for: —this is nearly a true statement of the case, but we do not know what it is that makes it be so" (Legge, 1962, p. 179). Thus, in dialogue, it is the sheer differentness of the other person's view that teaches me what I believe; my individual views arise not from within but from the connections between me and other persons.

This linkage means that harmony is best established when it is accepted and allowed. Leaders don't need to rule or to force the action. Instead, they lead, in a sense, by noninterference and by not thrusting themselves unnecessarily into an artificial center stage.

Two basic features characterize the implicit Taoist ethic in a conflict situation. First, because the sides are mutually dependent, to the extent that the sides are clearly seen *as* sides, as isolated, the underlying unity is not experienced. Instead, the self is deemphasized and transcended, although its uniqueness is constantly affirmed. Paradoxically, within such uniqueness is multiplicity; Lao Tzu said that "one who recognizes all men as members of his own body / Is a sound man to guard them," and that persons are "members of one another" (Bynner, 1962, pp. 32, 8). Taoism even suggests that a form of empathy can come from such experience: the Sage "does not view things as apprehended by himself, subjectively, but transfers himself into the position of the thing viewed. This is called using the Light" (Cooper, 1972, pp. 65–66).

Second, the attempt to force the other side into a predetermined position, capitulation, or solution is certain to fail. The more appropriate approach is *wu-wei*, which is occasionally misunderstood as nonaction or passivity, or noneffort. *Wu-wei* is more accurately described as "effortless effort," or more simply, effort that flows naturally from the demands of a situation. The ethical message of Taoism, often subtle and implicit, is to find the movement of the Tao and merge with it. Thus, the effective person is much like flowing water, the central symbol of Taoism; that person adapts personal action to already-existing channels, and finds that, like flowing water, he or she can shape the environment in turn. Water, the weakest, softest, and most pliant substance known to the ancient Chinese, therefore was also the strongest. The hardest substance, stone, was weak by comparison.

Interestingly, then, Taoism seems to blend pragmatics with ethics, the "what works" question with the "whether what works is right" question. In its emphasis on the interconnectedness of living systems, and its insistence that all facets of the world are always in a process of mutual definition, Taoism is similar to a modernday Western philosophy of dialogue.

dialogic ethics

In 1922, a small and intriguing book by Martin Buber (1958) called *I and Thou* appeared in German, and began to create its own groundwork for ethical discussion. Although Buber's writing style resembles mystical poetry at times, his views are rooted not in mysticism but in the concrete realities of everyday existence. The questions Buber asks about humanity are very practical ones.

Stated simply (perhaps too simply) in his **dialogic ethic,** Buber (1958) saw what is uniquely human as the relations between persons, not the individual persons themselves. As noted in Chapter 6, through concern for what Buber calls "the between," or the relationship itself, each of us can become for other persons a unique "you" (or, as it is usually translated, a unique "thou"), capable of being seen and respected in all our differences. Buber contrasts this person-with-person, *I-Thou,* relationship with the *I-It* relationship, which encompasses our approach to the objects and things that we use but do not communicate with in meaningful ways. I-It relations may be normal and natural for certain portions of our lives; a craftsperson, for example, "uses" tools to make furniture. But when the assumptions of I-It invade our consciousness when we're communicating, we renounce our human character and our potential to create a sense of community is diminished. As Buber (1958) explains:

L I N K

In Chapter 6 on communicative interdependence, we discussed the outlines of a dialogic theory or philosophy of human communication. Here, we examine the ethical dimensions of dialogue.

> If I face a human being as my *Thou,* and say the primary word *I-Thou* to him, he is not a thing among things, and does not consist of things.
>
> Thus a human being is not *He* or *She,* bounded from every other *He* and *She,* a specific point in space and time within the net of the world; nor is he a nature able to be experienced and described, a loose bundle of named qualities. (p. 8)

Clearly, the ethical implication of Buber's position is that we diminish others when we objectify or "use" them as we do objects. This implication also applies to the assumption that we can measure objectively the "qualities" or "nature" of human beings and the human spirit. Buber mistrusts *psychologism,* or the idea that all authentic human experience occurs in the inner self and can be measured or described by the concepts of psychology. Thus, from Buber's perspective, it may be unethical to reduce our concept of human existence to a series of individuals who can be measured and known objectively.

Our identity is not housed within our minds but in *the between;* it is from human relations that identity develops. In effect, then, we owe our *selves* to the grace of each other's speech, in Buber's (1958) view:

> Through the *Thou* a man becomes *I.* That which confronts him comes and disappears, relational events condense, then are scattered, and in the change consciousness of the unchanging partner, of the *I,* grows clear, and each time stronger. To be sure, it is still seen caught in the web of the relation with the *Thou,* as the increasingly distinguishable feature of that which reaches out to and yet is not the *Thou.* But it continually breaks through with more power, till a time comes when it bursts its bonds, and the *I* confronts itself for a moment, separated as though it were a *Thou,* as quickly to take possession of itself and from then on to enter into relations in consciousness of itself. (pp. 28–29)

In essence, we become human through our communication with others, and we are responsible for maintaining our humanity through communication.

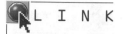

L I N K

Compare Buber's dialogic ethic to Goffman's theoretical concepts of impression management, discussed in Chapter 6. If these two scholars were to talk in dialogue, they might disagree about the fundamental nature of human existence. For example, Goffman might argue that an inherent part of human society is a kind of *seeming*, because we constantly dramatize ourselves for others. Yet Buber appears to position his theory against *seeming*. In your comparison, try to decide if this disagreement is based on genuine conceptual disagreement or just a different emphasis of terminology. Given your understanding of Buber's approach to *I-It* relations, would he ever see a valid role for *seeming* in social life?

In his distinguished career as a theologian, an intellectual, a political figure, an educator, and an author, Buber (1965b) developed the implications of his dialogic approach. Two distinctions he drew are particularly important. In one distinction, he described the difference between the conditions of "being" and "seeming" (1965b). The condition of *being*, he thought, was when persons respond to each other in terms of the demands of the immediate situation. It is basically an unstrategic condition or style of living and meeting others. In a condition of being, we do not decide beforehand how to behave or what to think or feel. These are simply outcomes of concrete situations, not objectified plans to be made and packaged. Interestingly, Buber's conception of authentic being includes the possibility that we may be called to oppose another; he was no hopeless romantic. In order to confirm our partners in communication, we must sometimes tell them directly that we believe they are wrong or misguided. Only in this way can we be real partners, real Thous, for the others. *Seeming*, in contrast, was a human choice growing out of the assumptions of I-It. In seeming, false impressions and guile are common and unquestioned strategies. When we are engaged in seeming, we give up the spontaneous authenticity of a meeting for the planned objectification of impressions. We try to manage and manipulate each other and each other's reactions.

Another particularly important ethical distinction growing out of Buber's writing is the problem of "imposing" ideas or actions on others compared with "unfolding" ideas for them (1965b). The person concerned with *imposing* a point of view is basically acting as a propagandist. It is the acceptance of the idea rather than the value of the idea itself or the relations of persons that is foremost in the mind of the propagandist. Such a person is ends-oriented, and in many cases, the means may be sacrificed for the desired ends. In contrast, someone interested in *unfolding* is primarily motivated by the relation itself. The unfolder stands on a personal ground of commitment, but makes no attempt to change, add to, or impose on the other as if the other were a thing to be shaped. Instead, one's perspective is offered (unfolded) as a relational invitation for the other's full consideration. This in no way contradicts the potential for opposition discussed in the previous paragraph. Two persons may engage in heated exchange from entirely different vantage points, each unfolding ideas while still respecting and addressing the experienced ground on which the other person stands.

This brings us to what is in some ways the most important of Buber's (1965b) ethical concepts—*inclusion*, or, as he sometimes called it, "imagining the real." Humans engaged in *inclusion* maintain their own perspective while simultaneously imagining the experienced reality of the other communicators from their perspectives. The dialogic communicator thus knows firsthand that reality is differently experienced depending on who, and where, we are. Perception is both here and there. Discussions and decisions are potentially more thorough and informed, as well as more emotionally sound, when we engage in inclusion. Of course, inclusion is not mind reading; rather, it is a tentative but educated guess at an alternate possibility of "rightness" that is not the same as our own. It thus verifies and confirms humanness, not just a single human being.

Inclusion, as Buber uses the term, appears to be essentially similar to what some social scientists and psychologists call *empathy* (Anderson, 1982; Ayres, 1984; Cissna & Anderson, 1990; Johannesen, 1990). However, some other authorities disagree, reserving the term "empathy" for an identification in which a person attempts to gain knowledge about the other by projecting into the other's experience (Arnett & Nakagawa, 1983; Stewart, 1983). The essential question for dialogue seems to be this: Does the dialogue partner try to meet the other person on the other's own terms without pretense, without abandoning his or her existential ground, and without judging the other by the perceiver's own external standards? This approach of inclusion is, according to Buber, the essence of maintaining a relationship. Ethical communicators understand the world as much as possible both from their own side and, imaginatively, from the other side.

Richard Johannesen (1990, pp. 62–63) has distilled the thought of Buber and other theorists into six characteristics of dialogue, which can also be considered ethical guidelines for communication:

1. *Authenticity*. Maurice Friedman (1960), a noted philosopher and Buber scholar, summarizes this feature: "Whatever the word 'truth' may mean in other spheres," he writes, "in the realm between man and man it means that one imparts oneself to the other as what one is. This is not a question of saying to the other everything that occurs to one, but of allowing the person with whom one communicates to partake of one's being" (p. 86).

2. *Inclusion*. A dialogue partner's life is included as a viable perspective from which someone can understand the world. Perception, therefore, can and should be more than a psychological phenomenon. Ethical communicators do not act as though they are isolated individuals.

3. *Confirmation*. In dialogue we verify each other's existence. Through speech and other forms of communication, we demonstrate that we notice others and take them into account, even if we might not agree with them. The very human need to be confirmed, unfortunately, may lead some communicators to adopt behaviors of seeming to be what they're not, and they try to fake sincerity, interest, or competence in order to make the right impressions.

4. *Presentness*. Johannesen (1990) explains that dialogue partners "demonstrate willingness to become fully involved with each other by taking time, avoiding distraction, being communicatively accessible, and risking attachment. One avoids being an onlooker who simply takes in what is presented or an observer who analyzes" (p. 63).

5. *Spirit of mutual equality*. Dialogic communicators avoid imposing their will on others; instead, they seek ways to allow and encourage other persons to express themselves more fully. The connection of dialogue to listening is affirmed by this spirit of mutuality. In fact, Buber and others have noted that the spirit most opposite to dialogue is that of monologue, in which a single voice dominates a situation. Perhaps more important, that voice—if spoken in the absence of mutuality—will discourage or pre-

L I N K

Seeming sometimes appears to be the preferred choice for media communicators, such as entertainers and broadcast journalists (see Chapter 9). For example, you'll rarely if ever hear about Peter Jennings's or Oprah Winfrey's headaches: although they may be sick or in pain, they've trained themselves to speak on-camera or on-stage in much the same way as when they feel healthy. Many widely admired broadcast interviewers also act as though they're friends with each interviewee, although you'll later discover the two had been feuding. Because many communication majors want to enter such fields, you might like to speculate about why audiences apparently believe that such impression management in professional roles doesn't involve ethical dilemmas.

clude thorough listening. Some rhetorical and argumentation theorists have described this condition as *bilaterality,* or the mutual access of communicators to all the resources of talk; in a dialogue both sides are heard.

6. *Supportive climate.* Judgment of the other person is not a central characteristic of dialogue. Rather, the ethic of I-Thou recognizes the essential connection of persons (symbolized by the hyphen in I-Thou) that makes dialogue more of a team effort than a transfer of psychologized meanings from one individual to another.

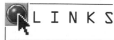

L I N K S

• See Chapter 6 for more information on how theorists and researchers in the human sciences have extended Buber's idea of confirmation to a wider range of interaction.

• Is *presentness* essentially similar to Mehrabian's concept of *immediacy,* discussed in Chapter 3? In which contexts do communicators have an ethical obligation to listen and speak in ways that are particularly "present" or "immediate"?

• Buber believed that ethical communicators invite others' talk and won't dominate communication by imposing their monologues upon others (see No.5, above). This suggestion is consistent with Habermas's concept of the *ideal speech situation* for deliberation, discussed later in this chapter.

Many writers have applied dialogic theory to analyses of ethical dilemmas— in society, in political arguments, in cross-cultural encounters, and in ordinary conversations. Recently, the attempts of communication scholars Charles Brown and Paul Keller (1979; Keller & Brown, 1968), of educator and philosopher Nel Noddings (1984), and of critical theorist Jurgen Habermas (1979, 1990) have been notable.

Brown and Keller (1979) describe their "interpersonal ethic" in terms of the choices communicators have, and are able to develop, as a result of their dialogue. This *choice criterion,* as they describe it, has much more to do with the attitudes persons demonstrate toward one another than with specific behaviors that might be prescribed or precluded. They agree with Buber that human interaction is not a matter of "do's and don't's." It involves genuineness and concern as imperfect persons do their best with imperfect means to give themselves and others a chance to make a difference in life. Thus, Brown and Keller (1979) show that a dialogic ethic ultimately comes down to the choice criterion: "The ethic we are proposing is imbedded in the assumption that *whatever enhances that which is uniquely human in participants is ethical; whatever dehumanizes is unethical.* This assumption finds expression in one of the values held most dear in a democratic society, namely, that conditions *of free choice* be created and maintained in which it becomes possible *for the individual to realize his or her potential.* This is achieved to the extent to which others . . . *do not* try to control, coerce, manipulate, maneuver, or exploit him or her" (p. 277). Further, Brown and Keller point out, such behavior is unethical not only because it harms the other but also because it subverts the growth of the manipulator.

Noddings has applied Buber's notion of dialogue to the **feminine ethic of care** she developed for everyday relationships. Her book, *Caring: A Feminine Approach to Ethics and Moral Education* (1984), has had a powerful effect on contemporary ethics as well as on the ongoing social conversation about gender relations. Noddings starts from a somewhat different premise than some other ethicists. She argues that caring is not just the outcome of an ethical relationship, but also is the genesis of ethics at its most elemental and crucial level. Further, she believes this insight is unusual within ethics because most ethical theory has been developed by men. Thus, many ethical systems are dominated by the enunciation of relatively detached principles and "can/can't" or "should/shouldn't" guidelines (a typically male perspective, Noddings suggests), rather than a more "feminine" assumption of the primacy of relational caring within social situations. From our earlier discussion, you should recognize Noddings's characterization of the male-dominated approach as primarily deontological. However, instead of arguing for a teleological criterion of judging the possible consequences of actions, she goes more or less outside the boundaries of the basic assumption. Noddings believes that women tend to approach moral problems from neither principles nor (necessarily) consequences, but from emphasizing the crucial reality of the relationship itself. This is how she describes the problems of *caring* and being *cared-for.*

Bear in mind that Noddings does not mean to suggest women are incapable of acting on principle or men are incapable of being relationally sensitive. Rather, she merely asserts that ethical decisions are not made hypothetically but are embedded in real situations. Studies of gender differences in real-life contexts have shown that men and women tend to solve problems differently. Men generally apply previously developed principles, whereas women generally inspect the situation and the relationships for more information about "feelings, needs, impressions, and a sense of personal ideal" (1984, p. 3). Men answer hypothetical or imaginary questions more readily because the principles from which they tend to operate are thought to be invariable (i.e., they try to describe the situation and apply the rule to get the right answer). Women tend to balk more at hypothetical descriptions of behavioral problems because they want more information about the relationships involved. Therefore, it makes a difference at the level of caring, for example, whether the people involved have been together for two months or two years, and it matters whether they feel strongly about each other or are only mildly attracted. It is from the immediacy of the more "feminine" condition that ethical caring develops, according to Noddings. In fact, she argues that an ethic of caring exists as a "natural inclination" once a person (female or male) is immersed in the immediacy of a given relation.

Like many other dialogic theorists, Noddings is suspicious of developing an action-based or a behavioral criterion for ethical living. What is right in one situation may be wrong or even destructive in another. The relation is primary, so the attitudes supporting relatedness are primary in moral dilemmas. As Noddings (1984) writes: "What we do depends not upon rules, or at least not wholly on rules—not upon a prior determination of what is fair or equitable—but upon a constellation of conditions that is viewed through both the eyes of the one-caring and the eyes of the cared-for. By and large, we do not say with any conviction that a person cares if that person acts routinely according to some fixed rule" (p. 13). An ethic of human communication instead requires *engrossment,* Noddings's term suggesting the dialogic conceptions of *inclusion, imagining the real,* and *empathy.* When we experience engrossment in another person, we also notice *motivational displacement* (pp. 17, 25). That is, motivation no longer seems to come from within ourselves, but seems to have been displaced to the "cared-for" person. Motivation is simultaneously within and outside the individual person; it is relational.

Noddings's ethic of caring is primarily applicable to situations of interpersonal communication. But her emphases on real-life situations, relational motivation, and suspicion of invariant principles also apply to other approaches to communication ethics in the mass media and across cultures.

Although Habermas's (1990) **discourse ethics** also recommends dialogue, it differs in interesting ways from other dialogic theories of ethics. Habermas, for example, stresses what he calls *communicative rationality* as a backdrop to social order.

He is especially interested in how problems are argued within the public sphere when communicators experience social and political conflict. As Habermas (1979) explains: "I . . . proceed on the assumption that 'moral consciousness' signifies the ability to make use of interactive competence for *consciously* processing morally relevant conflicts of action" (p. 88). For Habermas, then, unlike most other dialogic theorists, consensus is a desirable social goal that can best be achieved by communicators who choose clear rules for guiding the fairness of deliberations. Thus, Habermas's discourse ethics has been characterized as primarily a procedural system for guaranteeing rational access to dialogue for a wide variety of communicators.

Within the communication discipline, the most influential of Habermas's concepts has been the **ideal speech situation**. It describes what he considers the best dialogue conditions for argumentative deliberation. According to Habermas (1990), an encounter of "ideal speech" has four characteristics: (1) The "cooperative search for truth" results in a consensus, or a mutually agreed-upon interpretation, about that truth; (2) the "force of the better argument" transcends any kind of external or internal coercion; (3) all communicators have equal access to the discourse; and (4) all communicators have equal opportunities to question assertions, introduce their own assertions, and express personal attitudes and wants (p. 89). Over time, Habermas (1992) has clarified that he saw the ideal speech situation not so much as a set of concrete procedural rules, but as an attitude of inquiry through which rational people attempt to structure how they should address their problems: " 'Ideal speech situation' is somewhat too concrete a term for the set of general and unavoidable communicative presuppositions which a subject capable of speech and action must make every time he or she wishes to participate seriously in argumentation" (pp. 160–161). Further, it is "a description of the conditions under which claims to truth and rightness can be discursively redeemed" (p. 171). In conceptualizing an ideal speech situation, Habermas demonstrates his faith in procedures of dialogue for the purpose of attaining public justice. Discourse ethics seems to trust the creation of public argumentative norms over the clash of private values that may never contribute to a total consensus.

However, some scholars believe that this procedural faith combined with Habermas's assumption about the desirability of consensus may not always serve a pluralistic society well (see, e.g., Benhabib, 1990, 1992; Young, 1990; among others). Those arguers who are best able to articulate generalizable or universal interests in public can be expected to do better in Habermas's ideal speech situation than those who are uniquely and radically oppressed. In other words, although such critics may appreciate Habermas's dialogic tendencies, they fear that discourse ethics, almost paradoxically, is overly concerned with maintaining a public procedural image of consensus at the expense of the diversity of multicultural voices. To Iris Marion Young (1990), "such a desire for political unity will suppress difference, and tend to exclude some voices and perspectives from the public, because their greater privilege and dominant position allows some groups to articulate the 'common good' in terms influenced by their particular perspective and interests" (p. 118).

L I N K

· Social exchange theorists, discussed in Chapter 6, tend to assume that a norm of reciprocity guides our communication across contexts, and that we naturally communicate in reciprocal ways. However, Habermas (1979, pp. 88 ff.) does not agree that this norm characterizes all interaction. Instead, he believes that reciprocity is negotiated within ongoing relationships, and thus that communicative rationality requires our sustained attention to the procedures of dialogue.

BOX 10-2

FOUR APPROACHES
TO DIALOGIC ETHICS

- Buber's *I-Thou concept* stresses the uniquely human relation as the basis for ethics (not *psychologism* or individualism), and distinguishes between *being* and *seeming*, and *unfolding* and *imposing*
- Brown and Keller's *choice criterion* suggests that ethical communicating increases people's range of free choice
- Noddings's *feminine ethic* emphasizes that caring communicators reduce their reliance on deontological principles of ethical choice making; it also focuses on how the caring person experiences *engrossment* in particular relationships
- Habermas's *discourse ethics* elevates procedural standards for rational deliberation and advocates an *ideal speech situation* in which participants are equally able to contribute and to influence others.

L I N K

Although Habermas, to his credit, advocates that all speakers arrive at a dialogic bargaining table equally able to listen, to speak, and to articulate common concerns of a public, some cultural critics argue that such openness rarely reflects the real-world conditions of intergroup relations. Do you think there are times when dialogue may not be a reasonable ethical criterion? In light of the cultural theories of power and dominance you learned about in Chapter 7, do you think dialogic ethics can help guide communication forcefully in a pluralistic society? Why, or why not? If the critics of Habermas are right, how might their criticisms also apply to the theories of Buber, Brown and Keller, and Noddings?

In many situations, articulations of "common" concerns will be more favorable to particular groups in power, which could help keep dominated groups at the rhetorical margins of society. In South Africa, for example, for years whites were able to argue that because of their European culture and education system, white perspectives were better suited than black perspectives to represent the political common good. Often blacks were invited to participate and negotiate, but were not taken seriously. In many parts of the United States, too, the procedures for participation are in place, but dialogue by itself may not guarantee that marginalized groups will be heard adequately. Do the processes of consensus, compromise, and official dialogue themselves inherently favor some groups over others? Companies when faced with strikes by workers often have public relations departments that tell the public (1) it is in the common good for workers to keep their jobs (working for less money) rather than push for more money that could force the organization to its demise, and (2) while the company is open to listening to both sides and considering the "common good," workers are not dialogic in that they make "demands."

Other interpreters defend Habermas's sensitivity to less powerful groups, suggesting that decentering and empathy are important to his discourse ethics: "Habermas's discourse model, by requiring that perspective-taking be general and reciprocal, builds the moment of empathy into the procedure of coming to a reasoned agreement: each must put himself or herself into the place of everyone else in discussing whether a proposed norm is fair to all. And this must be done publicly; arguments played out in the individual consciousness or in the theoretician's mind are no substitute for real discourse" (McCarthy, 1990, pp. viii–ix). Genuine empathy would seem to create a more open ethical climate in which diverse voices are not only heard but also invited.

Obviously, many of the ethical systems we have surveyed thus far are not mutually exclusive. In most cases, they overlap enough so that their authors and other experts from "within" one system can find much to agree with in other perspectives. For example, although Martin Buber agreed with many of the philosophical aspects of Taoism, what he saw as its essential mysticism sent him to look for ethical insights in a slightly different direction. This different direction is not an entirely contradictory one, however. As we will see, several of our remaining ethical theories show a consistency of purpose even when theorists choose different terminology.

marketplace of ideas ethics

In a widely read journal article published over three decades ago, Karl Wallace (1963) suggested that the essence of human communication understanding ought to be ideas—the *good reasons* that people give in support of actions. All discourse can be called into question, at least potentially. When this happens, its "substance"—its conceptual content and essential subject matter—has to be justified as leading to acceptable human behavior. The ideational substance of discourse is basic to Wallace, much more basic than the style, ornamentation, organization, or form in which messages are presented. Some of us might argue about how important it is to create clear-cut distinctions between content and style because they are often interdependent in communication, but Wallace in his time responded to studies that took a narrowly pedagogical approach to rhetoric by emphasizing *how* things are said rather than *what* is said.

People constantly make requests of each other as they try to convince, appeal to, be accepted by, or gain compliance from their listeners. Richard Weaver (1971) captures this in a striking metaphor: language is "sermonic." It cannot be neutral. Each of us preaches. Human speech, even at its most objective, persistently asks to be believed. We normally think of religious rhetoric in this way, but Weaver expands the notion. Language is immersed in value orientations, and creates in both speakers and listeners a complex set of choices, values, and positions. Speech is inherently position–taking, and listening inherently involves developing positions as well.

But what kind of position-taking is Wallace advocating? If all rhetoric takes a position or expresses a value judgment, then society needs a way of evaluating such judgments. *Good reasons* are those freely expressed, rationally based, and consistent supporting materials for the positions people assert. They mix traditional rational argument with the recognition that human beings are emotional creatures. "Good reasons" are what we use to support our "ought" statements. As critic Wayne Booth (1974) points out, ". . . the philosophy of good reasons leads us to a reaffirmation of those central human values that other philosophies and religions have reached by other routes: of tolerance, of justice or fairness, of 'democratic' equality of vote in all matters that concern all men equally" (p. 149).

In an earlier article, Wallace (1955) had already laid the groundwork for his ethical approach. Drawing on Aristotle and classical rhetoric, Wallace asked if modern society has become too preoccupied with its ability to persuade and too often ignores questions of "ought" and "What would be better?" in favor of "what works." His concerns, among others, stimulated the questions with which we began this chapter. Communication theory and research should not settle for a body of "findings" that are not connected to a moral context of "good reasons." This doesn't mean that the same researchers have to conduct these kinds of ethical studies; rather, it means that communication scholars should not privilege one kind of study over the other, nor should they divorce the study of communication science from the study of value judgments.

Wallace (1955) suggests four practical principles for ethical rhetoric in a democratic society. Each of them, paraphrased here, has implications for communicators in all fields:

1. Communicators in a democratic society should uphold a *standard of knowledge*. Because audiences depend upon the information speakers present in public, ethical speech should demonstrate a thorough familiarity with the topic and its relevant implications. Communicators in public life must, in other words, have a knowledge base supporting their good reasons. We must know what we're talking about if we ask others to listen.

2. Communicators in a democratic society should exhibit a *habit of justice*. That is, they should be fair in their selection and presentation of facts. If public communicators are ethical in this way, their audiences will have a fair and reasonable opportunity to make up their own minds about the subject at hand. This idea is similar in many ways to a dialogic ethic. The habit of justice encourages the unfolding of ideas for others, rather than the imposing of ideas on them; it also preserves the choice-making criterion and reflects the concern for equal access in discourse ethics. If communication is ethical, it does not diminish the freedom of, or the equal treatment available to, its participants.

3. Communicators in a democratic society should enact a *habit of preferring public to private motivations*. An ethical speaker should be willing to discuss openly the sources for the positions offered by his or her rhetoric. This type of communicator does not merely speak, but in addition speaks about the very origins of his or her speaking. An audience has a right to ask something beyond "What do you know?" The listeners in a democratic ethic need to hear answers to "How did you come to believe this?" and "Why are you telling us this?" A willingness to disclose such matters speaks directly to the issue of communicator credibility.

4. Communicators in a democratic society should demonstrate a *habit of respect for dissent*. Following this ethical guideline, a communicator will not try to avoid or hide information that might counter her or his opinions. Rather, the communicator respects opposing positions, in the same way that beginning tennis players appreciate playing with more advanced players. It is the strength of the *other* position that ultimately can strengthen the communicator's position; after all, an untested belief has no strength or validity. This respect for dissent is not a passive tolerance but an active choice of communicators that supports dialogic principles and communicative rationality.

L I N K

See the discussion of *ethos* and credibility in Chapter 8. In what ways would more attention to *ethos* improve political campaigning? How might it improve the communication of teachers and students?

Wallace's four ethical principles for democratic rhetoric seem to elevate the needs of a communication system beyond the individual's needs within that system.

Wallace's suggestions for rhetoric in a free society presume that ideas must be freely developed, freely shared, and freely confronted. Recently, rhetoricians and other scholars drawing on legal opinions and interpretations have extended similar ethical perspectives in philosophical and pragmatic studies of free speech, creating what has become known as **marketplace of ideas ethics** (Haiman, 1981, 1991; Schauer, 1982). The metaphor implies that ideas, like commodities, are differently attractive and influential to various publics. Further, like a market economy, a marketplace of ideas gains strength or influence by encouraging maximum access to the market and by maintaining an adversarial or competitive system for testing ideas against each other. The censoring of ideas is viewed as an impediment to the marketplace in its quest for truth.

Franklyn Haiman has clarified and applied the marketplace of ideas notion within the communication discipline. His book, *Speech and Law in a Free Society* (1981), created one of the best extended justifications for the marketplace approach to free speech and ethical communication. In it, Haiman argues that a society is both energized and educated by the open interplay of ideas. While intervening to conceal or restrict discourse may occasionally be justified by a government in an emergency, in everyday affairs a relative openness is required for an informed citizenry to maximize its opportunities for making choices.

Ethicist Sissela Bok's highly regarded study, *Secrets* (1983), does not presume that all concealment is necessarily unethical, but it does suggest that secrecy should be carefully balanced against its consequences. Bok offers two "presumptions" or ethical guidelines for deciding whether secrecy or revelation is most appropriate: *equality* and *"partial individual control* over the degree of secrecy or openness about personal matters" (1983, p. 27; emphasis added). The controls over whether information is open or secret should be relatively equally distributed among members of a group or society, even though the kinds of information available to them may differ at times. Although some social roles grant high information access and, therefore, high control, Bok claims that such "special considerations" must be justified as valid exceptions to the presumption of equality. Her other presumption, partial individual control, articulates the relationship between information openness and personal choice. As a general rule, a just and free society grants individuals a large degree of control over information about private matters or personal experience. It sounds simple: Persons should, for the most part, be in charge of information that pertains to them personally. It is interesting to note one implication of this presumption: If in the interpersonal realm individual rights to privacy should be considered ethically primary, then the marketplace of ideas metaphor may be an inadequate rationale for requesting (or expecting or requiring) self-disclosure. However, as in Bok's earlier work (1979), public discussion and discussibility becomes the key criterion for ethical questions in communication. Extending Rawls's (1971) analysis, Bok argues that publicity and our willing submission to it are the best safeguards and checkpoints of

BOX 10-3

FIVE THEORIES OF ETHICAL COMMUNICATION

- The *virtue ethic* of the golden mean
- The *Taoist ethic* of noninterference
- The *dialogic ethic* of mutuality
- The *marketplace of ideas ethic* of individual freedom and justice
- The *narrative and communitarian ethic* of community coherence

---

ethical responsibility. "A moral principle must be capable of public statement and defense," Bok believes (1979, p. 97).

Four principles consistent with "public statement and defense" emerge from Haiman's (1981) study of cases and trends in American freedom of expression. Taken together, they can stand as propositions of a marketplace theory of ethical communication:

1. Unless the harm done by an act of communication is direct, immediate, irreparable, and of a serious material nature, the remedy in a free society should be more speech. The law is an inappropriate tool for dealing with expression which produces mental distress or whose targets are the beliefs and values of an audience.

2. Unless deprived of free choice by deception, physical coercion, or an impairment of normal capacities, individuals in a free society are responsible for their own behavior. They are not objects which can be triggered into action by symbolic stimuli but human beings who decide how they will respond to the communication they see and hear.

3. So long as there is a free marketplace of ideas, where the widest possible range of information and alternatives is available, individuals will be the best judges of their own interests. The law is properly used to enrich and expand that communications marketplace and to insure that it remains an open system.

4. Government in a free society is the servant of the people, and its powers should not be used to inhibit, distort, or dominate public discourse. There must be compelling justification whenever the government requires unwilling communication of its people or withholds information in its possession from them. (Haiman, 1981, pp. 425–426)

Haiman's four principles represent a synthesis of both sensitive political theory and sophisticated communication theory. Notice how his second principle, for example, depends on a symbolic interactionist approach to communication, yet Haiman attributes a unique and subtle responsibility to government for determining meanings. He concludes that people are actors, capable of determining their own symbolic realities. They are not, by and large, manipulable robots whose lives are determined and shaped by outside forces (as some propaganda theorists and strict psychological behaviorists might claim).

narrative and communitarian ethics

In recent years, theorists have rejuvenated an academic interest in stories and storytelling. Although some of them believe a full-blown explanation of human communication experience can come from narrative (Fisher, 1987), others seem to understand it primarily as a helpful organizing principle or metaphor (M. C. Bateson, 1984; Coles, 1989; Keen, 1970). *Narration,* the human tendency to organize experience into stories with plot, characterization, chronology, conflict, and resolution, becomes particularly helpful in understanding what is called **narrative ethics** (Hauerwas, 1981; MacIntyre, 1984).

As Arnett (1991) points out in his synthesis of the work of Fisher, MacIntyre, and others, narrative is ethically important because it removes ethical discourse from the sphere of expert judges and from distant rules and principles, and places it squarely in the experience of particular communities (pp. 65–68). A story does not and cannot develop merely as a product of one "teller," in other words; instead, a story can be considered a cooperative venture, in which individuals participate and to which they contribute. But the story is in many ways larger than what any single speaker or writer can tell, because what is heard, interpreted, and even imagined all contribute to the narrative as well. Because a story is more than its text and more than its telling, evaluating its power is not the province of experts but a collaborative community function. Stories invite evaluation through conversation. At its most basic level, then, narrative theory necessarily emphasizes conversational elements and (in the ways discussed in Chapters 2 and 6) transactional elements. It also portrays reality as constructed through talk and its consequences, through people seeking shared meaning.

We explore ethics, our sometimes painful decisions about right and wrong, by paying careful attention to the stories that characterize a given culture. Analysts of popular culture chart deep currents of thought from seemingly trivial and superficial sources like soap operas, sitcoms, and music videos. One psychologist demonstrates this through an interesting methodology. Bruner (1986) tries to understand cultural values by having subjects hear or read a single story, and then by asking them to "retell" the story. The same "actual text" (literal words of an "author") turns into quite different "virtual texts" (the interpretive experiences of the retellers). Thus, "telling back" a Joseph Conrad story, when "one reader will turn it into a yarn of adventure, another into a moral tale about duplicity, and a third into a case study of a Doppelganger" (p. 6). Yet a researcher won't discover an infinite variety of interpretations; the stories will reflect a limited number of social and cultural community visions. A story, despite an identifiable individual authorship, transcends individuals to implicate them into a community ethic.

One implicit narrative ethical principle, therefore, seems to be a tolerance for diversity, even an *invitation* to diversity. Precise formulas for social responsibility, in contrast, are not expected outcomes of narrative ethics. As Bruner (1986) explains, ". . . the function of literature as art is to open us to dilemmas, to the hypothetical, to the range of possible worlds that a text can refer to. I have used the term 'to subjunctivize' to render the world less fixed, less banal, more susceptible to recreation. Literature subjunctivizes, makes strange, renders the obvious less so, the unknowable less so as well, matters of value more open to reason and intuition" (p. 159). Narrative theorists might well ask: What will keep diverse people talking in spite of their differences? Making an "ethical" decision in some contexts might be nothing more than taking action to move the story along with the cooperative contributions of a given community.

Narrative principles are central to the recent development of a **communitarian ethic**. Communitarian ethicists downplay or reject the traditional liberal emphasis on individual *rights*, conceived as what persons should be able to do as individual moral agents. Communitarians shift the emphasis to different ethical ground on which questions of community coherence can be considered (Christians, Ferré, & Fackler, 1993; Etzioni, 1993; Glendon, 1991). Discussing Stanley Hauerwas's (1981) analysis of character and community, media scholars Christians, Ferré, and Fackler (1993) write that appropriate forms of community are "grounded in stories of substantive morality and not merely in formal rules of proper procedure. . . . Moral power is inseparably connected to a body of language given us as a legacy; the legacy moves us toward a moral horizon, and thereby holds the whims of autonomous individualism at bay. Communities are woven together by narratives that mediate their common understanding of good and evil" (p. 115).

A narrative ethic reminds us to elevate the values we hold to a more prominent decision-making position than the logical rationality we sometimes seek to protect. This is not an irrational approach but a holistic view of rationality. W. R. Fisher (1987) uses the term *narrative rationality* and describes it as intimately value-tied: "The concept of narrative rationality asserts that it is not the *individual form* of argument that is ultimately persuasive in discourse. That is important, but *values* are more persuasive, and they may be expressed in a variety of modes, of which argument is only one. Hence narrative rationality focuses on 'good reasons'— *elements that provide warrants for accepting or adhering to the advice fostered by any form of communication that can be considered rhetorical*" (p. 48).

Clearly, a narrative approach does not help you decide with precision whether a specific act you're contemplating will be "right" or "wrong" taken in isolation. In this sense, it has rather severe limitations as an ethical system (Rybacki & Rybacki, 1991, pp. 124–125). Instead of offering precision, the narrative paradigm contests the assumption that right or wrong can be isolated from the cultural context of stories in which decisions are embedded. Although this paradigm obviously denies a deontological (ethics-as-duty) assumption, it does not necessarily argue in favor of open relativism, in which all behaviors have the potential for being equally valid. Instead, ethical discourse is like a game played within the confines of ground rules—and the ground rules are constructed in the form of what Fisher calls "narrative rationality": stories that make sense, make a coherent

LINKS

• Communitarian scholars do not necessarily admire the procedural emphasis of Habermas's discourse ethics (discussed earlier in this chapter), but you can see how much of dialogic theory would help explain how communities construct meaningful narratives of their moral experience.

• To what extent does multiculturalism, discussed in Chapter 7, comprise the narrative of America's history? In what sense might multiculturalism be an ethical perspective, in addition to a political agenda?

• The individualism versus communitarianism controversy recapitulates the tension we've noted throughout this book's survey of communication theories: Is a sense of self or a personal identity prior to social communication, or vice versa? Or is it a dialectical tension (see Chapter 6) in which both sides are true at the same time? Communitarians argue that if social life and its communities are thought to be ontologically prior (i.e., fundamental for human existence), then the major ethical responsibility is to the community, not to protecting individual self-expression. What do you think?

community, and provide "good reasons" to support behaviors consistent with those stories.

TESTING THE CONCEPTS

"Early in the chapter, you imply that ethics is a 'gray area' for discussion. But if I choose the 'deontological' position, for example, doesn't that eliminate the ambiguity? Won't the principles I believe in determine my choices?"

Not necessarily. Some choices may be simplified, but you still need to decide when a principle should be invoked. All principles are subject to interpretation, as well, and even deontologists would find it hard to argue that *all* circumstances must be governed by rigidly defined duties. Christians are told "Thou shalt not kill," yet most Christians interpret this as referring to human life exclusively (relatively few are vegetarians), and others may exclude supposedly "just" wars. Still others who believe in the same principle—pacifists, for example—draw their lines of interpretation differently.

"Doesn't the teleological position invite rationalization or self-delusion? Couldn't such communicators always fool themselves into thinking that some 'greater good' will be served by whatever decisions are made?"

Yes, but any other ethical paradigm may be rationalized in a similar way. The domain of ethics is intensely rhetorical, in other words; people constantly justify, confront, and rejustify their decisions. What may be a choice to one person could be seen as an inevitability by another. What matters, we would argue, is not that rationalization *could* happen (after all, self-delusion is a persistent human frailty), but that communicators should refer to ethical criteria to evaluate their choices and to minimize merely self-serving or convenient decisions.

"Does Aristotle's 'principle of the golden mean' suggest that I *always* need to compromise a strongly held position?"

You may be committed strongly to positions without necessarily being unethical, according to Aristotle. He only reminds you to consider whether the stand you've taken is, in context, not close to the "vices" of *deficiency* or *excess*. Further, he does not suggest that, as a communicator, you should "always" compromise; rather, you should recognize the middle ground as a fertile territory for discussion. This, of course, is to some extent a "judgment call." But what isn't?

"It sounds like *wu-wei* might mean I should go along with unfair conditions even when I don't want to do so. How can this sort of noninterference be right or ethical? Didn't Nazi collaborators in France during World War II, for example, engage in *wu-wei?*"

Taoist philosophers urge that people can act in an organic way without interfering in the natural flow of their own experience, or interfering with or ma-

LINKS

• Interestingly, our study of ethics in this chapter brings us back to several themes discussed in the Introduction to *Questions of Communication.* For example, while the learning styles of men and women appear to be somewhat different, they also share certain similarities: They both move in the direction of an increasing acceptance of diversity and divergent points of view, as well as an increasing recognition that the individual is inherently important in the choices he or she makes. The direction most college students take in structuring their own learning also seems to reinforce the importance of searching for "good reasons," expanded choices within community, and a tolerance for different perspectives. Although some reports on our ethical climate are discouraging, colleges and universities provide an encouragingly active arena for ethical discourse in society.

• Based on what you know about the theory-building process and the normal characteristics of theories in Chapter 1, do you think theories of communication ethics can be evaluated in the same ways as other communication theories? Why or why not? What justifies these conceptual approaches as theories?

nipulating the behavior of others. Therefore, a primary Taoist response to your example would be to turn toward analyzing the Nazi invasion itself. From the individual's perspective, maybe the most ethical communication would be that in accord with one's own inner experience. That is, if you indeed feel that the conditions are unfair, then the natural flow of *your* action within this holistic context might be to resist those conditions.

"Are communitarian ethicists opposed to preserving individual rights in society?"
Not according to sociologist Amitai Etzioni (1993), perhaps the most prominent spokesperson for communitarianism in the social sciences, who states that "our call for increased social responsibilities . . . is not a call for curbing rights. On the contrary, strong rights presume strong responsibilities" (p. 1). Communitarian ethicists do fear, however, that "people treat rights-based arguments, unlike many others, as 'trump cards' that neutralize all other positions" (Etzioni, 1993, p. 7). In other words, they argue, by paying too much attention to the rights someone supposedly "has," we may obscure a kind of communicative (and other) violence that's done to a community. For example, if we affirm an individual right to privacy, does that mean that a community cannot require that neighborhoods be informed when a convicted (and later released) child molester moves in? Communitarians argue that the community is "ontologically prior" to individual rights, and that we achieve such rights within the context of the community in which we communicate.

Y O U,   T H E   R E S E A R C H E R

1. Public relations (PR) is an increasingly valuable organizational function in an information society. Organizations employ professional PR communicators to explain their internal policies, decisions, and dilemmas to external publics, and to decide on behind-the-scenes persuasive strategies for doing so. Occasionally, these professionals may find that their responsibility to the organizations they represent (e.g., corporations, government agencies, and school districts) conflicts with their responsibility to relay accurate information to the public. Therefore, the Public Relations Society of America (PRSA) has long emphasized the ethical dimensions of public communication.

   - Get a copy of the PRSA's Code of Professional Standards for the Practice of Public Relations from your college library, your instructor, or the PRSA.
   - Evaluate the document to see which theories of ethics are most consistently reflected in its recommendations.
   - Analyze the code. Would following the advice in some sections mean rejecting or ignoring the stipulations in some other sections? If so, in which contexts do such double binds most likely occur?

- Interview a PR professional. Ask what was the most vivid ethical dilemma he or she has ever faced, but do not press to find out what action was ultimately taken. Take careful notes.
- In class, discuss the incident with your instructor and classmates in terms of the dictates of the code. Take a personal position: What would *you* have done? (Later, you may want to follow up with the professional to discover how the situation was resolved.)

2. Videotape the television commercials shown during a local station's children's programing on any Saturday morning from 8 A.M. until 12 noon. How do these ads' persuasive appeals differ from prime-time ads designed for adults? Prepare a brief multimedia presentation for your class using the most illustrative commercials.

- What are the ethical implications of ads for toys, electronic gadgets, shoes, and clothes targeting children rather than parents?
- Is this basically a "bottom-line" financial issue, one you might accede to if you were a network executive? Or is it a moral issue of right and wrong, one you would attempt to change if you were a media decision maker? Or is this dichotomy too simplistic? Explain your reasoning in your class presentation.

3. Communication researchers often face their own kind of ethical decisions. Twentieth-century social science research, in fact, has often depended on the use of research confederates (e.g., "plants" in a group), invasions of privacy, misleading instructions, hidden cameras and microphones, dishonest role-playing, and other deceptive methods.

- Find a journal article in communication, psychology, or sociology that reports on a study in which you believe the deception of subjects was employed unethically or without justification. Which theory or approach to communication ethics best describes the criteria you use in making your judgment?
- Find another article on a similar research topic, but in this case you should agree with the researchers' use of deception as ethically justified. What, specifically, makes the deception of subjects seem ethical? Have you applied the same criteria as you did with the other article?

4. Sociologist Irwin Deutscher (1973) warns that the outcome of much of our theory and research in human studies is a "fiddling with people's lives" (p. 358), no matter how innocent or inoffensive individual research studies may be. Western culture does not lack manipulators willing to fiddle with others' lives. Therefore, theories in such areas as compliance-gaining, behavior modification, and public opinion polling, for example, may be misused by powerful groups seeking to intervene in social sit-

uations or to manipulate people and publics in order to satisfy their own goals.

What, if any, are the ethical responsibilities of the communication researcher seeking to identify interaction outcomes precisely and, perhaps, even predictably? Should such researchers be concerned with the potential misuse of their findings and the consequences for society in general? Or should we let science progress, "letting the chips fall where they may"?

Courtesy of the University of South Florida

discipline, interdiscipline, or field?

"how has communication *become a* respected academic major?"

Were you to trace any life, and study even the minute consequences, the effect, for instance, of a three-minute walk over a patch of grass, of words said casually to a stranger who happens to sit nearby in a public place, the range of that life would extend way beyond the territory we imagine it to inhabit.

SUSAN GRIFFIN, *A CHORUS OF STONES* (1992, p. 151)

The aspects of communication to which scholars attend . . . have blossomed into a rich assortment of intriguing questions for which we continue to seek answers. Answers lead to other questions, pose new problems for future inquiry, and attract the attention of new generations of scholars. The evidence of activity indicates a field of study that is very much alive, maturing, open to different styles and methods of inquiry, and accommodating to a mixture of philosophical perspectives and world views.

DENNIS S. GOURAN, "SPEECH COMMUNICATION AFTER SEVENTY-FIVE YEARS" (1990, p. 27)

We started this book with a concern for questions, and that's how we'll end it. Where will the study of communication take us? How can we describe to others the depth of our interest in learning more about communicating? How can we, as teachers and students, structure this learning in a way that makes sense to our many audiences? Can we readily explain our departments and courses to employers, parents, and people from other college and university units? You see, on almost all campuses and for almost all students, it matters what you choose as a major. Not only is communication study a preparation for a career, but it is inevitably a topic for everyday conversation. Communication majors want to find good ways to explain their choices. You could spend your time explaining theories, but theories are only some of the building blocks of a major subject.

Those theories exist within a context of academic structure and a system of academic expectations, which we'll introduce in this final chapter. Bear in mind that some topics discussed here stimulate many different opinions; your teacher, along with others, may disagree with some of our conclusions. We doubt that most scholars would argue much about the historical facts and trends we summarize, but interpretations of disciplinary status and evaluations of potential for the future are fair game for vigorous debate. This chapter will serve its purpose if it helps create a dialogue in which readers seriously explore and debate fresh positions.

STUDYING COMMUNICATION IN A DISCIPLINED WAY

You are studying a subject that is too complex, by far, to be contained within the boundaries of a limited list of classes. Ranging widely across the sciences, arts, and humanities, it challenges you to learn a variety of concepts, theories, and methods. Communication study is so broad, in fact, that some observers wonder whether it has any content that it can rightly call its own—whether communication should even be considered its own "discipline" of study. From this perspective, communication becomes a function of all disciplines, and needn't be the special focus of any of them. Communication, these observers say, isn't really a discipline but a broad field of interest. Although some observers don't distinguish closely between a *field* and a *discipline,* others stress the distinctive qualities of academic disciplines. A **discipline** in the latter sense is a branch of learning that possesses its own content and relatively distinct curriculum, and that prepares people for well-defined career responsibilities (e.g., engineering, physics, or accounting). A **field**, in contrast, may be defined as a loosely associated group of scholars working on similar problems, but not unified by consistently defined concepts and not necessarily tied to particular career responsibilities. For example, many campuses have cross-disciplinary programs in such fields as International Studies, Women's Studies, and African American Studies.

In some ways, communication—the process of developing shared meaning through messages—should be a part of all other disciplines. Accountants calculate figures, but they also have to communicate about them in order for their work to be meaningful. Astronomers look for and study distant solar systems, but they also have to coordinate their work daily with colleagues. Literature professors read novels in private, but their analyses of the novelists' skills in sketching characters and creating dialogue has to be based on real-life insight into everyday human communication. But if communication is part of everyone else's disciplines, why not let them teach it? Why do we need a separate communication department? Indeed, if one premise of *Questions of Communication* is correct—that communication theory is a broadly based liberal arts endeavor that can't be limited to research from one discipline—why should communication departments need to develop their own identities? Why not let the other disciplines study communication?

Give these questions some careful thought. Although the distinction between *discipline* and *field* appears tidy at first, that may be due primarily to the examples we've chosen. Consider the many other college departments we consider disciplines whose content and concerns cut across the broad intellectual landscape. For example, is psychology not a discipline because researchers in all areas of study have (presumably) developed a capacity for thinking? Does sociology not have a content of its own because humans in all disciplines work in groups? Is management not a discipline because all people manage their decision making? Does biology fail to qualify as a discipline because all human life is comprised of living systems? One prominent critique of the communication discipline created controversy a number of years ago because it was published in the *Chronicle of Higher Education,* a newspaper read by many faculty and almost all college ad-

BOX 11-1

COMMUNICATION AS A DISCIPLINE: VIEWING REALITY THROUGH TWO DIFFERENT LENSES

- "The pre-professional gains nothing . . . from a series of courses in Communication theory, each of which is a replica of the others; one learns only how to become a replica of the teacher. . . . But that's the problem inherent in taking a verb, transforming it into a noun, and calling it an academic discipline. 'Education' is a similar case. The words 'education' and 'communication' define acts, not bodies of knowledge. . . . Communication professors who claim that theory and technique by themselves form a subject matter and constitute a legitimate discipline are reduced not only to studying themselves, but also to testing students on proper pinky placement in their handshakes and awarding college credit to those who have mastered the inflection of 'Uh huh' " (Fischler, 1989, p. A28).

- "Communication, as an academic discipline, bridges the gap between the humanities and the social sciences. It focuses on the study of relationships among open systems, especially the relationships among persons, groups, and cultures, and the factors which influence the forming, changing, maintaining, and terminating of those relationships. Some of these factors are the nature of persons, the nature of groups and of cultures, symbolic discourse in various forms, communication media, and a variety of contexts or environments in which communication occurs. . . . In spite of the fact that communication has been the object of formal study for over two thousand years, there is still much to be learned. Communication in a changing environment with changing participants is not a fixed body of content that one can master, nor a closed system of laws or rules that one can acquire once and for all. Furthermore, advancing technology, cultural changes, increasing human mobility, and the mingling of persons from different socio-cultural backgrounds are placing ever-increasing stresses and strains on human relationships. It is, therefore, imperative that we continue to devote significant attention to this complex process in order to improve the effectiveness of communication, to enhance the quality of life for individuals, and to ensure the survival of the species" (Darnell, 1984, p. 11).

ministrators across the country. In Box 11-1, Alan Fischler (1989) asserts that communication isn't a discipline because its title names an "act" rather than a subject matter. Yet more than a few respected academic units that are typically considered disciplines are labeled in similar ways; management, nursing, and engineering come to mind. Interestingly, Fischler's own department, English, taken literally, is inherently neither a subject matter nor an act, but a language.

We suggest that some disciplines are characterized not only by a particular body of *content* (at least as content is usually defined), but also by a particular focus on *processes*. Many disciplines deal with the content of people talking with other people. In political campaigns, for example, economists follow the arguments closely for fiscal policy implications; doctors listen to the same political rhetoric to gain clues about what will happen in the health-care sphere; generals and admirals want to infer what a new president might do to military expenditure. Many thoughtful people attend to the content of politics, but they may focus on it differently, depending on their perspective. That's what we mean by process: emphasizing the *how* of our looking and the *how* of the relationships we study in addition to the content.

A discipline may be characterized by its unique focus, even if it overlaps other studies. In fact, a discipline might be seen as especially crucial if it has both (1) a well-defined unique focus on process, and (2) obvious threads of relevance stretching out to many other research and career traditions. To us, communication not only qualifies on the basis of these criteria, but also has the potential to become an even stronger contributor to campus life in the future. Perhaps because of the various threads of relevance connecting them to many other studies and professions, such disciplines as communication, English, sociology, and management might better be termed **interdisciplines**.

No one area of study can capture or package the knowledge that links the diverse applications to which we must put our knowledge. For example, economists must know about history, the psychology of consumerism, and the cultural habits of large social groups if they hope to understand the dynamics of a fiscal system. The categories of knowledge have thus begun to overlap as our world becomes more complex. Since all human activities in some ways converge in human interactions, communication might be the most fundamental of the interdisciplines that can respond effectively to an era of dissolving boundaries. In the rest of this chapter, we'll call communication a discipline (a familiar term on campuses), although we believe it best represents an interdiscipline—that special form of discipline that focuses on processes and linkages with other areas of study.

We'd like to help you theorize informally about your connection to communication studies. We suggest you begin to ask questions about the uniqueness of communication studies based on the two factors mentioned previously—focus and relevance. We've divided this final chapter into two main parts: The first part describes the growth and status of communication studies in higher education, and the second discusses several components of what we call "healthy" disciplines. Your class may want to compare perceptions of your communication department's role on campus and in the professional community.

COMMUNICATION DEPARTMENTS IN HIGHER EDUCATION

The communication department is a relative newcomer to colleges and universities in the United States. Its history can be traced by two trends—one emerging from humanistic concerns and the other born in social science. Much of the discipline was solidly influenced by the first trend, which included an emphasis on speech by a few English teachers, who in 1914 created an offshoot organization that later became for many years the Speech Communication Association (and which in 1997 became the National Communication Association). These teachers thought that the education of public speakers demanded different approaches, techniques, and content than what students learned in literature, rhetoric, and composition courses (see Reid, 1990). These scholars, many of whom traced their roots to Aristotle, established speech as a study of historical and critical methods for understanding persuasion in one-to-many public contexts. Later, speech scholars, influenced in part by the work of social psychologists, became interested in less formal face-to-face speaking and listening. Interpersonal communication thus blended the humanistic concerns of psychologists, the group dynamics interests of sociologists and organizational consultants, and the behavioral and quantitative methods of social science.

The discipline was further influenced at midcentury by another group of social researchers who would foresee a wider role for communication emerging from the powerful new electronic media. Their methods were not primarily those of historical or rhetorical criticism, but were developed from the powerful belief that society could be understood in scientific ways. As Cuzzort and King (1989) observed, from about the turn of the century people expressed the optimistic view that ". . . the entire range of human communal activities could be examined scientifically and that such scientific understanding would enable people to achieve better and more ideal social structures. The new society would be as radically rational and as well designed as a modern jetliner" (p. 7).

Scientific communication researchers borrowed concepts and quantitative methods from sociologists (also largely a twentieth-century discipline), from psychologists, from economists, and from other disciplines. (Of course, other disciplines also got their start by borrowing concepts and methods; scientific sociologists borrowed from economists and the natural sciences, psychologists borrowed concepts from philosophers, and political scientists borrowed insights from historians, for example.) Contemporary communication departments stress not only the humanistic principles that characterize English and other performance disciplines but also the systematic and often quantitative methods imported from the social sciences (see Powers, 1995). Later, many communication scholars interested in interpersonal communication primarily borrowed neither rhetorical methods nor methods for studying media effects; they focused instead on how social psychologists, psycholinguists, anthropologists, and other scientists did their work.

All disciplines borrow from other disciplines, or they ought to do so. Ideally, information is shared freely across disciplinary boundaries, without some groups either isolating themselves or marginalizing others. The research enterprise, in other words, is an *open system* (in terms of general systems theory). Yet, serious students wonder, if this is true, who decides how to categorize learning into coursework and students and faculty into departments on campuses?

carving knowledge into slices: who decides?

Coursework at universities everywhere probably has been influenced—historically and at least indirectly—by a system of dividing knowledge into neat and teachable content categories originally inspired by French Renaissance philosopher Peter Ramus. Ramus (see Ong, 1983) believed that all subjects could be categorized so that the content of one would not overlap with the content of others; what teachers need to do is to decide where the boundaries are and then teach the boundaries. You can imagine what this kind of logic, known as *Ramism*, would have to say about the study of what we call interdisciplines.

Traditionally, the faculty of a college or university is given the responsibility to structure the curriculum, which is the range of courses the institution offers. In faculty councils and senates across the country, teachers typically torture each other in lengthy disputes about which programs should be trimmed, or expanded, or even eliminated in any given year. Faculty members monitor their programs through internal and external reviews that are correlated with student needs, "market" patterns, and, perhaps most important, the traditional mission and structure of the academic institution. The twentieth century has seen, by and large, an increasing faculty acceptance of interdisciplinary ventures and an increasing suspicion of older, locked-in categories of learning.

Recently, however, many campuses have adopted a corporate administrative model in which faculty decision making about departments, majors, core curricula, general education, and similar matters has become less central. The trend in the 1990s has been to define campus decisions, even those involving coursework and majors, as administrative or consumer-based functions. Although this book is not the place to debate whether this trend is a good or bad one, students should understand that the shape of their department's offerings does not always reflect the preferences of all the faculty in that department. Occasionally, college and university administrations will combine or merge areas of study based on financial reasons or reasons of efficiency.

Thus, for a variety of reasons, communication departments are labeled differently. A few reflect a long-standing reliance on concepts and labels of Rhetoric. Others call themselves Speech Communication, reflecting a merged identity with a continued reliance on spoken symbolic interaction. Still others are known as Media Studies, Mass Communication, or Journalism departments. Recently, we've seen an expansion of departments (and even "schools" and "colleges") designated simply with the label Communication. Such blended departments, whether they're a result of a genuine appreciation of the overall interdiscipline or are simply enforced by administrators, emphasize what communicators have in common, whether the relationships they study are interpersonal, rhetorical, or mass mediated.

communication studies departments and majors

Certainly not all departments of communication are equally popular, effective, or useful. Yet in many ways they are all part of one of the great U.S. academic success stories of the century. In the academic year 1973–1974 (just after one of your authors started his university teaching career), U.S. colleges and universities awarded to communication students just over 17,000 bachelor's degrees, about 2,600 master's degrees, and 175 doctorates. The number of degrees has increased almost every year since then, so that in 1991–1992 communication students earned over 54,000 bachelor's degrees, over 4,100 master's degrees, and over 250 doctorates (SCA, 1995, p. 4). If you'd like to compare this growth with a somewhat similar academic discipline, consider that sociology granted about 36,000 bachelor's degrees in 1970 but only about 14,000 in 1993 (Rogers & Chaffee, 1993, p. 124).

Communication departments are now well established in most of the country's major universities and in the full range of public and private institutions at all levels. Communication students in these departments successfully prepare themselves for careers in advertising, education, the electronic media, journalism, public relations, the performing arts, and a wide range of private and government organizations.

A HEALTHY DISCIPLINE

It's hard to know how to gauge the health of a system—like a discipline or inter-discipline—that is so much larger than yourself, since your own perspective is, by definition, limited. Maybe the best you can hope for is to sample a wide variety of experiences within a system. As authors, we represent some of that variety. One of us started college right out of high school, whereas the other began college as a "mature student" after a series of successful job experiences. One of us attended a massive university, whereas the other started at a community college. We have taught at mid-sized state universities, large public research universities, a private research-based university, and a small Christian liberal arts college. Both of us define ourselves first as teachers and learners, then as writers and researchers. But we've also participated at almost all levels of university governance—directing programs, chairing departments and committees, and managing a radio station, among other duties. In addition, we've received a vivid education by talking with a wide range of students and colleagues about their experiences at different schools.

What follows, then, is an idiosyncratic but—we hope—realistic and accurate explanation of why we are optimistic about the discipline of communication. We basically respond to these kinds of questions: Where did we come from? Who are our intellectual neighbors? What do we study? What is our future? (See Box 11-2.)

BOX 11-2

A HEALTHY DISCIPLINE:

- Knows its *past* (it is aware of its own history).
- Knows its *neighbors* (it understands its pathways to related disciplines and how it is interdependent with them).
- Knows its *content* (it understands its distinctive core concepts).
- Knows its *potential* (it anticipates a productive future for itself).

knowing your past: a discipline that charts its history

Now that you have a sketchy impression about how communication departments got started, perhaps you're curious about more of the historical context for your learning.

Mark Twain is reputed to have observed, at about age eighteen, that his father was quite ignorant. At age twenty-one, Twain was more independent and amazed at how much his father had learned in just three years. One mark of maturity in adolescence seems to be the realistic recognition of how much the person understands relative to the wisdom of those who came before. Typically, young teenagers are not interested in genealogy or even in an informal family history, but beginning in the college years, adults express more curiosity about their roots, asking, "Where do I come from?"

A similar process occurs in institutions and academic disciplines. As they mature, they find themselves more realistically curious about and aware of where they came from and how they must rely on others. In individuals or institutions, *differentiation* is the process of developing uniqueness in the context of recognizing one's dependence on larger patterns (Lewin, 1951). Academic disciplines experience a differentiation that also recognizes how they depend on their own history while they're interdependent with those other influential groups. In this section and the following one, we chart some of these influences and give you other sources so you can follow your own curiosities.

The communication discipline is now actively charting its own history, as noted earlier in this chapter. Generally, that history reflects originally separated, but now increasingly merged, humanistic and social scientific concerns. This doesn't mean, of course, that each researcher or each department emphasizes qualitative, critical, and traditional social science research equally, as you will discover later in this chapter and later in your coursework.

We don't have the space in this book to summarize all of the projects that attempt to trace the history of communication departments and research traditions. We can, however, recommend several sources to you. Most of them bemoan the fact that we've so far been largely unreflective about our history; however, the fact that so many questions are being asked now is surely a good sign. For an overall comparison of the different strains of communication studies, see Delia's (1987) extensive and detailed summary or Pearce and Foss's (1990) more succinct account. If you're more curious about the rhetorical and humanistic origins of the side of communication studies that's usually associated with speech, you may want to start with Herman Cohen's *The History of Speech Communication: The Emergence of a Discipline, 1914–1945* (1994), Work and Jeffrey's (1989) brief anthology published at the seventy-fifth anniversary of the Speech Communication Association, and Loren Reid's (1990) informal account of his own contributions to, and perceptions of, how a discipline interested in elocution and speech performance has matured into a discipline of teachers and researchers of communication. Communication scholars have long staked their territorial claims to include both the practical and the theoretical; more recently, they have also examined how the distinction between practice and theory may be somewhat artificial.

 L I N K

Chapter 6 discusses the thinking behind a dialectical approach to interpersonal communication. Does the process of maturation which involves both differentiation (establishing a unique identity) and interdependence (relying on others to help shape identity and expecting that reliance in return)—seem to reflect a dialectical process? Why or why not?

Some scholars believe the discipline of communication gathered crucial prestige in the academic and political worlds when media systems began to be researched scientifically at midcentury. The foremost account of this social science strain of communication studies is Everett Rogers's *A History of Communication Study: A Biographical Approach* (1994). Interestingly, as Craig (1995) points out, Rogers's book overlaps only slightly with Cohen's history—even though they were published in the same year and even though the departments in which they'll be read are finding their concerns overlapping more and more.

knowing your neighbors: a discipline of connections, not boundaries

Although communication is a function in all disciplines, not all other disciplines are equally relevant for communication researchers and teachers. This can be illustrated by our own personal experience. Your authors have given presentations on communication on various campuses for students in management, psychology, physics, theology, education, sociology, and accounting departments, among others. We have enjoyed these talks and workshops immensely, and built a wide variety of satisfying friendships and professional relationships through them. Everyone, whatever their disciplinary affiliation, profits from improved communication. Some of the students and faculty members we've met correctly assumed that communication scholars would be unlikely to borrow basic concepts from them (e.g., accounting techniques are unlikely to be a source of conceptual insight for communication scholars, even though the accounting profession would be a good site for applied communication studies). However, others assumed *incorrectly* that we wouldn't be interested in their research and theories. Perhaps they thought we were only interested in the performance aspects of speaking or in the "hardware" of media technology. Or, in other words, perhaps they thought we weren't theorizing about what we study.

However, as you've seen throughout this book, communication scholars have always been interested in applying ideas from other specialists. Some critics call this "borrowing," perhaps suggesting a derivative status. But academic borrowing is not unique to communication, nor is it a shortcoming. Rather, it's a necessary academic habit in the contemporary world. In fact, communication as a discipline with permeable conceptual territories represents well the contemporary social condition that Clifford Geertz (1983) calls *blurred genres*. Geertz notes that it's getting harder to separate fields of knowledge because, for example, philosophy often resembles literary criticism, science writing resembles personalized essays, history resembles fiction (and vice versa), "parables pos[e] as ethnographies," "ideological arguments [are] cast as historiographical inquiries," and so on (p. 20). Moreover, working with ideas in interdisciplinary ways creates fresh forms of knowledge. As Geertz (1983) writes:

> What Clyde Kluckhohn once said about anthropology—that it's an intellectual poaching license—not only seems more true now than when he said it, but true of a lot more than anthropology. Born omniform, the social sciences prosper as the condition I have been describing becomes general.

> It has thus dawned on social scientists that they did not need to mimic physi-
> cists or closet humanists or to invent some new realm of being to serve as the
> object of their investigations. Instead they could proceed with their vocation,
> trying to discover order in collective life. . . . (p. 21)

When Geertz says that the social sciences were "born omniform," he means that
versatility and flexibility in moving among many disciplinary forms is part of the
identity of such disciplines. They thrive on pluralistic views.

Thus, as communication theorists, we try to know our closest scholarly
neighbors and to monitor what they consider important, even as we proceed with
our own work. Probably the neighbors closest to our current work are the social
sciences of anthropology, sociology, political science, and psychology; the humanities of philosophy, history, and literary criticism and composition studies in
English; and the professional applied disciplines that acknowledge communication research, such as education, management, social work, nursing, and law.

While scholars naturally borrow concepts, they simultaneously adjust those
ideas to fit the unique demands of a particular focus on the communicative relationship. Rarely is a theory or research tool simply imported by itself; instead, it
is utilized in a new way, tinged with new meaning, applied to fresh problems.

The borrowing goes both ways. Increasingly, scholars who teach in communication departments are cited in the wider academic and popular discussion of
politics and social policy. Rhetorical concepts have a widening influence in such
fields as the philosophy of science, economics, and international diplomacy. Communication scholars and their research are becoming widely quoted in other disciplines and in popular media treatments of public problems: Kathleen Jamieson
and Roderick Hart on political campaigning and media advertising, Molefi Asante
on Afrocentric theory, Cheris Kramerae on gender-based power relations, George
Gerbner on violence in the media, Lawrence Grossberg and Michael Eric Dyson
on cultural theory and criticism, and James Carey and Jay Rosen on the public responsibilities of journalism.

knowing your content: a discipline with core concepts

Any attempt to isolate basic ideas in a discipline as diverse as communication
seems a bit presumptuous at best and perhaps misleading at worst. Surely, important aspects of communication will be left out. However, some scholars have
been bold enough to attempt such a difficult task. In a recent essay, Stamp, Vangelisti, and Knapp (1994) explain why four concepts are especially "foundational"
for communication theorists in distinguishing a communication-based approach
from the approaches of other disciplines. Although they intend for their discussion to apply especially to interpersonal communication research, we see their
concepts of *meaning, relationship, process,* and *context* as also characterizing the discipline as a whole. In many ways, these have been recurrent themes in *Questions
of Communication* as well. Summarizing them here may help you put the entire
study of communication theory into a distinctive perspective.

meaning.   Communication theorists are especially interested in the question of where meaning is generated in human experience, and where it could be said to reside. Communication theorists, teachers, and researchers tend to assume that meanings are not the possession of a single person, but are "negotiated phenomena" that "do not belong to [persons]," and are "pluralistic endeavors negotiated by participants within their relationship" (Stamp, Vangelisti, & Knapp, 1994, p. 170). This is not to say that individuals don't have unique experiences, but that meaning (as communication scholars tend to use the term) is not simply a psychological or cognitive phenomenon. Further, most communication theorists do not imagine messages as containing meanings but as evoking meanings when understood in relationships. Therefore . . .

relationship.   The unit of analysis for a communication theorist generally is not the individual person, even though individual behavior is often studied. Instead, the acts of persons are consistently thought to be characteristics of the relationships in which the persons are involved, rather than mere expressions of innate tendencies or self-contained personalities. To communication theorists, it isn't very interesting or conceptually helpful to ask "What kind of person is she?" or "How does he act?" Rather, communication perspectives would reflect a curiosity about how he acts when he finds himself within a support group, or how she processes media messages on the evening news or in clothing ads, or how her presence affects others' talk. Relationships are hard to study, however, because they won't stand still for you to analyze them; they're always shifting in some way.

process.   Therefore, communication theorists are as interested in social structures and enduring institutions and organizations as other social scientists might be. They are as interested in rhetorical texts, such as speeches and documents, as literary critics might be. One aspect of the culture of communication inquiry over the past forty years, however, has been the emerging recognition that such phenomena cannot be viewed as static or immune to the influences of time. The process concept reminds scholars to look for evidence of change and changingness in whatever studies they conduct. We understand that today's IBM might resemble the "same" company we studied last year, but that subtle changes have affected its internal communication. When people talk—or read or write or listen—their communication changes them. In other words, the existing communication forms the basis for interpreting new communication messages.

context.   Therefore, no message can be understood apart from the context in which it is interpreted. Contexts could include the physical surroundings within which we communicate, the temporal aspect of interaction, the relational expectations within which we interpret each other's behavior, the influence of background messages (often nonverbal) in any relationship, and the number of people present, among many other factors. The tradition of communication scholarship stresses context so much that it is often frustrating to our students, our trainees, or our clients in consulting relationships. We are asked questions like these: "What do I do when I lose my place in presenting my speech?" and "How do I talk to my father?" There are no good answers to such questions without asking other questions. You've lost your place in the speech, but who is your audience? Is your previous relationship with your audience informal or formal? What time of day is it? What is the seriousness of your task? Why are people listening to you? People who don't understand the impact of context often assume that communication teachers are indecisive or nit-picking when they're unwilling to give a quick answer to subtle problems. They don't understand that context is for many communication experts a core concept of the discipline, one that can't be ignored.

knowing your potential: a discipline that anticipates a future

The future seems secure, at least in one sense, for a theoretically sophisticated discipline or interdiscipline of communication. If communication departments continue to explore and integrate theories emerging from data-based social science research and theories of meaning and ethical judgment from the humanities, blending them with respect for both qualitative and quantitative studies, the academic and professional worlds will listen carefully to us. Communication scholars and departments can make solid cases for their contributions. But this doesn't mean that the future of communication studies will remain unquestioned.

For example, the future of the discipline has been interrogated by a few administrators who assume that effective communicators in any given field can teach and research communication effectively enough, making departments of communication dispensable. Although this is hardly a nationwide trend, a few instances of departments being threatened by their administrators have left some students, faculty, and alumni agitated.

A second—and more healthy—form of questioning the future can be seen in the journals and books of the field. There we find a wide variety of clashing opinions about what shape that future should take. We regard this as healthy because out of this dialogue and its different visions will come a future that is tested and usefully challenged as it develops. We find regular examples of this dialogue in the vigorous discussions of the nature of the discipline in its journals (for example, see the two-issue *Journal of Communication* investigation titled "The Future of the Field—Between Fragmentation and Cohesion" [1993]). Because scholars disagree strongly, it's impossible to predict outcomes at this time. For example, some might deny the premise of this chapter—that communication should claim a disciplinary status, although Powers (1995) cites a study that concludes "the preponderance of communication professionals . . . believe we are already a discipline, and even more believe that we should be considered one" (p. 213). Some faculty want a blended approach to departments, while others want to retain the special character of a speech/rhetorical or a journalism emphasis. All we can feel safe in predicting is that the study of communication will be stronger for having had these kinds of discussions.

In our senior-level capstone classes, we remind students that the image they currently hold about who and where they'll be five or ten years into their career will shape in subtle ways the career they actually create during that time. If a female public relations student, for example, believes that the field is too low-paying, or too limiting in its opportunities for women, then that perception will affect the kinds of jobs she'll apply for, and thus will change her actual future. Quite apart from the realities of her perceptions (pay *can* be low at times and there *is* a residual sexism in many organizations), she will enfold her expectations into the realities of her jobs. Perhaps she'll limit herself too much. If a classmate has a different perception, her experience probably will become different, and perhaps more successful.

So it is with academic life. If communication teachers and students sit around wringing their hands wondering about how respected they are by others, this itself affects how we're seen. It affects how we're treated, too. How we talk about ourselves influences what we'll become. We talk ourselves into the future. The discipline of communication is alive and well, and certainly healthy enough to create a healthy rhetorical future.

With what you've learned in this book, we hope you'll feel more confident in entering the conversation of a vital, a vigorous, and an important discipline of study. We hope also that you're beginning to build the personal discipline to study it well, whatever direction it will take you.

Our final question for you: Which questions do you want to ask next?

TESTING THE CONCEPTS

"Even though I may know more about theories, and even more about the history of the communication discipline, how will this help me get a job?"

So many variables factor into job searches that it's impossible to cite only one as the crucial factor. Knowing the shape—and the theoretical status—of your own discipline is one issue, among many others, that will impress potential employers. Your writing and speaking skills are also important, but employers usually don't make their decisions on those bases alone, either, because so many applicants are good writers and speakers. Employers want to know if you're a curious and persistent learner who'll continue to make contributions to the organization. Some of our former students have returned to tell us that employment interviewers often ask questions like "Why did you choose to major in communication?" If your answer to this question is a thin "I don't know; it just seemed interesting" or "I'm a people person," you'll undercut your chances.

If you want to know more about career possibilities in communication, we recommend you read the latest edition of *Pathways to Careers in Communication*, a booklet published by the National Communication Association (the latest version appeared in 1995). Single copies of the booklet are available for $2 from the NCA, 5105 Backlick Road, Building E, Annandale, VA, 22003; multiple copies are discounted.

YOU, THE RESEARCHER

1. Look through past issues of three different communication journals, and find four articles that define the discipline of communication. In what ways do the authors advance similar positions? Or do they argue for different positions? How do you think these disciplinary disputes could affect you as a student, directly or indirectly? Your teacher may want you to discuss these questions in class.

2. Brainstorm with a group of other students to identify three questions you still have about the discipline or about national organizations within the communication professions. Access the National Communication Association's homepage on the World Wide Web: <*http://www.scassn.org*>. Try to find the answers to your questions either on the NCA's page or by tracking its links to other Web sites.

3. Interview five professors outside of the communication department. Ask them to define the discipline of communication or to describe what the communication department on your campus focuses on in its teaching. How are these professors' definitions similar or different? How do their definitions compare to your definition of the discipline?

4. At the library, obtain copies of catalogs from several other colleges and universities in your state or region. If possible, choose one catalog for each of the following types of institutions:

   - A community college (e.g., St. Louis Community College at Florissant Valley, Arapahoe Community College)
   - A small or mid-sized liberal arts college or university (e.g., University of St. Thomas, DePauw University)
   - A mid-sized state university (e.g., University of Northern Iowa, Central Connecticut State University)
   - A large research-oriented private university (e.g., Stanford University, Columbia University)
   - A large research-oriented public university (e.g., University of Arizona, University of Minnesota)

   Compare the catalog pages for the communication departments. Note: (a) how the department names differ, (b) how the departments describe the rationale for their programs, and (c) the kinds of required and elective coursework they offer. How do you explain the diversity of courses you find? What courses or areas of study seem to be especially common?

g l o s s a r y

an "access vocabulary" in communication theory

Several basic questions helped us decide what should be included in this glossary: Which terms are most important for beginning students as they prepare to enter the conversation in communication theory? When professionals and academics in communication talk about theory and research, which terms do they tend to use again and again? Which general concepts used in this book might be unnecessarily intimidating or mysterious to undergraduate students?

We realize that many faculty members who teach communication theory would create somewhat different lists, and surely our brief definitions will leave out important facets of some concepts. Some terms, too, seem to resist a definition that would be both reasonably accurate yet accessible enough for new readers in communication. We decided that we should not attempt to present concepts in as much detail and as specifically as subject-matter specialists would, but that we should provide for each term a conceptual handle that, if grasped, would give students preliminary "access" to the kind of research interests suggested by the label. Neither do we attempt to include definitions for all of the terms highlighted in the text, many of which are specialized concepts of particular theories and, we hope, sufficiently clarified in the context of those descriptions.

In addition to basic concepts in communication theory that might be found in any text, we've included a number of terms used somewhat uniquely in *Questions of Communication,* and that are unlikely to be found in most other treatments of communication theory. Many come from associated disciplines, and through them, we hope to encourage a broadly based liberal arts climate for studying theory. Taking a communication theory course is an especially inviting opportunity to notice how interconnected your studies can be.

access theory suggests that online communication habits subtly move us farther away from "directedness," transfer, or conduit assumptions about mediated communication. An access approach foregrounds the availability of many kinds of computer-mediated messages that aren't literally "sent to us" and emphasizes the active choices of communicators who were often conceived of previously as "receivers."

action assembly theory explains the cognitive process by which persons transform inner plans into communication behaviors. Representative theorist: Greene.

actional view of behavior assumes that behavior is attributable to active choices of persons, as opposed to being caused by outside forces acting on persons. See also *motional view of behavior.*

Afrocentricity places "African ideals at the center of any analysis that involves African culture and behaviors" (Asante, 1987, p. 6). Afrocentric theorists often contrast their concepts with Eurocentric tendencies to explain cultural phenomena only in terms of standards developed within traditional European art, science, literature, and philosophy. Representative theorist: Asante.

agenda-setting theory examines how mass media outlets' choice of stories and content "sets the table" for public talk, creating the prime information for public policy and entertainment. Media producers, therefore, are communication "gatekeepers," and the issues and stories they present (only a small fraction of the stories available) automatically provide a social and cultural "agenda" to which the public must respond.

articulation theory studies how ideas and cultural concepts are linked together through public discussion into complex clusters of meaning, which then appear to be unified and whole. Articulation in this approach suggests connectedness, in addition to its more common contemporary American meaning of the ability to verbalize. Representative theorist: S. Hall.

believing game the choice of approaching new information by assuming it has value and is sensible in the context of its authors or other communicators. Representative theorist: Elbow. See also *doubting game.*

borderlands describes physical and social regions where people's identities are affected by a blend of communication expectations originating on both sides of a given cultural border. Representative theorists: Anzaldúa; Rosaldo.

channel a medium or route through which a message is sent for the purpose of communication.

cognition the overall process of mind, including thinking, perceiving, judging, and consciousness.

cognitive consistency theory explains the means by which persons maintain inner balance, congruence, or consistency among attitudes, opinions, and beliefs. Representative theorists: Heider; Festinger; Osgood.

communication the mutual process through which persons interpret messages in order to coordinate individual and social meanings.

communitarian ethics emphasizes an ethical standard that elevates community good and community coherence above individual rights. Representative theorists: Christians, Ferré, and Fackler; Etzioni; Glendon. See also *narrative ethics.*

compliance-gaining the process of achieving—through promises, threats, or other interpersonal means—the assent, agreement, or cooperation of others. Representative theorists: Marwell and Schmitt.

concept a process labeled and categorized by scholars in order to study it more effectively; a concept (e.g., attitude) may have no tangible existence of its own, but is useful as an explanatory tool if theorists remain aware of the nature of the abstraction.

conduit metaphor the persistent bias within the English language toward assuming communication is a transmission of meanings "contained" in words sent from "senders" to "receivers." Representative theorists: Reddy; Lakoff and Johnson.

consistency theory see *cognitive consistency theory.*

constructivism a theoretical perspective explaining communication as a fundamentally interpretive process through which persons organize and create personal reality. It examines the complexity with which persons develop and organize different categories of perception called "constructs." Representative theorists: Kelly; Delia.

context in the study of communication situations, all features that frame or surround an analyzed object or event in time or space.

coordinated management of meaning (CMM) theory describes communication as persons' mutual attempts to blend or negotiate individualized rules and meanings in order to achieve coordination in their relationship. Representative theorists: Pearce and Cronen.

covering laws see *laws (covering laws) approach.*

critical theory explains and critiques social communication by examining the implications of power relationships; Marxist and feminist scholars usually approach theorizing with these assumptions. Often identified with cultural studies approaches. Representative theorists: Williams; Kramerae. See also *cultural studies.*

cross-cultural adaptation theory studies how individuals learn to reorient their communication assumptions when they become strangers in unfamiliar cultural systems. Representative theorist: Kim.

cultivation theory (cultivation analysis) explains media, especially television, not in cause-effect terms, but by describing the longer-term tendencies of audiences to adjust their expectations about reality in the direction of prevalent media content. Representative theorist: Gerbner.

cultural studies a broadly based approach to studying communication through its cultural implications; often studies in this tradition adopt the tone of social commentary or criticism; closely identified with critical theory. Representative theorists: Carey; Grossberg; S. Hall. See also *critical theory*.

cultural syndromes the tendencies or patterns developed within cultures to organize communicators' behaviors. Examples include complexity syndrome (complication of relational patterns), individualism syndrome (extent of reliance on individual rights), collectivism syndrome (extent of conformity with larger social groups), tightness syndrome (extent of behavior regulation through norms and roles). Representative theorist: Triandis.

culture a "set of human-made objective and subjective elements" shared by a group, and developed so that these persons might communicate more effectively and efficiently with each other (based on a definition by Triandis, 1994).

deontological ethics a philosophy that relies on duties and principles as bases for making ethical decisions.

dependency theory stresses the interdependent relationships among media, audiences, and social structures. Analyzes audiences' cognitive, affective, and behavioral dependencies on media information. Representative theorists: DeFleur and Ball-Rokeach.

dialectical theory examines how relationships develop from the interplay of perceived opposite forces or contradictions (e.g., autonomy/connection, openness/closedness, predictability/

novelty), and how communicators negotiate these ever-changing processes. Representative theorists: Baxter; Rawlins.

dialogic ethics advocates such conditions as open consideration of ideas, authenticity, and a caring respect for otherness as criteria for ethical communication. Representative theorists: Buber; Habermas; Noddings.

dialogue a condition of quality communication in which each partner respects the uniqueness of the other, and does not seek to predetermine outcomes of the interchange; the basic reality of human existence is assumed to be in "the between" of the relationship rather than in psychological variables. Representative theorists: Buber; Gadamer; Rogers.

discipline (academic) a group of teachers and learners sharing a common focus on the human condition. For example, the discipline of communication may be said to focus on the relationships and relational messages through which persons share meanings. Psychology, although its concerns overlap with those of communication, tends to focus on mind and mental or emotional processes and their effects on human behavior. Clearly, both deal with communication, and both deal with psychological processes—but their interests often tend to be different. See also *field*.

discourse ethics attempts to ground dialogue in a form of rational communication by which consensus about public problems can be reached. This involves trying to structure an *ideal speech situation* in which communicators have equal access to the sphere of public discourse, and procedurally equal opportunities to test arguments within the dialogue. Representative theorist: Habermas.

doubting game approaching new information by noting and analyzing its flaws, deficiencies, and inadequacies. Representative theorist: Elbow. See also *believing game*.

dramatistic pentad see *pentad*.

dramaturgical theory explains how human interaction can resemble theatrical and dramatic conventions in its reliance on impressions, roles, and performances. Representative theorists: Burke; Goffman.

dyad a two-person communication system.

egalitarian ethics relies on the criterion of human equality as a basis for making ethical decisions.

elaborated code communicators using elaborated codes supply a great deal of information, assuming message receivers do not necessarily have sufficient context or background for understanding. Representative theorist: Bernstein. See also *restricted code.*

ethics the value-based consideration of right and wrong in deciding how to frame communication messages.

ethnomethodology investigates the everyday sense-making rules of persons by violating their expectations of normality. Representative theorist: Garfinkel.

feedback any message that aids a communicator in evaluating the success of previous messages.

feminine ethic grounds ethical decision making in the particulars of caring relationships rather than in the principles and duties of deontological ethics. Although exceptions are common, relational engrossment is identified by Noddings with feminine styles, while attention to ethical duty and obligation tends to represent masculine styles. Representative theorist: Noddings.

feminist theory explains communication variables (e.g., language, nonverbal immediacy, media effects, and ethics) from the perspective of gender relationships; it often focuses on overt and covert power implications of cultural patterns. Representative theorists: Belenky et al.; Gilligan; Kramerae; Lakoff.

field (academic) a loose affiliation of scholars broadly interested in studying similar phenomena; a field is often contrasted with a discipline, which presumes a well-defined focus on specific content or processes. See also *discipline.*

FIRO theory explains the role of the human needs of inclusion, control, and affection in in-terpersonal communication. Representative theorist: Schutz.

gender a cultural and social concept based on how people talk about different kinds of male and female behavior; often, but not necessarily, related to the biological condition of sex.

general systems theory (GST) describes living systems by referring to the interdependence of their components and relationships among components. Representative theorists: Bertalanffy; Fisher.

generative theory explains a physiological basis for "deep structures" of language, regarding language as inherent in the human brain. Representative theorist: Chomsky.

golden mean, principle of suggests the avoidance of extreme positions ("vices") of deficiency and excess in the consideration of ethical decision making. Representative theorist: Aristotle.

hermeneutics investigates the interpretation of texts; in one form popularized by Gadamer, hermeneutics emphasizes the historical and inherently linguistic nature of experience in denying a transmissional model of communication. Representative theorist: Gadamer.

high-context (HC) culture emphasizes message processing in which relatively little meaning is obvious in explicit content and communicators are expected to rely heavily on context to interpret possible meanings. Representative theorist: E. T. Hall. See also *low-context (LC) culture.*

hypodermic needle approach see *magic bullet theory.*

hypothesis a tentative statement of expectation.

ideology a system of ideas so thoroughly accepted that communicators don't question its existence, validity, or importance.

immediacy theory demonstrates how persons signal the emotional responses of attraction, dominance, and arousal through nonverbal and verbal messages related to physical closeness; for examples, eye contact and movement toward another, indicators of immediacy, are correlated with desires for increased involvement. Representative theorist: Mehrabian.

inner speech theory a generalized perspective emphasizing the importance of language in cognitive information processing, the development of self, the anticipation of dialogue, and the like. Representative theorists: Bakhtin; Dance; Vygotsky.

interdiscipline (academic) a group of teachers and learners sharing a common focus on the human condition, but which simultaneously emphasizes its reliance on, and relevance to, a wide variety of other scholarly groups and disciplines. Compare with *discipline,* a more common designation. This book presumes that communication is both a discipline and an interdiscipline (see Chapter 11).

language a socially agreed-upon code by which objects and relationships in the world are symbolized.

laws (covering laws) approach searches for macroscopic, highly generalizable, and relatively invariant principles that apply across many different types of communicators and situations. See also *rules* and *general systems theory.*

linguistic relativity theory explains how the language of a culture affects (or, in the strong version of the theory, determines) the way a culture defines reality. Representative theorist: Whorf.

low-context (LC) culture relies less on context for understanding than on explicitly stated messages. Representative theorist: E. T. Hall. See also *high-context (HC) culture.*

magic bullet theory influential early perspective on media effects; held that media caused direct and measurable effects in individuals in the mass audience.

marketplace of ideas ethics advocates the open exchange of, and access to, divergent ideas in order to compare "good reasons" within a democratic climate. Representative theorists: Haiman; Wallace.

meaning the patterns humans create out of their interpretation of experience.

mediated place, theory of explains how electronic media alter the human experience of "place" by blurring traditional distinctions between public and private spheres. Representative theorist: Meyrowitz.

message a stimulus to which meanings are attributed in communication.

metacommunication the process of communicating about communication.

model a verbal or pictorial description or representation of a process.

motional view of behavior assumes that behavior is caused, or set "in motion," by outside forces—as opposed to being actively chosen from within persons. See also *actional view of behavior.*

muted group theory studies how women's voices can be "silenced" by the political dominance of men's interpersonal perceptions and behaviors. Representative theorists: S. Ardener; Kramerae.

narrative ethics locates ethical decision making in the context of group and community experience of common "stories," rather than within the traditional dictates of experts or logical rationality; narrative ethics elevates the consideration of values in the development of a "narrative rationality." Representative theorist: Fisher. See also *communitarian ethics.*

noise internal or external interference with the sending and receiving of messages.

nommo a reverence for the generative and spiritual power of the spoken word within Afrocentric theorizing.

organizational culture the communication habits, norms, and values within an organization that give it a distinct identity; this process is analogous to how larger cultures are distinguished by their unique patterns of social communication.

para-social interaction the tendency of some audience members to identify with media figures (celebrities, fictional characters) as though an interpersonal relationship had been established. Representative theorists: Horton and Wohl.

pentad, dramatistic a means of analyzing rhetoric in context by looking at five factors (pentad): act (what was done), scene (where it was done), agent (by whom it was done), agency (with what means it was done), and purpose (the goal that guided the action). Representative theorist: Burke.

perception the process by which an organism assimilates, interprets, and uses sensory data.

person-centered approach a dialogically based approach to interpersonal communication emphasizing genuine concern for the messages and self-concept of the other person; involves empathy, congruent behavior, and acceptance of the other's experience. Representative theorist: C. Rogers.

persuasion the communication process in which persons influence others' opinions, attitudes, beliefs, and actions. Communication scholars often, but not inevitably, study persuasion as an intentional process of affecting target audiences.

phenomenology the "study of phenomena, of things or events, in the everyday world . . . from the viewpoint of the experiencing person" (Becker, 1992, p. 7).

play theory explains how audiences use media messages to reinforce a tendency toward free choice and "subjective play." Representative theorist: Stephenson.

polysemy a characteristic of language through which multiple alternate meanings may be available at any one time for a message or set of messages.

postmodernism a theoretical position contesting the modernist view that reality is measurable and verifiable, that causes and effects can be specified, that meanings are stable and capable of being transmitted, and that science or other institutions can clarify the human condition rationally. Various versions of postmodern theory assume instead that meanings are contingent, transitory, and often contradictory, and that no grand narrative or story—including science—is capable of unifying the human experience. Representative theorists: Derrida; Lyotard.

praxis the interdependent unity of theory and practice. Theory that is practical becomes practice that is theoretically sound.

principle of the golden mean See *golden mean, principle of.*

process the condition of constant, dynamic change.

qualitative research investigation by which the qualities of phenomena are discovered, observed, described, and analyzed; some forms may be referred to as "naturalistic" or "interpretive" methods. See also *quantitative research.*

quantitative research investigation by which units of phenomena are isolated, measured, counted, and analyzed. See also *qualitative research.*

race a set of social distinctions based on how persons link, rightly or wrongly, cultural patterns of human communication to visible physical features such as skin color. Race, once thought to be a biologically inherited characteristic, has become increasingly suspect in recent years as a valid scientific concept.

reflection-in-action the constant adjustment of a communicator's theories while he or she is involved in practical interaction. It is based on a willingness to engage in an ongoing process of practical "research" from moment to moment, rather than relying on techniques. Representative theorist: Schön.

relational culture the phenomenon by which each interpersonal relationship develops many of the same kinds of patterns and features as do larger cultures. Representative theorist: Wood.

research question asks about what relationships between behaviors or processes could be found by doing a focused investigation.

restricted code speakers and listeners using *restricted codes* tend to believe they already have specialized verbal assumptions in common (e.g., specialized or workplace jargon) and therefore don't need to verbalize as much information in order to achieve understanding. Representative theorist: Bernstein. See also *elaborated code.*

rhetoric the study of communication messages designed to affect specific listeners or readers in particular ways.

rules theory explains the usually implicit understandings persons develop for how to act and speak in social situations. Representative theorists: Ganz; Garfinkel; Shimanoff.

semantics the study of the patterns of meaning within a language.

semiotics the study of how signs (an overall term for both symbolic and nonsymbolic signal messages) in human environments form patterns or codes within which people come to understand their daily lives. Representative theorists: Barthes; Eco; Leeds-Hurwitz; Peirce.

social exchange theory investigates how interaction is guided by the desire to maximize communication profits and rewards while minimizing communication losses and costs. Representative theorists: Blau; Roloff; Thibaut and Kelley.

social judgment theory explains attitude change as a process of evaluating messages in relation to an individual's ego-involvement in a topic and latitudes or categories of acceptable or unacceptable positions. Representative theorist: Sherif.

speech act theory studies how speech is essentially performative; that is, although words are often assumed in everyday life to be separate from actions, speech act theorists assume the opposite—that by saying words, we are really performing certain actions, such as vowing, promising, or nominating. Representative theorist: Searle.

spiral of silence theory explains how public opinion can minimize social expression of minority opinion while exaggerating the power of the majority. Representative theorist: Noelle-Neumann.

symbolic convergence theory explains how communicators cooperatively build shared fantasy themes to account for and order their common experience. Representative theorist: Bormann.

symbolic interactionism accounts for the development of self through the processes of social communication and symbolization, and through the relation of self to mind and society. Representative theorists: Blumer; Goffman; Kuhn; Mead.

system See *general systems theory (GST)*.

Taoist ethic a transactional philosophy that generally advocates allowing processes of communication to develop "naturally," avoiding interference or the artificial manipulation of results.

teleological ethics a philosophy that relies on an assessment of consequences and the "greater good" for the greater number of people as a criterion for making ethical decisions; also known as a "consequentialist" position.

theory a tentative but usually systematic explanation for a problematic situation; an educated guess open to change.

transaction a relationship in which each party simultaneously defines, and is defined by, the other. Representative theorists: Dewey and Bentley.

two-step flow theory asserts that media effects on audiences are not direct, but are influenced by the interpersonal communication of opinion leaders. An extension of this theory emphasized the many complex levels of the process, becoming known as the *multi-step flow theory*. Representative theorists: Katz and Lazarsfeld.

uncertainty reduction theory assumes that a basic motivation for communicators is to use interpersonal information to predict communication outcomes more accurately. Representative theorist: Berger.

uses and gratifications theory explains how media audiences use media content for their own gratifications and purposes. Major theorists: Blumler and Katz.

variable an object of study that can be measured quantitatively.

virtue ethics a philosophy that encourages communicators to adhere to the moral qualities that presumably enhance public life (e.g., justice, courage, gentleness, and wisdom). Representative theorist: Aristotle. See also *golden mean, principle of*.

references

Abelson, R. P. (1967). Modes of resolution of belief dilemmas. In M. Fishbein (Ed.), *Readings in attitude theory and measurement* (pp. 349–356). New York: Wiley.

Achebe, C. (1959/1969). *Things fall apart*. New York: Fawcett.

Acker, S. R. (1989). Designing communication systems for human systems: Values and assumptions of "social open architecture." In J. A. Anderson (Ed.), *Communication yearbook 12* (pp. 498–532). Newbury Park, CA: Sage.

Ames, A., Jr. (1951). Visual perception and the rotating trapezoidal window. *Psychological Monographs, 65*, 1–31.

Andersen, K., & Clevenger, T., Jr. (1963). A summary of experimental research in *ethos*. *Speech Monographs, 30*, 59–78.

Andersen, K. E. (1991). A history of communication ethics. In K. J. Greenberg (Ed.), *Conversations on communication ethics* (pp. 3–19). Norwood, NJ: Ablex.

Anderson, R. (1982). Phenomenological dialogue, humanistic psychology, and pseudo-walls: A response and extension. *Western Journal of Speech Communication, 46*, 344–357.

Anderson, R. (1994). Anonymity, presence, and the dialogic self in a technological culture. In R. Anderson, K. N. Cissna, & R. C. Arnett (Eds.), *The reach of dialogue: Confirmation, voice, and community* (pp. 91–110). Cresskill, NJ: Hampton Press.

Anderson, R. (1997). The new digital presence: Listening, access, and computer-mediated life. In M. Purdy & D. Borisoff (Eds.), *Listening in everyday life: A personal and professional approach* (2nd ed., pp. 139–161). Lanham, MD: University Press of America.

Anderson, R., Cissna, K. N., & Arnett, R. C. (Eds.). (1994). *The reach of dialogue: Confirmation, voice, and community*. Cresskill, NJ: Hampton Press.

Anderson, R., & McCleary, K. (1984). Pointing toward a poetic of personal growth. *ReVision: A Journal of Consciousness and Change, 7*, 35–48.

Anzaldúa, G. (1987). *Borderlands/La frontera: The new mestiza*. San Francisco: Spinsters/Aunt Lute.

Anzaldúa, G. (1988). Tlilli, tlapalli: The path of the red and black ink. In R. Simonson & S. Walker (Eds.), *The Graywolf annual five: Multi-cultural literacy* (pp. 29–40). Saint Paul, MN: Graywolf.

Appiah, K. A. (1992). *In my father's house: Africa in the philosophy of culture*. New York: Oxford University Press.

Ardener, S. (1978). *Defining females: The nature of women in society*. New York: Wiley.

Aristotle. (1947). *Introduction to Aristotle* (R. McKeon, Ed.). New York: Modern Library.

Aristotle. (1954). *Rhetoric and poetics* (W. R. Roberts & I. Bywater, Trans.). New York: Modern Library.

Arnett, R. C. (1981). Toward a phenomenological dialogue. *Western Journal of Speech Communication, 45*, 201–212.

Arnett, R. C. (1991). The status of communication ethics scholarship in speech communication journals from 1915 to 1985. In K. J. Greenberg (Ed.), *Conversations on communication ethics* (pp. 55–72). Norwood, NJ: Ablex.

Arnett, R. C., & Nakagawa, G. (1983). The assumptive roots of empathic listening. *Communication Education, 32*, 368–378.

Asante, M. K. (1980). *Afrocentricity: The theory of social change*. Buffalo, NY: Amulefi.

Asante, M. K. (1987). *The Afrocentric idea*. Philadelphia: Temple University Press.

Ayer, A. J. (1955). What is communication? In A. Ayer et al., *Studies in communication*. London: Secker & Warburg.

Ayres, J. (1984). Four approaches to interpersonal communication. *Western Journal of Speech Communication, 48*, 408–440.

Bakhtin, M. M. (1981). *The dialogic imagination: Four essays* (C. Emerson & M. Holquist, Trans.). Austin: University of Texas Press.

Bakhtin, M. M. (1986). *Speech genres and other late essays* (C. Emerson & M. Holquist, Eds.; V. McGee, Trans.). Austin: University of Texas Press.

Barker, R. G. (1968). *Ecological psychology.* Stanford, CA: Stanford University Press.

Barnlund, D. C. (1970). A transactional model of communication. In K. K. Sereno & C. D. Mortensen (Eds.), *Foundations of communication theory* (pp. 83–102). New York: Harper.

Barnlund, D. C. (1989). *Communicative styles of Japanese and Americans: Images and realities.* Belmont, CA: Wadsworth.

Barthes, R. (1989). *Empire of signs* (R. Howard, Trans.). New York: Noonday.

Bateson, G. (1980). *Mind and nature: A necessary unity.* New York: Bantam.

Bateson, G. (1991). *A sacred unity: Further steps to an ecology of mind* (R. E. Donaldson, Ed.). New York: HarperCollins.

Bateson, G., & Jackson, D. (1964). Some varieties of pathogenic organization. In D. McRoach (Ed.), *Disorders of communication* (pp. 270–283). N.P.: Association for Research in Nervous and Mental Disease.

Bateson, M. C. (1984). *With a daughter's eye: A memoir of Margaret Mead and Gregory Bateson.* New York: Washington Square.

Bateson, M. C. (1990). *Composing a life.* New York: Plume.

Bauer, R. (1964). The obstinate audience. *American Psychologist, 19,* 319–328.

Bavelas, J. B. (1995). Quantitative versus qualitative? In W. Leeds-Hurwitz (Ed.), *Social approaches to communication* (pp. 49–62). New York: Guilford.

Baxter, L. A. (1988). A dialectical perspective on communication strategies in relationship development. In S. W. Duck (Ed.), *Handbook of personal relationships* (pp. 257–273). New York: Wiley.

Baxter, L. A. (1990). Dialectical contradictions in relationship development. *Journal of Social and Personal Relationships, 7,* 69–88.

Baxter, L. A., & Montgomery, B. M. (1996). *Relating: Dialogues and dialectics.* New York: Guilford.

Becker, C. S. (1992). *Living and relating: An introduction to phenomenology.* Newbury Park, CA: Sage.

Belenky, M. F., Clinchy, B. M., Goldberger, N. R., & Tarule, J. M. (1986). *Women's ways of knowing: The development of self, voice, and mind.* New York: Basic Books.

Bellah, R. N., Madsen, R., Sullivan, W. M., Swidler, A., & Tipton, S. M. (1986). *Habits of the heart: In-dividualism and commitment in American life.* New York: Harper.

Benhabib, S. (1990). Models of public space: Hannah Arendt, the liberal tradition, and Jurgen Habermas. In C. Calhoun (Ed.), *Habermas and the public sphere* (pp. 73–98). Cambridge, MA: MIT Press.

Benhabib, S. (1992). *Situating the self: Gender, community, and postmodernism in contemporary ethics.* New York: Routledge.

Beniger, J. R. (1990). Who are the most important theorists of communication? *Communication Research, 17,* 698–715.

Berelson, B., & Steiner, G. A. (1964). *Human behavior: An inventory of scientific findings.* New York: Harcourt.

Berger, A. A. (1982). *Media analysis techniques.* Beverly Hills, CA: Sage.

Berger, C. R. (1977). The covering law perspective as a theoretical basis for the study of human communication. *Communication Quarterly, 25,* 7–18.

Berger, C. R., & Bradac, J. J. (1982). *Language and social knowledge: Uncertainty in interpersonal relations.* London: Edward Arnold.

Berger, C. R., & Calabrese, R. J. (1975). Some explorations in initial interaction and beyond: Toward a developmental theory of interpersonal communication. *Human Communication Research, 1,* 99–112.

Berger, P., & Luckmann, T. (1966). *The social construction of reality: A treatise in the sociology of knowledge.* New York: Doubleday.

Berger, P., Berger, B., & Kellner, H. (1974). *The homeless mind: Modernization and consciousness.* New York: Vintage.

Bergmann, G. (1957). *Philosophy of science.* Madison: University of Wisconsin Press.

Berlo, D. K. (1960). *The process of communication: An introduction to theory and practice.* New York: Holt.

Bernstein, B. (1960). Language and social class. *British Journal of Sociology, 11,* 271–276.

Bertalanffy, L. von (1968). *General systems theory: Foundations, development, applications.* New York: George Braziller.

Birdwhistell, R. L. (1970). *Kinesics and context: Essays on body motion communication.* Philadelphia: University of Pennsylvania Press.

Blair, C., Jeppeson, M. S., & Pucci, E., Jr. (1994). Public memorializing in postmodernity: The Vietnam Veterans Memorial as prototype. In W. L. Nothstine, C. Blair, & G. A. Copeland (Eds.), *Critical questions: In-*

vention, creativity, and the criticism of discourse and media (pp. 350–382). New York: St. Martin's.

Blakemore, C., & Greenfield, S. (Eds.) (1987). *Mindwaves: Thoughts on intelligence, identity and consciousness.* Oxford: Basil Blackwell.

Blau, P. M. (1963). *The dynamics of bureaucracy: A study of interpersonal relationships in two government agencies* (Rev. ed.). Chicago: University of Chicago Press.

Blau, P. M. (1964). *Exchange and power in social life.* New York: Wiley.

Blum, A., & McHugh, P. (1984). *Self reflection in the arts and sciences.* Atlantic Highlands, NJ: Humanities.

Blumer, H. (1969). *Symbolic interactionism: Perspective and method.* Englewood Cliffs, NJ: Prentice-Hall.

Blumler, J. G. (1985). The social character of media gratifications. In K. E. Rosengren, L. A. Wenner, & P. Palmgreen (Eds.), *Media gratifications research: Current perspectives* (pp. 41–59). Beverly Hills, CA: Sage.

Blumler, J. G., & Katz, E. (Eds.) (1974). *The uses of mass communications: Current perspectives on gratifications research.* Beverly Hills, CA: Sage.

Bohm, D. (1980). *Wholeness and the implicate order.* London: Routledge & Kegan Paul.

Bok, S. (1979). *Lying: Moral choice in public and private life.* New York: Vintage.

Bok, S. (1983). *Secrets: On the ethics of concealment and revelation.* New York: Random House.

Bolles, E. B. (1991). *A second way of knowing: The riddle of human perception.* Englewood Cliffs, NJ: Prentice-Hall.

Booth, W. C. (1974). *Modern dogma and the rhetoric of assent.* Chicago: University of Chicago Press.

Booth, W. C. (1990). *The vocation of a teacher: Rhetorical occasions, 1967–1988.* Chicago: University of Chicago Press.

Bormann, E. G. (1972). Fantasy and rhetorical vision: The rhetorical criticism of social reality. *Quarterly Journal of Speech, 58,* 396–407.

Bormann, E. G. (1983). The symbolic convergence theory of communication and the creation, raising, and sustaining of public consciousness. In J. I. Sisco (Ed.), *The Jensen lectures: Contemporary communication studies* (pp. 71–90). Tampa: University of South Florida.

Bormann, E. G. (1989). *Communication theory.* Salem, WI: Sheffield.

Borton, T. (1970). *Reach, touch, and teach: Student concerns and process education.* New York: McGraw-Hill.

Boulding, K. E. (1956). *The image: Knowledge in life and society.* Ann Arbor: University of Michigan Press.

Bozarth, J. D., & Brodley, B. T. (1986). Client-centered psychotherapy: A statement. *Person-Centered Review, 3,* 262–271.

Brand, S. (1988). *The media lab: Inventing the future at MIT.* New York: Penguin.

Brehm, J. W. (1966). *A theory of psychological reactance.* New York: Academic.

Bross, I. D. J. (1970). Models. In J. H. Campbell & H. W. Hepler (Eds.), *Dimensions in communication: Readings* (2nd ed., pp. 11–27). Belmont, CA: Wadsworth.

Brown, C. T., & Keller, P. W. (1979). *Monologue to dialogue: An exploration of interpersonal communication* (2nd ed.). Englewood Cliffs, NJ: Prentice-Hall.

Brown, J. A. C. (1963). *Techniques of persuasion: From propaganda to brainwashing.* Baltimore: Penguin.

Brown, R. (1973). *Rules and laws in sociology.* Chicago: Aldine.

Brown, R. H. (1977). *A poetic for sociology: Toward a logic of discovery for the human sciences.* Cambridge: Cambridge University Press.

Brown, R. H. (1987). *Society as text: Essays on rhetoric, reason, and reality.* Chicago: University of Chicago Press.

Bruner, J. (1979). *On knowing: Essays for the left hand* (Expanded ed.). Cambridge, MA: Belknap.

Bruner, J. (1983). *In search of mind: Essays in autobiography.* New York: Harper.

Bruner, J. (1986). *Actual minds, possible worlds.* Cambridge, MA: Harvard University Press.

Bruner, J. (1990). *Acts of meaning.* Cambridge, MA: Harvard University Press.

Bruner, J. S. (1960). *The process of education.* New York: Vintage.

Bruner, J. S., & Goodman, C. D. (1947). Value and need as organizing factors in perception. *Journal of Abnormal and Social Psychology, 42,* 33–44.

Buber, M. (1957). *Pointing the way* (M. S. Friedman, Trans.). New York: Harper Torchbooks.

Buber, M. (1958). *I and thou* (R. G. Smith, Trans.). New York: Scribner.

Buber, M. (1965a). *Between man and man* (R. G. Smith, Trans.). New York: Macmillan.

Buber, M. (1965b). *The knowledge of man: A philosophy of the interhuman* (M. Friedman, Trans.). New York: Harper.

Burgoon, J. K., & Hale, J. L. (1984). The fundamental topoi of relational communication. *Communication Monographs, 51,* 193–214.

Burgoon, J. K., Buller, D. B., & Woodall, W. G.

(1989). *Nonverbal communication: The unspoken dialogue.* New York: Harper.

Burgoon, M., & Miller, G. R. (1990). Paths. *Communication Monographs, 57,* 152–160.

Burke, K. (1967). Rhetoric—Old and new. In M. Steinmann, Jr. (Ed.), *New rhetorics* (pp. 60–76). New York: Scribner.

Burke, K. (1969). *A rhetoric of motives.* Berkeley: University of California Press.

Burns, E. (1972). *Theatricality: A study of convention in the theatre and in social life.* New York: Harper Torchbooks.

Bynner, W. (1962). *The way of life according to Laotzu: An American version.* New York: Capricorn. (Original work published 1944)

Campbell, D. T. (1969). Ethnocentrism of disciplines and the fish-scale model of omniscience. In M. Sherif & C. W. Sherif (Eds.), *Interdisciplinary relationships in the social sciences* (pp. 328–348). Chicago: Aldine.

Campbell, D. T. (1986). Science's social system of validity-enhancing collective belief change and the problems of the social sciences. In D. W. Fiske & R. A. Schweder (Eds.), *Metatheory in social science: Pluralisms and subjectivities* (pp. 108–135). Chicago: University of Chicago Press.

Carbaugh, D. (1989). *Talking American: Cultural discourses on "Donahue."* Norwood, NJ: Ablex.

Carey, J. W. (1989). *Communication as culture: Essays on media and society.* Boston: Unwin Hyman.

Carpenter, E. (1960). The new languages. In E. Carpenter & M. McLuhan (Eds.), *Explorations in communication* (pp. 162–179). Boston: Beacon.

Chen, G.-M., & Starosta, W. J. (1996). Intercultural communication competence: A synthesis. In B. Burleson (Ed.), *Communication yearbook 19* (pp. 353–383). Thousand Oaks, CA: Sage.

Cheng, C.-Y. (1987). Chinese philosophy and contemporary human communication theory. In D. L. Kincaid (Ed.), *Communication theory: Eastern and western perspectives* (pp. 23–43). San Diego: Academic.

Chesebro, J. W., & Bonsall, D. G. (1989). *Computer-mediated communication: Human relationships in a computerized world.* Tuscaloosa, AL: University of Alabama Press.

Chomsky, N. (1957). *Syntactic structures.* The Hague: Mouton.

Chomsky, N. (1975). *Reflections on language.* New York: Pantheon.

Christians, C. G., Ferré, J. P., & Fackler, P. M. (1993). *Good news: Social ethics and the press.* New York: Oxford University Press.

Christians, C. G., Rotzoll, K. B., & Fackler, M. (1991). *Media ethics: Cases and moral reasoning* (3rd ed.). New York: Longman.

Cissna, K. N., & Anderson, R. (1990). The contributions of Carl R. Rogers to a philosophical praxis of dialogue. *Western Journal of Speech Communication, 54,* 125–147.

Cissna, K. N., Cox, D. E., & Bochner, A. P. (1990). The dialectic of marital and parental relationships within the stepfamily. *Communication Monographs, 57,* 4–61.

Cissna, K. N. L., & Sieburg, E. (1981). Patterns of interactional confirmation and disconfirmation. In C. Wilder-Mott & J. Weakland (Eds.), *Rigor and imagination* (pp. 230–239). New York: Praeger.

Clark, G. (1990). *Dialogue, dialectic, and conversation: A social perspective on the function of writing.* Carbondale: Southern Illinois University Press.

Clark, K., & Holquist, M. (1984). *Mikhail Bakhtin.* Cambridge, MA: Harvard University Press.

Cody, M. J., & McLaughlin, M. L. (1985). The situation as a construct in interpersonal communication research. In M. L. Knapp & G. R. Miller (Eds.), *Handbook of interpersonal communication* (pp. 273–312). Beverly Hills, CA: Sage.

Cohen, H. (1994). *The history of speech communication: The emergence of a discipline, 1914–1945.* Annandale, VA: Speech Communication Association.

Coles, R. (1989). *The call of stories: Teaching and the moral imagination.* Boston: Houghton Mifflin.

Collins, P. H. (1991). *Black feminist thought: Knowledge, consciousness, and the politics of empowerment.* New York: Routledge.

Condit, C. (1993). The critic as empath: Moving away from totalizing theory. *Western Journal of Communication, 57,* 178–190.

Condit, C. M. (1989). The rhetorical limits of polysemy. *Critical Studies in Mass Communication, 6,* 103–122.

Cooper, J. C. (1972). *Taoism: The way of the mystic.* New York: Samuel Weiser.

Corsini, R. J. (Ed.). (1984). *Encyclopedia of psychology* (Vol. 1). New York: Wiley.

Cottone, R. R. (1992). *Theories and paradigms of counseling and psychotherapy.* Boston: Allyn & Bacon.

Coughlin, E. K. (1996, February 16). Not out of Africa. *Chronicle of Higher Education,* pp. A6, A7.

Craig, R. T. (1995). Review of: E. V. Rogers, *A*

history of communication study: A biographical approach and H. Cohen, *The history of speech communication: The emergence of a discipline, 1914–1945. Communication Theory, 5,* 178–184.

Cronen, V. E., Pearce, W. B., & Harris, L. M. (1982). The coordinated management of meaning: A theory of communication. In F. E. X. Dance (Ed.), *Human communication theory* (pp. 61–89). New York: Harper.

Cushman, D. P. (1977). The rules perspective as a theoretical basis for the study of human communication. *Communication Quarterly, 25,* 30–45.

Cushman, D. P., & Cahn, D. D., Jr. (1985). *Communication in interpersonal relationships.* Albany: State University of New York Press.

Cuzzort, R. P., & King, E. W. (1989). *Twentieth-century social thought* (4th ed.). Fort Worth: Holt.

Daly, M. (1973). *Beyond God the father.* Boston: Beacon.

Dance, F. E. X. (1967). Toward a theory of human communication. In F. E. X. Dance (Ed.), *Human communication theory: Original essays* (pp. 288–309). New York: Holt.

Dance, F. E. X. (1982). A speech theory of human communication. In F. E. X. Dance (Ed.), *Human communication theory* (pp. 120–146). New York: Harper.

Dance, F. E. X. (1989). Ong's voice: "I," the oral intellect, you, and we. *Text and Performance Quarterly, 9,* 185–198.

Dance, F. E. X., & Larson, C. E. (1976). *The functions of human communication: A theoretical approach.* New York: Holt.

Darnell, D. K. (1984, October). Communication. *Spectra, 20,* 11.

Davidson, M. (1983). *Uncommon sense: The life and thought of Ludwig von Bertalanffy, father of general systems theory.* Los Angeles: Tarcher.

Davis, O. (1969). The English language is my enemy. In N. Postman, C. Weingartner, & T. P. Moran (Eds.), *Language in America* (pp. 73–79). New York: Pegasus.

Deetz, S. (1982). Hermeneutics and research in interpersonal communication. In J. J. Pilotta (Ed.), *Interpersonal communication: Essays in phenomenology and hermeneutics* (pp. 1–14). Washington, DC: University Press of America.

DeFleur, M. L., & Ball-Rokeach, S. (1982). *Theories of mass communication* (4th ed.). New York: Longman.

Delia, J. G. (1976). A constructivist analysis of the concept of credibility. *Quarterly Journal of Speech, 62,* 361–375.

Delia, J. G. (1977). Constructivism and the study of human communication. *Quarterly Journal of Speech, 63,* 66–83.

Delia, J. G. (1987). Communication research: A history. In C. R. Berger & S. H. Chaffee (Eds.), *Handbook of communication science* (pp. 20–98). Newbury Park, CA: Sage.

Delia, J. G., O'Keefe, B. J., & O'Keefe, D. J. (1982). The constructivist approach to communication. In F. E. X. Dance (Ed.), *Human communication theory* (pp. 147–191). New York: Harper.

Denzin, N. K. (1992). *Symbolic interactionism and cultural studies: The politics of interpretation.* Oxford, UK: Blackwell.

Derber, C. (1979). *The pursuit of attention: Power and individualism in everyday life.* Oxford: Oxford University Press.

Derrida, J. (1982). *Margins of philosophy.* Chicago: University of Chicago Press.

Dervin, B. (1993). Verbing communication: Mandate for disciplinary invention. *Journal of Communication, 43*(3), 45–54.

Deutscher, I. (1973). *What we say/what we do: Sentiments and acts.* Glenview, IL: Scott, Foresman.

DeVito, J. A. (1986). *The communication handbook: A dictionary.* New York: Harper.

Dewey, J. (1927). *The public and its problems.* Denver: Alan Swallow.

Dewey, J. (1933). *How we think.* Boston: Heath.

Dewey, J. (1934). *Art as experience.* New York: Putnam.

Dewey, J., & Bentley, A. F. (1949). *Knowing and the known.* Boston: Beacon.

Dillard, A. (1975). *Pilgrim at Tinker Creek.* New York: Bantam.

Dillon, J. T. (1990). *The practice of questioning.* London: Routledge.

Douglas, M. (1975). *Implicit meanings: Essays in anthropology.* London: Routledge & Kegan Paul.

Druckman, D., Rozelle, R. M., & Baxter, J. C. (1982). *Nonverbal communication: Survey, theory, and research.* Beverly Hills, CA: Sage.

Dubin, R. (1969). *Theory building: A practical guide to the construction and testing of theoretical models.* New York: Free Press.

Duncan, H. D. (1962). *Communication and social order.* London: Oxford University Press.

Eco, U. (1976). *A theory of semiotics.* Bloomington: Indiana University Press.

Edelman, M. (1964). *The symbolic uses of politics.* Urbana: University of Illinois Press.

Eisenberg, E. M., & Goodall, H. L, Jr. (1993). *Organizational communication: Balancing creativity and constraint.* New York: St. Martin's.

Elbow, P. (1973). *Writing without teachers.* London: Oxford University Press.

Ellul, J. (1964). *The technological society.* (J. Wilkinson, Trans.). New York: Vintage.

Ellul, J. (1985). *The humiliation of the word.* (J. M. Hanks, Trans.). Grand Rapids, MI: William B. Eerdmans.

Ethics of young decried. (1992, November 26). *St. Louis Post-Dispatch,* p. 8D.

Etzioni, A. (1993). *The spirit of community: Rights, responsibilities, and the communitarian agenda.* New York: Crown.

Farrell, T. B. (1987). Beyond science: Humanities contributions to communication theory. In C. R. Berger & S. H. Chaffee (Eds.), *Handbook of communication science* (pp. 123–142). Newbury Park, CA: Sage.

Fay, B. (1996). *Contemporary philosophy of social science: A multicultural approach.* Oxford, UK: Blackwell.

Ferrarotti, F. (1988). *The end of conversation: The impact of mass media on modern society.* New York: Greenwood.

Festinger, L. (1957). *A theory of cognitive dissonance.* Stanford, CA: Stanford University Press.

Fischler, A. (1989, August 2). From the inferno: Reflections on a sojourn in a communication program. *Chronicle of Higher Education,* p. A28.

Fisher, B. A. (1978). *Perspectives on human communication.* New York: Macmillan.

Fisher, B. A. (1982). The pragmatic perspective of human communication: A view from system theory. In F. E. X. Dance (Ed.), *Human communication theory* (pp. 192–219). New York: Harper.

Fisher, W. R. (1987). *Human communication as narration: Toward a philosophy of reason, value, and action.* Columbia: University of South Carolina Press.

Fitzpatrick, M. A. (1993). Communication and the new world of relationships. *Journal of Communication, 43*(3), 119–126.

Flew, A. (1984). *A dictionary of philosophy* (Rev. 2nd ed.). New York: St. Martin's.

Frank, F., & Anshen, F. (1983). *Language and the sexes.* Albany: State University of New York Press.

Friedman, M. (1974). *Touchstones of reality: Existential trust and the community of peace.* New York: Dutton.

Friedman, M. S. (1960). *Martin Buber: The life of dialogue* (2nd ed.). New York: Harper Torchbooks.

Friedman, M. S. (1981–1983). *Martin Buber's life and work* (Vols. 1–3). New York: Dutton.

Fry, D. (1977). *Homo loquens: Man as a talking animal.* Cambridge: Cambridge University Press.

Gadamer, H.-G. (1982). *Truth and method* (2nd ed.) (G. Barden & J. Cumming, Trans.). New York: Crossroad.

Ganz, J. S. (1971). *Rules: A systematic study.* Paris: Mouton.

Garfinkel, H. (1967). *Studies in ethnomethodology.* Cambridge: Polity Press.

Garko, M. G. (1990). Perspectives on and conceptualizations of compliance and compliance-gaining. *Communication Quarterly, 38,* 138–157.

Gates, H. L., Jr. (1992). *Loose canons: Notes on the culture wars.* New York: Oxford University Press.

Geertz, C. (1983). *Local knowledge: Further essays on interpretive anthropology.* New York: Basic Books.

Geller, L. (1982). The failure of self-actualization theory: A critique of Carl Rogers and Abraham Maslow. *Journal of Humanistic Psychology, 22,* 56–73.

Gerbner, G. (1970). Cultural indicators: The case of violence in television drama. *Annals of the American Association of Political and Social Science, 338,* 69–81.

Gerbner, G. (1990). Epilogue: Advancing on the path of righteousness (maybe). In N. Signorielli & M. Morgan (Eds.), *Cultivation analysis: New directions in media effects research.* Newbury Park, CA: Sage.

Gerbner, G., Gross, L. P., Morgan, M., & Signorielli, N. (1980). The "mainstreaming" of America: Violence profile no. 11. *Journal of Communication, 30,* 10–29.

Gergen, K. G. (1969). *The psychology of behavior exchange.* Reading, MA: Addison-Wesley.

Gilligan, C. (1982). *In a different voice: Psychological theory and women's development.* Cambridge, MA: Harvard University Press.

Glatzer, N. N. (1966). Preface. In M. Buber, *The way of response: Martin Buber* (N. N. Glatzer, Ed.). New York: Schocken.

Glendon, M. A. (1991). *Rights talk: The impoverishment of political discourse.* New York: Free Press.

Goffman, E. (1959). *The presentation of self in everyday life.* New York: Doubleday Anchor.

Goffman, E. (1974). *Frame analysis: An essay on the organization of experience.* New York: Harper Colophon.

Goffman, E. (1981). *Forms of talk.* Philadelphia: University of Pennsylvania Press.

Goldenson, R. M. (Ed.) (1984). *Longman dictionary of psychology and psychiatry.* New York: Longman.

Goldner, V., Penn, P., Sheinberg, M., & Walker, G. (1990). Love and violence: Gender paradoxes in volatile attachments. *Family Process, 29,* 343–364.

Goodall, H. L., Jr. (1991). *Living in the rock n roll mystery: Reading context, self, and others as clues.* Carbondale: Southern Illinois University Press.

Goss, B. (1989). *The psychology of human communication.* Prospect Heights, IL: Waveland.

Gouran, D. S. (1990). Speech communication after seventy-five years: Issues and prospects. In G. M. Phillips & J. T. Wood (Eds.), *Speech communication: Essays to commemorate the 75th anniversary of The Speech Communication Association* (pp. 1–32). Carbondale: Southern Illinois University Press.

Gozzi, R., Jr., & Haynes, W. L. (1992). Electric media and electric epistemology: Empathy at a distance. *Critical Studies in Mass Communication, 9,* 217–228.

Granberg, D. (1982). Social judgment theory. In M. Burgoon (Ed.), *Communication yearbook 6* (pp. 304–329). Beverly Hills, CA: Sage.

Greene, J. O. (1984). A cognitive approach to human communication: An action assembly theory. *Communication Monographs, 51,* 289–306.

Greene, J. O. (1989). Action assembly theory: Metatheoretical commitments, theoretical propositions, and empirical applications. In B. Dervin, L. Grossberg, B. J. O'Keefe, & E. Wartella (Eds.), *Rethinking communication: Vol. 2. Paradigm exemplars* (pp. 117–128). Newbury Park, CA: Sage.

Gregory, R., & Miller, J. (1983). Visual perception and illusions: A dialogue with Richard Gregory. In J. Miller, *States of mind* (pp. 42–64). New York: Pantheon.

Griffin, S. (1992). *A chorus of stones: The private life of war.* New York: Anchor.

Gronbeck, B., Farrell, T. J., & Soukup, P. A. (Eds.). (1991). *Media, consciousness, and culture: Explorations of Walter Ong's thought.* Newbury Park, CA: Sage.

Grossberg, L. (1984). Strategies of Marxist cultural interpretation. *Critical Studies in Mass Communication, 1,* 392–421.

Grossberg, L., Nelson, C., & Treichler, P. (Eds.). (1992). *Cultural studies.* New York: Routledge.

Gudykunst, W. B., & Kim, Y. Y. (1984). *Communicating with strangers: An approach to intercultural communication.* Reading, MA: Addison-Wesley.

Gurwitsch, A. (1974). *Phenomenology and the theory of science.* Evanston: Northwestern University Press.

Habermas, J. (1979). *Communication and the evolution of society* (T. McCarthy, Trans.). Boston: Beacon.

Habermas, J. (1990). *Moral consciousness and communicative action* (C. Lenhardt & S. W. Nicholsen, Trans.). Cambridge, MA: MIT Press.

Habermas, J. (1992). *Autonomy and solidarity: Interviews with Jurgen Habermas* (P. Dews, Ed.). (Rev. ed.). London: Verso.

Haiman, F. S. (1981). *Speech and law in a free society.* Chicago: University of Chicago Press.

Haiman, F. S. (1991). Majorities versus the First Amendment: Rationality on trial. *Communication Monographs, 58,* 327–335.

Hall, E. T. (1959). *The silent language.* New York: Doubleday.

Hall, E. T. (1966). *The hidden dimension.* Garden City, NY: Anchor.

Hall, E. T. (1977). *Beyond culture.* Garden City, NY: Anchor.

Hall, E. T. (1992). *An anthropology of everyday life: An autobiography.* New York: Doubleday.

Hall, E. T., & Hall, M. R. (1987). *Hidden differences: Doing business with the Japanese.* New York: Anchor.

Hall, S. (1989). Ideology and communication theory. In B. Dervin, L. Grossberg, B. J. O'Keefe, & E. Wartella (Eds.), *Rethinking communication: Vol. 1. Paradigm issues* (pp. 40–52). Newbury Park, CA: Sage.

Hall, S. (1992). Cultural studies and its theoretical legacies. In L. Grossberg, C. Nelson, & P. Treichler (Eds.), *Cultural studies* (pp. 277–294). New York: Routledge.

Hall, S. (1996). On postmodernism and articulation (An interview with Stuart Hall; edited by L. Grossberg). In D. Morley & K.-H. Chen (Eds.), *Stuart Hall: Critical dialogues in cultural studies* (pp. 131–150). New York: Routledge.

Haney, W. V. (1973). *Communication and organizational behavior: Text and cases* (3rd ed.). Homewood, IL: Irwin.

Hanson, N. (1958). *Patterns of discovery.* Cambridge, MA: Harvard University Press.

Hardison, O. B., Jr. (1972). *Toward freedom and dignity: The humanities and the idea of humanity.* Baltimore: Johns Hopkins University Press.

Harper, N. (1978). *Human communication theory: The history of a paradigm.* Rochelle Park, NJ: Hayden.

Hart, R., & Ollett, O. (1991). *The distributed mind.* Thousand Oaks, CA: Sage.

Hart, R. P., & Burks, D. M. (1972). Rhetorical

sensitivity and social interaction. *Speech Monographs, 39,* 75–91.

Hasnain, I. (1988). Communication: An Islamic approach. In W. Dissanayake (Ed.), *Communication theory: The Asian perspective* (pp. 183–189). Singapore: Asian Mass Communication Research and Information Centre.

Hauerwas, S. (1981). *A community of character: Toward a constructive Christian social ethic.* Notre Dame, IN: University of Notre Dame Press.

Hauser, G. A. (1986). *Introduction to rhetorical theory.* New York: Harper.

Havelock, E. A. (1986). *The muse learns to write: Reflections on orality and literacy from antiquity to the present.* New Haven, CT: Yale University Press.

Hawes, L. C. (1975). *Pragmatics of analoguing: Theory and model construction in communication.* Reading, MA: Addison-Wesley.

Hawkins, R. P., Wiemann, J. M., & Pingree, S. (Eds.). (1988). *Advancing communication science: Merging mass and interpersonal processes.* Newbury Park, CA: Sage.

Hawley, A. H. (1986). *Human ecology: A theoretical essay.* Chicago: University of Chicago Press.

Hayakawa, S. I. (1941). *Language in action.* New York: Harcourt.

Heider, F. (1958). *The psychology of interpersonal relations.* New York: Wiley.

Heim, M. (1987). *Electric language: A philosophical study of word processing.* New Haven, CT: Yale University Press.

Heim, M. (1993). *The metaphysics of virtual reality.* New York: Oxford University Press.

Heisenberg, W. (1958). *Physics and philosophy.* New York: Harper.

Henley, N. M. (1977). *Body politics: Power, sex, and nonverbal communication.* Englewood Cliffs, NJ: Prentice-Hall.

Henley, N. M. (1995). Body politics revisited: What do we know today? In P. J. Kalbfleisch & M. J. Cody (Eds.), *Gender, power, and communication in human relationships* (pp. 27–62). Hillsdale, NJ: Lawrence Erlbaum.

Hickman, C. A., & Kuhn, M. H. (1956). *Individuals, groups, and economic behavior.* New York: Dryden.

Hoggart, R. (1972). *On culture and communication.* New York: Oxford University Press.

Hollinger, R. (Ed.). (1985). *Hermeneutics and praxis.* Notre Dame, IN: University of Notre Dame Press.

Holquist, M. (1990). *Dialogism: Bakhtin and his world.* London: Routledge.

Homans, G. C. (1961). *Social behavior: Its elementary forms.* New York: Harcourt.

Horton, D., & Wohl, R. R. (1956). Mass communication and para-social interaction: Observations on intimacy at a distance. *Psychiatry, 19,* 215–229.

Hovland, C. I., Janis, I. L., & Kelley, H. H. (1953). *Communication and persuasion.* New Haven, CT: Yale University Press.

Hurt, H. T., Scott, M. D., & McCroskey, J. C. (1978). *Communication in the classroom.* Reading, MA: Addison-Wesley.

Infante, D. A. (1980). Verbal plans: A conceptualization and investigation. *Communication Quarterly, 28,* 3–10.

Infante, D. A., Parker, K. R., Clarke, C. H., Wilson, L., & Nathu, I. A. (1983). A comparison of factor and functional approaches to source credibility. *Communication Quarterly, 31,* 43–48.

Infante, D. A., Rancer, A. S., & Womack, D. F. (1990). *Building communication theory.* Prospect Heights, IL: Waveland.

Innis, H. A. (1951). *The bias of communication.* Toronto: University of Toronto Press.

James, W. (1896). *Principles of psychology.* New York: Henry Holt.

James, W. (1982). An interview: Pragmatism—What it is. In H. S. Thayer (Ed.), *Pragmatism: The classic writings* (pp. 131–134). Indianapolis, IN: Hackett.

Janis, I. (1982). *Groupthink.* Boston: Houghton Mifflin.

Jensen, J. V. (1987). Rhetorical emphases of Taoism. *Rhetorica, 5,* 219–229.

Johannesen, R. L. (1990). *Ethics in human communication* (3rd ed.). Prospect Heights, IL: Waveland.

Johnson, J. R. (1984). The role of inner speech in human communication. *Communication Education, 33,* 211–222.

Johnson, K. G., Senatore, J. J., Liebig, M. C., & Minor, G. (1974). *Nothing never happens.* Beverly Hills, CA: Glencoe.

Johnson, W. (1946). *People in quandaries.* New York: Harper.

Jones, S. (Ed.). (1994). *Cybersociety: Computer-mediated communication and community.* Thousand Oaks, CA: Sage.

Kalbfleisch, P. J., & Cody, M. J. (Eds.). (1995). *Gender, power, and communication in human relationships.* Hillsdale, NJ: Lawrence Erlbaum.

Kaplan, A. (1961). *The new world of philosophy.* New York: Vintage.

Kaplan, A. (1964). *The conduct of inquiry: Methodology for behavioral science.* San Francisco: Chandler.

Kaplan, S. J. (1990). Communication technology and society. In G. M. Phillips & J. T. Wood (Eds.), *Speech communication: Essays to commemorate the 75th anniversary of The Speech Communication Association* (pp. 205–234). Carbondale, IL: Southern Illinois University Press.

Katz, E., & Lazarsfeld, P. F. (1955). *Personal influence: The part played by people in the flow of mass communications.* New York: Free Press.

Katz, R. L. (1963). *Empathy: Its nature and uses.* New York: Free Press.

Keen, S. (1970). *To a dancing god.* New York: Harper.

Keller, E. F. (1985). *Reflections on gender and science.* New Haven, CT: Yale University Press.

Keller, P. W., & Brown, C. T. (1968). An interpersonal ethic for communication. *Journal of Communication, 18,* 73–81.

Kelly, G. A. (1963). *A theory of personality: The psychology of personal constructs.* New York: Norton.

Kelman, H. C. (1966). Three processes of social influence. In M. Jahoda & N. Warren (Eds.), *Attitudes* (pp. 151–162). Baltimore: Penguin.

Kennedy, G. (1963). *The art of persuasion in Greece.* Princeton, NJ: Princeton University Press.

Key, M. R. (1980). Preface. In M. R. Key (Ed.), *The relationship of verbal and nonverbal communication* (pp. vii–viii). The Hague: Mouton.

Kiesler, C., Collins, B., & Miller, N. (1969). *Attitude change: A critical analysis of theoretical approaches.* New York: Wiley.

Killenberg, G. M., & Anderson, R. (1989). *Before the story: Interviewing and communication skills for journalists.* New York: St. Martin's.

Kim, Y. Y. (1984). Searching for creative integration. In W. B. Gudykunst & Y. Y. Kim (Eds.), *Methods for intercultural communication research* (pp. 13–30). Newbury Park, CA: Sage.

Kim, Y. Y. (1988). *Communication and cross-cultural adaptation: An integrative theory.* Clevedon, England: Multilingual Matters.

Kim, Y. Y. (1991). Intercultural communication competence. In S. Ting-Toomey & F. Korzenny (Eds.), *Cross-cultural interpersonal communication* (pp. 259–275). Newbury Park, CA: Sage.

Kincaid, D. L. (Ed.). (1987a). *Communication theory: Eastern and western perspectives.* San Diego: Academic.

Kincaid, D. L. (1987b). Communication east and west: Points of departure. In D. L. Kincaid (Ed.), *Communication theory: Eastern and western perspectives* (pp. 331–353). San Diego: Academic.

Kinneavy, J. L. (1980). *A theory of discourse.* New York: Norton. (Original work published 1971)

Klapp, O. E. (1962). *Heroes, villains, and fools: The changing American character.* Englewood Cliffs, NJ: Prentice-Hall.

Klapp, O. E. (1969). *Collective search for identity.* New York: Holt.

Klapp, O. E. (1978). *Opening and closing: Strategies of information adaptation in society.* Cambridge: Cambridge University Press.

Koestler, A. (1967). *The ghost in the machine.* New York: Macmillan.

Koffka, K. (1935). *Principles of gestalt psychology.* New York: Harcourt.

Koman, K. (1990, March 30). Oh, that mayor's mouth!. *St. Louis Post-Dispatch,* pp. 1, 4.

Kramerae, C. (1981). *Women and men speaking: Frameworks for analysis.* Rowley, MA: Newbury.

Kramerae, C., & Treichler, P. A. (1990). Power relationships in the classroom. In S. L. Gabriel & I. Smithson (Eds.), *Gender in the classroom: Power and pedagogy* (pp. 41–59). Urbana: University of Illinois Press.

Kress, P. F. (1970). *Social science and the idea of process: The ambiguous legacy of Arthur F. Bentley.* Urbana: University of Illinois Press.

Krippendorf, K. (1989). On the ethics of constructing communication. In B. Dervin, L. Grossberg, B. J. O'Keefe, & E. Wartella (Eds.), *Rethinking communication: Vol. 1. Paradigm issues* (pp. 66–96). Newbury Park, CA: Sage.

Kubie, L. S. (1961). *Neurotic distortion of the creative process.* New York: Noonday.

Kuhn, M. H., & McPartland, T. S. (1954). An empirical investigation of self-attitudes. *American Sociological Review, 19,* 68–76.

Kuhn, T. S. (1970). *The structure of scientific revolutions* (2nd ed.). Chicago: University of Chicago Press.

Laing, R. D. (1969). *Self and others* (2nd ed.). New York: Penguin.

Laing, R. D., Phillipson, H., & Lee, A. R. (1966). *Interpersonal perception: A theory and a method of research.* New York: Perennial Library.

Lakoff, G. (1987). *Women, fire, and dangerous things: What categories reveal about the mind.* Chicago: University of Chicago Press.

Lakoff, G., & Johnson, M. (1980). *Metaphors we live by.* Chicago: University of Chicago Press.

Lakoff, R. (1975). *Language and women's place.* New York: Harper.

Lakoff, R. T. (1990). *Talking power: The politics of language.* New York: Basic Books.

Landow, G. P. (1992). *Hypertext: The convergence of contemporary critical theory and technology.* Baltimore: The Johns Hopkins University Press.

Langer, E. J. (1978). Rethinking the role of thought in social interaction. In J. H. Harvey, W. Ikes, & R. F. Kidd (Eds.), *New directions in attribution research* (Vol. 2). Hillsdale, NJ: Lawrence Erlbaum.

Langer, E. J. (1989). *Mindfulness.* Reading, MA: Addison-Wesley.

Langer, S. (1951). *Philosophy in a new key* (2nd ed.). New York: New American Library.

Lanham, R. A. (1993). *The electronic word: Democracy, technology, and the arts.* Chicago: University of Chicago Press Expanded Book (hypercard version).

Lasch, C. (1979). *The culture of narcissism: American life in an age of diminishing expectations.* New York: Warner.

Lawson, H. (1985). *Reflexivity: The post-modern predicament.* London: Hutchinson.

Lazarsfeld, P. F., Berelson, B., & Gaudet, H. (1948). *The people's choice.* New York: Columbia University Press.

Leary, T. (1957). *Interpersonal diagnosis of personality: A functional theory and methodology for personality evaluation.* New York: Ronald.

Leeds-Hurwitz, W. (1990). Notes on the history of intercultural communication: The Foreign Service Institute and the mandate for intercultural training. *Quarterly Journal of Speech, 76,* 262–281.

Leeds-Hurwitz, W. (1993). *Semiotics and communication: Signs, codes, cultures.* Hillsdale, NJ: Lawrence Erlbaum.

Legge, J. (Ed.). (1962). *The texts of Taoism* (Vol. 1). New York: Dover. (Original work published 1891)

Levant, R. F., & Shlien, J. M. (1984). *Client-centered therapy and the person-centered approach: New directions in theory, research, and practice.* New York: Praeger.

Lewin, K. (1951). *Field theory in social science: Selected theoretical papers.* New York: Harper.

Lievrouw, L. A., & Finn, T. A. (1990). Identifying the common dimensions of communication: The communication systems model. In B. D. Ruben & L. A. Lievrouw (Eds.), *Mediation, information, and behavior* (pp. 37–65). New Brunswick, NJ: Transaction.

Lincoln, Y. S., & Guba, E. G. (1985). *Naturalistic inquiry.* Beverly Hills, CA: Sage.

Lippmann, W. (1922). *Public opinion.* New York: Free Press.

Littlejohn, S. W. (1982). An overview of contributions to human communication theory from other disciplines. In F. E. X. Dance (Ed.), *Human communication theory* (pp. 243–285). New York: Harper.

Littlejohn, S. W. (1996). *Theories of human communication* (5th ed.). Belmont, CA: Wadsworth.

Llinas, R. (1987). "Mindness" as a functional state of the brain. In C. Blakemore & S. Greenfield (Eds.), *Mindwaves* (pp. 339–358). Oxford: Basil Blackwell.

Luft, J. (1970). *Group processes: An introduction to group dynamics* (2nd ed.). Palo Alto, CA: National Press Books.

Luria, A. R. (1961). *The role of speech in the regulation of normal and abnormal behavior.* New York: Liveright.

Lynch, J. J. (1977). *The broken heart: The medical consequences of loneliness.* New York: Basic Books.

Lynch, J. J. (1985). *The language of the heart: The human body in dialogue.* New York: Basic Books.

Lyotard, J.–F. (1984). *The postmodern condition: A report on knowledge* (G. Bennington & B. Massumi, Trans.). Minneapolis: University of Minnesota Press.

MacIntyre, A. (1984). *After virtue: A study in moral theory* (2nd ed.). Notre Dame, IN: University of Notre Dame Press.

Marvin, C. (1988). *When old technologies were new: Thinking about electric communication in the late nineteenth century.* New York: Oxford University Press.

Marwell, G., & Schmitt, D. R. (1967). Dimensions of compliance-gaining behavior: An empirical analysis. *Sociometry, 30,* 350–364.

Masten, R. (1979). *Speaking poems.* Monterey, CA: Palo Colorado Press.

Matlon, R. J. (1992). *Index to journals in communication studies through 1990* (Vols. 1–2). Annandale, VA: Speech Communication Association.

McCarthy, T. (1990). Introduction. In J. Habermas, *Moral consciousness and communicative action* (C. Lenhardt & S. W. Nicholsen, Trans.) (pp. vii–xiv). Cambridge, MA: MIT Press.

McCombs, M. E., & Shaw, D. L. (1972). The agenda-setting function of the press. *Public Opinion Quarterly, 36,* 176–187.

McCroskey, J. C., & Burgoon, M. (1974). Establishing predictors of latitude of acceptance-rejection and attitudinal intensity: A comparison of assumptions of social judgment and authoritarian personality theories. *Speech Monographs, 41,* 421–426.

McFarlane, R. W. (1992, January 5). The art of asking questions. *New York Times Book Review,* p. 31.

McHugh, P. (1968). *Defining the situation.* Indianapolis: Bobbs-Merrill.

McLaughlin, M. L. (1984). *Conversation: How talk is organized.* Beverly Hills, CA: Sage.

McLuhan, M. (1962). *The Gutenberg galaxy.* Toronto: University of Toronto Press.

McLuhan, M. (1964). *Understanding media: The extensions of man.* New York: Signet.

McLuhan, M., & Fiore, Q. (1968). *War and peace in the global village.* New York: McGraw-Hill.

McPhail, M. L. (1994). *The rhetoric of racism.* Lanham, MD: University Press of America.

McQuail, D., & Windahl, S. (1993). *Communication models for the study of mass communication* (2nd ed.). London: Longman.

Mead, G. H. (1934). *Mind, self and society: From the standpoint of a social behaviorist.* Chicago: University of Chicago Press.

Mead, G. H. (1956). *The social psychology of George Herbert Mead.* Chicago: University of Chicago Press.

Mehrabian, A. (1981). *Silent messages: Implicit communication of emotions and attitudes* (2nd ed.). Belmont, CA: Wadsworth.

Meyrowitz, J. (1985). *No sense of place: The impact of electronic media on social behavior.* New York: Oxford University Press.

Miller, G. A. (1967). *The psychology of communication: Seven essays.* Baltimore: Penguin.

Miller, G. R., & Boster, F. (1988). Persuasion in personal relationships. In S. W. Duck (Ed.), *Handbook of personal relationships* (pp. 275–288). New York: Wiley.

Mitchell, J. N. (1978). *Social exchange, dramaturgy and ethnomethodology: Toward a paradigmatic synthesis.* New York: Elsevier.

Moerman, M. (1988). *Talking culture: Ethnography and conversation analysis.* Philadelphia: University of Pennsylvania Press.

Moffitt, M. A. (1993). Articulating meaning: Reconceptions of the meaning process, fantasy/reality, and identity in leisure activities. *Communication Theory, 3,* 231–251.

Montagu, A. (1962). *The humanization of man: Our changing conception of human nature.* New York: Grove Press.

Montagu, A., & Matson, F. (1979). *The human connection.* New York: McGraw-Hill.

Moon, D. G. (1996). Concepts of "culture": Implications for intercultural communication research. *Communication Quarterly, 44,* 70–84.

Mortensen, C. D. (1972). *Communication: The study of human interaction.* New York: McGraw-Hill.

Motley, M. T. (1990). On whether one can (not) communicate: An examination via traditional communication postulates. *Western Journal of Speech Communication, 54,* 1–20.

Moyers, B. (1989). *A world of ideas.* New York: Doubleday.

Murray, A. (1970). *The Omni-Americans.* New York: Vintage.

Natanson, M. (1963). Introduction. In M. Natanson (Ed.), *Philosophy of the social sciences: A reader* (pp. 3–26). New York: Random House.

Negroponte, N. (1995). *Being digital.* New York: Vintage.

Noddings, N. (1984). *Caring: A feminine approach to ethics and moral education.* Berkeley: University of California Press.

Noelle-Neumann, E. (1984). *The spiral of silence: Public opinion—Our social skin.* Chicago: University of Chicago Press.

Nofsinger, R. E. (1989). Collaborating on context: Invoking alluded-to shared knowledge. *Western Journal of Speech Communication, 53,* 227–241.

Nofsinger, R. E. (1991). *Everyday conversation.* Newbury Park, CA: Sage.

O'Keefe, D. J. (1975). Logical empiricism and the study of human communication. *Speech Monographs, 42,* 169–183.

O'Keefe, D. J. (1990). *Persuasion: Theory and research.* Newbury Park, CA: Sage.

Oliver, R. T. (1962). *Culture and communication.* Springfield, IL: Charles C. Thomas.

Olson, S. R. (1994). Renewed alchemy: Science and humanism in communication epistemology. In F. L. Casmir (Ed.), *Building communication theories: A socio/cultural approach* (pp. 49–85). Hillsdale, NJ: Lawrence Erlbaum.

O'Neill, D. (1990, March 30). Happy talk: Phils' Leyva stresses communication. *St. Louis Post-Dispatch,* p. 3D.

Ong, W. J. (1967). *The presence of the word: Some prolegomena for cultural and religious history.* New Haven, CT: Yale University Press.

Ong, W. J. (1982). *Orality and literacy: The technologizing of the word.* New York: Methuen.

Ong, W. J. (1983). *Ramus, method, and the decay of dialogue.* Cambridge, MA: Harvard University Press.

Osgood, C. E., & Tannenbaum, P. H. (1955). The principle of congruity in the prediction of attitude change. *Psychological Review, 62,* 42–55.

O'Sullivan, T., Hartley, J., Saunders, D., Montgomery, M., & Fiske, J. (1994). *Key concepts in communication and cultural studies* (2nd ed.). New York: Routledge.

Pacanowsky, M., & O'Donnell-Trujillo, N. (1983). Organizational communication as cultural performance. *Communication Monographs, 50,* 126–147.

Palmer, R. E. (1969). *Hermeneutics.* Evanston: Northwestern University Press.

Palmgreen, P. (1984). Uses and gratifications: A theoretical perspective. In R. N. Bostrom (Ed.), *Communication yearbook 8* (pp. 20–55). Beverly Hills, CA: Sage.

Palmgreen, P., Wenner, L. A., & Rosengren, K. E. (1985). Uses and gratifications research: The past ten years. In K. E. Rosengren, L. A. Wenner, & P. Palmgreen (Eds.), *Media gratifications research: Current perspectives* (pp. 11–37). Beverly Hills, CA: Sage.

Pearce, W. B. (1989). *Communication and the human condition.* Carbondale: Southern Illinois University Press.

Pearce, W. B., & Cronen, V. E. (1980). *Communication, action and meaning: The creation of social realities.* New York: Praeger.

Pearce, W. B., & Foss, K. A. (1990). The historical context of communication as a science. In G. L. Dahnke & G. W. Clatterbuck (Eds.), *Human communication: Theory and research.* Belmont, CA: Wadsworth.

Pearson, J. C., Turner, L. H., & Todd-Mancillas, W. (1991). *Gender and communication* (2nd ed.). Dubuque, IA: Brown.

Peirce, C. S. (1931–1958). *Collected papers of Charles Sanders Peirce* (Vols. 1–6, C. Hartshorne & P. Weiss, Eds.; Vols. 7–8, A. W. Burks, Ed.). Cambridge, MA: Harvard University Press.

Perry, W. G., Jr. (1970). *Forms of intellectual and ethical development in the college years: A scheme.* New York: Holt.

Philipsen, G. (1995). The coordinated management of meaning theory of Pearce, Cronen, and associates. In D. P. Cushman & B. Kovačić (Eds.), *Watershed research traditions in human communication theory* (pp. 13–43). Albany: State University of New York Press.

Phillips, D. C. (1976). *Holistic thought in social science.* Stanford, CA: Stanford University Press.

Pilotta, J. J. (Ed.). (1982). *Interpersonal communication: Essays in phenomenology and hermeneutics.* Washington, DC: University Press of America.

Plato. (1927). *Plato: Selections* (R. Demos, Ed.). New York: Scribner.

Polanyi, M. (1962). *Personal knowledge: Towards a post-critical philosophy.* Chicago: University of Chicago Press.

Polanyi, M. (1967). *The tacit dimension.* Garden City, NY: Anchor.

Poole, M. S. (1990). Do we have any theories of group communication? *Communication Studies, 41,* 237–247.

Popper, K. (1980). Science: Conjectures and refutations. In E. D. Klemke, R. Holliger, & A. D. Kline (Eds.), *Introductory readings in the philosophy of science* (pp. 19–34). Buffalo, NY: Prometheus.

Popper, K. R. (1968). *The logic of scientific discovery* (2nd ed.). New York: Harper.

Poster, M. (1990). *The mode of information: Poststructuralism and social context.* Chicago: University of Chicago Press.

Postman, N. (1985). *Amusing ourselves to death: Public discourse in the age of show business.* New York: Penguin.

Powers, J. H. (1995). On the intellectual structure of the human communication discipline. *Communication Education, 44,* 191–222.

Press, L. (1995). McLuhan meets the net. *Communications of the ACM, 38,* 15–20.

Putnam, L. L., & Pacanowsky, M. E. (Eds.). (1983). *Communication and organizations: An interpretive approach.* Beverly Hills, CA: Sage.

Rasmussen, K. (1976). A transactional perspective. In D. K. Darnell & W. Brockriede. *Persons Communicating* (pp. 28–35). Englewood Cliffs, NJ: Prentice-Hall.

Rawlins, W. K. (1992). *Friendship matters: Communication, dialectics, and the life course.* New York: Aldine de Gruyter.

Rawls, J. (1971). *A theory of justice.* Cambridge, MA: Harvard University Press.

Real, M. R. (1989). *Super media.* Newbury Park, CA: Sage.

Reardon, K. K. (1987). *Interpersonal communication: Where minds meet.* Belmont, CA: Wadsworth.

Redding, W. C. (1968). Human communication behavior in complex organizations: Some fallacies revisited. In C. E. Larson & F. E. X. Dance (Eds.), *Perspectives on communication.* Milwaukee: University of Wisconsin Speech Communication Center.

Reddy, M. (1979). The conduit metaphor. In A. Ortony (Ed.), *Metaphor and thought*. Cambridge: Cambridge University Press.

Reid, L. (1990). *Speech teacher: A random narrative*. Annandale, VA: Speech Communication Association.

Rice, R. E., & Williams, F. (1984). Theories old and new: The study of new media. In R. E. Rice & Associates (Eds.), *The new media: Communication, research and technology* (pp. 55–80). Beverly Hills, CA: Sage.

Richards, M. C. (1973). *The crossing point: Selected talks and writings*. Middletown, CT: Wesleyan University Press.

Ricoeur, P. (1981). *Hermeneutics and the human sciences* (J. B. Thompson, Trans.). Cambridge: Cambridge University Press.

Roberts, C. V., & Watson, K. W. (Eds.). (1989). *Intrapersonal communication processes: Original essays*. New Orleans: SPECTRA.

Rogers, C. R. (1959). A theory of therapy, personality, and interpersonal relationships, as developed in the client-centered framework. In S. Koch (Ed.), *Psychology: A study of a science: Vol. 3. Formulations of the person and social context* (pp. 184–256). New York: McGraw-Hill.

Rogers, C. R. (1961). *On becoming a person: A therapist's view of psychotherapy*. Boston: Houghton-Mifflin.

Rogers, C. R. (1980). *A way of being*. Boston: Houghton-Mifflin.

Rogers, E. M. (1994). *A history of communication study: A biographical approach*. New York: Free Press.

Rogers, E. M., & Chaffee, S. H. (1993). The past and the future of communication study: Convergence or divergence? *Journal of Communication, 43*(4), 125–131.

Rogers, M. F. (1983). *Sociology, ethnomethodology, and experience: A phenomenological critique*. Cambridge: Cambridge University Press.

Rokeach, M. (1960). *The open and closed mind: Investigations into the nature of belief systems and personality systems*. New York: Basic Books.

Roloff, M. (1981). *Interpersonal communication: A social exchange approach*. Beverly Hills, CA: Sage.

Rommetveit, R. (1987). Meaning, context, and control: Convergent trends and controversial issues in current social-scientific research on human cognition and communication. *Inquiry, 30,* 77–99.

Rosaldo, R. (1989). *Culture and truth: The remaking of social analysis*. Boston: Beacon.

Rosenau, P. M. (1992). *Post-modernism and the social sciences: Insights, inroads, and intrusions*. Princeton, NJ: Princeton University Press.

Rosenblatt, L. M. (1978). *The reader, the text, the poem: The transactional theory of the literary work*. Carbondale: Southern Illinois University Press.

Rosenthal, R., & Jacobson, L. (1968). *Pygmalion in the classroom: Teacher expectation and pupils' intellectual development*. New York: Holt.

Ross, S. (1996, November 11). More multinational firms sending execs abroad. *St. Louis Post-Dispatch,* p. 18BP.

Ruben, B. D., & Kim, J. Y. (Eds.). (1975). *General systems theory and human communication*. Rochelle Park, NJ: Hayden.

Rudner, R. S. (1966). *Philosophy of social science*. Englewood Cliffs, NJ: Prentice-Hall.

Ruesch, J., & Bateson, G. (1968). *Communication: The social matrix of psychiatry* (2nd ed.). New York: Norton.

Rybacki, K., & Rybacki, D. (1991). *Communication criticism: Approaches and genres*. Belmont, CA: Wadsworth.

Said, E. W. (1978). *Orientalism*. New York: Pantheon.

Said, E. W. (1981). *Covering Islam*. New York: Pantheon.

Said, E. W. (1993). *Culture and imperialism*. New York: Vintage.

Sanchez-Tranquilino, M., & Tagg, J. (1992). The pachuco's flayed hide: Mobility, identity, and buenas garras. In L. Grossberg, C. Nelson, & P. Treichler (Eds.), *Cultural studies* (pp. 556–566). New York: Routledge.

Saussure, F. de (1966). *Course in general linguistics* (W. Baskin, Trans.). New York: McGraw-Hill.

Schauer, F. (1982). *Free speech: A philosophical enquiry*. Cambridge: Cambridge University Press.

Scheflen, A. E. (1974). *How behavior means*. Garden City, NY: Anchor Books.

Schön, D. A. (1983). *The reflective practitioner: How professionals think in action*. New York: Basic Books.

Schultz, D. (1977). *Growth psychology: Models of the healthy personality*. New York: Van Nostrand Reinhold.

Schultz, E. A. (1990). *Dialogue at the margins: Whorf, Bakhtin, and linguistic relativity*. Madison: University of Wisconsin Press.

Schumacher, E. F. (1979). *A guide for the perplexed*. New York: Perennial Library.

Schutz, A. (1967). *The phenomenology of the social world.* Evanston, IL: Northwestern University Press.

Schutz, W. C. (1966). *The interpersonal underworld.* Palo Alto, CA: Science and Behavior Books.

Scott, R. L. (1977). Communication as an intentional, social system. *Human Communication Research, 3,* 258–268.

Searle, J. R. (1969). *Speech acts: An essay in the philosophy of language.* Cambridge: Cambridge University Press.

Shannon, C., & Weaver, W. (1949). *The mathematical theory of communication.* Urbana: University of Illinois Press.

Sherif, C. W., Sherif, M., & Nebergall, R. (1965). *Attitude and attitude change: The social judgment-involvement approach.* Philadelphia: Saunders.

Sherif, M., & Hovland, C. I. (1961). *Social judgment.* New Haven, CT: Yale University Press.

Shimanoff, S. B. (1980). *Communication rules: Theory and research.* Beverly Hills, CA: Sage.

Signorielli, N., & Morgan, M. (1990). Preface. In N. Signorielli & M. Morgan (Eds.), *Cultivation analysis: New directions in media effects research.* Newbury Park, CA: Sage.

Simons, H. W. (1976). *Persuasion: Understanding, practice, and analysis.* Reading, MA: Addison-Wesley.

Simpson, C. (1996). Elisabeth Noelle-Neumann's "spiral of silence" and the historical context of communication theory. *Journal of Communication, 46*(3), 149–173.

Singer, P. (1986). Morality, egoism and the prisoner's dilemma. In C. H. Sommers (Ed.), *Right and wrong: Basic readings in ethics* (pp. 192–199). New York: Harcourt.

Skinner, B. F. (1953). *Science and human behavior.* New York: Free Press.

Slack, J. D. (1989). Contextualizing technology. In B. Dervin, L. Grossberg, B. J. O'Keefe, & E. Wartella (Eds.), *Rethinking communication: Vol. 2. Paradigm exemplars* (pp. 329–345). Newbury Park, CA: Sage.

Slack, J. D. (1996). The theory and method of articulation in cultural studies. In D. Morley & K.-H. Chen (Eds.), *Stuart Hall: Critical dialogues in cultural studies* (pp. 112–127). New York: Routledge.

Smith, A. L. [M. K. Asante] (1973). *Transracial communication.* Englewood Cliffs, NJ: Prentice-Hall.

Smith, D. H., & Pettegrew, L. S. (1986). Mutual persuasion as a model for doctor–patient communication. *Theoretical Medicine, 7,* 127–146.

Smith, M. J. (1988). *Contemporary communication research methods.* Belmont, CA: Wadsworth.

Snyder, I. (1996). *Hypertext.* Melbourne, Australia: University of Melbourne Press.

Sokolov, A. N. (1972). *Inner speech and thought* (G. T. Onischenko, Trans.). New York: Plenum Press.

Solmsen, F. (1954). Introduction. In Aristotle, *Rhetoric and poetics* (W. R. Roberts & I. Bywater, Trans.) (pp. v–xxii). New York: Modern Library.

Sommer, R. (1969). *Personal space: The behavioral basis of design.* Englewood Cliffs, NJ: Prentice-Hall.

Sommer, R. (1974). *Tight spaces: Hard architecture and how to humanize it.* Englewood Cliffs, NJ: Prentice-Hall.

Speech Communication Association. (1995). *Pathways to careers in communication* (4th ed.). Annandale, VA: Author.

Spitzberg, B. H., & Cupach, W. R. (1984). *Interpersonal communication competence.* Beverly Hills, CA: Sage.

Stamp, G. H., & Knapp, M. L. (1990). The construct of intent in interpersonal communication. *Quarterly Journal of Speech, 76,* 282–299.

Stamp, G. H., Vangelisti, A. L., & Knapp, M. L. (1994). Criteria for developing and assessing theories of interpersonal communication. In F. L. Casmir (Ed.), *Building communication theories: A socio/cultural approach* (pp. 167–208). Hillsdale, NJ: Lawrence Erlbaum.

Stephenson, W. (1967). *The play theory of mass communication.* Chicago: University of Chicago Press.

Stewart, J. (1978). Foundations of dialogic communication. *Quarterly Journal of Speech, 64,* 183–201.

Stewart, J. (1983). Interpretive listening: An alternative to empathy. *Communication Education, 32,* 379–391.

Stewart, J. (1990). *Bridges not walls* (5th ed.). New York: McGraw-Hill.

Strauss, A. (1956). Introduction. In G. H. Mead, *The social psychology of George Herbert Mead* (A. Strauss, Ed.) (pp. iv–xvi). Chicago: University of Chicago Press.

Streff, C. R. (1984). The concept of inner speech and its implications for an integrated language arts curriculum. *Communication Education, 33,* 223–230.

Stubbs, M. (1983). *Discourse analysis: The sociolinguistic analysis of natural language.* Chicago: University of Chicago Press.

Sudnow, D. (1978). *Ways of the hand: The organization of improvised conduct.* Cambridge, MA: Harvard University Press.

Tannen, D. (1989). *Talking voices: Repetition, dialogue, and imagery in conversational discourse.* Cambridge: Cambridge University Press.

Tannen, D. (1990). *You just don't understand: Women and men in conversation.* New York: Morrow.

Taylor, M. C., & Saarinen, E. (1994). *Imagologies: Media philosophy.* London: Routledge.

Tehranian, M. (1988). Communication theory and Islamic perspectives. In W. Dissanayake (Ed.), *Communication theory: The Asian perspective* (pp. 190–203). Singapore: Asian Mass Communication Research and Information Centre.

Terkel, S. (1981). *American dreams: Lost and found.* New York: Ballantine.

Thayer, L. (1968). *Communication and communication systems.* Homewood, IL: Richard D. Irwin.

Theodorson, G. A., & Theodorson, A. G. (1969). *Modern dictionary of sociology.* New York: Thomas Y. Crowell.

Thibaut, J. W., & Kelley, H. H. (1959). *The social psychology of groups.* New York: Wiley.

Thomas, L. (1974). *The lives of a cell.* New York: Viking.

Thomas, L. (1983). *Late night thoughts on listening to Mahler's ninth symphony.* New York: Viking.

Toch, H., & MacLean, M. S., Jr. (1962). Perception, communication, and educational research: A transactional view. *AV Communication Review, 10,* 55–77.

Toch, H. & Smith, H. C. (Eds.). (1968). *Social perception.* Princeton, NJ: Van Nostrand.

Todorov, T. (1984). *Mikhail Bakhtin: The dialogical principle* (W. Godzich, Trans.). Minneapolis: University of Minnesota Press.

Triandis, H. C. (1994). *Culture and social behavior.* New York: McGraw-Hill.

Turner, V. W. (1986). Dewey, Dilthey, and drama: An essay in the anthropology of experience. In V. W. Turner & E. M. Bruner (Eds.), *The anthropology of experience* (pp. 33–44). Urbana: University of Illinois Press.

Ullmann, S. (1966). Semantic universals. In J. H. Greenberg (Ed.), *Universals of language* (2nd ed., pp. 217–262). Cambridge, MA: MIT Press.

Vangelisti, A. L., Knapp, M. L., & Daly, J. A. (1990). Conversational narcissism. *Communication Monographs, 57,* 251–274.

Vygotsky, L. S. (1962). *Thought and language* (E. Hanfmann & G. Vakar, Trans.). Cambridge, MA: MIT Press.

Wallace, K. R. (1955). An ethical basis of communication. *The Speech Teacher, 4,* 1–9.

Wallace, K. R. (1963). The substance of rhetoric: Good reasons. *Quarterly Journal of Speech, 49,* 239–249.

Walters, M., Carter, E., Papp, P., & Silverstein, O. (1988). *The invisible web.* New York: Guilford.

Walther, J. B. (1993). Impression development in computer-mediated interaction. *Western Journal of Communication, 57,* 381–398.

Walther, J. B. (1996). Computer-mediated communication: Impersonal, interpersonal, and hyperpersonal interaction. *Communication Research, 23,* 3–43.

Wann, T. W. (Ed.). (1964). *Behaviorism and phenomenology: Contrasting bases for modern psychology.* Chicago: University of Chicago Press.

Warnke, G. (1987). *Gadamer: Hermeneutics, tradition, and reason.* Stanford, CA: Stanford University Press.

Watts, A. (1975). *Tao: The watercourse way.* New York: Pantheon.

Watzlawick, P. (1984). Self-fulfilling prophecies. In P. Watzlawick (Ed.), *The invented reality: How do we know what we believe we know? (Contributions to constructivism)* (pp. 95–116). New York: Norton.

Watzlawick, P., Beavin, J. H., & Jackson, D. D. (1967). *Pragmatics of human communication: A study of interactional patterns, pathologies, and paradoxes.* New York: Norton.

Watzlawick, P., & Weakland, J. H. (Eds.). (1977). *The interactional view: Studies at the Mental Research Institute, Palo Alto 1965–74.* New York: Norton.

Watzlawick, P., Weakland, J., & Fisch, R. (1974). *Change: Principles of problem formation and problem resolution.* New York: Norton.

Weaver, R. M. (1971). Language is sermonic. In R. Johannesen (Ed.), *Contemporary theories of rhetoric: Selected readings* (pp. 163–179). New York: Harper.

Weitz, S. (Ed.). (1974). *Nonverbal communication: Readings with commentary.* New York: Oxford University Press.

Wenner, L. A. (1985). Transaction and media gratifications research. In K. E. Rosengren, L. A. Wenner, and P. Palmgreen (Eds.), *Media gratifications research: Current perspectives* (pp. 73–94). Beverly Hills, CA: Sage.

Wertsch, J. V. (1991). *Voices of the mind: A sociocultural approach to mediated action.* Cambridge, MA: Harvard University Press.

West, C. (1993). *Keeping faith: Philosophy and race in America.* New York: Routledge.

Westley, B. H., & MacLean, M. S., Jr. (1957). A conceptual model for mass communication research. *Journalism Quarterly, 34,* 31–38.

Wheelis, A. (1976). *How people change.* New York: Perennial Library. (Original work published 1973)

Whitehead, A. N. (1930). *Process and reality: An essay in cosmology.* New York: Macmillan.

Whorf, B. L. (1956). *Language, thought, and reality* (J. B. Carroll, Ed.). Cambridge, MA: MIT Press.

Williams, R. (1976). *Keywords: A vocabulary of culture and society.* New York: Oxford University Press.

Williams, R. (1981). *The sociology of culture.* New York: Schocken Books.

Wilmot, W. W. (1971). Ego-involvement: A confusing variable in speech communication research. *Quarterly Journal of Speech, 57,* 429–436.

Windahl, S., & Signitzer, B., with Olson, J. T. (1992). *Using communication theory: An introduction to planned communication.* London: Sage.

Wolf, G. (1996, January). The wisdom of Saint Marshall, the holy fool. *Wired,* 121–125, 182, 184.

Wolman, B. B. (Ed.). (1973). *Dictionary of behavioral science.* New York: Van Nostrand Reinhold.

Wood, J. T. (1982). Communication and relational culture: Bases for the study of human relationships. *Communication Quarterly, 30,* 75–83.

Wood, J. T. (1995). *Relational communication.* Belmont, CA: Wadsworth.

Wood, J. T. (Ed.). (1996). *Gendered relationships.* Mountain View, CA: Mayfield.

Wood, J. T., & Cox, R. (1993). Rethinking critical voice: Materiality and situated knowledges. *Western Journal of Communication, 57,* 278–287.

Work, W., & Jeffrey, R. C. (Eds.). (1989). *The past is prologue.* Annandale, VA: Speech Communication Association.

Yancey, W. L. (1977). Architecture, interaction, and social control: The case of a large-scale public housing project. In W. E. Arnold & J. L. Buley (Eds.), *Urban communication: Survival in the city* (pp. 65–81). Cambridge, MA: Winthrop.

Young, I. M. (1990). *Justice and the politics of difference.* Princeton, NJ: Princeton University Press.

Young, J. Z. (1978). *Programs of the brain.* Oxford: Oxford University Press.

Zhang, L. (1988). The myth of the other: China in the eyes of the west. *Critical Inquiry, 15,* 108–131.

Zukav, G. (1979). *The dancing wu li masters: An overview of the new physics.* New York: Morrow.

index